Greece and the Cold War

Greece and the Cold War presents a comprehensive analysis of Greek foreign and security policy in the Cold War, covering the key period from the country's accession to NATO in 1952 until the imposition of the Colonels' dictatorship in 1967. It also makes extensive references to issues of Greek internal politics which substantially affected the formulation of the country's Cold War policy.

Clearly dividing his analysis into three parts, 1952–55, 1955–63 and 1963–67, Evanthis Hatzivassiliou examines the following key themes: Greek foreign policy in the Cold War; threat perception; the NATO connection (including Greek–US relations, the rise of anti-Americanism, the economic dimension of security and the issue of US military aid); Greek policy towards the Soviet Bloc; and the regional dimension (mainly Greek policy towards Turkey and Yugoslavia, and the Cyprus crises), which greatly complicated Greek security obligations. Making extensive use of primary sources, this volume covers the whole of these key periods in detail and makes a major contribution to all the main debates, with a special focus on the Greek–US relationship, which continues to be hotly debated.

This book will be of great interest to students of Greek politics, Greek–Turkish relations, Balkan history, the Cold War and strategic studies.

Evanthis Hatzivassiliou is assistant professor of Contemporary History at the University of Athens. He is the author of *Britain and the International Status of Cyprus, 1955–59* (1997) and *The Cyprus Question, 1878–1960: the Constitutional Aspect* (2002).

Cass series: cold war history
Series editors: Odd Arne Westad and Michael Cox
ISSN: 1471-3829

In the new history of the Cold War that has been forming since 1989, many of the established truths about the international conflict that shaped the latter half of the twentieth century have come up for revision. The present series is an attempt to make available interpretations and materials that will help further the development of this new history, and it will concentrate in particular on publishing expositions of key historical issues and critical surveys of newly available sources.

1. **Reviewing the Cold War**
   Approaches, interpretations, and theory
   Edited by Odd Arne Westad

2. **Rethinking Theory and History in the Cold War**
   Richard Saull

3. **British and American Anticommunism before the Cold War**
   Marrku Ruotsila

4. **Europe, Cold War and Co-existence, 1953–1965**
   Edited by Wilfred Loth

5. **The Last Decade of the Cold War**
   From conflict escalation to conflict transformation
   Edited by Olav Njølstad

6. **Reinterpreting the End of the Cold War**
   Issues, interpretations, periodizations
   Edited by Silvio Pons and Federico Romero

7. **Across the Blocs**
   Cold War cultural and social history
   Edited by Rana Mitter and Patrick Major

8 **US Paramilitary Assistance to South Vietnam**
   Insurgency, subversion and public order
   William Rosenau

9 **The European Community and the Crises of the 1960s**
   Negotiating the Gaullist challenge
   N. Piers Ludlow

10 **Soviet–Vietnam Relations and the Role of China 1949–64**
   Changing alliances
   Mari Olsen

11 **The Third Indochina War**
   Conflict between China, Vietnam and Cambodia, 1972–79
   Edited by Odd Arne Westad and Sophie Quinn-Judge

12 **Greece and the Cold War**
   Frontline state, 1952–1967
   Evanthis Hatzivassiliou

Greece and the Cold War
Frontline state, 1952–1967

Evanthis Hatzivassiliou

LONDON AND NEW YORK

First published 2006
by Routledge
2 Park Square, Milton Park, Abingdon, Oxon OX14 4RN

Simultaneously published in the USA and Canada
by Routledge
270 Madison Ave, New York, NY 10016

Routledge is an imprint of the Taylor & Francis Group, an informa business

© 2006 Evanthis Hatzivassiliou

Typeset in Times by Wearset Ltd, Boldon, Tyne and Wear
Printed and bound in Great Britain by TJ International, Padstow, Cornwall

All rights reserved. No part of this book may be reprinted or reproduced or utilized in any form or by any electronic, mechanical, or other means, now known or hereafter invented, including photocopying and recording, or in any information storage or retrieval system, without permission in writing from the publishers.

British Library Cataloguing in Publication Data
A catalogue record for this book is available from the British Library

Library of Congress Cataloging in Publication Data
A catalog record for this book has been requested

ISBN10: 0-415-39664-6 (hbk)
ISBN10: 0-203-96963-4 (ebk)

ISBN13: 978-0-415-39664-6 (hbk)
ISBN13: 978-0-203-96963-2 (ebk)

To Constantinos Svolopoulos

Contents

List of tables	xi
Foreword by Theodore A. Couloumbis	xii
Acknowledgements	xiv
Abbreviations	xv
General map	xvii

Introduction	1

PART I
The era of regional initiatives, 1952–55 — 15

1	Attempting to adjust to the post-war world	17
2	A new NATO member, 1952–55	24
3	The regional balance: the tripartite Balkan pacts	36
4	Greece and peaceful co-existence	43
5	Disaster in 1955	50

PART II
The era of functionalism, 1955–63 — 55

6	The search for a long-term strategy	57
7	New security problems	66
8	Functionalism in action	80
9	The limits of functionalism: security and détente	98
10	The regional aspect of functionalism: Yugoslavia, Turkey, Cyprus	107

x   *Contents*

PART III
The era of multiple fronts, 1963–67   123

11 Facing new challenges   125

12 Multiple fronts   141

13 Maximalism and dead-end: the Cyprus entanglement   160

14 The effort to adjust Greece's Eastern policy   174

15 The mid-1960s: a re-evaluation   181

  Conclusions   184
  Notes   187
  List of sources   218
  Bibliography   221
  Index   223

Tables

2.1 Greek defence expenditure as a percentage of the GNP 1949–54   27
8.1 Greek defence expenditure as a percentage of the GNP 1955–62   89

Foreword

History is written in stages, with occasional leaps. First, a cluster of experts tends to reproduce mentalities and assumptions of its own era. These analysts normally reflect the official or semi-official orthodoxy of their time. At a later stage, a second group of scholars begins to question so-called orthodoxy and seeks to revise it. Yet, more often than not, this second group tends to push revisionism to the other end of the analytical spectrum. It takes a bit longer before a third wave of young and less emotionally involved scholars offers its own, more eclectic, versions. The latter seek to exhaust source material and reflect on the whole range of perceptions and prejudices of key protagonists that have led to decisions of war or peace. Cold War studies, in our days, are clearly moving in this third category.

For example, narratives of conflict, such as the Greek civil war, have been presented in three successive waves. The first wave, the orthodox, viewed the struggle as a heroic attempt of pro-Western, democratic forces to wrench Greece from the claws of international – Soviet controlled – Communism. The second wave, the revisionist, was produced after the collapse of the Colonels' dictatorship in 1974. It sought to reverse the images of orthodoxy. The vanquished, in this case, branded the victors as obedient instruments of British and American interests who had managed to suppress a genuine popular revolution. The third wave, the post-revisionist, has sought consciously to avoid black and white interpretations of history. Highlighting the dire economic circumstances of the time, pointing up the deficit of prudent leadership on both sides as well as the clashing interests of interfering Great Powers, the post-revisionists have tended to view the civil war in the form of an ancient Greek tragedy.

Evanthis Hatzivassiliou's excellent work neatly fits the post-revisionist model in its treatment of the post-civil war period. Making excellent use of archival material, reviewing exhaustively memoirs and related accounts, and digesting the gamut of secondary sources, the author offers his readers a worthy overview of Greece's foreign policy landscape. Resisting political preferences and other value judgments, he records the difficulties and the dilemmas facing the small country's policy-makers. Statesmen such as Constantinos Karamanlis and Evangelos Averoff emerge as central players in the conceptualization and implementation of Greek post-civil war policies. More pragmatic rather than ideological, both men focused on 'the threat from the north' (especially on the capability of Bulgaria, as Moscow's main Balkan ally, to threaten the northern Greek frontier) in purely geopolitical terms.

The author also discusses in depth the influence of Greece's major ally, the United States, which is a hotly debated question of contemporary Greek historiography. However, he insists that, on the whole, the origins of Athens' strategies (including mistakes) should better be sought in Greek realities, fears or expectations, rather than in the overwhelming influence of 'a sinister, conspiratorial and all-powerful foreign factor'.

One of the major preoccupations of the Greek leadership during the early 1950s was to prevent the creation of a solid Yugoslav–Bulgarian front that would target the long, narrow and virtually indefensible strip of territory in northern Greece. As the book clearly demonstrates, however, the situation became highly complicated when a second front – Cyprus – began emerging in the mid-1950s, reaching levels of high intensity in 1963–67 and virtual paroxysm in 1974. After 1955, confronted with worsening relations with key NATO allies (Great Britain, Turkey and the United States) the Greek political leadership predictably resorted to a policy of 'functionalism' vis-à-vis its Western partners and its northern Communist neighbours. Functionalism essentially called for the development of patterns of economic interdependence.

In sum, as Hatzivassiliou skilfully paints the picture, Greece emerges as a frontline state with multiple external fronts. Adding to its external woes, the small Mediterranean country was also hampered by the growth of internal polarization (partly an aftershock of the civil war and partly of older divisions) permitting the Throne and the armed forces to intervene in the political process, paving the way for the most damaging (in terms of foreign policy as well) military dictatorship of the 1967–74 period.

Among the many virtues of Evanthis Hatzivassiliou's scholarly volume is the systematic debunking of popular, but highly inaccurate, myths. In his detached – at times Thucydidean – style of writing, the author navigates through the turbulent decade and a half (1952–67) of contemporary Greek history, challenging a popular myth (mostly cultivated by left-wing commentators) alleging Greece's total dependence on external powers. In fact, as we read through the author's narration of the trials and tribulations of the early 1950s, we realize that the Papagos government in Athens – however imprudently – proceeded with a unilateralist and highly revisionist Cyprus policy which failed to conform with the practices and preferences of the United States. A fortiori, the second Greek front in Cyprus pitted a small country, which had just emerged from long years of Nazi occupation and civil war, against Britain (the colonial master of Cyprus), Turkey (a country of growing strategic importance) and the United States (the master of the Western alliance). Ultimately, a central benefit for the reader of this volume will be the wealth of evidence that questions single-factor explanations and/or convenient conspiracy theories.

Theodore A. Couloumbis
Director, Hellenic Foundation for European and Foreign Policy

Acknowledgements

This book is the result of many years of research on Greece's international policy in the post-civil war period. During these years I had the opportunity to seek and acquire the support of many people, to whom I would like to express my gratitude. Professor Constantinos Svolopoulos, to whom this book is dedicated, has provided invaluable advice, encouragement and assistance over a period of many years. It would indeed be difficult for me to exaggerate the importance of the assistance I received from Professor Theodore A. Couloumbis, who also offered to write the foreword. Professors John O. Iatrides, Thanos Veremis and Constantinos Arvanitopoulos have offered invaluable comments on the text. Dr Soterios Rizas of the Academy of Athens and Dr Photini Bellou of ELIAMEP generously gave their comments and support. I must also thank former Prime Minister Constantinos Mitsotakis, former Foreign Minister Constantinos Papaconstantinou and Ambassador Vyron Theodoropoulos for their enlightening interviews.

Many institutions have made their material available for my research: the Constantinos G. Karamanlis Foundation and especially the archivist, Dr Marietta Minotos, who, apart from being a colleague, is also a good friend; the Constantinos Mitsotakis Foundation; the Association of Friends of Panayiotis Kanellopoulos; and the Evangelos Averoff Foundation, especially Soterios Ioannou and Tatiana Averoff-Ioannou. The Alexandros S. Onassis Foundation provided me with a generous grant, without which it would be next to impossible to conclude this research.

I would also like to thank Professor Arne Westad of the LSE and Mr Andrew Humphrys of Routledge for their patience and encouragement. Last but not least, I need to express my gratitude to my wife, Mariana, for her endless understanding and support over a period of many years.

Abbreviations

AKEL	Rehabilitation Party of the Working People (Cypriot, Communist)
ASEA	Supreme Council of National Defence (Greece)
CAP	Common Agricultural Policy (EEC)
CFM	Council of Foreign Ministers
CPSU	Communist Party of the Soviet Union
CU	Centre Union (Greece, 1961–67)
DLF	Development Loan Fund
DPC	Defence Planning Committee (NATO)
DSE	Democratic Army of Greece (Communist, 1946–49)
EAM	National Liberation Front (Greece, 1941–44)
EDA	United Democratic Left (Greece, 1951–67)
EDC	European Defence Community
EEC	European Economic Community
EENA	Union of Young Greek Officers
EFTA	European Free Trade Association
ELDYK	Greek Forces, Cyprus (1959 agreements)
EMEK	Special Joint Staff for Cyprus (Greece, 1964)
EOKA	National Organization of Cypriot Fighters (1955–59)
EPEK	National Progressive Centre Union (Greece, 1950–61)
ERE	National Radical Union (Greece, 1956–67)
ERP	European Recovery Programme
GES	General Staff of the Army (Greece)
GNP	Gross National Product
GPR	Greek Parliamentary Records
IDEA	Sacred Bond of Greek Officers
IRBM	Intermediate Range Ballistic Missile
JCS	Joint Chiefs of Staff (US)
KEA	Movement of National Rehabilitation (Greece, 1960–61)
KKE	Greek Communist Party
KYP	Greek Central Intelligence Service
MDAP	Mutual Defense Assistance Program (US)
MLF	Multilateral Force (NATO)
NAC	North Atlantic Council

NATO	North Atlantic Treaty Organization
NSC	National Security Council (US)
OECD	Organization for Economic Co-operation and Development
PRM/SRM	People's/Socialist Republic of Macedonia (Yugoslavia)
SACEUR	Supreme Allied Commander Europe (NATO)
SAM	Surface-to-Air Missile
SHAPE	Supreme Headquarters Allied Powers Europe (NATO)
TEA	Battalions of National Guard Defence (Greece)
UN	United Nations
UNFICYP	United Nations Force in Cyprus
UNRRA	United Nations Relief and Rehabilitation Administration
USIS	United States Information Service

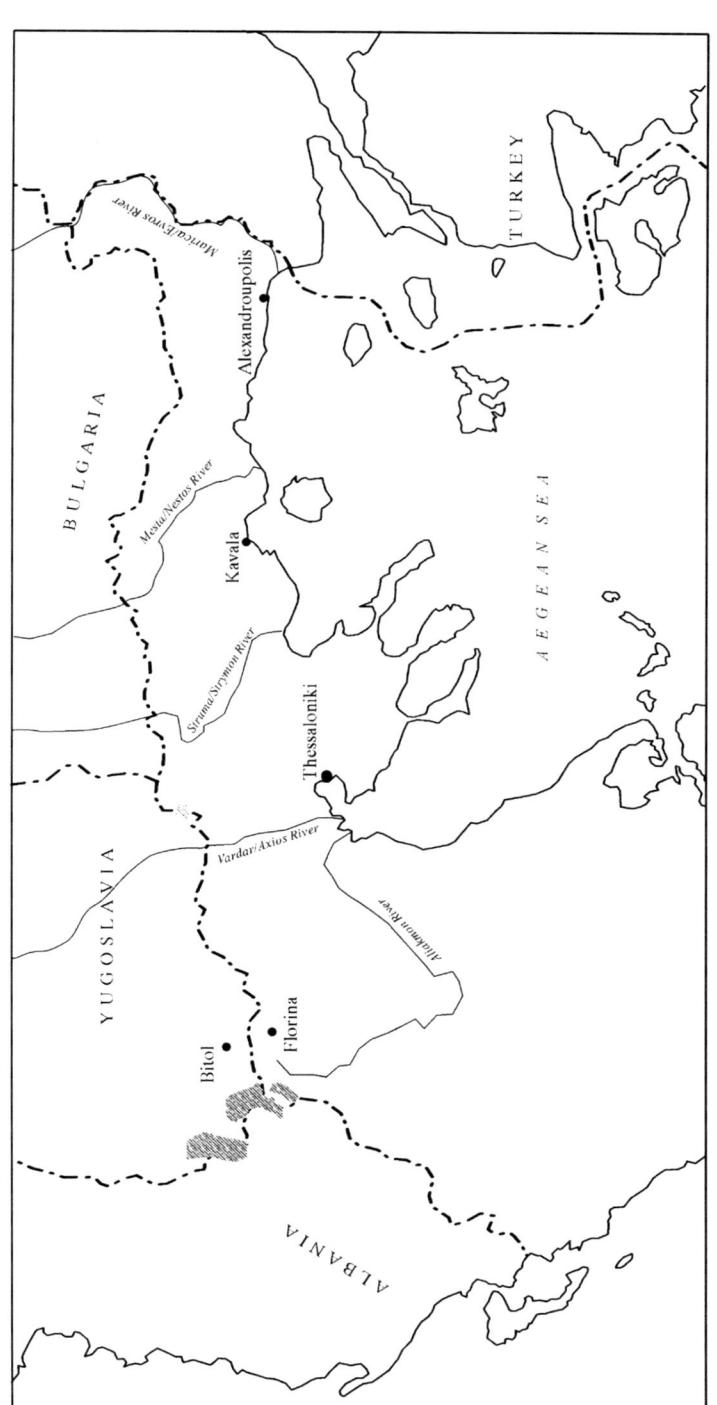

The northern Greek border.

Introduction

The aim of this book is to study Greece's policy in the Cold War from the country's accession to NATO in 1952 until the imposition of the Colonels' dictatorship in 1967. The book is divided into three parts, each corresponding with a phase of the security problem, but also with the lifetime of a government (or, in the case of 1963–67, with a period of internal instability). Each part will examine the personalities who dominated policy-making in the specific sub-period, and will critically present their analysis. The next chapters will study threat perception; defence policy and the financial problems of security; relations with NATO and with the Soviet Bloc; and Greece's regional policy – mainly its attitude towards the two peripheral powers, Turkey and Yugoslavia. In the case of the 1963–67 years, the additional military entanglement in Cyprus will also be examined as part of Greece's regional policy, which complicated considerably its overall international position. The book deals with Greek foreign and security policy in the Cold War; it does not analyse other issues such as Greek attitudes towards decolonization or the new states of the periphery. Moreover, it is not a history of Greek policy in the Cyprus question; the interested reader may turn to recent studies on this issue. However, this book will also deal with the problems that the Cyprus crises created for Greece's national security policy, such as strategic overstretch, the rise of anti-Americanism and the deterioration of Greek–Turkish relations.

The study of the grand strategy of a state (even of a small one) reveals the way that it understands the world, and as such it involves foreign policy, defence and the economy, as well as internal politics and the impact of ideological trends. In the case of Greece, a major aspect of its policy in the Cold War can be found in the perception that the country, a minor partner of NATO and in the front line of the Western world, faced a 'menace from the north'. However, one of the main arguments of the book is that Greek policy did not remain unchanged throughout the early Cold War period. It evolved according to two factors: the wider NATO strategy and the shifts in the regional balance of power in the Balkans and the Eastern Mediterranean. Indeed, the book aims to show that major changes in Greek foreign and security policy should be attributed to regional developments which directly affected the country.

The analysis starts with Greece's entry into NATO and ends with the imposition of the military dictatorship in 1967. The starting point, 1952, may trigger some disagreement: the 'menace from the north' existed as a security perception long before that; the country's liberation in 1944 or the end of the civil war in 1949 might be seen as better starting points. Yet, accession to NATO was also a major turning point. It created a new institutional framework for the shaping of foreign and defence policy: multilateralism was an entirely new experience for Athens. NATO accession provided Greece with a peacetime alliance with the great powers of the West, something which the country had not achieved even during the First and the Second World Wars. Moreover, Article 5 of the Treaty of Washington provided for a territorial guarantee. Thus, in more than one respect, NATO accession signalled a new era of Greek foreign and security policy. On the other hand, the fall of Greek democracy in 1967 meant that in the following years policy was being shaped in entirely different ways. Thus, 1967 is a logical date to end this story. Greek foreign policy in the years 1967–74 should be the subject of a separate volume.

This book indirectly draws a line between 'external' and 'internal' security which some may regard arbitrary. Indeed, the latter was a precondition for the former, if only for securing the rear. However, this does not mean that external and internal security were the same. During the post-civil war period internal security touched upon a different set of perceptions, fears or mentalities, which involved primarily the challenge posed by the Greek Communist Party (KKE), and which was being handled by different agencies of the state, including the Ministry of the Interior, the police and the intelligence service (KYP). The examination of the international dimension of the problem of security is not, therefore, intended to marginalize (much less to suppress) the unfortunate aspects of the political maladies of post-war Greece. Still, this book will also touch upon issues of internal security when these had a direct impact on external security.

Researching post-war Greek policy

One of the major problems in the study of post-war Greek history concerns the inaccessibility of many official (especially Greek) archival sources. Given the nature of this book, however, the damage is not irreparable: the basic principles of a state's grand strategy are usually declared publicly, mostly in Parliament, but also in other forms of public debate or in the press. Such public declarations offer a basis, but are not in themselves enough for a comprehensive analysis. Still, an important bulk of Greek primary and archival sources is now available; mainly private archives of important personalities, such as Constantinos Karamanlis, Panayiotis Kanellopoulos, Evangelos Averoff-Tossizza, George Papandreou, Constantinos Mitsotakis, and the Greek Cypriot leader, Archbishop Makarios.

Non-Greek archival material, such as the NATO Archive, the papers of the British Foreign Office and of the US State Department, was used in a manner complementary to Greek primary sources. The evidence found in British or US archives is indeed important, but does not necessarily reflect Greek attitudes.

The policies of Britain or the US were being determined by their governments' interests, priorities or understandings. Thus, at different moments, the US insisted on the formulation of a wider framework for the containment of communism, whereas Greece tended to emphasize regional, geographical or historical factors. On the other hand, especially after 1954, British attitudes were largely affected by London's priority to retain its dominant position in the Middle East, and especially in Cyprus, which was being claimed by Athens. Thus, after 1954 Greek policy was often seen in an unfavourable light in London. Last but not least, one has to note the existence of an important and growing bibliography on post-war Greek history. This includes works on post-war Greek foreign policy, the attitude of the political forces towards NATO, Greek–US and Greek–Turkish relations, the Cyprus question, internal politics or economic policy. The importance of these works is obvious for the present study.

The careful reader will have little difficulty in noting that this book has been substantially influenced by the works of British or American authors on the Cold War, but it is not an effort mechanistically to reproduce their methodology. There are important differences in the study of the policy of a small state, compared to the policy of a superpower such as the US. First, there is a crushing difference between the power of the two states; to put it simply, Greek policy was often a search for adjustment to international trends which the country had no means to control or influence substantially. Second, the policy-making process of the two states is completely different on the level of procedure, since Greece was a parliamentary democracy and the US a presidential republic. Moreover, US national security policy was much more solidly structured. There was nothing resembling the US National Security Council in the Greek case.

The implementation of the Greek or the US (or British) security policies also differed significantly. US policy dealt with a process of global dimensions, in which the points of tension (or those which could be lost) were not parts of the American metropolitan territory. On the contrary, Greek policy involved the defence of the homeland against more powerful adversaries (the Soviet Bloc) in the aftermath of a series of wars during which large parts of this national territory had been lost, even temporarily, with catastrophic consequences for the Greek populations there. Greek policy, therefore, reflected the sense of an often desperate weakness or vulnerability. This is another fundamental difference between great and small powers: the former usually engage in conflicts in 'grey' areas of the globe, away from their metropolis, and therefore can afford to promote compromises which do not cost them a lot – at any rate, such compromises do not involve their own territorial integrity. Therefore, the policy of the great powers often radiates a sense of clarity or calmness which cannot be found in the policy of smaller states. The latter need to adjust to decisions of larger players, while if something goes wrong they face nothing less than a national disaster.

Another major difference between great and minor powers involves the size of the field on which national security policy is being applied – and here, 'field'

4 Introduction

is more than a geographical reference. The British or the US Secretaries of State or Foreign Secretaries cannot deal personally with all the problems that arise in the vast geographical area that interests their country. Naturally, most of these issues are being handled by bureaucracies, which may acquire a major role in the formulation of policy, thus providing it with a solid sense of continuity. This is more so in the case of issues which do not determine the global balance of power – and these were usually the issues of Greek interest in the post-civil war period.

In the case of smaller states such as Greece, things are different. The leaders of a small state are being called to face specific issues in a particular geographical area; usually, their public opinion regards these issues as life-or-death affairs for the survival of the nation, and therefore these problems become important in the internal political scene as well. Thus, as a rule, the influence of the leader is usually larger in the policy-making of smaller states, and this certainly is the case for Greece. Of course, even in post-war Greece it was not possible for a single person to follow everything. Bureaucracies did have an important influence; no government could handle issues of security without the advice of officials, and there was no lack of capable analysts in the Greek diplomatic service or in the army. However, the role of the political leader was extremely important, and this is why it is possible to study Greek policy based on the personal archives of these personalities. Indeed, this is what happened in the study of previous periods of Greek foreign policy, for example the years of Eleftherios Venizelos (1910–20 and 1928–32). Fundamental works on Greek strategy were based on such material; later studies became more detailed or put forward new dimensions, but did not substantially alter the conclusions of earlier works.

Regarding institutions, apart from the Prime Minister, the Greek Foreign Ministry was the main policy-making centre, especially when it was under a strong Foreign Minister. The Foreign Ministry was not, however, an all-powerful body. There were instances when the bureaucracy's reservations were overruled by the main policy-maker, the political leader. This occurred in the cases of Greece's main mistakes in the Cyprus question, namely the decision to appeal to the UN in 1954 and the handling of the Cyprus crisis in 1963–64.

The military formed another influential group. Their influence has been hotly debated, mostly because of the military dictatorship of 1967–74; sometimes, they were described as a kind of 'parallel' government. However, this is an oversimplification. The army leaders had acquired a substantial degree of autonomy from political decisions in 1949–51, when General (then Field-Marshal) Alexandros Papagos was Commander-in-Chief. However, after Papagos' resignation the Centre governments re-established political control over the army, and this process was completed when Papagos himself became Prime Minister in late 1952. In 1952–63, the military dealt with the technicalities of defence and the military aspects of threat perception. Their views were important and were seriously taken into account, but they did not define grand strategy. This book will show that in 1953–63 there were cases when the governments and the military disagreed over *strategic* matters, and it was always the governments that prevailed. There is not a single example on record to show that these governments refrained from making a foreign policy or even a defence decision because they 'feared' the reaction of the army. On the contrary, in 1963–67 the role of the military seemed to change. This was a period of political instability, when civilian control relaxed, while the war scares over Cyprus gave to army leaders space for manoeuvre. Thus, this book will argue that the military's role was important yet limited during periods of governmental stability, but tended to be upgraded in times of crisis, especially in the mid-1960s, when the crisis was both internal and external and political authority seemed to weaken. Overall, this also stands for the role of the Palace. There is no evidence of Palace intervention in major grand strategy decisions during periods of governmental stability, for example in the decision to appeal to the UN over Cyprus in 1954, to seek Association with the EEC in 1959–61, to settle Cyprus in 1959. However, it is clear that the Palace sought a more active role during the crisis of the mid-1960s.

Finally, other institutions exerted influence in specific areas. This is the case of the Economic Ministries and the Bank of Greece. Their role was important in issues such as external trade, or relations with the EEC and the Western economic organizations. However, the economic institutions played an advisory rather than a decisive role in Cold War policy-making.

The origins of the 'menace from the north': Greek security after the Treaty of Lausanne

During the post-war period, Northern Greece (Greek Macedonia, Western Thrace and Greek Epirus) was one of the few borderlines of East and West, together with the infra-German border, Turkish Eastern Thrace and the Turko–Soviet border in Asia. In the case of Greece, though, this problem assumed even more complex dimensions, because a fusion occurred of Cold War enmities with older regional antagonisms. Greece's Cold War policy cannot be fully understood without taking earlier historical experience into account.

During the humiliating years of the 1967–74 military dictatorship, a part of Greek opinion held that the 'menace from the north' perception derived from the anti-Communism of the Greek state in the aftermath of the civil war. According to this view, the 'menace from the north' was an ideologically driven dogma, the other side of the coin of Greek anti-Communism, a tool for its legitimization in Greek society. Recent research – the Greek post-revisionism – projects a different picture. The 'Red Peril' certainly was used in an unfortunate manner by Greek anti-Communism for purposes of legitimization, but Greek foreign policy was much more refined than that. The 'menace from the north' was a pre-war concept – hence, for example, the building of the Metaxas Line fortifications along the Bulgarian border in the late 1930s, at a time when Bulgaria was anything but Communist. According to Greek post-revisionists, in the post-civil war version of the 'menace from the north' two different historical processes converged: the Cold War and the burdened legacy of the Balkan south, after more than fifty years of conflict, which ultimately involved the survival of Greek populations in the narrow geographical area between the northern shores of the Aegean and the mountain belt on which the northern Greek border lies. The post-war 'menace from the north' perception was founded on a triptych: history, geography and Cold War pressures.

Indeed, for Greek official and public opinion, the memories of the first half of the century were traumatic. The Greek–Bulgarian antagonism in the wider geographical area of Macedonia erupted in 1870 and by 1904–08 escalated in the Macedonian Struggle, a vicious guerrilla war between Greek, Bulgarian, Serb and Romanian bands, struggling for primacy in this Ottoman territory. In 1912–13, the Balkan Wars realized a great part of the Greek irredentist dream, the *Megali Idea*: Greece acquired the largest part of Epirus, the southern and part of the middle zones of the geographical area of Macedonia, the islands of the northern and eastern Aegean and Crete. In 1919, Greece also received Western Thrace. However, in the following decades defending the Macedonian and the Thracian territories of the country became the main foreign policy and security priority of the Greek state, especially because Bulgarian revisionism kept open the possibility of a new struggle for the control of the northern shores of the Aegean.

In 1922, the Greek army suffered a crushing defeat in Asia Minor at the hands of Kemalist Turkey. The 1923 Treaty of Lausanne and the compulsory exchange of populations between Greece and Turkey became a turning point for Greek foreign policy. This exchange of populations destroyed the ethnological basis of Greek claims over Turkish territory, put an end to the *Megali Idea* and turned Greece into a supporter of the *status quo*. Following this, there were no territorial disputes between Greece and Turkey until the eruption of the Aegean sea-bed question in 1973. Bilateral Greek–Turkish relations were fully normalized in 1930 thanks to the initiatives of Prime Ministers Eleftherios Venizelos and Ismet Inönü.[1] After that, Turkey was seen in Athens as a strategic partner in the effort to safeguard the *status quo*.

If the new eastern territories of Greece did not face a threat from Turkey, the northern ones (Greek Macedonia and Western Thrace) came under constant challenge, directly by revisionist Bulgaria and indirectly by Yugoslav hegemonism. The post-1919 Greek northern border was extremely difficult to defend: the land frontier had a length of 1,248 km, of which the Greek–Yugoslav border was 256 km and the Greek–Bulgarian one 531 km. However, the depth was minimal: Thessaloniki itself, the country's second largest city, lies at a distance of 50 km from the Greek–Yugoslav border, while in the Xanthi area in the east, the distance between the Bulgarian border and the sea is less than 30 km.[2] Thus Greece now had to protect a long and strategically thin land border, and this was a structural weakness which naturally affected the country's strategy. Moreover, apart from this 'continental' dimension of the Greek security problem, the country also had to protect an extensive coastline and its many islands. Thus, it was taken for granted that Greece needed to be on good terms with the great power which dominated the Eastern Mediterranean: Britain until 1947, the US after that.

The main security challenges came from the northern border. Three Bulgarian invasions of northeastern Greece took place in 1913, 1916 and 1941. In the 1920s the Yugoslavs claimed sovereignty over the Yugoslav free zone in the port of Thessaloniki, and asked for the establishment of a condominium on the railway line connecting Thessaloniki with the Yugoslav city of Gevgeli; it was only the enormous skills of Eleftherios Venizelos that managed to limit Belgrade's demands in 1929.[3] At the same time, both Bulgaria and Yugoslavia put forward claims over the small Slav-speaking population of northern Greece. Sofia and Belgrade tended to turn against Athens if the latter showed sympathy to the other side. There also was a nightmare scenario for Athens: a possible Bulgarian–Yugoslav axis or alliance, which could direct itself towards the Aegean ports of Thessaloniki, Kavala and Alexandroupolis. It was mainly to prevent such a Sofia–Belgrade rapprochement that Greece agreed to participate in the 1934 Balkan Pact. On another level, during the 1920s the Comintern recognized Greek Macedonia and Thrace as an area of Bulgarian interest.[4]

After the conclusion of the 1923 Treaty of Lausanne, Greece tried to safeguard the balance of power in the region and to prevent any regional power from acquiring a dominant position. Initially Athens placed much hope on the League of Nations, but it was soon disappointed by the international organization and reverted to a more traditional policy.[5] Athens formed an axis with Turkey in 1930, which was upgraded to an alliance in 1933. Greece also signed the 1934 Balkan Pact, together with Yugoslavia, Turkey and Romania. Thus, by 1934 four Balkan states combined against Bulgarian revisionism and their local superiority could not be contested. Yet by 1941, only seven years later, Bulgaria had occupied parts of Greece, Yugoslavia and Romania. Regional balances fell like a house of cards during the international crisis of the 1930s, when France could no longer contain revisionist Germany; in October 1940 Greece was left alone to face the Italian invasion. This showed that Greek security was directly connected with the wider European balance of power.[6] This conclusion, also a result of painful experience from the inter-war years, would play a major role in postwar security perceptions.

The 1940s was an extremely turbulent period: war with Italy in 1940–41; the German invasion and the fall of the country in 1941; triple occupation (German, Italian and Bulgarian) in 1941–44; famine in the winter of 1941–42; hyperinflation in 1944; and a danger of famine after Liberation, which was averted only thanks to aid by the United Nations Relief and Rehabilitation Administration (UNRRA). There was also civil war in 1943–44 between pro-Western and Communist-led resistance forces, while in December 1944 the Communist-led EAM forces were defeated in a fierce battle in Athens, by the government and British forces. Last but not least, a full-scale civil war erupted in 1946–49, when the Greek Communist Party was defeated by a grand coalition of Centre and Right political forces, supported by Britain and the US. By 1949 Greece had remained in the West, paying the price of a deep internal division.[7]

Furthermore, by 1944–45 Greece also faced new claims by its northern neighbours. In autumn 1944 the new Bulgarian Communist regime appeared

8   *Introduction*

reluctant to withdraw its troops from the Greek territories of Eastern Macedonia and Western Thrace, which its Fascist predecessor had occupied; the Bulgarians left only after strong Greek and British pressure.[8] In 1944–48, Yugoslavia sought the 'reunification' of Macedonia under its aegis and through the incorporation of the Greek and the Bulgarian parts of Macedonia into the newly created federative Yugoslav People's Republic of Macedonia (PRM). In 1946, during the Paris Peace Conference, the Yugoslavs officially claimed Greek Macedonia, while simultaneously supporting a new Bulgarian claim over Western Thrace.[9] The simultaneous claims of Bulgaria and Yugoslavia on Greek lands in 1946 shocked Greek policy-makers, convinced them that the Communist takeover had not changed the expansionist Bulgarian policy of the past, and confirmed that the 'menace from the north' continued, arguably in an even more dangerous form. It is true that during the Peace Conference Greece had itself asked for Northern Epirus (Southern Albania) and for the 'rectification' of the Greek–Bulgarian frontier. The latter claim was an effort by Athens to secure a defensible border. At any rate, the Greek claim was rejected, but Athens' fears about Sofia's (and Belgrade's) intentions remained.

During 1946–49, the Greek civil war was also connected in the minds of Greek policy-makers with an external threat. In the 1946–49 civil war, the Greek Communist forces were aided by the Communist countries of Eastern Europe.[10] Athens' accusations against its northern neighbours regarding intervention in the civil war became known as 'the Greek problem', and this was brought to the United Nations.[11] Furthermore, the Fifth Plenary of the KKE in January 1949, which reverted to the pro-Bulgarian Comintern line of the 1920s, convinced the anti-Communist forces in Greece that the civil war endangered both the social regime and the territorial integrity of the country.[12]

The threat against the Greek social and political order was repelled primarily thanks to massive Western, mainly US, military and economic aid. The reorganized Greek army took advantage of the Truman Doctrine. In 1949, under the leadership of General Alexandros Papagos (the victor of the Greek–Italian war of 1940–41), the Greek army reached a strength of 260,000 men and managed to defeat the Communist Democratic Army of Greece (DSE). The Tito–Stalin split led to the closure of the Yugoslav border to the Greek Communist forces in the summer of 1949 and contributed to (but did not cause, as the Greek Left subsequently claimed) their defeat.[13] Athens welcomed the Tito–Stalin split, which destroyed the prospect for a Bulgarian–Yugoslav understanding against Greece and thus significantly relieved the latter's strategic position.

The experience of the second half of the 1940s would not be forgotten so easily. Moreover, the persistence of the KKE that its forces were ready for a new 'round' of conflict further alarmed the Greek military, who insisted on the need for vigilance. After the civil war and throughout the period under examination, the KKE remained banned in Greece and moved its headquarters to the Soviet Bloc, while the banner of the Left within Greece was taken up by a new party, the United Democratic Left (EDA), founded in 1951. All pro-Western Greek political forces were alarmed by the perceived capabilities of the KKE and its possible intention to instigate another 'round' of civil war. The recent publication of Soviet documents about relations between the KKE and the Communist Party of the Soviet Union (CPSU) show that these fears were, to a large extent, ill-founded: the Soviet documents sketch a picture of a defeated and demoralized KKE, which was moving from one crisis to the other (from the 1955 Tashkent disturbances between party members to the 1968 split) and which was constantly in a difficult position, directing petty demands to the colossus of the CPSU which, after all, had half of the world to rule.[14] However, the Greek analysts and the 'civic' political parties had no means of knowing this; and in their post-civil war mentality, even if they had known it, they probably would not have believed it. This mentality, of course, had a deep impact on preparations for internal security.

Economically, the 1940s was a huge disaster. Greece's participation in the European Recovery Programme (ERP) since 1948 had ensured the flow of a large amount of US economic aid, but a large part of these funds was spent either on the war effort of 1948–49, or on repairing the additional destruction caused by the civil war. This meant that the positive effect of the Marshall Plan in the case of Greece was not as catalytic as in other European countries. Although indispensable, the Marshall Plan did not result in the building of a strong Greek economy which would be capable of lessening social tensions or of covering the cost of security.[15] In any case, in the post-war era the cost of defence spiralled because the necessary hardware such as tanks, artillery and jet planes was much more expensive. The Truman Doctrine, the Marshall Plan and the desperate need for foreign aid were combined with US penetration in the decision-making process in Athens, and caused a fierce debate regarding the dependence of the country on the US.[16]

All these meant that in the aftermath of the civil war, the Greek policy-makers and the Greek public understood the world in terms of an ongoing life-or-death struggle, involving threats which persistently originated in the north. During the first half of the century, the country had spent twenty years at war (1912–22 and 1940–49). During the 1940s Greece had suffered the worst destruction that a country could possibly sustain, short of the permanent loss of national territory. Finally, another factor coloured Greek perceptions regarding the new Communist north: until the late 1940s, Greek statesmen had never dealt with the Communist leaders of Bulgaria and therefore did not know much about them. Thus, the Greeks tended to see in their Communist neighbours either the old stereotype of *comitadjis* (nationalist Bulgarian fighters) or the equivalent of the Greek Communist revolutionaries, at the hands of whom non-Communist Greeks had suffered in 1943–49. This book will demonstrate that it was only after contact had been solidly established between Greece and the Soviet Bloc (roughly, by the early 1960s) that the Greek statesmen and officials adopted a more confident attitude towards their Bulgarian neighbours.

Thus, in the post-war era the legacy of regional antagonism met with Cold War realities, as well as with the political and psychological burdens of the civil war. Slowly, from 1946 to 1949, and especially after the outbreak of the Korean

War, the Western world came to interpret Soviet policy as a bid for world hegemony. The Greek civil war was perceived as a case of local Soviet aggression. Reserve about Soviet intentions was a general phenomenon in the West, but in Greece's case additional factors were coming into the picture and made things even more difficult. The Greek policy-makers and analysts were convinced that the post-war international order entailed an additional regional burden for Greek policy: the Cold War meant that traditional Bulgarian revisionism not only continued but had also acquired a new dynamic by becoming the main regional partner of a hostile superpower.

Apart from political and historical factors, the geographical and military realities of the region pointed to the existence of a 'menace from the north'. The northern borders of Greece had proved extremely vulnerable. The 1940 Italian invasion came from the Albanian frontier, the 1941 German invasion was launched from the Bulgarian one, while the Germans finally managed to break the front in the Yugoslav border and to invade Greece through the valley of the Axios/Vardar River, which meets the sea south of Thessaloniki. In terms of geography, the problems of post-war Greece seemed insoluble: cut off from the other Western powers, having to defend narrow and long northern borders, Greece faced the crushing sense of pressure from the Soviet Bloc, which extended from the Rhodope mountains, 30km from the Aegean, all the way up to the Baltic. This Soviet Bloc could mobilize the largest conventional military force in history, the Red Army, whose great capabilities had been vividly illustrated during the recent World War. The new geopolitical position of Greece was described accurately by Panayiotis Pipinelis, the Permanent Undersecretary of the Foreign Ministry during the late 1940s. A well known Realpolitiker, often cynical, Pipinelis described in 1948 'the relentless strategic and diplomatic data of the post-war period'. To make a long story short, Pipinelis noted, Greece had become a frontline state:[17]

> The Balkans was suddenly lost to us. The forward defensive line of the Danube and of the Balkan hinterland has disappeared. The enormous geopolitical pressures of continental Europe, which formerly were partially being checked on the Balkan territories of the Ottoman Empire and then on Yugoslavia or Bulgaria, now come to throw their full weight directly on our borders [...] The importance of Greece as a beach-head of the oceanic powers has multiplied, both for the oceanic powers and for the continental ones. The danger has become larger, the pressure on the country more tense.

Militarily, things were not better. Sofia re-armed in defiance of the demilitarization clauses of the Bulgarian Peace Treaty of 1947. Throughout the 1950s and 1960s the Bulgarian army was significantly stronger than the Greek, especially in tanks, artillery and jet planes. Bulgarian re-armament also sparked tense Greek fears, as it was reminiscent of the Bulgarian refusal to comply with the peace treaties after the First World War.

The lack of strategic depth in the northern Greek border, the overall superiority of the Soviet Bloc and the local superiority of the Bulgarian forces meant that it was impossible for Greek strategic planners to set up a credible system of defence: there simply was not enough space between the Bulgarian border and the Aegean to allow the Greek army to sustain an attack, hold it somewhere in the rear and mount a counteroffensive. The reign of mechanized armies had made it even more difficult to make a stand in this area. The experience of the Second World War had illustrated the inadequacy of static 'continuous' defence lines in the face of a well-organized and mechanized opponent, such as the postwar Bulgarian army. During the civil war, the US regarded Greece as the weakest part of the Northern Tier. After 1949, the Americans considered it better to aid the Greek army so that it could guarantee the *internal* security of the country (which means that, on the level of Greek external security, Washington felt that not much could be done). By the end of the civil war, both the Greek Prime Minister, Alexandros Diomidis, and the US Joint Chiefs of Staff (JCS) considered that, with Yugoslavia's position still unclear, the Greek borders were indefensible.[18]

Towards a partial solution of the security problem, 1950–52

Immediately after the end of the civil war Greece sought an official association with Western defence and, in spring 1950, together with Turkey, applied to join NATO. The Americans were not forthcoming; on the contrary, in 1949–50 they insisted that Greek land forces be reduced to 120,000 men, and encouraged a reluctant Athens to normalize relations with its northern neighbours. The US attitude changed after the outbreak of the Korean War in the summer of 1950. During the Cold War Washington tended to see Greece and Turkey 'as useful and mutually reinforcing outposts',[19] and their importance significantly increased after June 1950. Regardless of the debate about the post-1950 alarmism in the West, the Korean War signalled positive developments for Greek defence: the Americans became more benevolent regarding the prospect of Greek and Turkish accession to NATO, and in autumn 1950 the alliance invited the two countries to become 'associated' powers. In autumn 1951 the North Atlantic Council (NAC) approved their accession, which formally took place in February 1952.[20] Thus, probably beyond its wildest expectations, Greece managed to become a full member of a great alliance. This was a major success for the Centre coalition governments of the National Progressive Centre Union (EPEK) and the Liberal Party, especially the Liberal leader, Sophocles Venizelos, who, either as Prime Minister or as Foreign Minister, dealt with this issue from 1950 to 1952.

Furthermore, Venizelos sought to co-ordinate Greek and Turkish policy. This was not difficult, as both countries felt that they were being threatened by the Soviet Bloc. In 1950–52, Greece and Turkey co-ordinated their approaches to NATO: in 1950 the Turks pointed out to the Americans that, if left outside the Western alliance, Greece and Turkey could become easy targets of Soviet expansionism. On its part, Greece supported Turkey's claim to join NATO (and not to be left as part of a Middle-Eastern defence organization, as Britain had suggested). As Sophocles Venizelos told the British Foreign Secretary, Anthony Eden, in 1951, Greece did not want to be left alone in the front line of the Western alliance.[21]

On the other hand, the normalization of Greek–Yugoslav relations was delayed because of the insistence of Belgrade on appearing as the protector of the Slav-speaking minority in Greek Macedonia. Greece, like Bulgaria, did not accept that the population of the southernmost Yugoslav republic was the legitimate suitor of the whole geographical area of Macedonia, including the Greek and the Bulgarian parts. Furthermore, Athens could not forget that a part (though by no means all) of the Slav-speaking element in northwestern Greece first sided with Fascist Bulgaria and then with Communist Yugoslavia; autonomist pro-Yugoslav armed Slav-Macedonian groups had also taken part in the Greek civil war on the Communists' side. However, the full normalization of bilateral relations took place in December 1950, in the midst of the turmoil that the Korean War had caused. At that moment, Yugoslavia appeared eager to approach Greece; the two countries tacitly agreed not to raise the Macedonian issue, and this opened the road for a bilateral rapprochement.[22] This did not mean that all problems between the two countries had been solved: Yugoslavia was still a peripheral power under a *sui generis* Communist regime, and it was not inconceivable that it could revert to a pro-Soviet policy. Yugoslavia was the same country which had almost succeeded in undermining Greek sovereignty in the north of the country in the 1920s; it was the same regime, under the same leader, that had claimed Greek Macedonia in 1944–48.

During the early 1950s, though, it was becoming clear that both countries had much to gain from a bilateral rapprochement – a view that Sophocles Venizelos carefully and effectively projected. Greece hoped to increase its importance to the West by becoming its link to the Titoist regime. For Yugoslavia, a special relationship with Greece and Turkey seemed to be the only option, as Belgrade did not want to provoke Moscow further by approaching directly the great powers of the West. Moreover, Belgrade could not approach Italy, relations with which were strained because of the Trieste dispute. Thus, international balance in the Balkans seemed to stabilize: Greece and Turkey belonged to NATO; Bulgaria, Romania and Albania were parts of the Soviet Bloc; while neutral Yugoslavia held the balance.

On the military field there were new developments. Greece and Turkey sent troops to Korea, as a sign of their determination to support the UN and as a token of their loyalty to the West, at a moment when they were seeking entry into NATO. The Korean War strengthened the position of those Greek officials who wanted to retain a large army, especially the Commander-in-Chief, Papagos. On the contrary, the Foreign Minister, Sophocles Venizelos, and the Prime Minister, General Nicolaos Plastiras, insisted that the country could not maintain a large land army without facing economic collapse.[23] Papagos prevailed in this dispute: by late 1950, influenced by Korea, the Americans agreed to fund the maintenance of the Greek army at a strength of 160,000 men.[24] After his resignation from the army in May 1951, Papagos formed a new political party, the Greek Rally, and strongly criticized the Centre government for its willingness to reduce the land forces. This was the beginning of tense internal political disputes regarding defence expenditure, which continued until 1967.

The Korean War had further repercussions. In February 1951, the Americans changed their attitude regarding the future role of the Greek army: document NSC-103 of the US National Security Council (NSC) stressed that Greece was important for the West as a bridge to the Middle East and to Yugoslavia. Regarding the Greek armed forces, NSC-103 stressed that the Greek army should be able to resist a Bulgarian invasion, but that if Soviet forces participated in such a conflict the Greek army should simply try to delay their advance.[25] This new American line played a significant role in the evolution of Greek security policy: first, it laid the foundations for the country's accession to NATO; secondly, the Greek army would not limit itself to internal security duties but would focus on repelling external threats; thirdly, the road was opened for the continuation of US military aid. In late 1951, a bilateral Greek–US agreement provided for Greece's participation in the Mutual Defense Assistance Program (MDAP) through which the US offered military aid to their allies.

As the Marshall Plan was about to expire, emphasis was placed on military rather than economic US aid. During 1951, Greek officials kept stressing to their American counterparts that, because of the 1946–49 civil war, Greece had not managed fully to take advantage of the Marshall Plan. Without US military aid, the Greek officials insisted, Athens would have either to reduce its land forces or cover their cost, thus facing economic collapse.[26] This argument contributed to Greece's inclusion in MDAP, but internally it allowed Papagos to accuse the Centre government of trying to 'blackmail' the allies.

By late 1951 and early 1952, great steps had been made towards an amelioration of the country's security problem. However, geography and the balance of military power between Greece and Bulgaria meant that in operational terms the problem remained. It was impossible to hold a Bulgarian attack at the border; it was certain that in that case Eastern Macedonia and Western Thrace would be lost once more. Thus, Athens was constantly seeking to enhance its security: Sophocles Venizelos, in an interview to the *Daily Mail* in February 1951, aired the idea of an alliance between Greece, Turkey and Yugoslavia.[27] This would create a pro-Western combination enjoying regional supremacy over Bulgaria. The accession of Greece and Turkey to NATO seemed to make this idea attractive to Belgrade as well: in early 1952 the Yugoslavs indicated that they were willing to consider a new policy, and to defend the whole of their border with Bulgaria, abandoning their earlier plans to withdraw to the mountainous areas of Bosnia and Kosovo.[28] Thus there was going to be a geographical continuity of Yugoslav, Greek and Turkish forces, which made it possible to consider military co-ordination between them. This is a further reason why 1952 should be considered as a turning point in Greek security policy.

Part I
The era of regional initiatives, 1952–55

1 Attempting to adjust to the post-war world

The Centre coalition government under General Nicolaos Plastiras and Sophocles Venizelos remained in power until the autumn of 1952, but the aged Plastiras had suffered a stroke in March 1952 and Venizelos' political masterpiece, NATO accession, had already been completed. Other people now came to the forefront. In the November 1952 general election, the Greek Rally secured 49 per cent of the vote and won 240 out of 300 seats in Parliament; it then formed the first single-party government of post-civil war Greece. This signalled an important change in comparison to previous years: governmental stability, a huge parliamentary majority, the strong personality of the Prime Minister, Alexandros Papagos, and the achievement of high development rates as early as 1953 were the catalysts for the emergence of a new foreign policy that was much less sensitive to foreign influence or pressure. The 1952 election was the start of a period during which powerful personalities emerged in Greek politics (Papagos, Constantinos Karamanlis and George Papandreou). This significantly contributed to a lessening of the country's dependence on the US. At the same time, the decrease of US economic aid after the end of the European Recovery Programme pointed in the same direction. Washington itself, under President Dwight D. Eisenhower, sought to reduce its economic obligations abroad. Thus, the gradual assertion of relative Greek self-confidence and independence was also welcomed by the Americans, as it was in line with the decrease in US aid.[1]

A soldier-politician: Alexandros Papagos

The Prime Minister, Alexandros Papagos, was the pillar of the Rally: his personal prestige held the various factions of the party together. He has sometimes been criticized as being merely a father figure; according to this view real power rested with Papagos' powerful lieutenant, the Minister for Economic Co-ordination, Spyros Markezinis, who had played a crucial role in the formation of the Rally in 1951. However, this is an exaggeration: Papagos was in complete control of his government and was not dependent on Markezinis; in 1954 he even quarrelled with Markezinis, who then left the Rally and in 1955 formed his own Progressive Party. Markezinis never assumed a major role in the making of foreign or security policy; indeed, he later wrote that Papagos' refusal to make him

Foreign Minister was one of the causes of their quarrel.[2] In the developments examined in this book, Papagos is particularly important. Victor of two wars (the Greek–Italian war in 1940–41 and the civil war in 1949), an all-powerful Commander-in-Chief until 1951, the only Field-Marshal in the country's history, Papagos enjoyed enormous prestige. Furthermore, the army was loyal to him personally. The style of his leadership is vividly illustrated by a remark that he made to Lieutenant-General Solon Ghikas: 'Doubt should not be construed as innocence but as guilt'.[3]

Like all non-Communist Greek leaders, Papagos was convinced that only in the Western alliance could Greece hope to find security; credible defence could not be secured by the country's own means. Thus, allied solidarity was for Papagos a sine qua non for the Greek defence effort. As leader of the Opposition in 1951–52, he had relentlessly accused the Plastiras–Venizelos government of wanting to reduce the size of the army and of trying to 'blackmail' the allies in order to secure more military aid. In December 1952, presenting his government in Parliament, Papagos repeated that NATO and the UN were the pillars of the international policy of Greece.[4] On the first anniversary of his electoral victory, he again referred to the security which allied solidarity gave to Greece.[5] This was a permanent theme of his public declarations.

However, Papagos did not believe that NATO membership implied that Greece could now relax its defence effort. On the contrary, he held that the alliance would help only those who were willing to make a sustained defence effort. Thus, he repeatedly declared Greece's determination to resist a Soviet-Bloc attack. This was also important to underline the role of the Greek army as a trip-wire mechanism, which would ensure that Greece would not be left alone in a future war. In November 1951, as leader of the opposition, Papagos had stressed:[6]

> As I have repeatedly declared, Greece will defend its independence even alone, making every conceivable sacrifice. Its entry into NATO has a significant moral effect and also offers great military advantages, which however create additional obligations for Greece. Anyway, I strongly believe that the moral unity between the people and the armed forces is the guarantee that any attack against the country will find the nation in the battlements of honour and sacrifice.

Papagos also believed that the West should declare its determination to hold its ground: in November 1951 he insisted that 'only a sign of allied weakness could cause a war'.[7] And during his last interview to the Greek press, in February 1955, he noted:[8]

> I still think that we will avoid a war. But everything regarding the issue of peace is connected with unknown factors. Thus, Greece has to be ready for everything. I wish to stress that even if international tensions end up in a war, Greece, thanks to the continuous aid and the invaluable help of the

USA, thanks to its alliances, and finally thanks to the admirable organization and the wonderful fighting spirit of its armed forces, will be in a position to resist any aggressor and to play a prime role in the defeat of the forces of violence and barbarism, as it has done in all crucial moments of its history.

The Prime Minister also paid great attention to geography; however, his thinking did not involve a comprehensive geographically-oriented analysis (as would be the case in 1955–63); he focused on technical military issues. This is an interesting difference between the 'soldier' Papagos and his political successors. Papagos mainly stressed the strategic position of Greece and its possible contribution in case of war. In autumn 1953, speaking to a British journalist, he noted:[9]

> Greece occupies a most strategic position in the Balkans, as it links the Mediterranean with Central and Eastern Europe. The valleys of the Axios, Strymon, Nestos and Evros rivers, which end in the Greek ports of Thessaloniki, Kavala and Alexandroupolis, are natural roads for the transfer of troops either to the north or to the south. These three ports will be natural bases for any army operating in the Balkans [...] But even if we lose the Dardanelles, the flank position of Greece regarding the Straits, and the Aegean islands, which form numerous chains between the Greek and Turkish coastlines, allow us to block the entry of enemy naval units in the Mediterranean.

Papagos' attention to technical military detail is also evident in his constant care to ensure that Greek border defence would buy time for the completion of the mobilization; after all, the effective and swift mobilization under his own command had proved instrumental in Greece's victory against Italy in 1940. This emphasis on military issues must be regarded as natural in the thinking of a field-marshal. In a sense, it complemented the more politically oriented analysis of his two close associates, Panayiotis Kanellopoulos and Alexis Kyrou.

Strategy and ideology: Panayiotis Kanellopoulos

Panayiotis Kanellopoulos, one of Greece's most prominent intellectuals, was Minister of National Defence and, after December 1954, one of the two Deputy Prime Ministers. Yet his influence in security policy has been neglected, as most observers turned their attention to his other activities: some focused on his role as a leading anti-Communist intellectual of the early Cold War period; others centred on his leadership of the Greek Right (1963–67) or on his major role in the resistance against the 1967–74 military dictatorship; and others noted his calls for moderation after 1974. However, these aspects are fragmentary and there are very few comprehensive analyses of this impressive figure who greatly influenced Greek political history, although he never held power for long periods (he became Prime Minister for three weeks in late 1945 and for another three weeks in April 1967, until his government was toppled by the Colonels). It is also important to note that he steadily administered war ministries: the National Defence Ministry of the government-in-exile in 1942–43, and the Ministry of the Land Forces in the late 1940s during the civil war.

Serving under the imposing figure of Papagos, Kanellopoulos could take few substantial initiatives on military matters. Later, he also referred to the role of the ultra-conservative organization in the Army, the IDEA (Sacred Bond of Greek Officers), which distrusted him; he noted that such practices finally facilitated the imposition of a military dictatorship in 1967.[10] However, his role in security policy cannot be neglected. Indeed, Kanellopoulos expressed two diverse but important viewpoints regarding Greek security. First, he advanced an ideological interpretation, which was natural for one of the leading intellectuals of Greece: the ideological rivalries of the post-war world, and mostly the notion of the struggle between freedom and totalitarianism, could not leave him indifferent. Kanellopoulos also paid attention to the practical problems of defence. Thus, speaking at the Press Club in Washington during his visit to the US in spring 1954, he noted that 'the entry of Greece and Turkey into NATO was the result of a geographical and a moral necessity', while the two countries had the task of defending the 'historical corridor' of the Mediterranean.[11] 'Moral' was one of his favourite words, describing his concern for ideological consistency. Admittedly the combination of 'geographical' and 'moral' imperatives was unusual, but this expressed the search for a combination of the practical and the theoretical which characterized his thinking.

The most important example of this search can be found in Kanellopoulos' attitude towards the Greek–US agreement of October 1953, which provided for the setting up of US bases on Greek soil. Speaking in Parliament, he noted that the installation of US bases created a feeling of security for the people, and thus also facilitated economic development; the presence of US troops and of US air force units increased the practical guarantees for Greek security. Kanellopoulos then moved to his favourite 'moral' field, by stressing that the agreement was a manifestation of the spirit of friendship and co-operation which characterized Greek–US relations in an era of global ideological struggles. In March 1954, speaking at the Press Club in Washington, he noted that Greece did not regard that this agreement was concluded with a 'foreign power', because Greece did not regard the Americans as 'foreigners'.[12] His critics often used to point to such rhetoric exaggerations in order to argue that he was 'servile' to the Americans. However, such declarations resulted from his need to take a clear and unreserved position in the great 'moral' issue of his time, namely the ideological conflict of East and West. Kanellopoulos was not servile to the US. For example, he was the Defence Minister who ended the participation of US officers, with voting rights, in the Supreme Military Council, thus practically enhancing national control over the armed forces.[13] In the period examined here, Kanellopoulos plays a major role both as a person with deep experience on defence issues and as a major personality of the new Right, who also expressed the need to make a stand on the wider ideological problem of the post-war world.

A diplomat: Alexis Kyrou

The third important influence on the Papagos government's policy was that of Alexis Kyrou, a diplomat of Cypriot origin, brother of the owner of the influential pro-government daily *Hestia*. Kyrou is widely known for his role in the Cyprus question: in 1931, as Greek Consul General in Nicosia, and contrary to the instructions of Athens, he encouraged the Greek-Cypriot revolt of that year, the first violent confrontation of the Greek-Cypriot majority with British colonial authorities. Kyrou led the movement for the resignation of Greek diplomats from the Foreign Ministry after the fall of Greece to the Germans in 1941.[14] During the occupation he was a member of the Athenian conservative resistance organizations *Hellenikon Aima* and *Ethniki Drasi*, and it was then that he forged a close personal relationship with Papagos. He served as permanent representative of Greece at the UN from 1947 to 1953. In 1952–54 he was Papagos' main advisor on foreign policy; indeed, immediately after his electoral victory of November 1952 Papagos asked Kyrou to return to Athens and assume the duties of the Director General of the Ministry.[15] In 1953–54 Kyrou convinced Papagos to appeal to the UN, asking for the exercise of the right of self-determination in Cyprus, and presented Greece's case in New York in December 1954; following the Greek defeat in that debate, he resigned from the directorate general. In retrospect, it was Kyrou rather than the Foreign Minister, Stephanos Stephanopoulos, who exerted the greatest influence on Greek foreign policy, especially on issues such as Balkan affairs, the Soviet Union and Cyprus.[16]

Even during the 1940s, Kyrou had disputed the alarmist view which was then popular: to blame all Greece's security problems on an international Panslavist conspiracy. In 1944, in a pamphlet which he published as a member of *Hellenikon Aima*, he noted that the US, Britain and the Soviet Union should co-operate after the war; during the previous decades, he added, 'Panslavism had done to Greece less harm, compared to the harm caused by the exaggerated fear of Panslavism'.[17] Kyrou's views can be found in two books that he published in 1955 and in 1962. Of the triptych 'history–geography–Cold War', he placed his emphasis on history. According to him, the danger did not derive from devious international masterplans but from a more tangible source: Bulgarian nationalism.

Kyrou noted that Greek foreign policy was determined by 'its [the country's] geographical position, its economic needs, the historical experience, the realization of its role in the international community and more especially in the Balkans and the Eastern Mediterranean basin'. Mostly, Greek foreign policy was shaped by the need for security: 'the future of our country lies in the sea, provided that we will securely base our backs on old-Rhodope [a mountain range in the Greek–Bulgarian frontier]'.[18] According to Kyrou, Greece's security problem derived from a permanent Bulgarian aggressiveness, not from the communist nature of the regime in Sofia:[19]

> [The author – Kyrou] is personally of the opinion that Greek interests require the normalization of Greek–Bulgarian relations and the implementation of a

realistic policy towards this neighbouring state. At the same time, however, the author is also convinced that our guidance from the teachings of the past, recent and older, as well as the realization by the Bulgarians that we have decided not to forget such teachings, are elementary preconditions for the success of such realistic policy towards them, regardless whether today they are organized as a 'People's Republic' and whether, instead of Tsankov, they are being governed by comrade Chervenkov. Thus, neither hatred, nor rancour, nor unbending prejudices, nor insistent dislike. Simply cold logic and systematic reserve. We must make every conceivable effort to fully normalize Greek–Bulgarian relations, but we must also fully understand that the Bulgarians themselves will not allow this normalization to evolve into a true friendship. All the better if the future disclaims the past.

In other words, according to Kyrou (and on this he was representative of a wider tendency in the Foreign Ministry), Bulgarian policy was always aggressive towards Greece, regardless of the nature of the internal Bulgarian regime. This thesis was founded on the experiences of the three Bulgarian attacks on Greece (1913, 1916, 1941), as well as on the reluctance of the Bulgarian Communist government to evacuate northeastern Greece in 1944 and on the Bulgarian claim over Greek Western Thrace in 1946.

When referring to the other countries of the Soviet Bloc, though, Kyrou was much more moderate, and advanced a single precondition for the normalization of relations: the security of the Greek state. Thus, he was in favour of a 'careful policy towards Soviet Russia and the other states of the eastern bloc':[20]

> Our sentiments towards Soviet Russia are being guided – and have to be guided – by the experience of the last fifteen years [i.e. the civil war]; but they are not being influenced – nor should they be influenced – by prejudices arising from differences between our ideological views and the political, economic and social organization of the two states [...] These relations will always be guided, so far as Greece is concerned [...] by past experience and the pressing need to strengthen our security, external as well as internal (namely security even against subversive elements aided from outside), but never by ideological views.

His attitude towards Yugoslavia and Turkey differed, probably because these two countries were seen as natural partners of Greece in the quest for regional stability. He expressed some reservations concerning Yugoslav policy on the Macedonian question, but noted that a rapprochement between Athens and Belgrade was always possible.[21] He was also in favour of Greek–Turkish co-operation, although he put forward some preconditions for it:[22]

> Co-operation, thus, with Turkey, co-operation close and cordial; but co-operation on totally equal terms, co-operation based on mutual good will and on careful avoidance of those exaggerations which have led us into illu-

sive hopes [for a common attitude towards the 1941 German invasion of the Balkans] and sometimes into national humiliation. The same exaggerations have convinced some of our Turkish friends that their friendship is the only pillar of Greek foreign policy and that this makes Athens willing to become a *brillant* – or not even a *brillant* – *second* of Turkish diplomacy. We must understand, and then explain to our Turkish allies, that the value of Greece's friendship for Turkey is equal to the value of their friendship for us, and that our country does not wish to dominate the Balkans, but it does not accept the hegemony of others, knowing that it is eternal Greece.

Finally, Kyrou expressed a tendency to disengage from dependence on the US. In 1954 he insisted that Greece should appeal to the UN over Cyprus, ignoring British reactions and the warnings of the Americans that they would not support an appeal in New York. Serving in the Permanent Mission to the UN, Kyrou had gone through the bitter experience of the late 1940s, when Greek policy agonizingly sought the guidance of the US on every single issue. Now he wanted to reassert Greek independence, and in this he was in full agreement with Papagos.

In foreign and security policy, Papagos, Kanellopoulos and Kyrou represented a transition to a new era and a determined attempt at adjustment after the shocks of the civil war. The main guiding lines of their security policy included loyalty to NATO, the effort to deepen the relationship with the US (while at the same time displaying an increased measure of independence from Washington), and a regional policy aiming to achieve security from a historically defined and, therefore, permanent Bulgarian threat. Their policy proved effective until mid-1954, when the tripartite alliance between Greece, Turkey and Yugoslavia was signed. However, everything was to fall apart because of the Cyprus question after the Greek appeal to the UN. Had the achievement of relative security in 1952–54 made Greece less prudent than before? Were Ankara and Belgrade equally careless? Or was the 1953–54 Balkan entente inherently unstable? It is safe to assume that all these factors played a role in the developments that ensued.

2 A new NATO member, 1952–55

The Greek armed forces: strategy, cost and size

The Greek army expanded dramatically after the Balkan Wars of 1912–13 and assumed an active role in politics during the National Schism of Venizelists and anti-Venizelists in the 1910s. During the inter-war years, control of the army was an important aspect of the Greek domestic scene.[1] However, more internal crises occurred in 1941–52. During the Second World War, the old Venizelist and anti-Venizelist officers – roughly, the old Liberals and Conservatives – converged in an anti-Communist attitude, in view of the rise of the Communist-led EAM forces in occupied Greece. Anti-Communism led to the homogenization of the army during the civil war years. In 1949–51, when Papagos was Commander-in-Chief, the army acquired a great measure of autonomy from political control.[2] In May 1951, when Papagos announced his resignation from the army, some of his followers staged a coup, which was suppressed thanks to the reaction of King Paul and of Papagos himself; this incident brought to the forefront the issue of the existence of IDEA, a secret organization of officers who looked to Papagos for leadership.[3]

Immediately after his ascent to power Papagos dismissed his personal opponents from the army, such as Lieutenant-Generals Theodoros Grigiropoulos, Thrassyvoulos Tsakalotos, Th. Pentzopoulos and E. Vasilas. It may be noted that the Defence Minister, Kanellopoulos, and the US Embassy were against these changes. The US Chargé, Charles Yost, pressed Papagos not to make the changes, or at least not to make them immediately, but the Prime Minister went ahead with his plans. Yost cabled to Washington that Papagos felt so strongly on this issue that even a US ultimatum would not force him to change his mind.[4] Papagos elevated his own close associates to the highest positions in the army. Lieutenant-General Stelios Kitrilakis became Chief of the General Staff of National Defence, and was succeeded in December 1954 by Lieutenant-General Constantinos Dovas. Lieutenant-General Alexandros Tsigounis became Chief of the General Staff of the Army (GES), to be succeeded by Lieutenant-General Solon Ghikas. Furthermore, some of the officers who had been removed from the army after the abortive 1951 coup now returned, such as Lieutenant-General A. Natsinas, who became the head of the newly-formed Greek Central Intelligence Service (KYP). Throughout 1952–55, the opposition accused the government of tolerating IDEA. According to Kanellopoulos, the IDEA people were hostile towards himself and the three Undersecretaries of his Ministry.[5]

The institutional role of the army was also reformed. Following Papagos' resignation from the army in May 1951, the Centre governments had managed to re-impose a degree of civilian control over the armed forces. As head of the government, Papagos had no reason to encourage the army's autonomy, and in 1953 defence policy was placed under the control of the government and of the Supreme Council of National Defence (ASEA).[6] Decree 2387/53 set up a weak General Staff of National Defence, which was responsible for the overall planning and international relations of the Services, and a powerful General Staff of the Army, which was the operational leader of the land forces. Thus the most powerful figures of the Army in 1953–67 were the chiefs of the General Staff of the Army, not those of the General Staff of National Defence.

NATO accession also triggered significant changes, which were dealt with by the EPEK–Liberal coalition in 1952. The Greek armed forces were placed under the Naples Headquarters, although Athens pressed for the appointment of a US commander, since it was reluctant to place its forces under an Italian general, given the Greek memories of the 1940–41 war. The Greek navy came under the jurisdiction of the British officer who commanded the allied naval forces in the Mediterranean (after December 1952, this was Admiral Lord Mountbatten). Moreover, Athens sought to modernize its military equipment, giving priority to the air force and mostly to the replacement of old Spitfires with jet planes; the first F-84 jets arrived shortly before the November 1952 election.[7]

After November 1952, the Papagos government faced a difficult problem. Despite NATO membership, the Greek forces did not have the capability to repel a Bulgarian attack. The land army had a total strength of 143,000 men, but its equipment was out of date and came from the days of the civil war, when the army had fought against a guerrilla force, not against a modern mechanized opponent; Greece's few light tanks were no match for Bulgaria's armour. As Papagos stressed in Parliament on 19 March 1953, Bulgaria was estimated to have 235,000 men under arms, Albania 45,000, Turkey 350,000 and Yugoslavia 450,000 (Bulgarian forces comprised the tactical army of 170,000 and a 'border army' of 65,000 men).[8] The Greek army had 239 light tanks and 550 artillery pieces, while Bulgaria was considered to have 700 medium and light tanks and 2,000 artillery pieces.[9] The NATO force goals, which the country had difficulty in meeting, provided for an army of nine infantry divisions, *one-third* of an armoured division and six light-infantry regiments. Furthermore, NATO specialists noted the shortages of anti-aircraft defences, NCOs and specialists, as well as of support units, and the lack of an adequate recall training programme for reservists. Last but not least, the NATO specialists stressed that the country did not have the economic capabilities to expand its defence effort, and was dependent on foreign military aid.[10]

Greek strategy in case of war reflected these weaknesses. Papagos publicly referred to this strategy twice, in November 1951 and in March 1953. In his 1951 interview to *Kathimerini*, he stressed:[11]

Having in mind the strength of Bulgaria and Albania, a reduction of the army would create huge dangers. The army has as its main task to resist a sudden attack, to cover the mobilization and to secure internal order against any treasonous activity.

In March 1953, speaking in Parliament, Papagos made no reference to 'internal order', and noted that the army had to accomplish two tasks: 'to allow us to deal with a sudden attack and to cover the mobilization'.[12] A 'sudden attack' was a major fear of Greece and the other Western countries in the aftermath of the Korean War. In that case, the country had to ensure the completion of its mobilization, otherwise, it would run the risk of losing the war before having the chance to engage its full forces.

In a sense, the mission of the Greek army aimed to repeat Papagos' successful tactics of 1940–41: strong and well-organized units at the front would try to slow down the advance of the enemy, so that the mobilization could proceed, then the army would mount a counteroffensive. However, Papagos knew well that this was a profoundly theoretical concept. Bulgarian superiority in tanks and artillery meant that a Greek counteroffensive had little chance of success. Moreover, there was a second insoluble problem for the Greek strategic planners: the geography of the Greek–Bulgarian frontier was dramatically different from that of the Greek–Albanian border. In 1940, Greece's defence had strategic depth – a mountainous terrain, favourable for the defending forces – while in the Bulgarian border, behind the Falakron or the Rhodope mountains there was only the sea.

The Greek strategic planners had two options. In the first scenario, the defensive battle would not be fought at the border, with the front facing the north, but at the Strymon/Struma River (which divides Greek Eastern from Central Macedonia) with the front facing the east; this, indeed, was the unspoken assumption of the US NSC-103 document on Greece in 1951. However, even then the Greek army could not mount a counterattack with its limited mechanized means. Furthermore, a defensive line at the Strymon meant that the Greek army would concede a large part of the national territory from the very first days of the war: Eastern Macedonia and Western Thrace. The second option involved the implementation of a 'forward strategy', by moving the defensive line to the River Nestos/Mesta, which divides Eastern Macedonia from Western Thrace. Such an option would mean that the Greek army would abandon only Western Thrace, which the Greeks could realistically expect to regain through a concerted Greek–Turkish counteroffensive. Papagos was strongly in favour of this strategy, but the Greek army lacked the necessary weaponry to implement it, mainly medium tanks and jet planes, and the alliance would not provide them. Thus, the Greek defensive line remained on the Strymon. According to the Greek strategic planners, this meant that the country would not put up a forward defence; in case of war the whole of northeastern Greece would be overrun by the Bulgarians for the fourth time in a row.[13]

Defence co-ordination with Turkey was an idea of the 1930s, very popular in the Greek General Staff after the signature of the 1933 Greek–Turkish treaty for the guarantee of the common border (i.e. the Thracian one) and the 1934 Balkan Pact.[14] The participation of the two states in NATO made such a plan theoretically possible, but it is interesting that Papagos made a reference to it even before NATO accession, remembering that the 1933 treaty still stood.[15] In other words, Papagos wanted to turn the tables on the Bulgarians through the conclusion of a regional alliance. However, the Turks were reluctant to commit large forces in Turkish Eastern Thrace. Ankara indicated that this would be possible only if Yugoslavia decided to participate in the common defence, thus radically changing the balance of power with Bulgaria.[16] This was why the decision of the Yugoslavs in 1952 to defend their southern border with Bulgaria was so crucial for Greek strategy. In February 1953, the first tripartite pact between Greece, Turkey and Yugoslavia was concluded. This made it possible to plan the 'forward strategy' preferred by the Greek Prime Minister, or even to plan an offensive against Bulgaria during the early stages of a war – a tactic which naturally was attractive to a soldier like Papagos.[17] In May 1953 Papagos told the US Secretary of State, John Foster Dulles, that the Balkans could even threaten the Soviet flank in Central Europe.[18] Of course this was an exaggeration, and even in 1954 the US military did not fail to note Greece's 'negligible' offensive capabilities.[19] Yet a tripartite Greek–Turkish–Yugoslav entente could change the balance in the Balkans, and was the only way to deal with the military and geographical weaknesses of Greek defence against Bulgaria.

During its first year in office, the Papagos government tried to maintain the existing strength of the land army and to increase its firepower. In 1953, the old British artillery was partially replaced by more modern American equipment.[20] The air force was also strengthened: the old Spitfire fighters and the Helldiver light bombers were replaced by six squadrons of F-84s. There was an increase in ground crews, while new airports were being built, suitable to accommodate jet aircraft. However, Kanellopoulos also said in Parliament that there had been no progress in the replacement of the light Greek tanks, and this was a field in which Bulgarian supremacy could prove decisive. In 1954, the Greek air force also received F-86 jets.[21]

However, the effort to keep the land army at the strength of 140,000 men proved abortive, mainly for economic reasons. NATO accession did much to

Table 2.1 Greek defence expenditure as a percentage of the GNP 1949–54

Year	Percentage
1949	7.4
1950	7.6
1951	8.5
1952	8.3
1953	6.4
1954	6.9

Source: 'Military Spending and National Income' (tables), 27 April 1959, Karamanlis Archive, file 8A.

relieve the Greek economy, but could not solve the problem. Defence expenditure rose by almost 1 per cent in 1951 (see Table 2.1), after the outbreak of the Korean War, but was significantly reduced in 1953, after accession into NATO. Defence expenditure at the level of 8.5 per cent of the GNP in 1951 or 8.3 per cent in 1952 (which was a year of recession in Greece) was totally unacceptable, but even 6.4 per cent of the GNP in 1953 was crushing: 40 per cent of the budget was going to defence, and this still resulted in an army with inadequate firepower. For a country like Greece, which had the second lowest standard of living in NATO (higher only than Turkey's) and which had gone through a social revolution some years earlier, this was unbearable. Furthermore, after Papagos' electoral victory the issue of defence spending did not recede as an internal political problem. The Rally had attacked the Centre coalitions for wanting to reduce the strength of the army; now, the Centre parties attacked the Rally for keeping defence expenditure too high. During a Parliamentary debate in March 1953, Sophocles Venizelos noted that Greece could not maintain an army of more than 70,000 men. Papagos and Kanellopoulos insisted on the need for a large army, but the Defence Minister also mentioned that numbers could vary according to international developments.[22]

Of course, the easiest way of maintaining a large army was to have others pay for it – and there was only one candidate for such a role. US economic aid to Greece was substantially reduced after 1953, but military aid was regarded by the Greek governments as indispensable. The term 'military aid' describes a wide variety of packages: for example, military hardware such as guns, artillery, vehicles, tanks, airplanes, warships; consumables; training or technical assistance; and the defence support aid, which involved the transfer of funds directly to the Greek budget and was of great financial importance. In fact, defence support aid was not military aid proper but a kind of economic aid, which affected defence spending and was allocated through the procedures of military assistance. It was mainly defence support aid that would determine the capability of Greece to maintain a large army. However, the Americans were no longer forthcoming: the Eisenhower administration steadily reduced this form of aid, and this meant that Greece would have to cover the additional cost. It was not surprising, therefore, that aid was such an important topic in the discussions of the members of the Papagos government with their American counterparts. Kanellopoulos raised this issue when talking to the NATO Supreme Allied Commander Europe (SACEUR), General Alfred Gruenther, in April 1953, and Markezinis insisted on aid during his visit to Washington in May.[23]

In the spring of 1953, Stalin's death and the new Soviet policy of peaceful co-existence seemed to make Western fears of a sudden Soviet attack less pressing. Of course, neither the Western statesmen in general nor the Greeks in particular believed that Soviet aims had changed. The Greeks furthermore feared that, in a general East–West negotiation, their country could be abandoned by the West. Thus, in the April 1953 NATO ministerial meeting Kanellopoulos and Stephanopoulos called for greater solidarity among the Western powers. Kanellopoulos also referred to the financial burden of Greek defence expenditure, noted the deficiencies of the Greek army in modern equipment and asked for 'equitable burden sharing' among the members of the alliance.[24] In the following month, when Dulles visited Athens, the Greek leaders insisted that Soviet policy had not changed, and that Greece desperately needed more US aid in order to maintain its army at its present strength.[25] In NATO, Greece took the line that the alliance should not relax its defence effort.[26]

During 1953, NATO military leaders started expressing reservations about the strength of the Greek army. In May 1953, the British Secretary General of NATO, Lord Ismay, publicly stated in Athens that the alliance's effort should continue, but that it might be better to have smaller and better-equipped forces rather than large and ineffective ones.[27] This created some nervousness in the Greek government. In July Kanellopoulos publicly reiterated the government's determination to keep the army at 140,000 men, but in August he told the Americans that the country could not sustain such a large force and was studying its possible reduction.[28] In September 1953 the Deputy Supreme Commander of NATO Forces Europe, Field Marshal Sir Bernard Montgomery, visited Athens; in conversations with Papagos, Kanellopoulos and Lieutenant-General Kitrilakis, Montgomery noted that NATO had succeeded in deterring a sudden Soviet invasion and now had to adjust to the economic needs of a long Cold War. Montgomery did not ask for the reduction of the Greek army, but mentioned to Kitrilakis that the Greek army had too many guns and too few reserves.[29] Still, the Greek government continued to hope that the Americans would step in, offer the necessary funds and avert a reduction in the land army.

This soon proved an illusion. The adoption of the New Look strategy, which involved a heavier reliance on nuclear weapons, made it clear that the Eisenhower administration meant its words regarding the reduction of defence spending and aid. Moreover, since 1953 a catastrophic earthquake in the Ionian islands had created additional financial strain for the Greek budget, as money was needed for reconstruction.

It was clear in Athens that if the US was not going to provide extra funds, the Greek economy would not be in a position to support a large army. The first signs of a change of policy became evident during the NATO ministerial meeting of December 1953, when Kanellopoulos underlined that 'we will do our best in order to implement them [the alliance force goals] within our financial capabilities'.[30] In late January 1954, Papagos visited Paris and had the opportunity to meet Ismay, General Alfred Gruenther (the SACEUR), and Montgomery. The Greek Prime Minister noted that either a 'more economic organization' of the army should be found, or NATO itself should pay to keep the Greek army at its present strength. It was decided that the alliance should review the issue. Evidently, by that time the Greek government believed that the army could be reduced to 100,000–105,000 men without undermining national defence. On their part, the military planners of the alliance thought that this was the minimum number which would be compatible with NATO planning.[31] Thus, Papagos was now implementing exactly the policy for which he had criticized the previous Centre government: he intended both to reduce the army and to blackmail the alliance. To be sure, the Prime Minister took into account some additional elements, such as the new strategy of the alliance (the New Look policy and 'massive retaliation'), and the fact that the alliance plans already called for smaller and better armed and trained conventional forces.[32] In short, the new Greek policy was not incompatible with NATO policy. Still, Papagos' volte face was remarkable. As the influential Conservative daily *Kathimerini* noted, the army's numerical strength was not 'under the circumstances of today's defence programs, a necessary and exclusive element of security'.[33] Sophocles Venizelos could not have said it better.

Having decided to adopt a new policy, Papagos made a dramatic gesture: on 24 February 1954 he gave the US Ambassador, Cavendish Cannon, a memorandum outlining the economic difficulties of Greek defence and warning that the Greek army would be reduced if the country did not receive additional aid.[34] The Greek press considered that the reduction of the army had already been decided. On 21 March, *Kathimerini* noted that numbers were not significant if the firepower of the army could be strengthened, while 'the endurance of the Greek tax-payer has reached its breaking point'.[35] In March and April 1954, Kanellopoulos visited the US and again raised the issue of aid with US officials, including Eisenhower himself, but he did not get additional funds.[36] This made the reduction of the army inevitable. After Kanellopoulos' failure in Washington, and as the political effects of Markezinis's recent resignation from the government were still unclear, Papagos announced a *unilateral* decision to reduce the land army. It should be remembered that this took place at a moment when the issue was supposed to be discussed in NATO, but Papagos did not wait for these deliberations to end. By early May, reservists were released from service. This was estimated to bring the land army down to a strength of almost 105,000 men.[37]

The Centre opposition noticed that Papagos was now doing exactly what it had accused the Centre governments of wanting to do. In practice this was an understatement, since Papagos additionally disregarded an alliance procedure. The unilateral character of the Prime Minister's initiative also made the Americans nervous: in a meeting with Papagos, Ambassador Cannon reminded him that the issue was being discussed in the alliance. Papagos stepped up the pressure, though, noting that without additional aid for 1955 Greece would reduce its army further, even to a level of 70,000 men.[38] This line was aggressively supported by the conservative press, which held that even an army of 105,000 men was too big for Greece's purse: 'All these years, this country has done nothing else but to arm itself [...] The army is being fed by the flesh of the nation', *Kathimerini* commented on 13 June.[39] It is interesting that now, when the conservative press was turning against the idea of a large army, the United States Information Service (USIS) offered to assist the government in a campaign to educate the Greek public about the necessity of the common defence effort.[40]

NATO officials were strongly against a further reduction. In the summer of 1954, Gruenther himself insisted on the need to maintain a force of 105,000 men and suggested that the Greek army could concentrate all its armoured vehicles in order to form a 'special' infantry division.[41] Thus the SACEUR indirectly conceded that the Greek army did not have adequate armour to form an 'armoured' unit. According to NATO's annual review of 1954, the Greeks proposed the formation of an armoured division, but the term 'special' was preferred because it was 'more descriptive of its actual status'.[42] Still, the government repeated that if more aid were not given, the army would be further reduced. Thus, the Americans finally agreed to provide an additional $10 million, in order to keep the Greek army at 105,000 men.[43]

In the following year, 1955, new developments negatively affected Greek security. A destructive earthquake in Thessaly meant that the budget needed to deal with additional expenditure; Papagos fell ill in March; and the alliance asked for the increase of the Greek army to 120,000 men because of the further strengthening of the Bulgarian army and the opening of the new Soviet leadership to Tito. The Greek government again asked for more US aid. This was supported by the US Embassy, with the argument that Greece was a world-wide symbol both of US resolve to resist communism and of the positive effects of US aid.[44] Washington assented and an agreement for additional aid was signed in the summer of 1955; thus, the Greek army returned to a strength of 120,000 men.

With such financial difficulties, the Greek navy was relatively neglected, despite the insistence of analysts and retired naval officers that a country like Greece was dependent on its navy for the smooth completion of its mobilization.[45] Kanellopoulos limited his efforts to the modernization of the Hunt-class destroyers that Greece had received as a loan from Britain, but even this did not materialize.[46] Moreover, a proposal to build a large NATO naval base in the island of Leros in the Dodecanese did not produce results: although this would have enabled the alliance effectively to close the Aegean to an advancing Soviet fleet, the proposal was vetoed by Turkey on the grounds that the Dodecanese should remain demilitarized, and was definitely abandoned by 1956.[47] The Greek air force, which had been modernized in 1953–54, reached a relatively satisfactory strength of twelve squadrons by 1955. However, there still were problems in the warning system and in training.[48]

Last but not least, the Greek government also expressed interest in the possible role of NATO in aiding its less developed members. The Foreign Minister, Stephanos Stephanopoulos, who was an economist, raised this subject in almost all of his interventions in the NATO ministerial meetings.[49] He stressed that underdevelopment and poverty could create instability, thus reducing Greek defence capabilities. This was a constant argument of the Greek government in these years.

The agreement for the installation of US bases

Aid was not the only issue in Greek–US relations. The Papagos government wanted to establish a more tangible bilateral defence relationship with Washington. In the spring of 1953, the Americans encouraged Athens to ask officially for the establishment of US bases on Greek soil. The Americans wanted the initiative to come from the Greek side. Papagos immediately put this request in a letter to Eisenhower, which Markezinis personally delivered to the US President in May 1953. In his letter, Papagos did not raise the issue of US aid – an indication that Athens did not want to put forward any preconditions for such an agreement. The negotiations started in August 1953, and were concluded within some weeks. The only issue that caused some difficulty was the fear of the Americans about possible leaks of the secret texts which accompanied the treaty. The Americans asked the Greeks not to ratify the agreement in Parliament, but Athens rejected this.[50] The agreement was signed on 12 October 1953 by Stephanopoulos and Ambassador Cannon. The communiqué mentioned that the agreement was made in the context of the obligations set out by the NATO Treaty. The text of the agreement provided that the US could create military installations, which both governments would consider as necessary for the implementation of the approved plans of the alliance. The US forces would be free to move on Greek territory. A special procedure was also set up, which provided that US personnel in Greece could only be tried by US courts and could not be prosecuted in Greece. This last provision, 'extraterritoriality', later sparked strong reactions in Greece. The 1953 agreement allowed for the installation of the large US bases in Hellenikon and Herakleion (air force), Suda Bay (naval and air) and Nea Makri (communications), the installations of the Voice of America and a number of smaller bases.[51] Since King Paul was away from the country and the Parliament was not in session, the agreement was ratified by the Cabinet, and the Special Committee of the Parliament was summoned to approve it a few days later.

The reactions of the opposition varied. The Liberal Party welcomed the agreement, but expressed doubts about the ratification procedure; the EPEK and the Democratic Party expressed some reservations; while the United Democratic Left (EDA) and the KKE, now exiled in the Soviet Bloc, strongly denounced it as enslavement of Greece to the Americans. During the Parliamentary debate on 22 October 1953, the government speakers, Constantinos Vovolinis and Kanellopoulos, emphasized that the agreement was tangible proof that the US would not abandon Greece in a crisis. The opposition speaker, Constantinos Mitsotakis of the Liberals, said that his party would vote in favour of the agreement, but also criticized the ratification procedure and noted that extraterritoriality would insult the Greek people and could have adverse effects on bilateral Greek–US relations – which proved an accurate prediction. George Papandreou, who had recently become co-leader of the Liberal Party, said that the reservations of his party regarding the ratification procedure could not balance the positive effects of the agreement: 'The US is coming to Greece as a security guarantee. We salute it.'[52]

The conclusion of the agreement also sparked reactions from the Soviet Bloc: the Soviet Union, Albania and Bulgaria protested the stationing of US forces on Greek soil. In its reply, Athens pointed to the attitude of its neighbours during the civil war and to Sofia's re-armament contrary to the 1947 Bulgarian Peace Treaty. Athens immediately indicated to the Americans that it was facing Soviet-Bloc pressure because of the agreement, and therefore needed more 'solidarity' from the West. In late October, Stephanopoulos, who accompanied the Greek Royals to the US, mentioned to Dulles that these Soviet-Bloc pressures called for increased US aid to Greece.[53]

It is clear that the installation of US bases was immensely important for Greek security policy. Despite public references to the NATO Treaty, it is doubtful whether the agreement directly derived from the obligations of Greece as a NATO member. Greece wanted to grant the bases; it was not obliged to do so. Of course, the stationing of the armed forces of a superpower on the territory of a minor ally entailed a de facto imbalance; in practice it would be difficult for Greece to object to the use of the bases, especially in times of crisis. Even so, the Greek government regarded this as secondary, since Athens wanted to make sure that US forces would anyway be committed in case of a Soviet-Bloc attack against Greece. Until then, the fear had often been expressed in Greece that the alliance viewed the country as a forward post which could be easily abandoned in case of a general war. Similar questions were often asked of NATO officials during their visits to Greece; this happened even in October 1953, a few days before the announcement of the agreement.[54] The Greek–US agreement partially eased this fear of abandonment: the presence of US forces in Greece would act as an additional trip-wire mechanism in case of a Bulgarian attack. This may explain why the Greek government did not make additional aid a precondition for the conclusion of the agreement. Thus, the installation of US bases complemented NATO accession, militarily as well as psychologically.

Relations with Western European allies

The Papagos government also sought to revive relations with the Western European members of the alliance. As early as 1953 Markezinis initiated economic deliberations with West Germany, which soon emerged as Greece's main European commercial partner. The bilateral rapprochement with West Germany was crowned by the visit of the West German Chancellor, Konrad Adenauer, to Greece in March 1954, a visit that was returned by Papagos in June.[55] Yet there also was an internal political side-effect: Markezinis's handling of the Greek–West German economic negotiations became the pretext for his quarrel with Papagos in April and November 1954. Papagos visited France, Holland and Belgium early in 1954. Moreover, he revived contacts with Italy: the Italian Prime Minister, Alcide de Gasperi, visited Athens in January 1953, and Papagos went to Rome in September. This was an impressive development, since Papagos had commanded the Greek army during the 1940–41 Greek–Italian war.

This European opening of the Papagos government was primarily economically oriented: it aimed to attract foreign capital after the end of the Marshall Plan. On the level of defence, few things could be done together with these states. In 1951–54 the debate about the formation of the European Defence Community (EDC) brought disappointments for Greece, which was not invited to participate; indeed, the EDC would not cover Greek territory. In 1951–52 the Centre governments protested about this, but there was little that could be done.[56] In March 1952, the Undersecretary for Foreign Affairs, Evangelos Averoff-Tossizza, minuted that Greece sought the closest possible association with the West and thus was favourable towards any effort for closer co-ordination among the European states. Averoff also noted that Greece should closely monitor discussions on the EDC, since their course depended 'on many factors and developments, including the attitude of states whose defence position is analogous to our own'.[57] Thus, Athens kept hoping that it could somehow take advantage of the EDC. The Papagos government also expressed its support for the EDC,[58] but the whole project was killed by the French National Assembly in mid-1954.

Greece was strongly in favour of German re-armament. As the British Embassy in Athens noted in March 1954, in the aftermath of Adenauer's visit to Athens, Greek support for German re-armament was directly connected with the Greek security problem:[59]

> I do not doubt that threatened as they are along their own borders by the military power of the Soviet bloc, and seeing as they do that France, and for that matter no other continental country outside the Iron Curtain, Germany apart, appears to possess even the potential strength to resist this military power, the Greeks will increasingly look to Germany to supply the high-quality troops which could withstand aggression from the East.

The Greek Foreign Minister, Stephanopoulos, presided over the October 1954 NAC ministerial meeting, which approved the London Accords, providing for German re-armament and West Germany's entry into NATO. Stephanopoulos and Kanellopoulos expressed their deep satisfaction that the democratic West Germany was taking its place among the Western powers.[60] As usual, Kanellopoulos successfully pointed to the wider political issues: he had studied in Heidelberg during the years of the Weimar Republic and had been prominent in the resistance against the Nazis in the 1940s. In his speech he expressed the basis of Athens' policy towards the West German state, namely the confidence that the Bonn Republic represented the revival of a democratic and liberal country, the presence of which would be indispensable for the shaping of post-war Europe. There was more than security concerns or economic interests in the Greek attitude towards West Germany.

Athens also showed some interest in the proposed Middle-Eastern defence organization, but this was not welcome to Britain for a variety of reasons: Greece was not a Middle-Eastern power and could play little role in military developments there. Athens also had to protect the large Greek community in Egypt, and this made the Greeks vulnerable to pressures from Cairo. Last but not least, the eruption of the Cyprus question in 1954–55 placed Greece and Britain on a collision course. In 1953 Papagos and Kanellopoulos, speaking in Parliament, referred to the bonds with France and Britain,[61] but this reference was not repeated in the following year, when Cyprus was becoming a major issue negatively affecting Anglo–Greek relations. In 1954 these relations seriously deteriorated, and visits of British warships to Greek ports were cancelled. It has indeed been suggested that the ascent of the Papagos government was a major step in the process through which US influence definitely prevailed over the British one in Greece. Papagos was on bad terms with the Palace (which had excellent contacts with London), and the Cyprus question sped up the decline of British influence in Greece, which had started with the Truman Doctrine in 1947. Clearly, the role of the US in Greece's system of alliances remained irreplaceable.

3 The regional balance
The tripartite Balkan pacts

An automatic guarantee?

In the Balkans, the Papagos government scored one of its major successes and suffered one of its greatest failures. The success was the setting up of the tripartite Greek–Turkish–Yugoslav entente in 1953–54; the failure involved its demise in 1955.

As mentioned above, deliberations for a tripartite rapprochement had started before Papagos' electoral victory. Tripartite co-ordination was absolutely crucial for Greece. Without Yugoslav participation in common defence, the Turks would not commit large forces in Eastern Thrace and Greece would be left alone to face the Bulgarians. In that case, the Greek territories of Eastern Macedonia and Western Thrace would be lost in the opening stages of a war, given that the Greek army did not possess the necessary armour to counterattack and regain them. To put it simply, tripartite defence was the best possible option for Athens.

By early 1952, as they were becoming NATO members, Greece and Turkey tried to co-ordinate their policy. Venizelos visited Ankara in late January, while the Turkish Prime Minister, Adnan Menderes, and the Foreign Minister, Fuat Köprülü, returned the visit in April; these discussions also dealt with possible defence co-operation with Yugoslavia.[1] Then, in June 1952, King Paul and Queen Frederica visited Turkey; they were accompanied by the Undersecretary for Foreign Affairs, Evangelos Averoff-Tossizza. He, on his return, noted that there was ample space for the development of Greek–Turkish relations, and stressed that Cyprus was the only issue which could endanger bilateral relations.[2] In December 1952, the President of the Turkish Republic, Çelal Bayar, visited Greece.

At the same time, discussions were taking place between the Greek and the Yugoslav military. It was during these deliberations, in the spring of 1952, that the Yugoslavs had indicated that they intended to defend the whole of their southern border; this opened the road for tripartite defence co-ordination. This Yugoslav communication was received with jubilation in Athens, although publicly the Greeks tried to react cautiously. In the summer, the Permanent Representative to NATO, Panayiotis Pipinelis, noted that Athens should not give the impression that it was dependent on Turkish and Yugoslav support, as this would weaken its negotiating position; at the same time, Pipinelis continued, Athens and Ankara should not hurry, so as not to expose Tito to Soviet pressures.[3] Contacts on the military level continued. A Yugoslav military delegation visited Athens and Ankara in September 1952, a Greek delegation went to Belgrade in November, and a Turkish one followed in December. The Yugoslavs, who had formerly seemed to prefer informal defence co-operation, now indicated that they were thinking in terms of a tripartite defence agreement. This change in Yugoslav policy has been attributed to Belgrade's desire to strengthen its regional position in the face of the Trieste dispute.[4]

The process was not without its problems. For example, in 1952 Athens returned as unacceptable Yugoslav note verbales referring to the Slav-speaking minority in Greece.[5] Athens regarded these Yugoslav references as an indication of Belgrade's ambition to view Greek Macedonia as an area of Yugoslav interest. However, the Greek governments also considered that the Yugoslav federal government and Tito himself would not allow anything to block a bilateral rapprochement. It is indicative that, despite such incidents, the Papagos government authorized in 1953 the re-opening of the Yugoslav free zone at the port of Thessaloniki.[6] Thus a basic tendency of post-war Greek–Yugoslav relations was becoming evident: facing a common threat from the Soviet Bloc the two states drew closer, but the effect of older animosities arising from the Macedonian question threatened to hamper this process.

A tripartite defence agreement posed an additional problem regarding the extent of the obligations that it would lay down, especially the nature of the guarantee. Indeed, the credibility of an alliance tends to grow if it sets out an automatic guarantee, providing that an attack on one of the signatories would automatically be regarded as an attack on all. However, Greece and Turkey were NATO members and such an automatic guarantee would indirectly expand NATO obligations to Yugoslavia. Athens and Ankara did not seek such an advanced provision, which could prove very embarrassing to them, especially if the Trieste dispute culminated in an Italian–Yugoslav conflict. Moreover, an automatic guarantee could entangle Greece and Turkey in a localized crisis between Yugoslavia and a Soviet ally other than Bulgaria – for example, in a Yugoslav–Hungarian conflict in Central Europe. An automatic guarantee would result in Yugoslavia acquiring all the advantages of NATO membership without undertaking any of its obligations. The Western powers wanted indirectly to associate Yugoslavia with NATO, but they would not give a blank cheque to Belgrade, allowing it to draw the whole of the West into a crisis that would only involve Belgrade's interests. Last but not least, with the Trieste question open, Italy was certain to react against an automatic tripartite guarantee. It was not easy to accommodate all these conflicting pressures. By late 1952 the US Secretary of State, Dean Acheson, noted that his country was favourable to the continuation of military talks, but did not support the conclusion of an official alliance which could create problems for Greece's and Turkey's position in NATO.[7]

The continuation of the Italian–Yugoslav dispute over Trieste made Greece anxious. Athens had taken a neutral attitude on this issue, and wanted to revive its relations with Italy, which after all was the western neighbour of the country as well as a NATO partner. In January 1953, Alcide de Gasperi's visit to Athens was a major step for the normalization of bilateral relations. The Italians stressed that Rome would not participate in a Balkan pact, but would not object to its conclusion, provided that such a pact would aim to strengthen resistance against a Soviet-Bloc attack and that it would be compatible with NATO. The Greeks considered that the Italian position was reasonable.[8] However, this also meant that a tripartite treaty should not lay down an automatic guarantee.

It was the Turks (probably with US approval) who suggested a way out: in late January 1953 the Turkish Foreign Minister, Fuat Köprülü, visited Belgrade and Athens, and proposed to circumvent the problem by signing a pact of friendship. At that time Greece and Turkey even regarded Yugoslavia's future accession to NATO as possible, and therefore that the problem of the guarantee might never arise. In February Stephanopoulos went to Belgrade, where the holding of talks was announced, including military deliberations. Indeed, military talks were held in Ankara on 17–20 February. By now the Yugoslavs had tried to establish some form of automatic guarantee, by inserting the provision that future agreements of the Chiefs of General Staffs would be regarded as part of the agreement. This was rejected by Athens and Ankara, while a Greek draft only mentioned an obligation to deliberate in times of crisis. However, the US intervened, asking that it not go even as far as that. This angered Belgrade, but did not block the conclusion of the agreement.[9]

The Greek–Turkish–Yugoslav Pact of Friendship and Collaboration was initialled in Athens on 25 February 1953, and was formally signed in Ankara three days later. The preamble declared the will of the signatories to defend their independence and territorial integrity, to step up their efforts to make common defence more effective, and to deliberate and co-operate on matters of common defence in case of unprovoked attack. The Pact set up a Council of Foreign Ministers which would meet once a year, opened the road for formal co-operation between the three General Staffs, provided for the development of economic, technical and cultural co-operation, referred to the peaceful settlement of disputes and set out the obligation of each signatory to avoid interventions in the internal affairs of the others. The Pact also forbade the participation of each signatory to alliances or activities directed against another.[10] This was an entente, but not an alliance. Even so, the very fact of the Pact's signature, the reference to future co-ordination of defence policy, and the continuation of military talks directly affected Balkan balances. It is indicative that during a debate in the Greek Parliament on 6 March and then during the debate for the ratification of the pact on 23 March, the view prevailed that this was primarily a security arrangement.[11]

The road to Bled

Almost immediately after the conclusion of the tripartite Pact of Friendship, Balkan developments were affected by Stalin's death, as well as by the policy of peaceful co-existence which his successors proclaimed. Like other NATO members, Greece did not regard this new Soviet policy as 'sincere'. The possibility of a new Soviet opening to Tito made Greece and Turkey nervous. Athens and Ankara were also afraid that, in an overall negotiation with Moscow, the West could sacrifice the Balkan entente in exchange for gains on other fronts, such as Germany. Last but not least, Papagos' June 1953 visit to Turkey aimed, among others, at assessing whether Turkish policy could be influenced by Moscow's recent initiative to abandon its claims in the Turko–Soviet border. The Ankara talks eased Greek fears. The two governments also agreed to support Yugoslav entry into NATO and to continue co-operation with Belgrade, but only up to a point which would not affect their obligations as NATO members.[12]

In June 1953 delegations of the three General Staffs met in Athens; the talks centred on the selection of locations where the defensive battles would be fought, the units which would be engaged and the defence of Thrace. An idea for the creation of a standing joint high command was aired but not adopted.[13] According to the available evidence, by that time Yugoslavia seemed ready to accept a more advanced defence agreement, but Greece, also echoing US reservations, wanted to delay this. Athens' position is not surprising: Greece had got what it wanted – namely, de facto regional superiority vis-à-vis Bulgaria – through the emergence of a tripartite entente. From Greece's point of view, a formal agreement would not add much and could additionally complicate the international obligations of Athens and Ankara. Then, in July 1953, the Balkan Pact Council of Foreign Ministers held its first meeting in Athens, with the participation of Stephanopoulos, Köprülü and the Yugoslav Undersecretary for Foreign Affairs, Alexander Bebler. The three ministers declared the desire of their countries to advance military co-operation, and to respond collectively to the Soviet peace offensive; an agreement for the setting up of a permanent secretariat of the Pact was reached in principle. This was finally signed in November.[14]

However, in September 1953 there was again some uncertainty regarding Greek–Yugoslav relations. In early September Athens resented Belgrade's initiative to respond positively (and without consulting Greece and Turkey) to a Bulgarian proposal for normalization of relations. At the same time, a minor crisis occurred in Greek–Yugoslav relations over the recent Greek decree on the border resettlement programme, which was denounced by the Yugopress Agency as a programme of 'colonization' of Macedonian lands. This in turn caused resentment in Athens: the Greeks held that the Yugopress reaction violated the pact of 28 February, which ruled out interventions in the internal affairs of another signatory. Indeed, officials of the Greek Foreign Ministry told the Americans that Athens could consider a Yugoslav approach through diplomatic channels, but this public denunciation of Greek policy was unacceptable. The

40 The era of regional initiatives, 1952–55

Greeks suspected that the Yugopress reaction had much to do with Yugoslav nervousness over Papagos' scheduled visit to Italy. At that moment, it was Alexis Kyrou who stepped in from New York and made sure that Greek policy returned to a calmer line: Kyrou suggested that the incident was not as important as Athens suspected, and noted that the Yugopress line did not necessarily reflect official Yugoslav policy. He was quickly vindicated: in the following days Yugoslav officials assured their Greek counterparts that the Yugopress had overreacted. Anyway, the border resettlement programme soon led nowhere, as few citizens wanted to return to that area.[15]

Papagos' visit to Italy in late September 1953 was a clear sign that the two countries aimed to set aside their past as enemies during the Second World War. The Greek Prime Minister insisted that closer Greek–Yugoslav co-operation would not adversely affect Greek–Italian relations. The Italian leaders referred to Trieste and warned the Greeks about the 'bad faith' of the Yugoslavs, but noted that they would not try to upset the Greek–Turkish–Yugoslav co-operation; the British Embassy in Rome described this position as 'realistic'.[16]

Another major step towards co-ordination of tripartite defence was made on 20 November: during a new round of tripartite talks in Belgrade between representatives of the General Staffs, a common defence plan against a surprise Bulgarian attack was discussed and agreed in principle. The plan did not provide for automatic intervention and was also discussed during a new meeting of military delegations in late March 1954; the Greeks put forward the idea of creating a common headquarters, but this was rejected by Belgrade, which did not want to place its forces under the command of a NATO officer.[17] These military deliberations again raised the issue of automatic engagement of the armed forces of the three countries in a future conflict. Furthermore, the Yugoslavs again pressed for the conclusion of a formal alliance. The Greek leaders constantly made clear that they would not accept an automatic guarantee. Speaking with Dulles in October 1953, Stephanopoulos expressed reservations about the effects of a formal Balkan alliance on Greek–Italian relations (in the autumn of 1953 there was another crisis over Trieste).[18] In November 1953, in Parliament, Kanellopoulos indicated that a guarantee should not be automatic; he referred to the efforts to co-ordinate the defence of the three countries, 'in case – and please take note of every phrase and every word I say – in case they would sustain an attack in the common area and in case they would become co-belligerents'.[19] During his January 1954 visit to France, Papagos himself noted that Greece sought defence co-ordination with Yugoslavia, but rejected an automatic guarantee which was not compatible with Athens' obligations in NATO.[20]

However, Athens was finally forced to accept a defence pact. In April 1954, during Tito's visit to Ankara, Yugoslavia and Turkey announced their intention to go ahead with the conclusion of an alliance, if Greece also agreed. Athens was taken aback, but decided that it could not torpedo such a public proposal. Indeed, an Italian attempt to delay the signature was brushed aside by Papagos himself, who indicated that Greece would not make its decisions dependent on the course of Italian–Yugoslav relations.[21] At the same time, the US, the French and the West German governments asked Greece to delay the process; this request was received unfavourably both in Athens and in Belgrade.[22]

Tito visited Greece in June 1954. Although he was the Yugoslav leader who had claimed Greek Macedonia in the 1940s, he was triumphantly received in the Greek capital. Indeed, on 3 June the Conservative daily *Acropolis* called him 'a symbol of resistance against red imperialism'. During the Greek–Yugoslav talks, which were also attended by the Turkish Ambassador, Kemal Taray, it was decided that the new treaty should be ready by July. After the visit, *Kathimerini* wrote that the alliance 'could be regarded as an accomplished fact'; the signature was merely a 'formality'. It obviously was not (since the nature of the guarantee had not been agreed), but the leading newspaper was correctly describing the jubilant climate in bilateral relations.[23] Immediately afterwards Adnan Menderes went to Athens, accompanied by the Ministers of Foreign Affairs (Köprülü) and Defence (Ethem Menderes). The Greek and the Turkish leaders discussed the issue of the guarantee, trying to form a common attitude as NATO members. By that time Papagos had already decided to appeal to the UN over Cyprus, and tried to discuss this with Menderes, but the Turkish side indicated that it did not want to touch this issue.[24]

The new pact was drafted by a committee consisting of Kyrou, Bebler and the leading Turkish diplomat, Nuri Birgi. Yugoslavia proposed an automatic guarantee, which was rejected by the other two parties. Greece proposed an automatic guarantee, especially in case of a crisis with Bulgaria, but this was rejected by Turkey and Yugoslavia, with the argument that the provision of two different processes would weaken the alliance. Anyway, even such an automatic guarantee could still be contradictory to Greece's and Turkey's position as NATO members. Throughout this process Greece and Turkey remained in touch with the Americans and NATO, trying to ease anxieties about possible conflict between the two arrangements.[25] Yet, in early July the US intervened in Athens and in Ankara, pointing out that the draft included a form of automatic guarantee which might force other NATO powers to declare that they would not come to the assistance of Greece and Turkey were the latter to become involved into a war because of their new obligations; according to the Americans, this would dangerously weaken the credibility of NATO.[26]

In this rather confused atmosphere, a more serious problem occurred: in mid-July the Turks proposed to delay the signature of the pact so that Italy could also participate in it. This move greatly upset the Yugoslavs, who always suspected Rome. Kyrou told British diplomats in Athens that the Yugoslavs were in a dangerous mood and that it might be better if Athens and Belgrade signed a bilateral defence agreement.[27] Indeed, in an effort to appease Belgrade, Papagos publicly asked for an immediate signature of the tripartite pact, while *Kathimerini* suggested that, if Turkey persisted in this attitude, Greece and Yugoslavia should conclude a bilateral agreement.[28] It has to be noted that the Turks did not mean to create any problem for the negotiations; they merely tried to make sure that the new pact would secure the full support of the other NATO members.[29] Thus, after the Turks fully explained their position, the text of the pact was finalized.

The Treaty of Alliance, Political Co-operation and Mutual Assistance was signed by the three Foreign Ministers on 9 August in the Yugoslav city of Bled. It had a duration of twenty years, and set out an obligation of the signatories to offer help, including military assistance, to another signatory who came under attack, and not to conclude a separate peace. The signatories would also co-operate with the object of enhancing their defence capabilities. On the issue of the guarantee, the text was evasive: the signatories would consult and then react in common in case of an armed attack against one of the contracting parties; they would only consult in case of a deterioration of the situation in areas which interested the contracting parties and in case of an armed attack against a third country with which one of the contracting parties had an obligation for mutual assistance (namely, against any other NATO member).[30]

The Bled Treaty formed an alliance, but did not set out an automatic guarantee. Later, in 1959, when the revival of the pact was discussed, Lieutenant-General Dovas, who had taken part in the drafting of the Treaty, was asked by the Greek Foreign Ministry about this and replied that there was no automatic guarantee; he also noted that there had been no explicit agreement on the automatism of the guarantee.[31] Indeed, according to the pact, consultation was necessary before the three countries committed their armed forces. On the other hand, the pact indirectly associated Yugoslavia with NATO, without creating insurmountable problems: to give an example, if the Soviets attacked Norway, which was a NATO member, the Western alliance (including Greece and Turkey) would find itself at war with Moscow (according to the procedure of Article 5 of the NATO Treaty) while Yugoslavia would have to consult with Athens and Ankara. No similar obligation existed for Greece and Turkey, since Yugoslavia was not connected by an alliance to any other state. It was a clever formula.

Even with such deliberately evasive wording, the 1954 Bled Treaty was important for Balkan balances, something which was underlined in the Greek Parliament during the debate for its ratification.[32] In September 1954, a meeting of the Chiefs of the three General Staffs was held, while additional talks between delegations of the three armies followed until April 1955.[33] In late February 1955, the Balkan Pact Council of Foreign Ministers met in Ankara and also agreed to the establishment of a Consultative Assembly. Simultaneously, non-military co-operation was also attempted. This included the possible setting up of a Balkan cultural foundation and of a Balkan Festival of Folk Music, a system for the exchange of books, the translation and publication of works of Balkan writers, co-operation on the fields of cinema and radio, contact between the academies of the three countries as well as their unions of writers and journalists, the co-ordination of the positions of the three countries in international economic negotiations, co-ordination of their policies on tourism, etc.[34]

It has been perceptively suggested that '[t]he fall of 1954 found Greece at the peak of its effectiveness in its system of international alliances, which were aimed toward guaranteeing internal and external security'.[35] Never before and never after 1955 would Greece find itself in such a favourable position. However, all these advantages would be swept aside in the vortex of the developments of the following year.

4 Greece and peaceful co-existence

Bordering the Soviet Bloc created a variety of problems. Even after the end of the civil war, the Greek government kept fearing possible infiltration of former Communist guerrillas through Bulgaria. Athens also was anxious about the activities of various (non-Communist) Bulgarian-Macedonian organizations in the US, which could become vehicles of a future Bulgarian revisionism. Greek analysts did not rule out the possibility that the US might try to 'buy' the Bulgarians with promises for territorial gains in the Balkans, perhaps at Greece's expense. This fear was founded on the experience of the First World War, when the entente powers had tried to lure Bulgaria by promising Greek Eastern Macedonia to it.[1]

Greece had not re-established diplomatic relations with Bulgaria and Albania; many Greek soldiers who had been taken prisoners during the civil war were held in Eastern Europe (Athens estimated them at about 4,000).[2] Last but not least, there was the very delicate problem of the children who had been taken by the Communist DSE army during the civil war and moved to the Communist states. Initially Athens had insisted on their return, but from 1950–51 the Greek authorities changed their attitude, estimating that the children had already been indoctrinated. Many children held in Yugoslavia were returned in 1950–52, during the full normalization of bilateral relations.[3]

Stalin's death in March 1953 and the implementation of the new policy of peaceful co-existence – or, as the West called it, the Soviet 'peace offensive' – naturally affected a frontline state such as Greece. Athens considered that Soviet aims had not changed, but at the same time, peaceful co-existence seemed to open some new prospects. In spring 1953 Greece was stepping up its effort for economic development, and could not disregard the possibility of exports to the East. Indeed, starting with Poland in 1952, Greece slowly re-established commercial relations with the Soviet-Bloc countries. In 1953–54 Greece concluded commercial agreements with all members of the Soviet Bloc save Romania and Albania, but including East Germany; 1953 has been called 'a decisive turning point' in the development of Greece's Eastern trade.[4] This first Greek opening to the Soviet Bloc was under the effective direction of Alexis Kyrou: since Greece had not re-established diplomatic relations with many Soviet-Bloc countries, most of these contacts took place through the UN and were handled by the Permanent Mission and Kyrou personally.

The first Soviet opening to Greece

Greek–Soviet relations were the first to be fully normalized. The two countries had not broken their relations, but since 1948 they had withdrawn their ambassadors, and their diplomatic missions had remained downgraded. In spring 1953, immediately after Stalin's death, Alexis Kyrou asked Athens to consider the exchange of ambassadors with Moscow. He insisted that after the conclusion of the tripartite pact with Turkey and Yugoslavia, Greece's international position had been strengthened, and that it would now be useful to have a full Embassy in Moscow and a similar contact through a Soviet ambassador in Athens. Papagos hesitated and asked US advice on this.[5] However, in July a commercial agreement was signed with the Soviet Union, and in September Alexandros Kountoumas took up his position as Ambassador to Moscow, while Mikhail Sergueev became the Soviet Ambassador to Athens.

Sergueev's personality played an important role in Greek–Soviet relations. A capable diplomat, fluent in Greek, Sergueev cleverly left political issues on the sidelines, knowing that these could make the Greeks suspicious: it is indicative that he did not insist on the issue of the Greek–US agreement on the installation of US bases. On the contrary, he placed emphasis on the development of commercial and cultural relations. He stated that his country was ready to buy large quantities of Greek tobacco, which had been facing great difficulties in these years because of the competition with American tobacco. He also visited Thessaloniki and even announced that the Soviet Union would participate in the city's International Fair in 1954. The US Embassy anxiously noted that the Greeks were interested in Soviet proposals:[6]

> After the suffering which the Soviets directly and indirectly inflicted on Greece in the recent past, the only kind of bait which would have any attraction for the Greek people as a whole would be an offer to call off hostilities. This offer is implicit in the recent Soviet gestures and however sceptical local observers may be, the majority are inclined to think their country could not afford to pass up any possibilities. They, the Government included, are inclined to think that they can take whatever the Soviets have to offer without any danger to themselves pending receipt of the answer to the basic question. They perhaps tend to underestimate what the Soviets can accomplish through infiltration tactics once they have a foothold, believing as they do that communism cannot easily fool them again. This frame of mind presents a potentially serious menace both to Greece and to the American interest in the country.

The report tended to exaggerate the problem, but this was the first time for years that the US Embassy faced a full Soviet Embassy in the country, so some anxiety is not surprising. The British were more accurate when they noted that Athens was out to get whatever it could on the economic level, without making any political concessions.[7] Papagos, the British and the Americans were also worried about Sergueev's propaganda activities.[8] It was propaganda, with its medium-term psychological effects, that was regarded as most dangerous.

However, the Soviet Ambassador slowed down his activity in the following months: the major Soviet interests in the Balkans concerned Yugoslavia, not Greece; and in any event, Athens was the target of Bulgaria's own peace offensive. Furthermore, it seems that the Soviets significantly delayed their deliveries according to the 1953 commercial agreement, which reduced their credibility in Greek eyes. In early 1954 Sergueev visited Thessaloniki again, but was more careful regarding his promises for the purchase of Greek tobacco, and it appears that the major aim of his trip was to help the leader of the left-wing EDA party, Yiannis Passalides, who was a candidate in a by-election there.[9] In March 1954 Greece stopped the delivery of goods to the Soviet Union and Poland, claiming that these countries were unreliable in their commercial dealings (although the opposition accused the government of slowing down Eastern trade for political reasons). Still, in September 1954 the Greek–Soviet commercial agreement was renewed.[10]

It was only in late 1954 that the Soviets managed to make a new breakthrough, by supporting the Greek appeal on Cyprus at the UN; all NATO members save Iceland voted against Greece. In July 1955 Sergueev regained the initiative, by proposing a greater bilateral commercial agreement; a less ambitious one was finally signed.[11] However, soon the disasters of Greece's Cyprus policy (see Chapter 5) caused a serious crisis in the country's relations with NATO, and offered even greater opportunities to the Soviets.

The Bulgarian peace offensive

The major effort of the Soviet Bloc to approach Greece was made in the field of Greek–Bulgarian relations. It was no coincidence that in September 1953, immediately after the Bulgarian proposal to Greece and Yugoslavia for normalization of relations, the US Embassy in Athens commented: 'the dazzling sun of the Moscow peace offensive has now focused its deadly rays with renewed intensity toward the Balkans'.[12]

Regional rivals since the end of the nineteenth century, enemies in three wars between 1913 and 1944, members of opposing worlds since 1944, Athens and Sofia had not re-established diplomatic relations after the Second World War. The 1947 Bulgarian Peace Treaty had not settled things: Bulgaria kept violating the disarmament clauses; Sofia had not paid to Greece the agreed sum of reparations, $45 million at 1938 rates. Furthermore, the wars of the past had left bitter memories as well as practical problems: in 1941, when Sofia annexed Greek Eastern Macedonia and Western Thrace, the Bulgarians had destroyed the frontier pyramids (border markers), and this meant that after 1944 there were disagreements regarding the exact location of the dividing line; often such disputes culminated in frontier incidents. To make matters worse, there were disputed islets on the River Evros in Thrace which also caused frontier incidents, the most important of which led to an artillery conflict in July 1952. A new artillery battle took place in March 1953. These were very dangerous incidents, since they involved direct engagement of NATO and Soviet-Bloc forces. In the summer of 1953, in New York, Kyrou proposed the setting up of a mixed commission which would redraw the frontier line. The Bulgarians accepted the proposal and the commission started its work.[13] The Bulgarian 'peace offensive' began exactly at that time: August–September 1953.

Sofia's move was a clever response to regional developments. The Bulgarian army was the cause of deep concern in Athens, but Sofia had to deal with its own fears: the February 1953 tripartite Greek–Turkish–Yugoslav pact had placed Bulgaria in a strategic disadvantage. Thus, in early September 1953 the Bulgarians proposed, through the UN, the immediate full normalization of relations with Greece and Yugoslavia.

The Greek officials considered that this Bulgarian peace offensive aimed to disorganize the Greek–Turkish–Yugoslav entente. Athens exchanged views with Turkey and Yugoslavia, while it also consulted with the Americans; the latter said that they would not normalize their relations with Sofia, but Greece would have to decide on its own response. The Greek government then decided to test Bulgarian 'sincerity'.[14] Athens could either demand that Bulgaria comply with the disarmament clauses of the Peace Treaty, or that it pay reparations. Realizing that it was too much to ask Bulgaria to disarm, Athens focused on reparations. This way, the issue of Bulgarian reparations became, for Greece, the testing ground for Bulgarian sincerity.

Athens indicated that the reparations issue should be settled prior to the re-establishment of diplomatic relations. Sofia replied that this could be settled *after* the re-establishment of diplomatic relations, and additionally stressed that it intended to raise its own financial demands from the inter-war period (the 1927 Kafantaris–Moloff agreement, which provided for the compensation of Bulgarians who voluntary emigrated from Greece). Meanwhile, in December 1953 a bilateral commercial agreement and another regarding the exact location of the frontier line were signed.[15] The next important step was made in Paris in May 1954, when Greece and Bulgaria issued a communiqué stating that they agreed to re-establish diplomatic relations; yet, ambassadors would not be exchanged prior to a settlement on reparations. At this stage, the negotiations on reparations led nowhere. Bulgaria offered to pay a first instalment of reparations; Athens realized that it would not secure the whole sum of $45 million but was also afraid that, if it consented to an exchange of ambassadors, Sofia would spin negotiations out indefinitely. Thus, in 1955 the Greek–Bulgarian talks led to a dead end.[16] However, in the summer of 1954 Greece consented to the withdrawal of UN observers from the Greek–Bulgarian border. It is notable that on this issue the Greek government overruled the objections of the General Staff of National Defence.[17] The presence of the observers was no longer needed after the recent agreement on the frontier line, while the lessening of tension between the two countries was compatible with Papagos' decision to reduce the size of the land army.

The Greek decision to re-establish diplomatic relations with Bulgaria is indicative of Athens' Balkan priorities. When the Americans asked Greek

Foreign Ministry officials why Athens consented to re-establish relations with Bulgaria but not with Romania (with which there also were economic differences), the Greeks replied that Bulgaria was a neighbouring country in which Athens needed to have representation in order to monitor it better. Papagos himself noted that since Romania did not have a common border with Greece, his government could wait.[18]

Greek–Albanian relations: the conflict between irredentism and pragmatism

On Greek–Albanian relations, the Papagos government took a tougher line. Formally, a state of war had existed between the two countries since 1940. In the 1946 Peace Conference, Greece had claimed Northern Epirus or Southern Albania, but the Soviet support to Tirana ensured that no territorial change took place. Bilateral relations were further complicated by the support of Albania to the Greek communists during the civil war, by the persistence of Greek governments in claiming Northern Epirus, and by the fact that many Greek military who had been taken prisoners during the civil war were held in Albania.

Still, in the early 1950s there seemed to be important incentives for Greece to pursue a different policy. The Centre coalition government discouraged the Yugoslavs from attacking Albania in case of a general war; the Greeks argued that this would distract the much needed Yugoslav units from other fronts. There were other motives as well. As Averoff said during the Greek–Turkish discussions of April 1952, there were many reasons why Albania had to survive as an independent state: to avoid the enlargement of Yugoslavia to the point that it would be uncontrollable; to prevent the control of the eastern coast of the Adriatic by a single power; and even to prevent a strong Italian reaction to such a Yugoslav operation.[19] In the summer, the Defence Minister, George Mavros, made similar remarks, speaking to the Americans.[20] By early 1953, many officials in the Greek Foreign Ministry considered that Greece should resume diplomatic relations with Tirana.[21]

After his ascent to power, Papagos reiterated the position of the previous governments that the claim on Northern Epirus would be pursued by peaceful means only.[22] Athens wanted to avoid any destabilization in the Balkan mainland. On the other hand, Northern Epirus had been taken by the sword in 1940–41 (notably, Papagos' sword), and the Greek public opinion felt strongly about it. Moreover, Papagos was on bad terms with the Palace, which was known to favour the claim over Northern Epirus, and the Prime Minister evidently did not want to open a new quarrel with King Paul.

However, in 1953 there seemed to be other options as well. The Greek–Turkish–Yugoslav rapprochement had made Albania vulnerable. It appears that the Western powers, especially the US, considered an operation aiming to topple the Communist regime in Tirana. A committee for Free Albania, consisting of Albanians hostile to the Communist regime, would take the lead in this effort to 'roll back' Communism. The Americans asked the

48   *The era of regional initiatives, 1952–55*

Greeks to assist in this operation, implying that the Greek claim over Northern Epirus actually helped the Albanian Communist leader, Enver Hoxha, to rally his people behind him. Athens appeared willing to consider US views. In May 1953, a Greek memorandum repeated to the Americans that Greece persisted in claiming Northern Epirus through peaceful means; yet, Athens wanted to facilitate the emergence of an independent and friendly Albania. The Greek memorandum stressed that not all non-Communist governments in Tirana would be considered as friendly to Athens; the Greeks would only regard an Albanian government as 'friendly' if it recognized the existing international obligations of that country towards the Greeks of Northern Epirus, namely the autonomy status agreed in 1913; furthermore, a friendly Albanian government should return the Greek military who were being held in that country.[23] A similar Greek document was given to the British.[24]

Then, in the summer of 1953, discussions took place in New York between Kyrou and the pro-Western Albanian committee. Kyrou proposed an agreement which would provide for ending the Albanian persecution of the Greeks of Northern Epirus; this way, Kyrou indirectly yet clearly indicated that Athens would withdraw its territorial claim if a non-Communist Albania agreed to safeguard the rights of Northern Epirot Greeks. This failed to satisfy the Albanians, who wanted a clear-cut denunciation of the Greek claim since, from their point of view, any other position would make them appear less patriotic than Hoxha in the eyes of the Albanian people.[25] Still, publicly, the Greek position did not change: in the communiqué issued after the Balkan Pact Council of Foreign Ministers in the summer of 1953 there was a reference to Albanian independence, but not to its territorial integrity, exactly because of the Greek claim over Northern Epirus.[26]

It appears that the projected Western operation in Albania embarrassed the Greeks. The Italians had already indicated their support for the territorial integrity of Albania and had warned that they would intervene if the Yugoslavs moved against Tirana (this was also connected with the Italian–Yugoslav confrontation over Trieste).[27] According to the British Embassy in Athens, the Greek Foreign Ministry officials realized that their claim over Northern Epirus would not be met, and aimed to deter Italian or Yugoslav involvement in that country; the Greeks also realized that if Yugoslavia ever managed to control Albania, Athens would not be in a position to claim rights for the Greeks of Southern Albania without sparking demands by this enlarged Yugoslavia regarding Greek Macedonia.[28] From Athens' point of view, a crisis in Albania could destabilize the whole system of international relations in the south of the Balkans. Anyway, the effort to topple Hoxha failed and, with Hoxha in power, discussions about autonomy or human rights were profoundly theoretical.

In the summer of 1953, the Albanian government proposed to the Greeks, through the UN, the re-establishment of the frontier pyramids marking the border between the two states. This was met by an intransigent Greek response: again through the UN, the Greeks replied that the two countries still were in a state of war, and that the Albanian General Staff should communicate with the

Greek one, asking for the conclusion of a Peace Treaty.[29] The Albanians assumed a new initiative towards Athens in the summer of 1955, at a moment when the Papagos government was falling apart, and while similar openings to Greece were attempted by the Soviets and the Bulgarians: in July 1955, Tirana proposed the resumption of diplomatic relations, noting that no Peace Treaty was necessary. The Greeks approached the Americans, who replied that this was for Athens to decide. Simultaneously, the Greek Foreign Ministry suggested that the government accept the Albanian proposal and resume diplomatic relations: the diplomats stressed that the Italians and the Yugoslavs already had Embassies in Tirana, while the Greeks were absent, and the claim over Northern Epirus blocked any contact with the pro-Western Albanian organizations which could one day rule that country. Once more, however, this pragmatic view did not prevail. The American Embassy noted that the memories of 1940 were too recent; it was not possible for the Greek government to take initiatives at a time when it was under opposition attack for its Cyprus policy.[30]

Thus, in August 1955, Athens replied that the Albanian General Staff should ask for peace; Greece maintain its position regarding 'pending territorial issues'; and Albania return the captured Greek military, and stop facilitating the infiltration of wanted Communists into Greece. The Albanian news agency commented that these terms were 'insulting'. Tirana then came back with a new proposal for the normalization of relations, which made a direct reference to the territorial integrity of the country and was rejected by Athens.[31] This exchange evidently helped Albania to become a UN member in December 1955. However, the opportunity for the normalization of relations – if it had ever existed – had been lost: in the following years, the Karamanlis government, constantly accused of having been 'appointed' by the US in order to 'sell out' Cyprus, could not make a radical turn in its Albanian policy, either by withdrawing the claim over Northern Epirus or by normalizing relations with Tirana.

5   Disaster in 1955

Cyprus and Balkan pressures

Starting late in 1954, the two pillars of the Greek security system – NATO and the tripartite Balkan alliance – received serious blows. By the autumn of 1955, this system had come to the brink of collapse. In December 1954, the Greek appeal to the UN over Cyprus was discussed and defeated in the General Assembly. The decision to appeal to the UN was made in April 1954, during a meeting of Papagos and some of his close associates: Stephanopoulos, Kyrou and some other diplomats; only the Ambassador to London, Vassilios Mostras, disagreed and pointed to the dangers inherent in confronting a Western great power. Furthermore, the Greek appeal ignored Turkish reactions, as well as US objections: during his visit to Athens in June 1954, Menderes declined to discuss Cyprus with Papagos, and subsequently Ankara took a tough line at the UN. The Americans did not rule out the possibility of Enosis (union of Cyprus with Greece) in the future, but twice in 1954 – early in the year and in July – indicated to Athens that they were against an appeal to the UN, which would allow Moscow to become involved in an infra-NATO dispute.[1] Even the Yugoslavs, who eventually supported the Greek case in New York, disagreed with the Greek appeal, on the grounds that it could weaken the tripartite Balkan pacts.[2] The appeal to the UN simply did not take into account international realities.

In the December 1954 UN debate, the British and the Turks strongly resisted the Greek claim for the application of the right of self-determination in Cyprus. The General Assembly decided not to discuss the issue 'for the present', a phrase added at the insistence of the Americans as a face-saving formula for the Greeks.[3] Following this defeat, Kyrou resigned from the post of Director General of the Foreign Ministry. The December 1954 defeat had serious repercussions: all NATO members except Iceland came out against the Greek item; the Greek public, who had not been informed about the US attitude regarding the UN, felt that the Americans had 'betrayed' Greece. In Athens, the UN debate was followed by large demonstrations against the Western powers. In an effort to ease Greek feelings, the government, King Paul and even the standard-bearer of the Cypriot case, the daily *Hestia*, reminded the public that the opponent in the Cyprus question was Britain, not the US. However, the public pressures tended to become even greater, since the thorny issue of 'extraterritoriality' (involving the US personnel in the bases) had started surfacing at exactly the same time.[4]

In the following months, pressures became evident in the regional pillar of Greek security as well. In May 1955, the Soviet opening to Tito was crowned by the visit of Nikita Khrushchev and Nikolai Bulganin to Belgrade. This made the Yugoslavs distance themselves from the tripartite pacts: having received tangible proof that its 'heresy' could be tolerated by the Soviets, Belgrade did not want to provoke Moscow further by coming closer to the two NATO countries of the Balkans. In the summer of 1955 Tito publicly referred to a change of circumstances, and to the secondary importance that the 1954 alliance now had for Yugoslavia.[5] The Soviet opening to Yugoslavia made Athens extremely anxious. A possible return of Belgrade to the Soviet Bloc would dramatically redress Balkan balances and make the Greek security problem absolutely insoluble.[6] Indeed, it appears that in early summer 1955 Greece was alarmed by some NATO studies regarding the Yugoslav position, and even advanced troops to the Yugoslav border.[7] The Greek fears were partially eased early in September, when King Paul visited Yugoslavia; the Yugoslav officials assured him that although they no longer placed their emphasis on the military aspect of the Balkan entente, they would not change their international policy.[8]

By then, gigantic problems had occurred on other levels. Papagos fell ill in March 1955, and he was abroad for a month for medical examinations. Even after his return he was no longer in a position to co-ordinate his government. This sparked a succession struggle in Athens, between Kanellopoulos and Stephanopoulos. On 1 April 1955, EOKA (the National Organization of Cypriot Fighters) started its armed campaign against the British in Cyprus. The disorganized Greek government, without Papagos and without Kyrou, and in the midst of a vicious succession struggle, could no longer control developments. Then, in June, the British government invited Greece and Turkey to a Conference in London, which would examine security issues in the Mediterranean, 'including Cyprus'. This coincided with a worsening of Papagos' health, angered the Greek Cypriots who denounced the British invitation as a trap, and caused even greater problems to the Greek government, which had to make a decision whether to attend or not. It finally decided to attend, but the whole issue revealed to the public the bad state of the Prime Minister's health and the great problem of co-ordination within the government. The US advised Greece to attend the Conference.[9]

The London Conference and its aftermath

The London Tripartite Conference opened in late August and collapsed on 7 September, following the riots against the Greek Orthodox minority and the Ecumenical Patriarchate in Istanbul, as well as incidents against Greek officers in the NATO Headquarters in Izmir.[10] These events dealt a severe blow to Greek–Turkish co-operation for the first time since 1930. The September 1955 pogrom and the London Tripartite Conference completed the process of the weakening of the 1953–54 Balkan pacts, on which the Greeks based their regional policy: with Yugoslavia reluctant to provoke the Soviets further and with Greek–Turkish relations in a shambles, there was little prospect for common action of the three states in case of a Soviet-Bloc attack. Given the strength of the Bulgarian forces, Greece reverted to a situation of hopeless military inferiority.

However, more was to come. During the same month, September 1955, a serious crisis erupted in Greek–US and Greek–NATO relations. In the aftermath of the Istanbul riots, the Greek public felt that the country had been abandoned by the US; the leader of the Liberals, George Papandreou, drew the attention of the US Embassy Counselor, Ray Thurston, to this dangerous development.[11] The other opposition parties took a tougher line. EPEK and Sophocles Venizelos' new party, the Liberal Democratic Union, asked for a re-examination of Greek foreign policy, while the centre-left Democratic Party indirectly referred to possible withdrawal from NATO. These were the very political forces which had secured Greece's accession to the alliance. Things became worse when, on 18 September, Dulles sent identical messages to Papagos and to Menderes urging restraint.[12] The Greek press accused the US of putting in the same position the victim and the culprit of the September events. The opposition came out even more strongly. The Democratic Party stated that the people 'now see the value of the country's external bonds such as NATO, and the effects of its one-sided external orientation'. The EDA, the left-wing party, asked for a 'radical change' in foreign policy. The former Prime Minister Constantinos Tsaldaris, who was the leader of the Right during the civil war, declared that Greece should not be trapped in the dilemma 'east or west', and that 'there are other options, as the king's recent trip has shown'; this meant neutral Yugoslavia.[13]

On 21–23 September, at the United Nations, the Greek request for the inscription of Cyprus at the agenda of the UN General Assembly was rejected. The Western powers, including the US, again voted against Greece. The Americans believed that, at that moment, a debate on Cyprus would make matters worse, and thus gave in to British pressure and voted against inscription. This caused even stronger anti-Western reactions in Greece. The opposition launched a full-scale attack on the government, as well as on NATO. Venizelos' Liberal Democratic Union openly wondered whether NATO membership was 'security or danger for Greece', and asked that the country seek additional guarantees 'even beyond today's alliances'. The Democratic Party turned against the US, and the EPEK noted that 'where things are, Greece has to reconsider its foreign policy and to re-examine the whole system of its alliances'. The EDA leader, Ioannis Passalides, asked for a policy of equal friendship to East and West.[14] On 23 September, the prominent Centre daily, *Eleftheria*, attacked the governing party of the Greek Rally, calling it 'the fatal world of slave-minded traitors', while three days later an *Hestia* editorial referred to dark forces which wanted to set up a 'government of Quislings'.[15] Even the Conservative *Kathimerini* wrote on 24 September that the country had only one option, 'to immediately end its co-operation with the west', and in other articles noted that Greece no longer had friends, that the Atlantic partners 'are not our allies', that NATO was simply another 'Holy Alliance': 'We do not need NATO, we do not need the Greek–Turkish alliance, we do not want bonds which have proved to be chains'.[16] As the internal crisis worsened, the pressure on the international policy of the country also grew. On 3 October, speaking in Thessaloniki, Sophocles Venizelos himself, the man who had taken Greece into NATO, also asked for a policy of 'equal friendship' to East and West.[17]

Thus, by late September and early October 1955, Greece's system of alliances had come under a vicious and public attack. The tripartite alliance with Turkey and Yugoslavia had practically dissolved, while the country's NATO membership had also been publicly disputed. This was the climate at the moment of Papagos' death on 4 October. On the following day, the King appointed Constantinos Karamanlis, a leading successful Minister of the Rally, as Prime Minister. Although in later years it was alleged that Karamanlis' appointment was sponsored by the US, recent research has shown that it was an initiative of the King, who needed a popular leader capable of containing public excitement. The Americans did not cause Karamanlis' ascendancy; on the contrary, on the very day of his appointment the US Embassy cabled to Washington that Stephanopoulos would probably become Prime Minister.[18] The new leader, Karamanlis, had to face an extremely difficult situation: the Balkan alliance was a thing of the past, and the Cyprus question was entering an explosive phase. The government would have to keep Greece in the West, facing a wounded and excited public opinion, as well as an extremely offensive opposition press, which did not hesitate to refer to the Cyprus question, speaking of 'slave-minded traitors' or of 'Quislings'.

Part II
The era of functionalism, 1955–63

6 The search for a long-term strategy

Constantinos Karamanlis and Evangelos Averoff

In the new sub-period, the triptych history–geography–Cold War continued to form the basis of Greek foreign policy analysis. However, the emphasis now focused on a 'deeper force': geography. Two people played a major role in policy-making: the Prime Minister and leader of the National Radical Union party (ERE), Constantinos Karamanlis, who also was Defence Minister from October 1955 until the February 1956 election and again in 1958–61; and Evangelos Averoff-Tossizza, who served as Foreign Minister from May 1956 to June 1963. Kanellopoulos also entered the government as Deputy Prime Minister early in 1959, but this time he played little role in defence policy. In 1956–61 Constantinos Tsatsos served as minister for the Prime Minister's Office, and he was acting Foreign Minister when Averoff was away from Athens, yet he mostly dealt with Cyprus. Panayis Papaligouras was the Minister for Economic Co-ordination in 1961–63 and a man of exceptional abilities, but on foreign affairs his field was mostly European integration, not national security. Thus, Karamanlis and Averoff were the main policy-makers on foreign and security policy.

Karamanlis had a degree of personal involvement in the security debate. A Macedonian Greek and son of a fighter of the 1904–08 Macedonian Struggle, Karamanlis had lived through the bitter Greek–Bulgarian antagonism over Macedonia and had seen his home town – Proti, in the Serres region of Eastern Macedonia – taken by the Bulgarian army three times in his own lifetime, in 1913, 1916 and 1941. Proti, furthermore, lies east of the Strymon, in the most vulnerable area of the northern Greek frontier.

Karamanlis did not belong to the traditional Athenian political establishment; he was the first northern Greek to assume the premiership. He was elected in Parliament in 1935 as an MP for Serres with the People's Party (the anti-Venizelists), but in the following year the Metaxas dictatorship put a sudden, though temporary, stop to his political career. During the 1941–44 occupation he remained in Athens, practised law and was a member of the 'Socialist Union', the circle of the prominent intellectual Constantinos Tsatsos. Karamanlis also participated in the Committee of Macedonians and Thracians under Law

58 *The era of functionalism, 1955–63*

Professor Alexandros Svolos, which in 1943 resisted the projected expansion of Bulgarian occupation to parts of Greek Central Macedonia.[1] Thus, Karamanlis' personal memories and experiences made him extremely sensitive to threats coming from the north. However, Karamanlis was not sentimental. His thinking was based on a mild form of realism and was guided by the need to place the security issues into a wider framework of the country's aims in the post-war world. He also was a very efficient administrator; his impressive success as Minister for Public Works in 1952–55 had gained him popularity as well as a reputation for relentless efficiency, which played a crucial role in his selection for the premiership by King Paul in the difficult days of October 1955.

On security issues, Karamanlis distanced himself from ideologically oriented analysis quite early. He was Defence Minister for a few months in the short-lived Sophocles Venizelos government in the autumn of 1950, when Greece's association with NATO was achieved. At that time, Karamanlis described the nature of the threat, including the recent civil war, in terms mainly geographical: 'A huge power, setting out from the farthest north and ending at the mountain crests of Beles [in the northern Greek border], attempted to crush our country and to enslave our people'.[2] It is also interesting that, as early as 1950, Karamanlis put forward an alternative interpretation regarding the capabilities of the Greek Communist Party. In an interview with Reuters on 30 September, he was asked whether the KKE could destabilize Greece. He replied: 'The KKE itself cannot now threaten the security of Greece. But there is the danger that it will regain such capability in the future, if the civic parties do not pursue a more prudent policy.'[3] Karamanlis believed that the stability of the Greek political and social system could not be achieved only (or even mainly) by repressive or military means, but by economic and political ones, namely through economic development, which alone could prevent the emergence of a new revolutionary climate in the country.[4] This was at the heart of his reformist orientation.

On the other hand, Karamanlis was not prepared to ignore the historical element altogether. The recent experience of the country made it even more important in his mind to constantly show 'prudence', another keyword in his discourse. Thus, when in summer 1956 the Soviet Foreign Minister, Dmitri Shepilov, visited Athens and suggested a reduction in Greek defence expenditure, Karamanlis replied, rather coldly, that since Bulgaria had invaded Greece three times in a generation, this was out of the question.[5] In September 1957, rejecting the proposal of the Romanian Prime Minister, Chivu Stoica, for the holding of a Balkan Conference, Karamanlis explained that mutual trust had not been restored among the Balkan states, and indirectly pointed to Bulgaria's past policy: '[Even before 1945] Greece had faced the unprovoked hostility of some of its neighbours, who either invaded its territories, or became puppets of other aggressors and as such declared their intention to annex Greek lands'.[6]

Karamanlis' thinking regarding the nature of the threat became clear during his discussion with Archbishop Makarios on 19 September 1958, at a moment when the British Macmillan Plan was being implemented in Cyprus despite Greek and Greek-Cypriot opposition. Makarios suggested that Greece leave

NATO 'even temporarily', in order to show to the West the strength of its feelings. The Prime Minister replied:[7]

> If these are your views, then indeed there is a disagreement between us, because the government, protecting the wider interests of the nation, is not willing to pursue a policy of withdrawal from NATO. You must take into account the geographical position of Greece which is being pressed by the bulk of the Slav and the communist world; you must take into account the permanent Slav threat for the creation of an Aegean Macedonia, in order to perceive the dangers that Greece will face if it detached itself from the west. Allow me simply to say that Yugoslavia itself offers its friendship to us, on the condition that we maintain the Balkan Pact and remain in NATO.

Geography loomed large in Karamanlis' argument when speaking with the West German Economics Minister, Ludwig Erhard, in November 1958 in Bonn: '[Greece's] people are in a dramatic position, facing pressure from the north and defend themselves literally on a rock to preserve themselves as a nation'.[8] This was even more evident during Karamanlis' meeting with US President Eisenhower, in Athens, in December 1959:[9]

> Greece ideologically belongs to the West, but geographically and ethnically is isolated. Surrounded by Slavs, it faces their pressure for centuries. This pressure has lately combined with communism, which unites them [the Slavs] even more. Therefore this pressure has become more tense and dangerous.

In April 1961, during his discussion with the US President, John F. Kennedy, Karamanlis 'underlined the crucial geographical position of Greece and the Slav communist threat that it faced from the north';[10] the parallel use of the words 'Slav' and 'communist' is again indicative. Karamanlis constantly stressed that the threat was deeply rooted and that it involved the relentless and unchangeable factor of geography.

The Foreign Minister, Averoff, also tended to focus on the effects of the 'deeper forces'. Averoff's views on foreign policy can be found in *Lost Opportunities*, his book on the Cyprus question, which has been published in English. His tendency to emphasize these deeper forces had become apparent since his youth. Because of his bad health (he had three crises of tuberculosis by the age of forty) he went to Switzerland for treatment, and then continued his studies there. His PhD thesis, from the School of Social Sciences of the University of Lausanne, dealt with the preconditions of Balkan co-operation (geographical, economic, monetary, legal, technical, administrative and psychological), received an award by the Carnegie Foundation and was published in Paris in 1933.[11] His second academic work was a study on the demographic development of Greece, and received an award from the Academy of Athens in 1939.[12] During the 1941–44 occupation, Averoff played a major role in the resistance in

Thessaly and in Epirus, against Italian and Romanian attempts to form a separatist Vlach state in Greece (Averoff belonged to a prominent Vlach family). In 1942 he was arrested and deported to Italy; but after the Italian surrender in 1943 he escaped, went to German-occupied Rome and formed a Greek resistance organization which facilitated the escape of Greek and allied soldiers; for this action, he received the British MBE. After the war, Averoff joined the Liberal Party and became one of Sophocles Venizelos' closest associates: he served as head of home front ministries, but in 1951–52, as Greece was entering NATO, he became Venizelos' Undersecretary in the Foreign Ministry. He joined Karamanlis' new party, ERE, at the time of its foundation in January 1956. Averoff was one of the young Liberals who followed Karamanlis in ERE and helped him shape a new Centre-right.[13]

Averoff's insistence on the importance of geography was evident in his writings. In 1973, in the very first sentences of his book on the civil war, Averoff offered a geographically-based interpretation for the factors which determined Greece's position in the world:[14]

> The struggle was local, the stakes worldwide. Now, as in the past, the Greek peninsula stands at one of the great crossroads of Europe and of the world. Today a crossroad of ideologies, once of religions. It is, and always has been, a crossroads of continents, of maritime routes and of the races of man.

In April 1961, after the visit that he and Karamanlis paid to the US, Averoff put forward a similar view in a newspaper article:[15]

> Greece, finding itself in the most spectacular, perhaps, cross-roads of the globe, in the cross-roads where three continents and important maritime routes, races and religions meet, has experienced intensely all the major crises of humankind. I could argue, pointing to many historical precedents, that Greece has experienced these crises not only intensely but also as a vanguard, for many of these crises erupted as crises of Greece, before even becoming crises of humankind in general. Allow me to mention only one contemporary example: the horrible bandit war of 1946–1949 was initially regarded as a crisis of Greece, but it then was recognized as the beginning of the terrible crisis which the whole of humankind experiences today, in the form of the conflict between the totalitarian and the liberal ideologies.

A comprehensive picture of Averoff's views on Greek foreign policy can be found in his lecture to students of the US War College in Athens in May 1958. He said that Greece needed the support of larger states in its age-long effort to hold back the 'Slav tide' (he did not even use the term 'Communist'). He referred to the importance of Greek–Turkish co-operation, which would surely be restored after a Cyprus settlement, and spoke of the 'desirability' to 'neutralize' a part of Greece's land border through friendship with Yugoslavia. Finally,

Averoff mentioned that Greece needed a 'backdrop or rear echelon', which could be found in relations with the Arab world.[16]

However, military inferiority and geographical vulnerability were not the only factors which shaped the Karamanlis government's policy. On the contrary, this government made a commercial opening to the East in 1956–57, while it sought the support of the Soviet Bloc in the UN debates over Cyprus. The basis of this new policy can be found in an important minute by Averoff to Karamanlis in the summer of 1956, shortly before the unofficial visit of the Soviet Foreign Minister, Shepilov, to Athens. Averoff argued that Greece had to recognize the reality of the ascendancy of Soviet power and to adjust to the new international climate. Once more, his analysis was primarily based on a reading of the map:[17]

> One has to note that we cannot, as a small country in a geographically crucial position at the cross-roads of continents, interests and great roads, ignore the fact that we are near a real colossus, the size, political and material development of which has reached a stage which it had never reached before, and continues to grow. Indeed, the Soviet Union politically reigns in areas which in the past were hostile to it, while today it is highly regarded in other neighbouring regions (Yugoslavia, Arab countries, the Far East), and economically it experiences an unprecedented take-off. The reports of our ambassador to Moscow, a good observer, are quite characteristic regarding economic development, and he believes that after the forthcoming sixth Five Year Plan, Russia's economic capabilities will be immense. Considering also that a balance in thermonuclear weapons seems to have been reached, it is obvious that one needs to deal with the future of one's relations with the Soviet Union with extreme care and concern. I of course have to categorically stress that there is for me no question of loosening our alliance bonds. Perhaps what I have noted above leads me to the conclusion that we must strengthen our alliances; but no doubt we must also develop, as far as this is possible, better relations with the Soviet Union.

In other words, Karamanlis and Averoff held that Greece faced a situation which is classic in international analysis: Greece controlled the narrow coastal areas and faced the pressures of the 'masses' of the interior who strove to secure an exit to the sea. The term 'Slavs' was used as a geopolitical expression, not as a racial description – hence their readiness to establish a strategic partnership with the strongest Slav country of the Balkans, Yugoslavia, which had quarrelled with Moscow. The threat from Bulgaria did not stem from a perception that the Bulgarians were 'bad', but because it was deemed 'natural' that in their given geographical position (and with their Soviet allies) they would seek an exit to a southern sea. The 'Red Peril' was a part of this threat, and certainly made it even more dangerous (since Communism 'united even more' the peoples of the interior), but did not create it. For Karamanlis and Averoff, the problem derived from a combination of the political realities of the post-war world with geography. A geographical problem was more difficult to solve than a political one.

A new perception of national security

Exactly because Greece was geographically cut off from the West and in a position of permanent military inferiority, it could not solve its security problem through military force alone. Thus, Athens tried to employ other means, mainly diplomatic, in order to create a system of credible deterrence. This was also attempted by previous governments, but under Karamanlis and Averoff the policy acquired much more systematic forms and embraced new fields of activity, such as European integration. This is why their approach to national security is defined here as 'functional'. 'Functionalism' describes a variety of elements: the emphasis on the economy and the geographical realities, rather than on rigid ideological rivalries with the East; the effort to take advantage of the formal multilateral NATO context, but also of its practical functions and guarantees, military and political, on a multilateral as well as bilateral level, and in particular moments and situations; a more outward-looking attitude towards the Soviet Bloc; and last but not least, the importance that they attached to European integration as an option of strategic importance for the long-term future of the country. Karamanlis and Averoff gave to Greek policy a flexibility and an emphasis on multilateralism which would have been unthinkable in previous periods. At the same time, there was one important, non-negotiable, guiding line: the unyielding persistence of the government in Greece's integration in the West. Nothing was to be allowed to endanger the latter aim. It will be shown that in 1955–58 this policy was implemented in spite of the hostile background of the rise of anti-Americanism in the country. Moreover, this general principle of integration with the West ensured that the pragmatism inherent in functionalism would not degenerate to opportunism.

Still, one should not go as far as suggesting that the Karamanlis government did not regard the very Communist nature of the Soviet Bloc as a threat. A post-civil war Greek government could hardly do otherwise. However, two additional factors must be taken into account when discussing the Karamanlis government's analysis: first, the ideological aspect of the threat was regarded as complementary to the major one, the geographical; second, the Karamanlis government regarded that the containment of Communism would be accomplished more successfully through economic development, rather than military means. An indicative example of this attitude can be found in the records of the discussions of Greek statesmen and officials with James Richards, the US envoy on the Eisenhower doctrine for the Middle East, in the spring of 1957:[18]

> At this point, Mr. Richards asked Ambassador Hadjivassiliou: 'and what about international communism?' Mr. Hadjivassiliou replied that since Greece won the guerrilla war in the autumn of 1949, we speak in this part of the world more about reconstruction and economic development, rather than 'international communism'.

The internal challenge seemed to grow after the May 1958 general election, when the left-wing EDA party received almost 25 per cent of the vote and became the major opposition force with seventy-nine MPs in Parliament. The rise of the Left, only nine years after the end of the civil war, was facilitated by the emergence of neutralism in the country because of the public's disappointment at the West's policy over Cyprus. This created a further problem for the government as well as for the non-Communist opposition. It is no coincidence that on 14 May 1958, three days after the election, the Greek Permanent Mission to NATO submitted to the alliance's Joint Working Group on Information Policy and Cultural Co-operation a note calling for the establishment of a 'committee for the study of Soviet propaganda'. The Greek note stressed that not all NATO members had adequate services for protection against psychological warfare, and suggested that the alliance should acquire a mechanism for concerted reaction to Soviet propaganda.[19] It is also notable that on 14 May 1958 there was a caretaker government in Greece; Karamanlis formed his third government on 17 May. Although the alliance set up a Working Group to study the Greek proposal, this was not taken further, as many NATO countries felt that this issue should be dealt with at national level. Still, in the following years, during NATO meetings, the Greek ministers kept insisting on the need for a concerted Western reaction to Soviet propaganda tactics.[20]

In December 1959 Averoff made a reference to the view of the British Foreign Secretary, Selwyn Lloyd, that Western public opinions were satisfied by NATO. Averoff said that he understood his British colleague's position: 'He lives in Britain. He allies with a whole group in the Commonwealth, [he has] a rich, powerful, isolated country'. Averoff noted that the position of other states of the alliance was very different; Greece had gone through the experience of a civil war some years ago and was geographically and economically vulnerable, while Turkey had extensive land and maritime borders with the Soviet Union itself; 'So, for the love of God, let us not have this impression that the psychological domain has been covered'.[21] Thus, even on the level of propaganda and psychological warfare, for the Karamanlis government the threat was becoming more tense, because of Greece's geographical exposure and economic problems.

On the practical level, there were two important initiatives which marked the new era of functionalism: the reform of Greek foreign policy which started in 1956 and the reform of defence policy in 1957. The 1956–57 reshaping of Greek foreign policy has already been researched.[22] It was partially instigated by Greece's need to respond to Makarios' exile by the British, which showed that the Anglo–Greek dispute would be a long one and thus the country needed to seek additional international support. Only for the year 1956, this reshaping of foreign policy included an opening to the Arabs, a commercial opening to the Soviet Bloc, the resumption of diplomatic relations with Hungary, the exchange of ambassadors with Czechoslovakia, the normalization of Greek–Romanian relations, the bilateral rapprochement with Yugoslavia (starting with Karamanlis' visit to Belgrade in December 1956), new contacts with Western Europe (for example, the visit of King Paul and Queen Frederica to France and the visit to

Athens of West German President Theodor Heuss) and, last but not least, Karamanlis' first visit to the US.

The peak of this reform came with Athens' interest in European integration. This was the climax of functionalism: it involved nothing less than the search for a long-term orientation of the country or, to put it differently, for a new place in the world. The major success of this policy can be found in the Treaty of Association of Greece with the European Economic Community (EEC), which was signed on 9 July 1961 in Athens.[23] Greece's participation in European integration also indirectly involved security. After the signature of the Treaty of Association on 9 July 1961, Karamanlis stated to the EEC statesmen who participated in the ceremony:[24]

> In the minds of the Greeks, the European Economic Community is not simply an economic community of interests, but an entity with a wider political role and importance. If we were the first to seek association with the Community, we did so under the conviction that the economic unification of Europe will lead to real European unity, and through this to the strengthening of democracy and peace throughout the world [...] We believe that the time will come when Europe will include all the free European peoples without exception. A united and powerful Europe will become a guarantee not only for its [Greece's] survival, but also for the prevalence of freedom in the world. For here, in Europe, the fate of the free man will finally be decided.

In 1961-62, Greece sought to participate in the European Political Cooperation envisaged by the Fouchet Plan; the Greeks noted that their participation 'will enhance the external security of the country, by making it even more clear to its neighbours that Greece forms part of a unified European political community'.[25]

Indeed, to understand fully Karamanlis' and Averoff's functionalism, it is important to note the two different roles that they attributed to the two major Western organizations, NATO and the EEC: the former was the shield; the EEC could not provide defence, but the Greeks saw it as a catalyst for the emergence of a strong Western Europe. The EEC would also give Greece a sense of direction in the post-war world. To put it simply, since the country's security problem derived from the unchangeable facts of geography and Greece's distance from the hard core of the West, association with the EEC was a means of achieving integral, 'functional', participation in the West. This was the only way to solve the fundamental problem of geography.

The policy in the armed forces was another part of functionalism. The 1957 reform of defence policy will be examined in Chapter 7. In a large part of the relevant literature, much is made of the fact that by 1958 some younger officers had formed a new clique within the army, the EENA (Union of Young Greek Officers), and used former IDEA channels to acquire better appointments; this group included many of the officers who toppled Greek democracy in 1967.

However, the 1967 coup took place in a completely different political climate many years later; in 1958 EENA did not have the power, nor the chance, to threaten Greek democracy. On the contrary, in 1955–63 the internal situation of the army seemed to be better compared to previous periods. Karamanlis continued Papagos' policy of not allowing the Palace to control the army. Indeed, Constantinos Choidas, the head of King Paul's Political Office, insisted later that the Palace brought the Karamanlis government down in 1963 exactly to be able to control the army.[26] On another level, though, Karamanlis distanced himself from Papagos' policies: Karamanlis used some of the officers whom Papagos had removed in 1952–53, such as Lieutenant-Generals (retd) Grigoropoulos as Greek military representative to NATO and Tsakalotos as ambassador to Belgrade. Moreover, decree 4028/1959 revised Papagos' legislation which had removed other officers from the army, and promoted them (without however bringing them back to active service).[27] It was a kind of partial rehabilitation. The relative calmness in the internal affairs of the army in 1955–63 could also be attributed to the fact that major changes had already been made by Papagos, and therefore the political cost had fallen on the previous government.

7   New security problems

Following the collapse of the Balkan pacts in mid-1955, Greece's security problem was radically transformed. It is possible to distinguish two different sub-periods. The years 1955–59 were a time of uncertainty, both regionally as well as internally. Then, the Cyprus settlement removed the major source of strain from Greece's relationship with NATO, but this led to an intensification of pressures from the Soviet Bloc; in 1959–63, Greece was afraid that it could become the victim of localized Soviet-Bloc aggression.

Years of uncertainty, 1955–59

In 1955, the collapse of the tripartite Greek–Turkish–Yugoslav alliance destroyed the regional basis of the Greek security system. Thus, the fundamental geopolitical weakness of Greek defence – a strategically thin northern border and the difficulty to face a stronger mechanized enemy, solidly entrenched in the interior – again rendered the country extremely vulnerable. To make matters worse, during the years of the Cyprus dispute, Turkey also verbally threatened Greece with war (for example in the summer of 1956, and at the time of Makarios' arrival in Athens from exile in April 1957). Averoff, in his usual assertive tone, replied that Greece would face a Turkish attack with all its military power.[1] This was also used as a form of deterrence, but solving the problem was not as easy as that. In 1955–59, the Greek armed forces had to cover the northern frontier and to retain some capability to cover the eastern borders as well. It was very difficult to do both. In 1958, the alliance's MC 70 document provided for the use of tactical nuclear weapons by the smaller members of the alliance and asked for the reduction of their armies; this would involve a 20 per cent reduction of the numerical strength of the Greek army. The alliance planned for a smaller but technically more advanced (and therefore more expensive) Greek force. Athens agreed to take the tactical nuclear weapons, but kept the army at its present strength; the Americans considered that this was because Athens felt the need to maintain a large force in a period of crisis in Greek–Turkish relations.[2]

Despite tension over Cyprus, in the 1950s a Greek–Turkish war was not regarded as probable: neither Greece nor Turkey could ignore the Cold War, and they could not afford a clash among themselves. NATO itself considered such a war as unthinkable. Thus, one week after his ascendancy to the premiership and one day after he had won the vote of confidence in Parliament, Karamanlis told the chief of the alliance planners, US General J. Lawton Collins, that Greece now had to take into account the Greek–Turkish balance of power as well; NATO no longer covered all eventualities.[3] According to the relevant US document, though, General Collins noted that in the event of a Greek–Turkish war, Article 5 of the North Atlantic Treaty (namely, the collective guarantee) would be activated:[4]

> With reference to the inference of Turkey as a possible military threat to Greece, he [Collins] emphasized that war between Turkey and Greece is unthinkable under any conditions present or future. While NATO countries have jointly agreed to come to the defence of any member no matter what quarter attack may come from, without or within NATO, the present threat to peace is Russia. Purpose of NATO is to build common defence so strong that Russia would have no temptation to attack.

However, one should not place excessive emphasis on General Collins' view regarding Article 5 of the NATO Treaty. The alliance guarantee covered the Soviet threat, and the issue of attacks from within had not been debated in the alliance; it is notable that the Greek record of the conversation does not mention Collins' view on Article 5. Nor was General Collins competent to make such a far-reaching interpretation of the Treaty. Collins' position was strictly on the lines of the 'unthinkable war' thesis, and as such was regarded as satisfactory in Athens. Even so, during the second half of the 1950s the possibility of Greek–Turkish war, however remote, could not be ruled out, and thus the Greek defence planners had to deal with this additional problem. This meant that the Greek security problem had severely deteriorated.

The difficulties also spread to the internal political scene. The September 1955 riots in Turkey, the collapse of the London Tripartite Conference on Cyprus and their aftermath sparked a wave of anti-Americanism. This was further fuelled by developments in the following two years: Makarios' exile in March 1956, executions by the British of EOKA members starting in May 1956, the British espousal of the principle of partition of Cyprus in December 1956, the British Macmillan Plan of June 1958 and the failure of the NATO allies to support the Greek UN appeals over Cyprus.

In the aftermath of Makarios' exile in March 1956, large demonstrations were organized in Athens and other Greek cities, with anti-Western slogans supporting withdrawal from NATO, neutrality and an Athens–Belgrade–Cairo axis. On 16 March the US Ambassador to Athens, Cavendish Cannon, reported to the State Department that the political atmosphere in Greece was even more explosive than during September 1955.[5] In May, three demonstrators and a policeman were killed during clashes in the capital. Karamanlis himself, speaking to American journalists in March 1956, commented that 'the west spreads butter on the

Russian bread [regarding Greek public opinion]'.[6] And Averoff, speaking with the Counselor of the US Embassy, Ray Thurston, in August 1956, immediately after the British had rejected an EOKA offer of a truce in Cyprus, noted: 'I told him that if, replying to the stupid and unfortunate English response, the prime minister had stated that Greece withdraws from NATO, all the Greek people, except some 2,000 Athenians, would applaud. Mr. Thurston admitted as much.'[7]

In the late summer of 1956, one of the first opinion polls conducted by the American Embassy in the Athens area confirmed these conclusions. Asked whether Greece should withdraw from NATO if the allies continued the same policy in Cyprus, an astonishing 74.16 per cent replied affirmatively; only 13 per cent wanted the country to remain in the alliance and 12.84 per cent refused to answer. Asked whether NATO membership covered Greek interests, 33.16 per cent replied affirmatively and 49.67 per cent negatively.[8] The wording of the questions was peculiar, something that the British Embassy immediately noted, especially regarding NATO membership: a 'yes' answer meant support for exit from NATO. Still, the results were indicative of the strength of Greek feeling. As has been stressed in the bibliography, the Cyprus question had a 'disintegrative effect' on the Greek public's attitude towards NATO.[9]

A new USIS poll, in autumn 1957, was even more alarming: NATO membership was endorsed by 37.5 per cent of those asked, while 47 per cent preferred a neutralist policy. This second poll was more important than the previous one: it was more detailed; it was held after Makarios' release and at a time when no executions of EOKA members were taking place in Cyprus; mostly, it confirmed a persistent tendency in the Greek public. The autumn 1957 poll greatly alarmed the US Embassy. The US Chargé, James Penfield, sent a long report to the State Department, noting that in the past year and a half (namely, since Karamanlis' first electoral victory in February 1956) Greece had disengaged from the 'essentially "American" policy which she has followed since the end of the Second World War'. The Penfield report stressed that Karamanlis himself was worried about the rise of anti-Western feeling, but this feeling could lead Greece to a neutral position outside the two major blocs, 'where, we have reason to fear, a growing number of Greeks today already feel themselves psychologically'. The report also noted the intense activity of pro-Soviet Leagues in the country, the increasing contacts of Greeks and Soviets, and the dramatic increase of Greek–Soviet-Bloc commercial exchanges in the past year, and commented:[10]

> Stated baldly, this means, if true, that we are not winning the battle for the Greek mind; that those who are devils on the international scene to us are not devils to the Greek; that increasingly frequent approaches by the Greek Government and by individuals to the Soviet Bloc would not be unpopular with two out of three Greeks. It could mean that many Greeks today are already ideologically and philosophically in the neutral bloc. It could mean that he [the Greek] either has forgotten the lesson that ended only seven years ago [the civil war] or that he never learned a lesson at all.

Significantly, in the autumn of 1957 the State Department had been obliged to recall its Ambassador to Athens, George Allen, after the latter had said that the Muslim minority of Western Thrace could ask for the right to self-determination, just as the Greek Cypriots were doing. The issue caused an uproar in the Greek press. Allen was not hostile to Greece, and his statements were simply careless, though provocative for a Greek public who were highly agitated. The USIS poll came on top of this incident. The US Embassy in Athens did expect some assertion of relative Greek independence, as the country was developing economically. This had been noted in two US National Intelligence Estimates in early 1955 and mid-1956, while in the summer of 1957 the US National Security Council had referred to this eventuality as a healthy development.[11] However, American officials did not anticipate that half of the Greek public would prefer a neutralist policy.

This was not all. Penfield made the mistake of repeating his observations during discussions with Greek politicians, who were convinced that the Americans wanted to overthrow Karamanlis. This played a role in the internal ERE revolt which (with some support from the Centre and circles close to the Palace) brought the Karamanlis government down in February 1958 and subsequently led to the May 1958 election. The Americans did not intend to cause this; but Penfield's remarks were misunderstood by Greek politicians (though not by the two major rebels of February 1958, Cabinet Ministers George Rallis and Panayis Papaligouras) as encouragement to overthrow Karamanlis. It is ironic that Karamanlis, who publicly was being accused by the opposition for being a puppet of the Americans, was toppled because his opponents regarded that he had distanced himself too much from the US.

The feeling that his observations had been misunderstood led Penfield to write another long report in April 1958, during the Greek electoral campaign. This time he was not alarmist: he noted that there was a controllable psychological disengagement of the Greeks from the West, he stressed that the emergence of a more independent Greek policy on Cyprus, Eastern Europe and the Middle East was a healthy phenomenon, and he simply expressed reservations as to the possibility that, in trying to assert this independence, Greece might come too close to the East.[12] However, by spring 1958 it was already late: the anti-Western spirit had acquired a dynamic of its own. In the May 1958 general election Karamanlis' ERE easily prevailed, receiving 42 per cent of the vote, but the left-wing EDA Party came second with almost 25 per cent, leaving the Liberal Party in third place. This was largely the result of the disappointment of the Greek public regarding Western policy on the Cyprus question.[13] After the 1958 election, the USIS provided advice to the Greek government to intensify anti-Communist propaganda in the countryside and in the army.[14] However, the problem had assumed great dimensions.

At the same time, the military balance was extremely unfavourable. By late 1955, the NATO planners estimated that the military capabilities of the Soviet Bloc had improved significantly.[15] In 1955 the Greek intelligence service estimated the strength of the Bulgarian armed forces at 275,000 men, including the police and the so-called border army; the Bulgarian army had almost 800 tanks, a formidable artillery and the support of a large number of jet planes (Bulgaria, under its Peace Treaty, was not allowed to have an army larger than 65,000 men). Albania had 40,000 men under arms, including police.[16] At that moment, the Greek army numbered 120,000 men.

The Greek military leaders focused on armour: Greece had only 110 Chaffee light tanks and 110 tank destroyers (which were primarily a defensive weapon). Turkey had 330 M-47 medium and thirty Chaffee light tanks, and 250 tank destroyers. Yugoslavia had 900 medium tanks (M-47 and Shermans), 500 tank destroyers and an unspecified number of German and Soviet tanks. Bulgarian armour was estimated at 750 medium T-34 tanks and forty Stalins, the best medium and heavy tanks of the Second World War.[17] The NATO annual reviews for 1955 and 1956 noted that although Greece made a considerable effort to meet the alliance's requirements (set out in document MC 48), there were serious problems, such as inadequate control and reporting systems, the lack of all-weather fighters in the air force, obsolete vessels in the navy, and the shortage of essential material and regulars in the land forces.[18] There were also the Battalions of the National Guard Defence (TEA). In 1958, the Americans estimated their strength at 84,000 men, of whom about a third were situated in the north; however, TEA were local lightly-armed units, which were not credible in case of a full-scale war.[19] At any rate, when Greek perceptions are examined, one also has to take into account the unfavourable geography of the Greek–Bulgarian border and the estimated Bulgarian supremacy regarding the readiness level of the units, which meant in the first crucial days of a war Sofia would be in a position to engage more units than Athens. Even allowing for some Greek alarmism regarding Bulgarian military power, the problem of the 'indefensibility' of the Greek border persisted.

To be sure, figures have to be considered together with additional aspects. Thus, Turkey and Yugoslavia had large armies but they also had larger areas to cover against the Red Army itself (the Turko–Soviet border or Central Europe). The presence of the US Sixth Fleet in the Mediterranean meant that there was a huge air power which could support the Western forces. However, according to NATO strategy, the Sixth Fleet would first concentrate its forces in the western Mediterranean and would then launch air-strikes. Thus its intervention would cause delay for a few days, which could prove crucial in the Greek front. As has been perceptively noted, from the Greek point of view this meant that the Sixth Fleet would, in fact, avenge Greece rather than defend it.[20] For the Greek defence planners, there was a simple conclusion to be drawn: after the collapse of the Balkan pacts there was no common front against Bulgaria and therefore Greece's military inferiority vis-à-vis Bulgaria created even greater dangers. This led Karamanlis, during his first meeting with an American officer, General Collins, on 13 October 1955, to ask for additional military aid, especially tanks.[21] On the next day, 14 October, in a letter to the US Ambassador, Cannon, Karamanlis asked for speedier delivery of US military aid; a little later, in a memorandum to the US government, Athens stressed that it spent almost 7 per cent of its GNP on defence at a time when the Greek standard of living was the second lowest in the Western alliance.[22]

Similar requests were repeated in the following months. In the autumn of 1956 Karamanlis paid his first visit to the US, and tried to convince the Americans to provide more military aid, especially hardware. He noted that in the case of a Bulgarian attack, the Greek army would have to withdraw west of the Strymon, conceding Eastern Macedonia and Western Thrace to the Bulgarians and leaving the left flank of the Turkish forces in the Straits unprotected.[23] According to the Greek military, this was 'forward defence' only in name. A little later, in January 1957, the Greek government repeated its request for increased military aid in a memorandum to the American committee for US aid abroad: Athens stressed that it played a major role in the defence of the Straits and of the Middle East, had an excellent relationship with Yugoslavia and the Arabs, and was a model for the positive effects of US aid.[24] These arguments were supported by the US Embassy, which cabled to Washington: 'The far greater tank and combat air capability available to Bulgaria means Greece would become a sitting duck in the event of war, committed to a static defense and eventual certain defeat, unless it had the means for counterattack'.[25] The Greek government was asking the US to help it acquire exactly this capability to counterattack.

The Greek persistence brought results. In March 1957, the Armour Report to the US Senate, dealing with the programmes of US assistance abroad, stressed that Greek defence was crucial for the security of the United States and of the West, as well as for the effective defence of Turkey and the Straits; if Greece ever fell under Communist control, it could pose a threat to the Middle East as well as to Western European security.[26] The Armour Report was hotly debated in Greece for another reason: it mentioned that a possible overthrow of the Karamanlis government would be damaging to US interests, because this government would probably be replaced by a coalition in which pro-Communist forces would also participate. Even on this point, though, it was the British who were angered the most, since they regarded this part of the report as a blank cheque to Karamanlis over Cyprus. Still, the Armour Report was important because it signalled a major success of the Greek government in its efforts to convince the US to provide additional military aid.

It was exactly thanks to this aid that the reform of defence policy became possible in 1957, in consultation with NATO military authorities. This reform started with a new positioning of Greek units, which was announced in February 1957. Moreover, the US agreed to speed up the delivery of hardware to Greece, mostly M-47 tanks and artillery, and this made it possible for the Greek army to set up a new armoured division (XX). This meant that the Greek army now acquired the means to counterattack. The reform also involved the strengthening of the air force as well as of the radar systems.[27] In 1958, following repeated Greek requests, the alliance agreed to help create a tank battalion in each Greek infantry division. This decision was not implemented until the early 1960s, because of the shortage of tanks.[28] A few years later, Lieutenant-General Petros

Nicolopoulos, who was chief of the General Staff of the Army in 1957, described the essence of the 1957 reform: 'A major change was effected in the location of the units, the power of the active Army was increased, new weapons were acquired and the defence of some vulnerable border areas was strengthened'. Nicolopoulos added that a new mobilization plan was drawn. As a result, 'the defensive power of the National Army almost doubled'.[29] Furthermore, since 1957 Greece had acquired warships, including minesweepers, two submarines, four destroyers and another two destroyers after 1962. Last but not least, new squadrons of F-84s were delivered.[30]

The 1957 reform was a turning point in Greek security policy. Although Greek military documents are still classified, the essence of the new strategy can easily be assessed: the Greek forces would fight a defensive battle on the Strymon River. The army would then counterattack to regain lost ground; and it was exactly this capability to counterattack that the XX Armoured Division offered. Thus the XX Armoured Division played a major role in the defence reform. Of course, the capabilities of this unit were not comparable to those of a US armoured division, and the Americans themselves used to refer to it as a 'brigade' rather than a 'division'. The Greek strategic planners kept noting that a defensive line at the Strymon meant that large Greek territories would have to be abandoned, while the XX Armoured Division was still not powerful enough to regain them. Regardless, this unit was vital for the new security policy.

This, together with the close Greek–Yugoslav defence co-operation after 1957, gave Athens a relative sense of self-confidence during the years of the Cyprus crisis. In July 1958, Lieutenant-General Dovas, the Chief of the General Staff of National Defence, indicated to Karamanlis (who now also held the post of the Defence Minister) that the Greek position in Greek Macedonia and in Western Thrace was interdependent with the Turkish position in the Straits and in Eastern Thrace. Dovas noted that if Turkey did not fight, the position of Greece would be extremely difficult; however, if Greece fell, Turkey's position would be desperate, since the Turkish army would be cut off from the other NATO forces.[31]

At any rate, the 1957 defence reform should not be overestimated. Even so, the Greek army could not balance the local superiority of the Warsaw-Pact forces. The 1957 NATO annual review noted the significant stepping up of the Greek defence effort; however, it also noted that there was a shortage of regulars, while the reserve training programme was not fully implemented due to financial difficulties; spare parts and fuel stocks were also below NATO standards. The lack of trained technicians in the armed forces was considerable, as there was competition between the army and the industry for skilled manpower. Mostly, there were serious problems regarding command communications: Greece had submitted a request to the NAC for international assistance for their improvement. The NATO annual review argued for the continuation of foreign military aid.[32]

Similarly, in August 1957 an NSC paper on Greece stressed that the country was important strategically because of its proximity to the Soviet Union and the

Middle East, its NATO membership, its links with Yugoslavia, and also because it formed (together with Turkey and Yugoslavia) a barrier between the Soviets and the Mediterranean. The NSC insisted that in case of war, Greece would put up a forward defence and would cover the Turkish position in the Straits; however, the Greeks, although 'good warriors', faced a shortage of material and, with their present force of eleven infantry divisions, one armoured 'brigade' and thirteen regiments of light infantry, could put up a limited defence against a satellite attack. Even after full mobilization, the Greeks could only undertake a short 'delaying action' against an attack in which the Red Army would participate.[33] Thus, the NSC insisted that Greece was essentially indefensible in case of a Red Army attack. Indeed, in the autumn of 1957 the Americans considered the possibility of pressing for the reduction of the Greek army's size.[34] In other words, the Greek security problem could not be solved by military means alone. The combination of geography and military balances always pointed to a painful Greek operational disadvantage. Karamanlis' and Averoff's functionalism tried to deal with this structural military weakness through the employment of other means, diplomatic and political.

The return to NATO normalcy and the problem of localized war, 1959–63

The 1959 Cyprus settlement removed the strain from Greece's relationship with the West, but also had other side-effects. The Cyprus settlement did not lead to the revival of the 1954 tripartite Balkan alliance: by 1959 Yugoslavia was not prepared to abandon its position in the non-aligned movement, while the May 1960 military coup in Turkey complicated things further, and Greek–Yugoslav relations went through a crisis in 1961–62. Thus, after 1959 there was no 'common' Greek–Turkish–Yugoslav force in the south of the Balkans. On the other hand, the re-establishment of Greece's relations with the West sparked strong Soviet-Bloc pressures on Athens. Thus, in May 1959 Moscow pressed Athens not to accept US missiles on its soil; this Soviet demarche was followed by similar approaches by Bulgaria and Romania. Then, in June 1959, Khrushchev visited Albania and stated that the Greek people could pay 'in blood' for the bad decisions of their government on the issue of US missiles.[35] In the summer of 1959 the Greek–Soviet 'stamps war' broke out (this will be mentioned in Chapter 9), and in the autumn Khrushchev stated that the capitalists should be ashamed to have oppressed 'the best children of Greece' during the civil war; this caused the strong reaction from the Centre opposition as well.[36] In its deliberations with the NATO allies, the Greek government often noted the pressures exerted upon Athens by Moscow Radio, other state radios in the East, or the Greek Communists' radio, based in Bucharest. Athens regarded that it was under constant psychological and political pressure from the Soviet Bloc, and also pointed out alleged Soviet assistance to the EDA Party within Greece.[37] The climax of Soviet pressures came with Khrushchev's statement in August 1961 about the nuclear weapons which would spare 'neither the olive trees nor

74 *The era of functionalism, 1955–63*

the Acropolis'.³⁸ In September 1961, the Soviet Ambassador in Athens, Mikhail Sergueev, protested about the holding of a NATO exercise in northern Greece; this also angered the Americans, since it was unusual for the Soviets to protest about NATO manoeuvres.³⁹

According to Athens, all these indicated that Moscow was intending to divide Greece from the alliance. The Greek leaders and strategic planners were particularly afraid of a Bulgarian localized attack, which could succeed because of Bulgarian military superiority, before the West would have the chance to intervene. A localized attack became more probable, in Greek eyes, because 'massive retaliation' was abandoned by the Americans in those years and was replaced by the 'flexible response' strategy, which called for a strengthening of the conventional capabilities of NATO armies. To put it simply, Greece was in no position to put up forward defence, while the alliance was in no position to come quickly to Greece's aid. As Averoff told the NAC in December 1959, NATO had to show military as well as political vigilance, not mere 'solidarité en paroles'.⁴⁰ This was why the Greeks also monitored with interest the SACEUR's ideas to set up a mobile force which could be deployed in exposed areas of the alliance.⁴¹ As the US NSC noted in its paper on Greece in early 1961:⁴²

> Greek policy towards the USSR and its satellites in Eastern Europe is based on deep distrust and fear of the Soviet Bloc's policy of alternating threats and blandishments [...] The Greek Government fears any serious movement in the direction of Free World–Soviet Bloc detente because such a detente, it believes, would result in leaving Greece exposed to Bloc pressures and in reducing the importance which the Free World attaches to Greece.

Finally, the possibility of a local war could be combined with another scenario, namely infiltration by former Communist guerrillas; the Greek press often carried reports about the training of such persons in Eastern Europe. Karamanlis mentioned this issue during a Parliamentary debate in 1960, while similar fears were expressed in 1962 by George Papandreou, now the leader of the Centre Union Party, in a conversation with members of the US Embassy.⁴³ For its part, the Kennedy administration did not believe that a localized attack on Greece was probable, and repeatedly (though unsuccessfully) tried to ease Greek fears.

The Greek fear of localized war peaked on two occasions. The first was during the crisis of the building of the Berlin Wall in August 1961: this coincided with tension in Greek–Bulgarian relations, as well as with Khrushchev's blunt remarks about nuclear weapons, olive trees and the Acropolis. Speaking to US diplomats, Averoff indicated that Moscow could spark a crisis in Greece in order to divert Western attention from Berlin.⁴⁴ The Greeks again feared a local Bulgarian attack during the Cuban missile crisis, when Athens regarded itself as the most probable point of Soviet retaliation in the case of a US strike on Cuba. During the crisis, the Greek and the Bulgarian armed forces were put on maximum alert.⁴⁵

Moreover, Greece's post-1959 relations with the Warsaw-Pact powers constantly fell victim to the unstable character of Khrushchev himself, who used to alternate threats and offers at immense speed. The sudden changes in Khrushchev's mood and the fact that he seemed to single out Athens and Bonn (two frontline states of NATO) for his pressures irritated a leader like Karamanlis, who focused on his interlocutor's credibility. In a memorandum that Karamanlis gave to US Secretary of State, Christian Herter, in the spring of 1960, the Greek government stressed: 'As peace is one and indivisible, détente too cannot but be one and indivisible. It is not possible to have détente in Washington, in Paris, in Rome, in Ankara, but [have] aggressive tension towards Athens'.[46]

At exactly the same time, 1958–61, the Greek Left and a part of the Centre opposition accused the government of being opposed to détente because it wanted to take advantage of the 'Red Peril' internally. This debate also involved Greece's commerce with the East, and will be examined in Chapter 9. However, it is important to stress that the government sincerely believed that the country was facing a pressing danger. The Greeks were raising this issue in their conversations with the Western leaders; it was not a pretext for internal political purposes. Moreover, it will be shown that this fear was shared by the Centre governments even after 1963.

Of course, Athens finally accepted the prospect of détente. It was the Foreign Ministry that took the lead on this. As the Director General, Christos Xanthopoulos-Palamas, minuted in the summer of 1960, for the Soviet Union détente did not entail the abandonment of its ultimate aim to destroy the Western world: 'As a tactic, détente does not annul the cold war. In fact it is a form of cold war [. . .] If the Free World lost this war, i.e. if it lost the peace, all its military potential will prove useless'. The Director General indicated that Moscow was forced to adopt this new tactic because it needed to concentrate on its economic effort, and because the Korean War had shown that expansion would be impossible without the danger of a general war. Xanthopoulos-Palamas stressed that the West should preserve its unity and its military potential, but it should also pursue, through NATO, a policy of active ideological and political confrontation with the East:[47]

> A proper handling of détente tactics may strike at the sensitive points of communist order and of the communist regimes [. . .] The Iron Curtain is a cuirass of safety for the East. Its demise and the wider communication of people and ideas create problems which for the Soviet Union have proved dangerous.

There was another senior diplomat who criticized the government's attitude on détente: the former Director General of the Ministry and by that time Permanent Representative to the UN, Pavlos Economou-Gouras. In a report from New York in March 1961 he noted that if the Cold War climate prevailed, Greece would be covered by NATO and the US; however, if détente ensued, Greece would have to be prepared to adjust to it. In a context of détente,

Economou-Gouras argued, the two blocs would inevitably seek compromises 'in which we will run the risk to be asked to pay an unexpected price, since we are one of the weakest allies of the United States'. Thus Greece had to develop a 'decent but mild' policy towards the Soviet Union, to display 'perfectly good will for the development of almost friendly relations' with Moscow's allies, but also to 'clarify' to the US the Greek interests in the Balkans, 'in order not to facilitate the forgetfulness of Greek interests in a future negotiation, a forgetfulness to which often our great allies tend'. Economou-Gouras strongly criticized the government for not restoring Greek–Albanian diplomatic relations.[48] The most important argument in his report lay elsewhere, however; he showed that Greek interests could be more easily ignored by the West if Athens failed to adjust to détente.

Averoff adopted these arguments. In an important minute, shortly before his and Karamanlis' visit to the US in spring 1961, the Foreign Minister stressed that since the Soviets had acquired the capability to hit the US metropolitan territory with nuclear weapons a local crisis had become more probable, but if the West remained united, détente and its pressures would be manageable.[49] Thus, in the following two years the unity of the West became the basis of the Karamanlis government's effort to adjust to détente. 'Allied solidarity' became a central theme in Athens' approaches to its allies: it was also important as an assurance that the alliance would not abandon Greece in case of a localized crisis.

During 1959–63, the military situation remained difficult. In 1958, the NAC discussed and approved the new alliance planning for 1959–63, as set out by document MC 70. This involved the integration of nuclear capabilities in the NATO shield forces (not only in the retaliatory forces). The greatest problem manifested itself in NATO's central region, where forces were below the required strength. For the southern region of NATO, MC 70 meant a reduction from a force of forty-seven divisions to thirty-two divisions.[50] MC 70 called for new weapons, advanced technical capabilities, higher combat readiness and modernization of the units. This policy involved a sharp qualitative improvement of NATO armies, and thus entailed a significant increase of defence expenditures, which made many NATO members anxious about its implementation.[51]

For Greece, this qualitative leap and the additional cost posed severe problems. First, MC 70 required a reduction of forces under national command but an increase of the forces placed under NATO command. Until the 1959 Cyprus settlement Athens was reluctant to implement this programme, although it indicated that it would give priority to the build-up of those forces required by MC 70. After the Cyprus settlement, Athens agreed to implement the new policy fully, but still insisted that it should keep some forces under national command. However, problems remained regarding the modernization of war material, the shortage of regulars and specialists, and shortages in ammunition stocks and electronic equipment. In 1958–60 Greece made significant progress in these fields (something which the NATO military authorities also noted), but the result still was below the standard required by MC 70.[52] Second, Greece found it difficult to cover the additional cost for the implementation of the new policy, which, according to NATO authorities would involve an annual increase of 16 to 20 per cent in defence expenditure. Greek ministers repeatedly told the NAC that, even taking into account the impressive growth of the Greek economy, this could not be done without foreign aid.[53] The Turks also made similar comments. This was a further reason why both countries intensified their efforts to convince the alliance to provide economic assistance. As the Chief of the General Staff of National Defence, Lieutenant-General Athanassios Frontistis, wrote to Karamanlis in April 1960, the alliance was asking contradictory things from Greece: 'there is a widening economic gap between our needs and the alliance's demands'.[54]

However, Greece's effort to comply with the MC 70 requirements brought some results, mainly a new wave of modernization of Greek war material in the early 1960s. This involved the re-organization of the infantry divisions, which would now be smaller in size but would also have armour and greater firepower. However, this 'new' infantry division still was not mechanized and was more expensive than the 'old'.[55] In 1961, the NATO military authorities remarked that the Greek contribution to common defence and the Greek efforts to meet the requirements of the alliance were 'gratifying'. The 1961 NATO interim review noted an increase of the manning levels of army formations, an improvement of combat readiness in the navy, the plan for establishing a second all-weather fighter squadron in the air force, progress in infrastructure works, as well as significant improvement in the control and reporting units. However, the document pointed to the vulnerability of the Greek air force in case of a surprise attack, as well as to the usual problems – shortages of specialists and of ammunition and the obsolescence of much of the equipment; the Greek defence effort was 'to a large extent dependent on continued, or, rather, increased assistance from Greece's allies'.[56] Still, the Greek General Staffs continued to note that, on the whole, Bulgarian superiority remained.[57]

The revival of Greek–Turkish co-operation after 1959 also seemed to open opportunities for a common response to the problem of localized attack, but in practice not much was done. In July 1961 a common meeting of the General Staffs of Greece and Turkey took place under the chairmanship of the American commander of the Izmir Headquarters, but the meeting led nowhere, as the Americans and the Turks wanted the Greek army to concentrate its forces in Western Thrace in order to cover the Turkish position in the Straits. This was not accepted by the Greeks, who argued that their front could break west of that area, leaving the rest of Greek territory defenceless.[58] Thus, Greek–Turkish co-operation did not solve the problem of confronting a localized conflict.

Further difficulties occurred in 1962–63: the US decided to stop defence support aid to Greece (see Chapter 8). In January 1962 the Greeks even threatened that if defence support aid were terminated, the Greek army would be reduced. This decision was not implemented in 1962, but was indicative of the conflicting pressures regarding defence and the economy.[59] It should also be stressed that NATO planning took it for granted that Greece would receive *increased* military aid, yet US defence support was terminated exactly then.[60] In

March 1962, the Greek General Staff of National Defence notified the alliance that, in view of these financial difficulties, Athens had to reduce the forces that it assigned to the alliance command. The SACEUR, General Lauris Norstad, regarded this as unacceptable, and in the following months the Greek military authorities produced a new plan, the project 'Athena'. According to Norstad, this project 'sets forth the minimum acceptable force goals and minimum standards required to maintain the level of defence effort to permit the Hellenic Armed Forces to fulfil the missions currently assigned to them'. The project 'Athena' provided that many improvements in the Greek forces would be deferred, in order to reduce costs, but even this project would require an expansion of Greek defence expenditure and additional aid.[61] This was why, in December 1962, the NAC decided to offer Greece extraordinary defence support aid of $23.5 million.

In short, in 1962 the problem of the 'widening gap' between NATO requirements and Greek capabilities intensified. This caused some anxiety in the Greek Defence Ministry. In early 1962 the Defence Minister, Aristeides Protopapadakis, complained to the Americans that the US would not come to Greece's aid in case of war, because the alliance preferred to concentrate its forces in Central Europe.[62] The wording of the Greek Minister was strong, but also displayed the intensity of the Greek defence dilemma: the country could not increase its military expenditure. It is interesting that in 1962 the delivery of US F-100 jets to Greece was cancelled, because Athens could not undertake the cost for their maintenance.[63] It took a personal appeal by Karamanlis to the US Vice-President, Lyndon B. Johnson, during the latter's visit to Athens in September 1962, to get a US promise for the delivery of F-104s and of additional M-47 tanks.[64]

However, by 1962–63 the Bulgarian war material was also partially modernized, and this meant that the military balance again deteriorated. According to Athens' estimations, the Greek armed forces had a total of 162,000 men, of whom 120,000 were in the land army; the Bulgarians had 254,000 men under arms, the Yugoslavs 341,000 and the Turks 458,000.[65] There was more than numbers involved. In the spring of 1963, Protopapadakis wrote to Karamanlis that the 'immediate opponent, Bulgaria', had radically improved its mechanized means and now had a superiority of three to one in the common border; Bulgaria had 'twice as many and better tanks than we have, twice as many artillery pieces and three times more jets, supported by twice as many airports'. According to Protopapadakis, the Bulgarian forces had changed their defensive positions to offensive ones, while the Yugoslav and the Turkish attitudes in a local crisis were not predictable. The Defence Minister stressed that Greece should be able to mount a counterattack to regain lost territory and to give NATO time to intervene; but whereas the NATO Council had suggested that the Greek armed forces (land, navy and air) be kept at a strength of at least 167,000 men, the projected cuts in defence support aid meant that this number should be reduced to 139,000 men. Thus, Protopapadakis continued, the army would be obliged to fight its defensive battle at the Aliakmon River, south of the second largest Greek city,

Thessaloniki; to avoid this, new requests should be made to NATO for aid, and the modernization programme should be accelerated.[66] The Protopapadakis memoranda did not mean that, at that moment, Greek defence planned a battle at the Aliakmon; but explained that this option could become inevitable some time in the future.

In short, by 1963 the problems of Greek defence and its co-ordination with NATO appeared in new (and arguably more pressing) forms. Greece was not only unable to put up 'forward defence', but additionally faced the prospect of having to draw its major defensive line further to the south than previously. Athens found it increasingly difficult to meet NATO demands, at a time when the Americans decided to terminate defence support aid. Moreover, Greece continued to regard a local crisis as possible because the unfavourable balance of military power could attract the Soviets or the Bulgarians.

Last but not least, it was not only regional factors that made Athens anxious in those years. The Greek leaders and analysts regarded that one of the major challenges for the West was to maintain its unity in the face of Soviet tactics. However, this meant that Greece would inevitably be affected by a crisis which could start in another part of Europe or the globe. Berlin was a telling example. The Karamanlis government strongly supported West Germany in issues of German reunification. The prospect of another crisis in Berlin after the November 1958 Soviet ultimatum brought Athens firmly to the side of Bonn. During the December 1958 NAC ministerial meeting, Averoff argued for a 'very firm' Western response on Berlin.[67] Throughout 1958–62, in the NAC, Averoff kept expressing his country's strong support for West Germany over Berlin. The Greek government regarded that the issue of the former German capital had two important dimensions: first, it was a problem of self-determination, in which anything else than full support for the German people was unthinkable; second, Athens also regarded Berlin as the testing ground for the cohesion of the Western alliance. The Greeks were upset to realize that Western solidarity on Berlin in the summer of 1961 was not satisfactory.[68] In September 1961, the Permanent Representative to NATO, Michael Melas, cabled to Athens that if the West were defeated in Berlin, 'the dissolution of NATO and the definite victory of the Soviets would be a matter of time'.[69] As Averoff put it, in 1962, with his usual aggressive wording, 'retreat in Berlin amounts to total retreat'.[70] The West German argument in 1961 that 'the defence of Kavala will take place in Berlin'[71] was fully accepted by Athens. Of course the danger of escalation was inherent in such a crisis, but Athens was willing to take the risk – both because an important principle was at stake, and because allied solidarity seemed to be the only way to deal with the pressing problems of military inferiority, unfavourable geography and the possibility of local war.

8 Functionalism in action

Resisting neutralism, 1955–58

Greece's integration in the West was the major priority of the Karamanlis government and, not surprisingly, NATO membership was a crucial part of this policy. Presenting the programme of his first government to Parliament, in October 1955, Karamanlis stressed that 'the history and geography of Greece have determined its place in the side of the western democracies'.[1] However, the new Prime Minister had to implement this policy at a time when the Cyprus question had turned Greek public opinion against NATO. Throughout 1955–59, the government persisted in pursuing a Cyprus policy 'in the framework of the country's alliances' (namely, without breaking relations with the West), but this concept was viciously attacked as a sell-out by parts of the opposition and of the press. During a period when the Greek public opinion experienced bitter disappointments by Western policy on Cyprus, Greece's position in the alliance was not to be taken for granted.

The Greek public resented the fact that the NATO members voted against Greece in the UN debates on Cyprus. In late 1956, NATO adopted a resolution for the peaceful settlement of disputes, but Athens refrained from submitting Cyprus to this procedure, fearing that the disappointment of the Greek public by a decision of the alliance could prove fatal for Greece's Western orientation. However, research has shown that when Greece played its cards cleverly, NATO could become an asset in this conflict: for example, NATO's Secretary General, Paul-Henri Spaak, was very active in 1957 against the concept of the partition of Cyprus and in 1958 in trying to amend the British Macmillan Plan which Greece had rejected.[2] Karamanlis himself repeatedly stressed in public that NATO membership maximized Greece's capabilities on the Cyprus question. Conversely, a Greek withdrawal from the alliance would have been a spectacular own goal: in that case, NATO, the US and Britain would lay even more emphasis on Turkey. However, these arguments were not always convincing for the Greek public.

As Minister of Public Works in the Papagos government, Karamanlis was known to favour a more prudent Cyprus policy. On 13 September 1955, in the immediate aftermath of the Istanbul riots, he made a strong intervention in

Cabinet. Karamanlis criticized the Cyprus strategy of the Papagos government; he pointed out that the UN appeal had been decided by Papagos and some of his close associates and had never been approved by the Cabinet, while the whole enterprise had been undertaken without adequate preparation at the international level. Mostly, he continued, Athens had ignored US warnings that Washington would not support Greece in the UN: the Americans had been 'perhaps unjust but sincere towards us'. Karamanlis suggested that, where things stood, Greece had to explain itself clearly:[3]

> There can be little doubt that, as things have evolved, there is for Greece an issue of re-examination of its foreign policy. But this must be debated later; now, we must make it clear to the Americans that we are thinking along these lines, and monitor their reactions. Especially regarding Turkey, we cannot revive our relations with it, even if we wanted to, unless the Greek people, who have been deeply hurt, receive a kind of satisfaction.

In mid-September 1955, with the Greek press and most of the opposition parties angrily denouncing the US and NATO, this was not a popular position. A month later, as Prime Minister, Karamanlis took some initiatives to show to the Western allies that Greek sensitivities had been badly hurt: within a single month, his government refused to participate in NATO manoeuvres together with Turkey if the latter did not show its regret for the September pogrom; the Greek detachment from Korea was withdrawn; and negotiations started for the termination of the 'extraterritoriality' status of US military personnel in Greece (this was also a decision of the previous government). Some results were achieved; for example, in the autumn of 1955, in the NATO Headquarters at Izmir, a Turkish military detachment presented honours to the Greek flag which the demonstrators had insulted during the September events. These partially checked the anti-Western spirit in the country. Karamanlis' electoral victory in February 1956 was greatly facilitated by his staunch pro-Western position and by the feeling that the opposition alliance, the Democratic Union, in which the left-wing EDA party also participated, was a kind of a Popular Front. During the electoral campaign, Karamanlis put forward a comprehensive view for national security. Thus, in his Thessaloniki speech, he said:[4]

> Our country, always facing pressure from the North – a pressure of which Northern Greece has bitter experience – associated itself with the western world for security reasons. All the governments and all political parties in this country have followed this policy. Our relationship with the west is founded on historical and political grounds; but this does not mean that this relationship cannot be revised, if the security of our country, our national dignity and the interests of our people called for this. Yet the assessment of such factors is a huge issue and must be done with prudence, and at any rate not in the midst of an electoral campaign. Prudence is all the more necessary, because lately on the international scene, tension follows détente and

82   *The era of functionalism, 1955–63*

détente follows tension with such speed that the future appears unclear and full of agonies.

Karamanlis' electoral victory seemed to confirm that the Greek public approved this position, despite recent disappointments with the West over Cyprus. However, immediately after the election the situation dramatically deteriorated. In March 1956, the British deported Makarios to the Seychelles. This ended the negotiations between the archbishop and the Governor of Cyprus, Field-Marshal Sir John Harding, which had sparked hope for a settlement of this dispute. In May 1956 the British started the executions of EOKA members in Cyprus, which again upset the Greek public. Thus, in spring 1956, all hell broke loose in Greece: large demonstrations took place in Athens and the major cities, with anti-Western and neutralist slogans. The Greek-Cypriot leaders and the opposition publicly accused the Foreign Minister, Spyros Theotokis, of hostility towards the exiled Makarios, and by the end of April motions of censure were piling up in Parliament. In a Parliamentary debate, Karamanlis disclosed that after Makarios' deportation the Greek-Cypriot leaders had suggested that Greece withdraw from NATO, but he stressed that the government rejected this, and the government alone was responsible for deciding the foreign policy of the country.[5] Later on, in late May, Theotokis resigned and was replaced by Averoff, who tried to renew contacts with the Greek-Cypriot leaders. In October, Averoff summarized the view of the government in a telegram to the Consul General in Nicosia, Angelos Vlachos, asking him to pass it on to the Greek Cypriots:[6]

> To prepare ourselves for the worst and to create anxiety, we have made an opening to the east. But because our people are strongly dissatisfied with the west, this opening could lead us very far, especially if we are not prudent. While I think that we now have an active Arab policy, and up to a point a notable policy towards the east, I believe that Hellenism will disarm itself if it ever left the west, in the framework of which, and there alone, the Cyprus question could be satisfactorily solved.

The rise of neutralism in 1956–57 has been mentioned in the previous chapter. In the summer of 1957, at the time of the Turko–Syrian war scare, the Greek press suggested that Greece should not come to Ankara's assistance in case of war. This created consternation among senior Greek diplomats: as the Permanent Representative to NATO, Michael Melas, sarcastically noted, Greece was the only one that stood to lose by such a loosening of allied solidarity.[7] In autumn 1956 and autumn 1957, the EOKA leader, Colonel (retd) George Grivas, from Cyprus, asked that Greece withdraw from NATO, provoking strong reactions by Averoff, who noted that the government alone was responsible for Greek foreign policy.[8] In the autumn of 1957, as the new USIS poll showed the persistence of neutralist spirit in the country, the EDA Party launched a campaign against the installation of US intermediate-range missiles in Greece. Last but not least, the electoral success of EDA in the May 1958 election was directly connected with the dissatisfaction of the Greek public with Western policy in Cyprus. EDA constantly called for Greece's disengagement from NATO.

Thus, his discussion with Makarios in September 1958 was not the first time that Karamanlis received a suggestion to leave NATO. In fact, in a letter to Spaak a few days earlier, the Greek Prime Minister had indicated that the implementation of the British Macmillan Plan could endanger the cohesion of the Atlantic Alliance and peace in the Eastern Mediterranean.[9] This letter caused Spaak's intervention in the Cyprus question in September and October 1958. However, one could legitimately wonder whether Karamanlis was being contradictory on these: if he had already 'threatened' withdrawal from NATO, why did he react so strongly to the similar suggestion by Makarios a few days later?

To fully understand Karamanlis' attitude, one has to take into account the fears of Athens at that specific moment: the government had repeatedly stressed to the British and to the Americans that it would be forced to resign if the Macmillan Plan were implemented; since there was no governmental alternative from the Centre (which had been crushed in the May 1958 election), and since the only governmental alternative would be the left-wing EDA, the resignation of the government would probably lead to a military coup, and a military dictatorship could withdraw Greece from NATO in an effort to gain popularity.[10] In other words, Karamanlis warned the alliance that there was a danger of a drift from NATO, *contrary* to the wishes of the government; this was the essence of his letter to Spaak. He was not prepared to take the initiative in leaving NATO, though: Karamanlis did not like bluffs, nor was he prepared to allow Makarios to dictate policy to him.

This was as far as Karamanlis and Averoff were prepared to go: they strongly believed that if the country ever left the Western alliance, all its aims, including Cyprus, would collapse. All this took place against a background of anti-Western sentiment in Greece, though, which could easily lead to uncontrollable developments. The public probably never realized how close the country came to a drift from the Western world in those days. This is a further reason why the 1959 Cyprus settlement was so crucial in the evolution of Greek foreign policy: it removed the strain from the country's relationship with the West and checked the rise of the neutralist spirit in the country.

NATO and functionalism

As noted above, NATO was the shield to which Greece entrusted its defence. It also offered additional advantages: Greece participated in military aid programmes, and was part of the wider strategic planning of a great alliance; the Greek ministers were taking part in multilateral deliberations regarding Western defence, and had the opportunity for closer contact with their Western counterparts. Averoff himself had a notable presence in the NAC ministerial meetings, and enjoyed the respect of his colleagues. Michael Melas, who served as permanent representative to NATO in 1956–62 and was not a person given to exaggeration, noted in his memoirs that the Greek General Staffs, mostly the General Staff of National Defence under Lieutenant-Generals Constantinos Dovas and Athanassios Frontists, were respected in the alliance.[11]

However, the analysis would be incomplete if it only emphasized the importance of NATO as a deterrent, a source of aid or a channel for diplomatic activity. In 1955–63 Athens also projected more refined perceptions regarding the alliance, the overall organization of the Western world and Greece's possible place in it. As noted above, the Karamanlis government searched for a long-term orientation for the country. This was found in the 1961 Association Agreement with the EEC, but before the creation of the EEC this search also involved NATO as a tool for the country's integration (including economic integration) in the West. In 1956–58, the Karamanlis government became immensely interested in the debate regarding the deepening of economic co-operation within the alliance.

As noted above, in 1952–55 Greece had shown interest in the possible function of NATO as a source of economic assistance. However, now Greek policy went beyond its previous positions. In the December 1955 and the May 1956 NAC ministerial meetings, the Foreign Minister, Spyros Theotokis, stressed that NATO should become a field for economic co-operation and should provide guidelines to its members, rather than a simple technical co-ordination.[12] During his autumn 1956 visit to the US, Karamanlis noted to the Americans:[13]

> The purely military shape of NATO needs to expand. Today, the bonds that tie the NATO members together are very loose. The member states accept the Alliance as an emergency measure. But if NATO's field is expanded on these levels [economic and technical], we will create a real community of interests and a real solidarity between the member states.

In December 1957, addressing the NATO summit in Paris, Karamanlis noted that NATO was not simply a military alliance, but a union of free nations which had rallied together to safeguard freedom and peace, and to secure justice and prosperity. Thus, Karamanlis continued, NATO had to improve its military organization, but also to form a framework of co-operation between its members on the technical, scientific and mostly on the economic levels; it also had to offer economic assistance to its less developed members in order to help them fulfil their obligations.[14] In November 1958 Greece strongly supported closer economic co-operation within NATO, jointly submitting a memorandum together with Turkey on this.[15] It should be noted that this joint Greek–Turkish move took place before the conclusion of the Cyprus settlement, arguably at the worst moment of the Cyprus crisis.

After 1959, things changed. Although some persons in the Greek establishment kept referring to NATO's possible 'unifying' or 'supranational' role, the government turned its attention to the EEC as a route for eventual integration in the West. The Greek application to become an associated member of the EEC was submitted in the summer of 1959. Regarding NATO, Athens focused on the possibility of local war, and thus tended to stress the need for allied solidarity rather than for closer economic co-operation. During his December 1959 conversation with Eisenhower, Karamanlis only referred to allied solidarity in the face of Soviet unreliability.[16] In December 1960, in a letter to Spaak, Karamanlis suggested the holding of a new alliance summit, and mentioned 'economic defence' as a front of the Cold War and as a field in which allied solidarity should be shown (through more aid), but did not put forward economic co-operation as an aim of the alliance.[17]

During his April 1961 visit to the US, Karamanlis stressed to John F. Kennedy and to the Secretary of State, Dean Rusk, that the alliance should be strengthened: 'The weaknesses of NATO are mostly the lack of unity, the frequent disagreements on fundamental points and the lack of solidarity'.[18] During his Washington talks, the Greek Prime Minister repeated his request for military aid, but did not mention his old position on the role of NATO as a field of closer economic co-operation; this was already being done for Greece through the EEC. As will be shown, in these years Greece and Turkey also jointly made a sustained effort to convince the alliance that they needed economic assistance. Thus, the Greeks kept calling for a more active role of NATO on the fields of economic assistance and of the proportional sharing of the defence burden, but there were no arguments for an expanded role for NATO regarding economic integration.

Thus, the Karamanlis government did not see NATO merely as an instrument of collective defence or as a source of aid, but also as an important route through which Greece's major aim of integration in the West could materialize. Initially, until 1958, Athens regarded NATO as a possible tool for economic as well as military integration. After 1959, when it turned towards the EEC, Athens kept stressing the need to strengthen NATO bonds even beyond the military field. Of course, allied solidarity was a natural argument for a country which feared a localized attack and asked for more military aid; even so, it is clear that the Karamanlis government saw NATO as a medium for integration in the West.

Bilateral relations with the Western allies and the relationship with Gaullist France

NATO's role as a shield was absolutely necessary, a sine qua non for Greece's security and international position. However, the formal guarantee through Article 5 of the North Atlantic Treaty was not considered to be sufficient. The Karamanlis government tried to use NATO's multifaceted framework – military planning, aid, multilateral deliberations within the alliance, as well as bilateral relations and even personal contacts. Athens sought to receive guarantees, less formal, but also important, on a bilateral basis as well. In early November 1956, as the crises were mounting in Hungary and in Suez, Athens faced turmoil both from the north and from the south. At the same time, there were rumours of a possible Soviet attempt to aid Nasser by dispatching aircraft to Egypt, which would have to pass through Greek air space. Thus, Averoff asked the Americans to issue a statement guaranteeing the independence and the territorial integrity of Greece.[19] A unilateral US guarantee, additional to that of NATO, was obviously regarded as very important. Averoff did not manage to get such a statement in 1956, but in 1961 J.F. Kennedy gave such an oral assurance, trying to ease Karamanlis' fears about a possible Bulgarian surprise local attack.[20] In August 1961, during the crisis of the Berlin Wall, when the Greeks again feared a Bulgarian strike, Rusk, through the US Embassy in Athens, assured the Greeks that a Soviet-Bloc attack would activate Article 5 of the NATO Treaty. Karamanlis welcomed Rusk's assurance, but added to the US Ambassador, Ellis O. Briggs, that a NATO guarantee was dependent on alliance procedure, including the limited automatism of Article 5. Karamanlis indicated that Athens would like to have a US assurance. The Americans did not move further than that.[21] Still, these US assurances through bilateral contacts were considered as important in Athens, because they were seen as complementary to the basic NATO guarantee.

At the same time, the Karamanlis government was also interested in the re-emergence of the Western European power centres. Already by 1957, Athens welcomed the reappearance of West Germany as 'an important factor' in NATO.[22] In the following years, both Athens and Bonn felt that, as frontline states of the West, they faced strong Soviet pressures, and this made their interests converge. The bilateral rapprochement with Bonn reached its climax in autumn 1958, when Karamanlis visited the West German capital.[23] A little later, in spring 1959, an opening was made to Gaullist France: the Greek Ambassador to Paris, Philon Philon, acting on Karamanlis' instructions, met the French President, General Charles de Gaulle, and expressed Athens' wish that France regain its role as an important player in the Eastern Mediterranean.[24] By 1960, when Karamanlis and Averoff visited Paris, there even was an exchange of visits on the level of General Staffs.[25] In May 1963, de Gaulle visited Greece – one of his few visits abroad. These openings to the two major Western European continental countries helped Greece's effort to become an associate member of the EEC, and also aimed at balancing the one-sided dependence on the Americans. Yet, Greece's interest in Paris and Bonn was mainly political and economic.

In 1962–63, the Karamanlis government also tried to reach a closer understanding with France on the level of security. Thus, in May 1963, when de Gaulle visited Greece, he also went to Thessaloniki. Karamanlis referred to the importance of de Gaulle's presence in the country's second largest city, so close to the border:

> For the whole nation, but also for me, who have been born here, your visit to Northern Greece is an event of particular importance [...] When the French soldiers, whose graves you will visit today, fell [during the First World War at the Macedonian Front], this country had been the victim of a brutal invasion. Unfortunately, this was not the first, nor the last such invasion. Its rich valleys, its coasts stretching along the Mediterranean, have constantly been seen as a prize [...] Here, where the voice of history is

more clearly heard, you will understand even better why this land is for us the heart of our country, for which we are prepared to tolerate no improper thought by anyone; this land is also an invaluable bastion for freedom and for the western civilization.

This appeal to de Gaulle's sense of pride and honour was not left unanswered: he replied that 'I do not think that we could find a better place to manifest the Franco–Greek friendship to all'. The Greek–French communiqué stressed that 'the visit of the President of the French Republic to Thessaloniki has by itself underlined the interest which France has in the security of Greece'.[26] This reference was so strongly worded, it caused a Bulgarian protest.

On the other hand, it has been alleged that Karamanlis fell from power in June 1963 because the Americans intervened against him, fearing that he would 'replace' Greek–US bonds with Greek–French co-operation. Such a view is not supported by the evidence now available. Karamanlis and Averoff were Atlanticists and Europeanists at the same time, and regarded these two aspects of Greek policy as complementary; they repeatedly indicated this publicly. They did not agree with de Gaulle's tactics to cause trouble in NATO; in fact, during a period when Greece focused on allied solidarity, it felt anxious about the loosening of allied solidarity which de Gaulle's policy could entail.

Karamanlis tried to play down the importance of de Gaulle's disagreements with the other NATO members. During his April 1961 visit to the US, the Greek Prime Minister told Kennedy that NATO should give de Gaulle 'some satisfaction, harmless for the alliance, to get his acquiescence on more important points'.[27] At the same time, Karamanlis indicated to the French that harm to alliance should be avoided. During a visit to Paris in February 1961, he told the French Prime Minister, Michel Debré, that NATO and the US were indispensable for European security.[28] In April 1962, Karamanlis told Spaak, who was now the Foreign Minister of Belgium, that 'without the US, Europe cannot survive. Let us not make experiments; there is no time for such things.'[29] During the first months of 1963, Karamanlis pleaded with both French and Americans to reach a compromise which would not endanger NATO. In March 1963 in Paris, and in May in Athens, Karamanlis asked de Gaulle to seek an understanding with the US. In April 1963, talking to L. Merchant, Kennedy's envoy on the projected NATO Multilateral Force, the Greek Prime Minister urged that the US seek a settlement with France, because alliance cohesion was in danger. He even asked Merchant whether the Americans wanted him to communicate something to de Gaulle, and stressed that '[t]he existing antagonistic economic interests and national pride, which are the weaknesses of our alliance, should retreat in the face of the abiding need to safeguard our common security'.[30]

It is true that when in the spring of 1963 Karamanlis asked de Gaulle whether Greece could consider itself covered by the French nuclear deterrent, he got an affirmative reply. However, Karamanlis made it clear that he was talking of a guarantee which would be complementary, not antagonistic, to that of NATO. In the early 1960s, Karamanlis would not abandon the huge potential of US deterrent power in exchange for a French deterrent which would be developed in the future (the *force de frappe* did not become operational until the 1970s). On the contrary, it was de Gaulle who encouraged the Greek Prime Minister to regard the French nuclear forces as the main pillar of Greek security.[31] In May 1963, in an interview for *Le Monde*, Averoff was asked whether Greece wanted to form a bilateral defence relationship with France; but he stressed that Greek security had been entrusted to NATO.[32]

Thus, it is clear that the relationship with France was not antagonistic to the Greek–US bonds. The opening to Gaullist France aimed, among others, at balancing foreign (mainly American) influence in the country, but there never was any case of *replacing* US influence with French. The Americans knew this and welcomed Greece's new bonds with the EEC (which would channel Greek aid requests to the Europeans), and anyway they played no role in the resignation of the Karamanlis government in June 1963; in fact, the US Embassy expected a Karamanlis victory in the November 1963 elections.[33]

The economic aspect of security: the issue of military aid

Economic development was a prerequisite for Greece's integration in the West, and thus played a major role in the shaping of the foreign policy aims of the Karamanlis government; in 1955–63 the Greek economy showed impressive development rates.[34] However, although the cost of defence remained enormous, it was important to create a sense of security in the country, without which development was deemed impossible. This is why the role of US military aid was important in the overall policy of the Karamanlis government: defence support aid, in particular, provided for funds for the Greek budget, and thus was a great contribution to the Greek development effort. It is not easy to make an exact estimate of defence expenditure as a percentage of the GNP, if only because the Greek side often exaggerated its defence spending in order to support its requests for more aid. At any rate, according to figures from the Karamanlis Archive, Greek defence expenditure continued to be enormous (see Table 8.1).

In the late 1950s the country annually attributed almost $170 million to defence, while its Public Investment Programme (the pillar of its development effort) rose to $35–40 million.[35] Defence support aid was about $20 million, and this shows what could have happened to the Greek economic effort if the investment programme had ever had to cover this additional cost. Throughout 1955–63, Athens insisted that if military aid were reduced then the consequences for the country would be disastrous: either the army would have to be cut down to unacceptable levels, or Greece would have to increase its defence spending to a point which the Greek economy could not sustain.

The Greeks tried to take advantage of every possible argument to support their requests for more military aid: for 1956 alone, this included arguments such as Bulgarian military superiority, the pressures created by the Cyprus question, and Soviet offers for economic co-operation. Indeed, in the summer of that year, the US Embassy in Athens and the State Department noted that Karaman-

Table 8.1 Greek defence expenditure as a percentage of the GNP 1955–62

Year	Percentage
1955	6.4
1956	7.3
1957	6.2
1958	6.1
1961	5.2
1962	5.0

Source: 'Military Spending and National Income', 27 April 1959, Karamanlis Archive, file 8A; Minute, 'Defence Expenditure as a Percentage of the GNP' (1963), Karamanlis Archive, file 20A.

Note
Between 1955 and 1962, the Greek GNP rose at an estimated 70 per cent. This suggests that defence expenditure actually increased.

lis was having a difficult time resisting neutralism and Soviet economic offers, and had to be helped.[36] In the autumn of 1956, the Greek Prime Minister presented his request for aid during his visit to Washington. In early 1957 the Greeks repeated their arguments to the Armour Committee, which examined US economic obligations abroad: 'even a relatively minor economic turmoil could easily end our progress and destroy everything that has been achieved'.[37] The Armour Report accepted these arguments; the 1957 NSC paper on Greece accepted Athens' view that a decrease of military aid could have destabilizing effects on the Greek economy; and in 1957 US military aid actually increased.[38] This made the 1957 reform of Greek defence policy possible.

Greek requests for military aid reached a climax after the May 1958 election, in which the left-wing EDA emerged as the second largest party. On 26 May, two weeks after polling day, a Greek memorandum to the US Embassy noted:[39]

> It is impossible to escape anyone's attention that the political and defensive capability of a nation depends on the people's morale, on material means, but also on the people's standard of living [...] Greece is determined to make every effort to maintain and improve its political and defensive capability. But without a solid economic base for such an effort, there is the danger that the people's endurance will be stretched to its limits.

In another Greek document of August 1958, unemployment was expressly mentioned as a source of 'huge social dangers' which could impair Greek defence; the government also noted that it could not maintain its policy of monetary stability without some assistance from the West.[40] Similar arguments were put to the SACEUR, General Lauris Norstad, in late August; to the US Secretary of Defence, Neil McElroy, in November 1958; and to George McGhee, member of the committee for the US military aid programme in January 1959.[41]

To a large extent, Greek persistence paid off. According to US figures, military aid to Greece rose dramatically after 1957: in 1953–56 Greece had received $215.6 million as economic aid and $219 million as military aid, but in 1957–60 Greece received $219.4 million as economic and $414.7 million as military aid.[42] According to a US brief given to President Kennedy in the spring of 1961, US military aid to Greece in 1955 was $58.9 million, but went up to $134.4 million in 1958, and in 1961 fell to $88.8 million; the document noted that Greece had received very favourable treatment compared to other NATO members.[43] Indeed, it has been suggested that the economic aspect of the New Look was not finally implemented with regard to Greece.[44]

Since US military aid almost doubled in 1957–60, it is also possible to draw another conclusion: the claim that the US used aid in order to blackmail Greece to settle on Cyprus in 1959 is unfounded. Exactly the opposite is the case: the Americans regarded that military aid (especially defence support) could act as a brake on the rise of neutralism in the country. It was the Greeks who used the Cyprus question to press the Americans into giving more military assistance. Moreover, at least twice, in May 1956 and in December 1957, Karamanlis suggested to the Americans that the US should use aid to press Turkey into being more accommodating on Cyprus; in December 1957, John Foster Dulles replied that his country would not use aid in this way.[45]

The reduction of US aid occurred *after* the Cyprus settlement had been reached. In September 1959, as the US Congress approved significantly smaller funds for military assistance, the Greek Ambassador to Washington, Alexis Liatis, sent a long report to Karamanlis noting that, for internal political and economic reasons, US aid would decrease in the future. Liatis stressed that the US military disagreed with this policy, but would not have their way; in the following years, Greece would find it increasingly difficult to acquire defence support aid, and its security policy should be adjusted to this eventuality.[46] Liatis correctly predicted future developments, but his suggestion entailed a reduction of Greek defence capabilities. Karamanlis did not want to accept this. In 1959, Lieutenant-General Theodoros Grigoropoulos (one of the military whom Papagos had summarily thrown out of the army in 1952) was recalled to active service, and was appointed Greece's military representative to the alliance and a member of NATO's military committee; Grigoropoulos was entrusted with the issue of military aid.[47] In December 1959, during Eisenhower's visit to Athens, the Greek government repeated its arguments on military aid: Greece faced a pressing need for effective economic reform, which would be impossible without US assistance on defence expenditure. This was a problem which Greece had 'to solve or else perish by it'.[48]

The discussions with Eisenhower brought a short-term result: in early 1960, after the President's visit, a small increase in defence support aid and a new Development Loan Fund (DLF) loan were announced.[49] However, this was a temporary improvement: in April, the new US Secretary of State, Christian Herter, indicated to Karamanlis that Washington was moving towards the idea of ending defence support aid.[50] Karamanlis and Averoff also raised the issue of aid during their April 1961 visit to the US. A March 1961 brief presented the basis of their argument:[51]

Without it [defence support aid], the budget would not be in a position to deal with the various needs that it has to cover; and additionally, the balance of payments would not be in a position to cope without creating deficits which would be dangerous for a developing economy such as the Greek [...] By its history and geography Greece is posted to cover its crucial position, and does not have the luxury to divide its limited resources between needs of defensive and non-defensive character. Greece is exposed to many dangers, and the creation of a sense of security to the people is directly connected with popular psychology and thus with the dynamics of economic development.

In May 1961 Karamanlis made his anxiety clear, talking to the US Vice-President, Lyndon B. Johnson: 'the next three or four years will be crucial, because it is then that the economic rehabilitation will be completed and the Greek economy will become self-sustainable'.[52] In the following months Karamanlis repeated these arguments in successive letters and memoranda to Rusk; he noted that, according to the new NATO defence policy (in line with flexible response), the NATO members had to increase their defence capabilities and Greece simply could not afford this.[53] In essence, it was a hopeless effort. Washington had already opted to terminate defence support aid, which the Kennedy administration regarded as an outdated form of financial assistance. In 1962, the termination of defence support to Greece was decided.

However, by 1962 this issue had acquired even greater political significance. Aid was always important in internal Greek politics, as many observers rushed to use it as a testing ground for the support of a Greek government by the US. Such conclusions were usually totally unfounded and embarrassed the US Embassy, but bad habits die hard in the Greek political system. These became even more important by late 1961, when the Centre opposition, united after many years of internal quarrels, started its 'relentless struggle' against the Karamanlis government. The Centre accused the Right of rigging the recent election (this was despite the fact that Karamanlis was not in power during the election, as there was a caretaker government). Anyway, in this context a reduction of US aid could easily create the impression that the Americans favoured the overthrow of Karamanlis. Furthermore, the Centre Union's 'relentless struggle' brought to the forefront the issue of social policy and the burdens of defence expenditure. In January 1962 the Karamanlis government repeated to the Americans that if defence support were terminated, a reduction of the size of the army would be inevitable. This would entail a reduction of Greek defence capabilities, but, as Athens noted, social and political upheaval could prove even more dangerous.[54] This was obviously an effort to repeat Papagos' 1954 successful blackmail of the Americans, and the new US Ambassador, Henry Labouisse, used exactly this word – 'blackmail' – to describe the Greek line.[55] However, even this argument – that the country was entering a period of social unrest – brought no result. Of course, US aid in hardware continued in the following years.

However, more painful disappointments were about to come, not only from the US but also from NATO. As shown above, after 1959 Greece did not regard NATO as a vehicle for economic integration in the West, but kept arguing for allied solidarity on the economic field and for a more proportionate sharing of the defence costs. In this, Athens was always in agreement with Ankara. The two countries had raised the issue in the NAC in late 1958, but their effort led nowhere: the NATO experts recognized that Greece and Turkey faced problems, but went no further than suggesting that the members of the alliance should examine ways to assist these two countries.[56] The problem became more difficult, as both countries found it difficult to implement the MC 70 force goals. In early 1961, following a Turkish proposal, a NATO ad hoc study group was set up to examine the economic problems of the two countries. The study suggested that the issue should be referred to a committee of experts,[57] something which was regarded as satisfactory in Greece and in Turkey. Then, in the May 1961 NAC ministerial meeting, Averoff and the Turkish Foreign Minister, Selim Sarper, suggested the creation of a common NATO military fund, which would assist the less developed members in their defence effort. The proposal was repeated in the December NAC ministerial meeting by the Greek Minister of Economic Co-ordination, Panayis Papaligouras.[58]

In May 1961, the NAC agreed to set up a committee of experts (Edgar Faure, Hans Karl von Mangoldt-Reiboldt and John H. Ferguson) to study the economic problems of the two countries.[59] In March 1962 this committee concluded its report (the so-called Report of the Three), which noted Greece's great efforts to meet the cost of its defence and to continue its economic development. It considered that the country was economically successful and would achieve the suggested target of a 6 per cent growth rate annually, and thus it would be possible to sustain its defence burden if it received long-term loans. This was the important point in the report: it considered that Greece could cover the cost of defence with little foreign economic assistance in the form of long-term loans, rather than aid. The committee proposed the setting up of a consortium which would assist Greece in these fields.[60]

This was a great disappointment for Athens: the Committee failed to suggest aid for the country, whereas it argued for such assistance to Turkey; more importantly, this occurred simultaneously with the US decision to terminate defence support aid to Greece. Athens already had problems in meeting the force goals required by NATO; moreover, the NATO military authorities always drew their plans for Greece on the assumption that these could not be implemented unless the country received substantial aid. Thus the Report of the Three represented a serious blow for the Greek government, which was left with increased requirements from the military authorities of the alliance; with a fear of local war; and with no defence support aid, which the NATO military authorities considered necessary for their planning. As could be expected, Karamanlis strongly reacted against the recommendation of the Report of the Three, and made his position clear to the US Ambassador, Labouisse. Karamanlis was reputed to have a legendary temper, but seldom can one detect such evidence of an explosion in official documents:[61]

The conclusions of this report are outrageous [...] I find it impossible to understand how countries like Portugal, Spain and Turkey, which did not fight in the war, did not suffer destruction and on the contrary exploited the Second World War for their own ends, are being favourably treated, while Greece has the feeling that it does not get the support that it was its right to expect. [and when Labouisse hinted that the opposition could take advantage of the report]: I do not care what the opposition will say. During the 27 years that I am in politics I have never allowed myself to resort to demagoguery. But the view that everyone except Greece is entitled to support insults my personal and my national dignity.

The Centre opposition – the Centre Union Party – duly accused the government of both maintaining defence expenditure at high levels, and failing to ensure the continuation of defence support aid. According to the CU, Karamanlis had turned Greece into an American 'protectorate' and did not have the stomach to press for more aid. On its part, the Karamanlis government made every effort to block the conclusions of the Report of the Three. The Greek position was supported by the new NATO Secretary General, Dirk Stikker, by Ambassador Labouisse, by the US Permanent Representative to NATO, Thomas Finletter, and by the SACEUR, General Norstad.[62] However, the decision did not change. Greece considered rejecting the report, but finally decided to accept it and try to get some additional advantages. In April 1962 Stikker suggested that a consortium would not solve the Greek financial problem, and proposed to offer Greece defence support from NATO members.[63] This created some hope for a short-term solution of the problem. Karamanlis spoke to Rusk during the May 1962 NATO ministerial council, which was held in the Greek capital:[64]

The Greek economy is now at that delicate point, in which it needs a not very large assistance to become self-sustainable. Our prospects are encouraging. It will prove disastrous to abandon our economic effort at this stage, and will require many more funds to redress this mistake.

In May 1962 the NAC decided to set up an international consortium through the OECD (not NATO), which would assist the Greek economic effort. The alliance also agreed to examine the possibility of offering to Greece extraordinary defence support aid for the years 1963 and 1964.[65] Stikker then suggested undertaking a review of the minimum strength of the Greek armed forces which would be compatible with NATO requirements; he also suggested setting up a working group to examine NATO financial assistance to Greece for the years 1963–64.[66] His proposals were accepted. The Greek government agreed to devote more resources to defence (according to the project 'Athena'), and the working group finally accepted the suggestion to offer extra economic assistance to Greece through NATO.[67] Following a conversation between Averoff and Rusk in December 1962, the NAC agreed that Greece should receive an extra $20 million of defence support aid from the alliance (not the US), especially for the year 1963.⁶⁸ In January 1963 the Greek government notified NATO that it would increase its defence expenditure by $7 million, but would not be in a position to commit itself on the exact strength of its armed forces without knowing the exact amount that NATO members would contribute to the Greek defence effort according to the December 1963 decision.⁶⁹

Greece and nuclear weapons, 1957–63

Until 1957 the minor partners of the US had not needed to formulate a position on nuclear weapons, but things changed with the Sputnik flight in the autumn of 1957, which rendered 'massive retaliation' outdated and pushed the alliance to consider the installation of US intermediate range ballistic missiles (IRBMs) on the soil of its European members. Greece accepted the value of nuclear deterrence, and its position was summed up in a reply to a Soviet Note in June 1959:⁷⁰

> The Greek Government does not believe that it is possible in principle to isolate the issue of atomic weapons and missiles from the wider issue of the effective defensive preparation of each country. These form an integral unity. As for the countries which do not possess atomic weapons and missiles, this issue emerges in the form of their need to modernize their defence, in the face of the terrible danger arising from the fact that other countries possess such weaponry.

However, this was a rather theoretical position. In practice, things proved much more difficult. As a first instance, there was the question of tactical nuclear weapons according to NATO military doctrine. Athens accepted those weapons, which partially balanced the conventional superiority of the Warsaw Pact and played a major role in deterrence. In 1958 Greece agreed to acquire Honest John missiles, and in 1959 signed two agreements with the US which provided for the storage of tactical nuclear warheads in the country under a dual-key system, which was the standard US practice with its allies: the warheads were controlled by the Americans and the delivery systems by the Greeks, so the co-operation of both was needed to use a nuclear armed missile.⁷¹ Thus, the issue of tactical nuclear weapons was settled.

Things were more complicated regarding IRBMs, which could be launched from Greece and target countries of the Soviet Bloc or the Soviet Union itself. This issue finally combined with the pressures of the Cyprus question and caused great difficulties to the government. In the spring of 1957, as it appeared that NATO would consider the deployment of nuclear weapons, the Soviet Ambassador, Sergueev, had warned Averoff that the installation of US missiles on Greek soil would turn Greece into a target for Soviet retaliation; Moscow radio carried a similar warning.⁷² In the same year, the Romanian Prime Minister, Chivu Stoica, proposed the holding of a Balkan Conference (at a later stage, the Romanians also proposed the establishment of a nuclear-free zone in the

Balkans).[73] A Romanian Foreign Ministry document which was given to the Soviets in the summer of 1957 suggested that the Stoica proposal aimed at loosening Greece's and Turkey's bonds with NATO, at the definite neutralization of the tripartite Balkan pacts of 1953–54, and even at the mobilization of the 'democratic forces' within the Western countries if they rejected the proposal.[74] Thus, the Stoica proposal aimed, among other things, at creating an internal political problem in Greece and Turkey. At any rate, the West rejected these proposals. In his reply to Stoica, Karamanlis noted that confidence between the Balkan states had not yet been re-established. As Averoff noted, for Greece it didn't matter whether it was hit by nuclear weapons coming from within or without the Balkan area.[75]

In the autumn of 1957, the Sputnik flight demonstrated that the Soviets could now strike at the American homeland. After this, the installation of US IRBMs on the soil of NATO members was discussed, to balance the perceived Soviet supremacy in intercontinental ballistic missiles. The Permanent Representative to NATO, Michael Melas, stressed to the government that installation of US missiles in Greece could underline allied solidarity and thus would be beneficial for Greek strategy.[76] The military also favoured acceptance of the US missiles.[77]

However, great problems occurred. In the autumn of 1957, Greece supported the Western position during the UN discussions on disarmament, but avoided any quarrels with the Soviets. As the Foreign Ministry put it, this aimed at 'not upsetting the communist delegations prior to the discussion of the Cyprus issue at the UN'.[78] The Cyprus dispute limited the options of Greek diplomacy. At the same time Greek public opinion took a strongly neutralist position in the USIS poll, while the left-wing party, EDA, accused the government of accepting 'US missile bases'. According to a perceptive assessment, 'The matter of nuclear bases came to a head early in 1958 and developed into a full-fledged controversy under the chilling shadows of disintegration caused by the now chronic Cyprus dispute'.[79]

The government and the largest part of the Centre opposition wanted to accept the US missiles, but this was becoming increasingly difficult after the new manifestations of the neutralist spirit in the autumn of 1957 and after the launching of the EDA's campaign. By early December, as the NATO summit approached, many retired military officers, most of them friendly to the Centre, wrote articles in the press arguing in favour of accepting the US missiles. They noted that this would cement allied solidarity towards Greece, while even if the country declined these weapons it would still be a target of the Soviet arsenal.[80] The publication of these articles seems to have been encouraged by the government, and is an example of an agreement between the Centre and the Right in post-war Greek history. However, it produced no result.

The decision to install US missiles in Europe was made during the alliance summit in December 1957. The Greek government wanted to accept these weapons, but finally, pressed by the EDA campaign, decided to decline. During the summit Karamanlis put forward the principle of 'universality', suggesting that the Greek government would accept US missiles if all the other countries of the alliance did so; since it was certain that at least some of the NATO members would decline, this amounted to a rejection.[81] During his meeting with Karamanlis on 18 December, Eisenhower himself showed 'understanding' for the 'difficulties' of the Greek government which had led it to such a position.[82]

The issue of US missiles also created strain in Greece's relations with the Soviet Bloc. Shortly before departing for the Paris NATO summit, Karamanlis received a letter from the Soviet Prime Minister, Nikolai Bulganin, who warned that installation of US missiles could bring hardship to a country which accepted them. Karamanlis replied on 5 February 1958: although Greece had not accepted the IRBMs, he noted that the Western European countries had the right to proceed with such a measure.[83] Meanwhile, in January 1958 another incident occurred, when the Hungarian Ambassador to Athens raised the issue in a conversation with the Permanent Undersecretary of the Foreign Ministry, Pericles Sceferis, but then leaked the conversation to the press. The government was extremely angry at this incident, which was perceived as an attempt by the Hungarians to aid the EDA campaign with the Greek public.[84]

EDA chose to make the US missiles a major issue of its 1958 electoral campaign. In early May 1958, one week before the election, Khrushchev himself intervened with an interview in a major Greek newspaper. The Soviet leader said that Greece's membership of the 'aggressive coalition' of NATO threatened to involve Athens in 'dangerous adventures'. This was probably intended to become another stimulant of the EDA campaign, and was renounced by Karamanlis as an intervention in Greece's internal affairs.[85] However, the 1958 election resulted in a triumph for EDA, which crushed the divided Centre and came second with almost 25 per cent of the vote. The Greek Left's campaign on the US missiles and the neutralist tendencies which had appeared in the country evidently helped its case with the public.

The Cyprus question then moved to another crisis, when the British announced their Macmillan Plan for Cyprus, and thus the Karamanlis government's room for manoeuvre was again limited. In June 1958 the Greek government indicated to the US that it could not accept the US missiles. Indeed, after the 1958 election the US Embassy itself noted that acceptance of the missiles could have wider political repercussions. The Americans raised the issue again in early 1959, but once more backtracked when Soviet, Romanian and Bulgarian pressure on Greece began in May and June 1959.[86] At the same time, in May 1959, a major figure of the opposition, Spyros Markezinis, visited Moscow and upon his return publicly supported a 'third' policy which would retain Greece in NATO but would also accept the prospect of a nuclear-free zone in the Balkans.[87] Thus the pressures on the government came from many different quarters, and evidently Karamanlis decided that at that moment – when Cyprus had been settled and there was hope of overcoming the neutralist spirit – it was better not to further provoke the public with installation of the controversial missiles. Indeed, by the summer of 1959, and also in view of the Greek reserve, Eisenhower himself doubted as to whether the installation of the IRBMs in 'flank' positions such as Greece would be advisable.[88] A recent study criticized the Karamanlis government for its inability to accept the missiles; according to this view, the government gave in to public pressure and lost a major opportunity to emerge, even for a few years, as a part of the US nuclear deterrence.[89] However, exactly because the government wanted to accept the missiles and finally felt unable to do so, it may be argued that this was the EDA's major victory over the pro-Western political forces in Greece throughout the post-civil war period.

The issue of nuclear weapons and their installation in Greece continued to come up in various forms even after 1959, with the government reminding the public that it had not accepted US missiles and the opposition accusing Karamanlis of being hostile to the prospect of détente.[90] This was a constant embarrassment for the Karamanlis government. However, Khrushchev's August 1961 statement that the nuclear weapons would not spare the olive trees or the Acropolis came at a time when Greece was moving towards a general election, and was largely seen in Athens as an attempt to repeat the Soviet leader's intervention in the 1958 election. Khrushchev's threat of a nuclear attack on the Acropolis was hardly a gesture which the Greek public would appreciate, and it finally backfired: détente was not a major issue in the 1962–63 'relentless struggle' of the Centre against the conservatives. In a sense, Khrushchev himself solved this problem for Karamanlis.

The debate on nuclear weapons was transformed in the early 1960s, as flexible response replaced massive retaliation in US strategy. Flexible response entailed a greater emphasis on conventional forces, which called for some kind of US assurance to the European allies that they would not be abandoned in case of crisis. The Karamanlis–Kennedy meeting in April 1961 took place during a period when the US was eager to provide such assurances, and this is perhaps why the Greeks were so enthusiastic about the US President's attitude. At any rate, Greece accepted the US proposal for the NATO Multilateral Force, pointing out that this could also prevent unilateral initiatives by alliance members on nuclear weapons.[91] The Karamanlis government knew that it had little say in such a matter, but saw the whole issue as a tool for cementing allied solidarity. However, Greek positions did not remain unchanged throughout these years. As de Gaulle made it clear that he would oppose the MLF, Athens tried to find a new position which could reconcile US and French views. In early 1963, the government suggested that the MLF should not limit the independence of those countries which had already developed atomic weapons.[92] This was obviously intended to ease French anxieties.

Greece also favoured measures against the proliferation of nuclear weapons. The Karamanlis government had good contacts with the Third World (with which it had forged relations during the UN debates on Cyprus), but did not want these countries to become nuclear powers. Thus Athens signed the Test Ban Treaty in August 1963, during the lifetime of the Pipinelis government. The very fact that there was no internal controversy over this treaty shows that a kind of consensus existed between the Right and the Centre; the EDA's agreement to the treaty should be taken for granted.

9 The limits of functionalism
Security and détente

Greece and the Soviet Bloc: the years of the Cyprus crisis, 1955–59

The Karamanlis government's policy towards the Soviet Bloc can be divided in two sub-periods. In 1955–59, a time of trial for Greek–NATO relations, the Soviets made impressive offers for economic co-operation. In the summer of 1956, the Soviet Foreign Minister, Dmitri Shepilov, paid an unofficial visit to Athens. This was the first high-level Soviet visit to Greece since 1917. Shepilov put forward proposals for extensive bilateral economic co-operation, which the British Foreign Office described as 'a take over bid'.[1] At the same time, the Soviet Ambassador to Athens, Mikhail Sergueev, was very active especially on bilateral cultural relations; this was underlined by the US Chargé, James Penfield, in his November 1957 report to the State Department which was leaked to Greek political circles and thus contributed to the overthrow of the Karamanlis government in early 1958.

Athens faced this new Soviet 'peace offensive' with a high degree of caution. The Greek government tried to acquire and maintain the support of the Soviet-Bloc countries over Cyprus at the UN, and worked for the increase of commercial exchanges with them, but strove to avoid dependence on Eastern markets, which could have turned Greece into a hostage of Moscow. Athens also rejected multilateral political co-operation, such as the Romanian suggestions for a Balkan conference or a nuclear-free zone. The development of commercial relations acquired a new dynamic. In 1956 and until early 1957 Greece concluded commercial agreements with all the Soviet-Bloc states save Albania. In the summer of 1956, Greek–Romanian relations were normalized and a bilateral agreement was reached on compensation for Greek properties destroyed during the war. The climax of this process came with the large Greek–Soviet commercial agreements in 1957 and 1958. This opening to the East focused on commercial relations and has been described as 'limited',[2] but it involved a new, much more flexible Greek policy, seeking adjustment to the realities of that era.

Even during these years, the clumsiness of Soviet diplomacy became evident. Thus, shortly before the February 1957 UN debate on Cyprus, the Soviet Permanent Representative, Vassili Kuznetsov, told Averoff that the Soviet-Bloc's votes would depend on progress on Greek–Bulgarian and Greek–Albanian relations. The reactions of the Greek statesmen were revealing: Averoff suggested to Karamanlis that Greece should appear more accommodating towards Albania (not Bulgaria), but Karamanlis rejected the idea and instructed Averoff to make it clear to Kuznetsov that a favourable Eastern vote on Cyprus would create a favourable atmosphere in Greece's relations with these two countries.[3] The Soviet Bloc finally supported Greece in that UN debate, but this attempt at blackmail intensified Greek reserve. The suggestion by Averoff to make progress with Albania but not with Bulgaria is very interesting. Averoff, who had taken similar positions in 1952, as Venizelos' Undersecretary in the Foreign Ministry, was an MP for Epirus; a possible leak of his position could have easily destroyed him politically (more so since the opposition always accused him of treachery on Cyprus). However, both he and Karamanlis excluded concessions under pressure to Bulgaria, the main source of threat to the country's security.

Indeed, as long as Sofia was reluctant to pay reparations according to the 1947 Peace Treaty, and since it continued violating the disarmament clauses of that treaty, Athens was not prepared to place confidence on the 'sincerity' of Bulgaria. Greece refused to agree to an exchange of ambassadors without a prior settlement on reparations. Bulgaria appeared willing to pay a first instalment of $2 million, provided that ambassadors would be immediately exchanged, but Athens regarded that the Bulgarians would then spin out the negotiations indefinitely and refuse to pay any more money. In 1958 the Greek government indicated that it would agree to an exchange of ambassadors if Sofia agreed to pay an instalment of $6 million, which Sofia was not prepared to do. The negotiations stagnated on this issue. To be sure, co-operation developed on other levels, including commercial relations; in 1957 the Greek government, overriding objections of the General Staff of National Defence, agreed to reopen the Sofia–Thessaloniki road for commerce. However, tensions did not dissipate. In 1958 Sofia reacted strongly to the visit to Greece of the former King of Bulgaria, Symeon; this caused an equally sharp Greek reply. The British Foreign Office commented that the Bulgarians, who hosted Greek Communist former guerrillas from the civil war years, were hardly in a position to put forward similar complaints.[4]

On the other hand, Greek views regarding relations with Bulgaria were not monolithic. There were officials or services which supported a quick normalization of bilateral relations. An indicative example can be found in a meeting of officials under the chairmanship of the Director General of the Foreign Ministry, Pavlos Economou-Gouras, in October 1958. Two officials favoured the quick normalization of relations: the Chargé to Sofia, Constantinos Tranos (who in the early 1960s became Greece's permanent representative to the EEC), and the representative of the Ministry of Commerce, Ioannis Komitsas (who in 1958–61 became a member of the delegation which negotiated Greece's association with the EEC). Tranos and Komitsas stressed (correctly, as it turned out) that time was working against the Greek claim for reparations, and that finally Greece would get even less than the sum it could secure at that moment. Their position was supported by an unnamed representative of the Greek Central Intelligence

(KYP), who noted that commercial relations would create no security problem, whereas 'the Bulgarian space is very important to Greece and we cannot close the Bulgarian door; it is from there that the attack will come and we must be able to gather information'. However, the normalization of relations was opposed by the representative of the Foreign Ministry, the influential Ambassador Alexandros Matsas (who later headed the Ankara and the Washington Embassies). Matsas argued that Bulgarian goods would penetrate the Greek market and would 'familiarize the Greek public with communism, especially Bulgarian communism'. Matsas also insisted that the meeting should include representatives of the military and the Ministry of the Interior, two departments expected to oppose normalization of relations.[5] The meeting was inconclusive; in October 1958 there was another severe crisis in Cyprus, Averoff was in Paris for the NATO mediation effort and this was not a moment when Athens could turn its attention to Sofia. After the February 1959 Cyprus settlement, though, the new deterioration of Greece's relations with the Soviet Bloc again blocked progress on Greek–Bulgarian relations.

Greek–Albanian relations also continued to stagnate: there still was a state of war between the two countries, diplomatic representation was non-existent and the Greek minority in Albania was being persecuted. In 1956–57, the Albanians freed many Greek soldiers who had been held since the days of the civil war; the two countries also agreed to clear the Corfu Straits of mines (for Greece this was important for the development of the tourist industry in Corfu).[6] Throughout these years, Athens maintained its claim on Northern Epirus or Southern Albania, despite the fact that the Foreign Ministry and Averoff personally considered that nothing could come out of this. The diplomats favoured the normalization of diplomatic relations, which would allow Greece to have an observation post in this neighbouring state. The Americans agreed with this view, although repeatedly, when asked, they told Athens that the decision was up to the Greek government.[7] There were other centres that remained committed to the claim on Northern Epirus, especially the Palace. The government did not agree with such a prospect: Averoff himself repeatedly stressed that there no longer existed a Greek majority in Northern Epirus, because many Greeks had fled this territory since the Balkan Wars. After the Cyprus settlement, the government coldly and abruptly brushed aside suggestions for a 'national liberation struggle' in Albania.[8]

Waiting for détente, 1959–63

In 1959 the re-establishment of Greek–NATO and Greek–Turkish relations evidently irritated Moscow; it was no coincidence that Soviet, Bulgarian and Romanian pressures on Greece on the issue of nuclear weapons were stepped up in May 1959, immediately after the successful visit of Karamanlis and Averoff to Ankara and Istanbul, which marked the revival of Greek–Turkish co-operation. The bad habit of the Soviets of alternating between threats and friendly gestures made the Greeks even more uncertain and suspicious.

Although the country's security was based mainly on diplomatic and military deterrence, in those years the Karamanlis government also used psychological means to counter Soviet-Bloc tactics. In 1959–63, Athens appeared very combative rhetorically, and consistently responded to Soviet-Bloc challenges by escalating verbal exchanges. It did so, for example, after Khrushchev's threatening statements in Albania in June 1959 and from Moscow in August 1961. This also became evident in the case of the so-called 'stamp war' in 1959: when the Soviet Union issued a stamp bearing the picture of Manolis Glezos, a leading left-winger who had been sentenced to death for espionage, the Greeks published a stamp with the picture of Imre Nagy, the Hungarian Prime Minister of 1956, who had just been executed.[9] Glezos was not executed, but this was one of the most provocative responses by a small NATO member to a Soviet challenge throughout the Cold War. The climax of these Greek tactics of 'defiance' came during the Cuban missile crisis, when Averoff appeared extremely rigid in his conversation with the Soviet Ambassador, N. Koriukin.[10] This tendency to employ strong language can easily be explained: the Greeks did not want to show weakness, believing that this could actually encourage a Soviet-Bloc strike. Moreover, the Greeks wanted to shout as loudly as they could, to ensure that NATO would not be in a position to abandon them if the threat materialized. It was a part of the trip-wire mechanism that the Greek government used as deterrence.

In 1959–61, Greek–Eastern European commercial relations also emerged as an internal political problem. The left-wing EDA, which had become the major opposition party, attacked the government for being hostile to détente. (Admittedly, in the conservative wing of Karamanlis' party, as well as among many Centrists, there was the view that tension with the Communist East and talk about the 'Red Peril' paid off internally, especially in 1958–61, when the EDA was the major opposition.) As noted in Chapter 8, in the spring of 1959 a prominent opposition figure with strong anti-Communist credentials, Spyros Markezinis, the head of the Progressive Party, visited Moscow and then argued in favour of expanding commercial or even political relations with the Soviet Bloc. However, it should be noted that the issue of relations with the East also became a part of the infra-Centre struggle for dominance in those years. In the summer of 1960, the Liberal leader, Sophocles Venizelos, went to the Soviet capital. He then published four prominent articles on his discussions with the Soviet leadership, as well as an even more ground-breaking article calling for the legalization of the Greek Communist Party.[11] At the same time, Venizelos 'lent' his party's MPs to George Grivas, the former leader of the Greek Cypriot EOKA who tried to enter Greek politics through accusations against Karamanlis of treachery in Cyprus. These were contradictory moves (Grivas was an extreme right-winger) and Venizelos' enterprise collapsed in 1961, thus leaving George Papandreou as the victor in the internal Centre dispute and as the leader of the newly-formed Centre Union. But the issue of commerce with the East created substantial pressures on the government.

Indeed, trade with the East was indispensable for the Greek development effort. In 1955, 4.7 per cent of Greek exports were directed to the Soviet Bloc, but by 1958–59 this had spiralled to 16.2 per cent and by 1961 to 21 per cent. The government felt that further increase of exchanges could lead to dependence on the Soviet-Bloc markets. Moreover, Northern Greece was a border area and a region of particular electoral appeal for Karamanlis' party, yet, it produced exactly the kind of goods that the Soviets were buying, such as tobacco, and its population was extremely sensitive regarding trade with the East.[12]

The major political battle regarding trade with the Soviet Bloc was fought during the Parliamentary debate of 24–30 November 1959. The leader of the EDA, Ioannis Passalides, the leader of the Democratic Union, Elias Tsirimokos, Sophocles Venizelos and Markezinis accused the government of being hostile to détente, and suggested that Greece expand its Eastern trade in order to relieve its farmers. The government's case was presented by Averoff and the Minister for Economic Co-ordination, Aristides Protopapadakis, who pointed out that Eastern trade had multiplied in the previous years. However, it was essential that the government position was also supported by Panayis Papaligouras (who was not an ERE MP in 1958–61) and by George Papandreou.[13] The Greek Parliament debated trade with the East again in April 1960, when the EDA tabled a motion of censure against the government. This time, it was the EDA's most eloquent speaker, Elias Eliou, who spoke on its behalf. The government speakers accused the EDA of being populist in its rhetoric to the Greek farmers. The Liberals and Markezinis's Progressives criticized government policy but also distanced themselves from the EDA's motion of censure, which they described as inopportune. George Papandreou again supported the government.[14]

The problem was definitely solved through Greece's Association with the EEC, which provided for the long-term orientation of the Greek economy towards Western Europe; it also dealt with Greek agricultural exports and thus removed any danger of dependence on Soviet-Bloc markets. Karamanlis himself had pointed out this danger in a letter to his EEC counterparts in autumn 1960.[15] The Association with the EEC also brings to light important details regarding the development of Greek external trade. In December 1960, the US Ambassador to Athens, Ellis O. Briggs, intervened in Athens' requests for lowering EEC tobacco tariffs for Greek products; Briggs even said that if Greece persisted in its demands, Greek–US co-operation would be adversely affected. Of course, Greek and American tobacco were considered as competing products (the American Virginias were winning over the markets against Greek Eastern tobacco), but the small quantities of Greek tobacco posed little problem to the US, and the American demarche seemed to be a gross exaggeration. The Director General of the Foreign Ministry, Christos Xanthopoulos-Palamas, rejected the US demand:[16]

> This issue is of vital importance to Greece, while it certainly has no such importance for the US economy. [Xanthopoulos-Palamas] stressed that the tobacco problem is a fundamental economic problem for the Greek economy. Simultaneously, it also is a serious social problem. In the tobacco-growing areas of Northern Greece, the tobacco issue is a major

issue in the communist propaganda attack, and this region is extremely sensitive on this. It would be a mistake if people in Washington believed that the problem of tobacco-growing and exports is merely of an economic character and could be judged through a narrow technical approach. It is primarily a political problem; the Greek government was obliged to consider all the repercussions and effects from the handling of this problem, or even from today's US demarche.

Karamanlis also rejected the US demand; then, the Minister for Economic Co-ordination, Protopapadakis, discussed the issue with the US Undersecretary of State, Douglas Dillon. The US accepted the Greek arguments. In January 1961, immediately after the Kennedy administration took over, a new US approach to the Six encouraged them to conclude negotiations for Greece's association.[17]

The January 1961 change of US policy probably did not play a major role in the Greek–EEC negotiations, but came at the right moment. In late December 1960, evidently in an attempt to press Greece, the Soviet Union refused to renew the bilateral commercial agreement; this created strong fears in Athens regarding exports of agricultural products.[18] In the summer of 1961, during the Berlin Wall crisis, the Greeks feared that the West might respond with a trade embargo against the Soviet Bloc.[19] In late 1961, NATO examined the possibility of providing assistance to three member states which would be hurt in case of the application of economic countermeasures against the Soviet Bloc: Iceland, Greece and Turkey.[20] This shows that a degree of dependence on Eastern markets was already there. In short, Greece managed to associate itself with the Community, before becoming dependent on Moscow regarding agricultural exports.

For a number of reasons, after the October 1961 election trade with the East was not a major issue in the campaign of the Centre Union against the government. First, the new opposition party, the CU, turned its attention to accusations against the government of undemocratic behaviour; on foreign policy the CU criticized Karamanlis for subservience to the Americans, for his Cyprus policy and for his alleged soft line on Yugoslav attempts to create a Macedonian problem. Second, in August 1961 Khrushchev had stated that he was ready to target the Acropolis with nuclear weapons; after that, the issue of détente could not pay off in the internal political scene. Third, Venizelos, the main supporter of further Eastern opening, had been defeated politically: George Papandreou, the leader of the CU, had always been more reserved towards the Communist world. Last but not least, the CU, a strongly pro-Western party, naturally wanted to distance itself from the agenda that the left-wing EDA had put forward during the previous years.

At the same time, after the October 1961 election the Karamanlis government's initially reserved attitude towards détente begun to change. As shown in Chapter 7, the Foreign Ministry and Averoff strongly supported the view that the country could face even greater dangers if it failed to adjust to the new

104 *The era of functionalism, 1955–63*

international climate. More importantly, Greece's association with the EEC removed the danger of dependence on Eastern markets. Participation in the process of European integration brought Greece closer to the hard core of the West, and boosted Greek confidence. Evidently, the Greeks were also relieved to see the US resolve during the Cuban missile crisis. The new Greek attitude was summed up by Averoff in a letter to Rusk in December 1962. Averoff indicated that Khrushchev obviously did not want a war 'today or so long as the balance of forces is against him'; the Soviet leader was facing important challenges from other Communist leaders, including Tito, and the major problem of the Sino-Soviet split; Khrushchev thus might welcome an understanding with the West. However, Averoff continued, such an understanding should cover points of interest to both worlds, and Moscow would have to make concessions on issues of Western interest. Significantly, this position was remarkably close to a 'linkage' perception of an East–West negotiation. Averoff concluded:[21]

> I am not at all sure that we should expect an agreement [with the Soviet Bloc] in our time. If it is advanced that we must expect agreement, I do not place my hopes either on the 'good' Mr. Khrushchev, or on his 'better' or more probably worse successor. I place them *only* on the development of pressure from below inside the Soviet Union, which has for some time helped to make Mr. Khrushchev 'good'. But this development depends very much on the evolution of the standard of living in the USSR, on developments in other communist states, and on the strength, cohesion and initiatives of the Free World.

On bilateral relations, Bulgaria remained at the centre of Greek diplomatic activity. In December 1960, a new round of Greek–Bulgarian negotiations produced no result. But the climate was beginning to change, especially as the new Bulgarian leader, Todor Zhivkov, consolidated his position in power and appeared ready to offer the assurances of good will that Greece expected. In the summer of 1960, the Greeks reacted favourably to a Bulgarian proposal for common exploitation of the waters of the rivers running through the two countries. In May 1961, a Bulgarian proposal for the development of technical and economic co-operation was regarded as interesting by Athens. Still, the Greeks were afraid that, if they accepted such proposals, the Bulgarians would have little motive to pay reparations. And in the summer of 1961 Greek–Bulgarian relations took a turn for the worse when Greece and Bulgaria exchanged accusations of espionage, and the Bulgarian Prime Minister, Anton Yugov, made a strong verbal attack on Karamanlis' policy. This coincided with the Berlin Wall crisis as well as with Khrushchev's threats regarding nuclear weapons and the Acropolis, and thus Athens once more considered that it could fall victim to a Bulgarian invasion, designed to draw Western attention away from Berlin. The turning point in Greek–Bulgarian relations came in 1962. By that time, Athens was certain that the Bulgarians needed bilateral economic co-operation because they faced serious economic shortages. Thus, first in April, talking to the Bulgarian Chargé, N. Minchev, and then in December in a note to the Bulgarian government, Averoff suggested linkage: the two countries should seek a package deal which would simultaneously solve all pending problems and initiate economic and technical co-operation. This would assure each side that its interests would be safeguarded: economic and technical co-operation for the Bulgarians, reparations for the Greeks. This proposal became the basis for the normalization of bilateral relations: Sofia accepted it in August 1963, during the lifetime of the Pipinelis government, and the final settlement was reached in 1964.[22]

On Greek–Albanian relations, there was some activity in the early 1960s which led nowhere. Nevertheless, this activity revealed interesting aspects of Greek strategy in the Balkans. In 1961 Enver Hoxha's Albania quarrelled with the Soviet Union, and this created doubts as to whether the Tirana regime would survive. Athens did not regard this as an opportunity to advance its claim on Northern Epirus. On the contrary, by spring 1961 the Greek government was afraid that Yugoslavia would receive a green light from Moscow to topple the Albanian rebel regime and impose its control on the country.[23] This scenario made Athens extremely anxious: the Greek government was afraid of a possible regional strengthening of Yugoslavia, which would upset the delicate Balkan balance of power. In late 1961, Averoff told the British and the Americans that it was very important, for Greece, to retain Albania and Yugoslavia as separate political entities.[24]

This Greek support for Albanian independence brought some results: in December 1961 Tirana released 123 Greek soldiers held since the civil war; Athens was embarrassed (as it regarded that these persons had already been indoctrinated), but anyway this was a notable Albanian gesture.[25] Then, the Greek Embassy in Paris approached the Albanian Embassy. According to British officials, the Greeks were out to normalize relations with Tirana: an Embassy at Tirana could give Athens the opportunity to influence events in case trouble ensued.[26] However, the Greek opening led nowhere, mostly because of the unusual extremism of the Albanian Communist regime: at a time when Hoxha accused Khrushchev of having Western contacts, he would not initiate relations with a NATO member; the Soviets themselves were dismayed at the intransigence of Tirana towards Athens.[27] The second factor was the Northern Epirus question: during a visit to Belgium in the spring of 1962, Averoff publicly stated that he favoured the resumption of Greek–Albanian relations, which would not entail the abandonment of the Greek claim. However, Tirana insisted that Athens had formally to renounce this claim prior to any move on the diplomatic front.[28] This rendered progress impossible: Greece could not renounce its claim without securing some improvement for the Greeks of Northern Epirus, and this was a rather distant prospect, taking into account the nature of the Hoxha regime.

The window of opportunity, if it ever opened, closed rather quickly. The xenophobia of Hoxha's regime soon led Albania to complete international isolation. The downfall of the Karamanlis government had similarly adverse effects. Ironically, the partition of Albania between Greece and Yugoslavia was publicly suggested by Panayiotis Pipinelis in a book published in the US in 1963: Pipinelis advocated that Greece should receive Northern Epirus and Yugoslavia the rest.[29] In June 1963, though, Pipinelis became Prime Minister and Foreign Minister. He ascended to the premiership exactly because he had little power in the governing party and thus could not threaten Karamanlis in his dispute with the Palace; but the Albanians were certain to focus on the new Prime Minister's call for the partition of their country. Moreover, in August and September 1963, Pipinelis appeared anxious to promote the Greek claim on Northern Epirus: he publicly stated that the international climate favoured the projection of the claim. He went as far as to inquire from the Foreign Office whether Britain continued to regard the four-power Council of Foreign Ministers, established in the aftermath of the Second World War, as competent to deal with Northern Epirus. London officials were amused by the suggestion and in any event Pipinelis left office soon thereafter, when new elections were proclaimed.[30] The Pipinelis government was a quasi-caretaker administration which made significant progress on Greek–Bulgarian relations; but it did a lot to derail Greece's Albanian policy, which was already not based on very solid ground.

In conclusion, Athens was initially reserved towards détente; the emphasis of Karamanlis and Averoff on 'prudence' prevented them from taking enthusiastic initiatives towards the East. However, in 1962–63 the Karamanlis government tried to adjust to the new international climate. The December 1962 package deal proposal to Bulgaria, the debate on Greek–Albanian relations in the spring of 1962, the settlement of the Greek–Yugoslav crisis over the Macedonian issue in December 1962 (see Chapter 10), and the conclusion of new commercial agreements with Yugoslavia, Poland and Hungary in 1962–63 were parts of this policy. Yet the Karamanlis government fell before having the time to implement this line fully. The adjustment of Eastern policy was left to the Centre governments of the mid-1960s.

10 The regional aspect of functionalism
Yugoslavia, Turkey, Cyprus

Regional developments were immensely important for the Karamanlis government. Relations with Turkey were strained in 1955–59 because of the Cyprus dispute. In 1959–60 the establishment of a Cypriot state created further obligations for Greek foreign and security policy. Yet, the main initiatives of Athens during these years involved Tito's Yugoslavia. After the 1955 Istanbul riots and the deterioration of Greek–Turkish relations, Yugoslavia became Athens' only option for a regional partnership. Belgrade should be kept outside the Soviet Bloc at any cost; in the opposing case, Greece could never balance a Yugoslav–Bulgarian combination. Even after the conclusion of the 1959 Cyprus settlement, it was imperative to ensure Yugoslav neutrality. Karamanlis explained the Greek view on the strategic importance of Yugoslavia, during his 1959 visit to Turkey:[1]

> We have three choices: to push Tito towards Russia; to make him our ally; or to keep him outside both blocs. The first is disadvantageous, the second impossible. The third choice is the only one that remains and we have to go for it.

But Yugoslavia's position in Greece's system of alliances was peculiar: lecturing, in May 1958, to students of the US War College, Averoff spoke of the 'abiding need' for good relations with Turkey, but only mentioned the 'desirability' of neutralizing a part of the country's extensive land border through friendship with Belgrade.[2] This was indicative of the caution with which Greek officials confronted this powerful peripheral power, which had claimed Greek Macedonia as recently as the 1940s. The same picture also clearly emerges from Karamanlis' comments to President Kennedy in the spring of 1961: 'Regarding Yugoslavia, Mr. Karamanlis said that although we cannot fully trust it, we must nevertheless help it maintain its policy of neutrality between east and west'.[3]

Throughout the post-war period, the Greek–Yugoslav relationship was determined by two sets of considerations: the need of both countries for a strategic partnership which would help them balance the Warsaw-Pact powers; and the Macedonian question, on which they could not possibly agree.

Forming a bilateral partnership with Belgrade, 1956–58

The Greek initiative for the formation of a bilateral axis with Yugoslavia derived from the grave strategic problems that Athens faced after the deterioration of Greek–Turkish relations in 1955. Greece could not continue its defence effort or even its policy to integrate in the West, if it were fully isolated regionally. The bonds with Turkey and Yugoslavia, or at any rate with one of them, were absolutely necessary for Greek foreign policy. Initially, until the autumn of 1956, Athens hoped that the tripartite relationship with Turkey and Yugoslavia could be re-established. In the summer of 1956, the Greek government undertook some initiatives which could lead to the revival of tripartite co-operation. Thus, it put forward a proposal for the implementation of the principle of self-determination in Cyprus, in a manner which would take into account Turkish anxieties: the Greek proposal included demilitarization of Cyprus except for the British bases, recognition of special minority status for the Turkish Cypriots, and the creation of free ports for Turkish trade.[4] The government also tried to brush under the carpet the issue of the planting of a bomb in the Turkish Consulate in Thessaloniki in September 1955, which had been the pretext for the anti-Greek Istanbul riots. Although the Greeks had evidence that the bomb had been planted by Turkish citizens and a member of the Muslim minority of Western Thrace, the government released the Turkish nationals, while the Thracian Muslim, Octay Engin, 'escaped' from prison (the US Consulate in Thessaloniki reported this by putting the word 'escape' within quotes).[5]

The Greek government also examined alternative options, in case its Turkish opening failed. In the summer of 1956, Karamanlis and Averoff held talks with Tito in Corfu. The Greeks and the Yugoslavs agreed that every effort should be made to revive tripartite co-operation, but if this proved impossible they would re-examine the situation.[6] Thus Athens left its options open, hoping to achieve its major aim, namely a Cyprus settlement and the revival of Greek–Turkish friendship. However, this was not to be. In the autumn of 1956 it became clear that Turkey insisted on the partition of the island, which Athens could not accept. At the same time, October and November 1956, tactical differences between Athens and Belgrade were relegated to secondary importance in the face of the Soviet invasion of Hungary which naturally worried the Yugoslavs; once more Tito was forced to seek indirect links with NATO through Greece. The fact that Greece and Yugoslavia took almost identical positions in the two major international crises of autumn 1956 – Suez and Hungary – also contributed to bringing them closer.

Thus, when Karamanlis and Averoff visited Belgrade in early December, everything was in place for a bilateral rapprochement. During the Belgrade talks, Karamanlis reminded Tito that they had agreed to seek the re-establishment of tripartite co-operation, but this had not worked; although the 1953–54 tripartite pacts had to remain 'dormant', Greece and Yugoslavia needed to form a bilateral partnership. Tito and the Vice-President of the federal government, Edvard Kardelj, agreed with this analysis. Thus, the two countries decided to initiate close bilateral political and military co-operation.[7] Significantly, the US Embassy in Athens did not initially realize the importance of the Belgrade talks: in a mid-December 1956 report, the Embassy suggested that the Karamanlis visit had not produced impressive results.[8] This shows that the Greek–Yugoslav rapprochement was not recommended or managed by the Americans.

Karamanlis' and Averoff's visit to Belgrade was the turning point for the creation of a bilateral strategic partnership in the south of the Balkans. This process was completed in 1957–58, when high-level contacts continued: in April 1957 the Vice-President of the Yugoslav government, Svetozar Vukmanovic-Tempo, visited Athens; in July the Greek Royals went to Brioni, in October Kardelj went to Athens, and in 1958 the Speaker of the Greek Parliament, Constantinos Rodopoulos, visited Belgrade. Then, in July, Averoff participated in the Brioni conference with Tito and Nasser. In late 1958, the two countries started negotiations for the expansion of bilateral economic and technical co-operation.

Some problems continued to emerge. Thus, a Yugoslav proposal for a renewal and possible expansion of the pre-war agreement on border traffic in the Florina–Bitol area embarrassed the Greeks. Athens was afraid that old Communist guerrillas from the days of the civil war, who lived in that area, could benefit from it. The military, the Ministry of the Interior and the intelligence service were against such an agreement, although the Foreign Ministry considered that Greece could not block it indefinitely. Furthermore, in February 1957 Kardelj, speaking to the Greek Ambassador, raised the issue of the Slav-speakers of Greek Western Macedonia.[9] However, a large part of these people identified with Greece, while such Yugoslav initiatives could spark deep-rooted concerns in Greece, which always feared Yugoslav hegemonism. Athens fired some warning shots on that issue. During Kardelj's visit in October 1957, the two governments agreed on almost all international issues; they disagreed on the recent Romanian proposal for a Balkan Conference (Yugoslavia was in favour of acceptance), but they also showed understanding for the other party's position. It was Karamanlis who stressed that the issue of border traffic could create problems. He said that there were people in the Yugoslav south who in the 1940s had threatened Greek territorial integrity:

> I have to speak openly, so that there will be no grounds for misunderstandings. If Yugoslavia were in our place, it would certainly have similar reservations. This whole affair is very embarrassing. In Skopje, perhaps without the knowledge of the federal government, some thoughts are being cultivated which can create misunderstandings.

Kardelj assured Karamanlis that both Belgrade and Skopje were in favour of good relations with Greece; Athens should not place undue importance on views of individuals or on 'insignificant' matters. At any rate, the Greek Prime Minister made it clear that the only problem for the bilateral relationship could come from inept handling of the Macedonian issue.[10]

The Greek–Yugoslav partnership also had a tangible military dimension. In

1957–58 there were frequent exchanges of visits of Greek and Yugoslav military: four such visits took place in 1957 alone. It was not a coincidence that in 1957 Athens appointed as ambassador to Belgrade one of the best Greek military leaders, Lieutenant-General (retd) Thrassyvoulos Tsakalotos, who had also served as Chief of the General Staff of the Army. In 1958 the British Foreign Office noted that the Yugoslavs protested about the acquisition of US missiles by the Italian army, but said nothing about the similar acquisition of Honest Johns by the Greeks.[11] In the summer of 1958, asked by the British whether Athens would pursue the conclusion of a bilateral military agreement with Belgrade, officials of the Greek Foreign Ministry replied that military co-operation had already developed so much, that there was no need for a formal arrangement.[12]

This 'special relationship' was crucial for Greek policy in those years. The Greek–Yugoslav rapprochement prevented the regional isolation of Greece, and at the same time helped Tito to keep his distance from Moscow and Sofia. Furthermore, through this bilateral rapprochement Athens managed to isolate Turkey in the Balkans – something which the British were quick to note.[13] Yugoslavia gave invaluable support to the Greeks during the UN debates on Cyprus. Last but not least, the Greek–Yugoslav relationship allowed Greece to develop a regional role as a NATO power, by becoming the link between the West and Tito. Belgrade could not turn to Italy, a regional rival in the Adriatic, with which there were older as well as more recent points of tension. More importantly, this role of Greece as a link with Tito was recognized by the US: two NSC papers on Greece, in 1957 and 1961, noted that Athens had excellent relations with Belgrade and thus formed (together with Turkey) a barrier to Soviet expansion southwards; the 1957 document expressly mentioned the 1953–54 Balkan pacts, a reference which did not appear in the 1961 paper.[14]

It should be noted that this worked both ways: Greece's NATO membership also made it a credible partner for Belgrade. Thus, during the tripartite Greek–Yugoslav–Egyptian talks in Brioni, in the summer of 1958, Tito brushed aside Nasser's idea for the formation of a neutralist axis between the three countries.[15] In September 1958, when fears were expressed that Greece would drift out of NATO because of British policy in Cyprus, Tito urged Karamanlis to remain in the Western alliance.[16] The Greek Prime Minister used this to rebuff Makarios' suggestion for a 'temporary' exit from NATO. As the Greek Foreign Ministry noted in February 1959, 'the value of Greek friendship would drastically be reduced for them [the Yugoslavs] if the bonds between Greece and the western powers became looser'.[17]

To be sure, both Greece and Yugoslavia faced difficulties in their international positions, and this tended to bring them closer. As the British Foreign Office noted in late 1957, there was a genuine community of interests between Greece and Yugoslavia: the former was a 'relatively rebellious' NATO member, and the latter a leading non-aligned state.[18] Some months later, in April 1958, the US Embassy in Athens pointed out that for a number of reasons Tito was popular with the Greek public: Yugoslavia supported the Greek case on Cyprus, while the dispute with Turkey tended to convince the Greeks that Belgrade was their only friend in the Balkans. Many Greeks felt admiration for Tito's neutrality, at a time when they regarded that the West had let them down on Cyprus. Greek–Yugoslav friendship did not conflict with the neutralist spirit which had developed in the country.[19]

The peak of the Greek–Yugoslav rapprochement, 1959–61

In 1959, the scene changed significantly. The February 1959 Cyprus settlement opened the road for the re-establishment of Greek–NATO and Greek–Turkish relations, while Yugoslavia was seeking a new international role as a leader of that international combination which would later be called the non-aligned movement. At a time when the two countries were finding new international roles, they had to redefine the aims of their partnership. Still, facing new pressures by the Soviet Bloc, Greece was not prepared to abandon its relationship with Belgrade; and Yugoslavia was not ready to trade its partnership with Greece for links with the non-aligned, which had not yet been fully forged.

In February 1959, in the immediate aftermath of the Cyprus settlement, the Greek Foreign Ministry prepared for Karamanlis a series of minutes on Greece's external relations. Regarding Yugoslavia, the Ministry considered that the bilateral negotiation on economic and technical issues (which had started in December 1958) was primarily a political issue and a tool for deepening the bilateral relationship. The Foreign Ministry was concerned about the possible effects of Albanian irredentism in Kosovo, which was fuelled not only by the Soviet Bloc but also by Turkey, and intensified pressures on Belgrade by Moscow and its allies. The Foreign Ministry feared that Yugoslavia would now be pressed by the Soviets to formally renounce the 1953–54 tripartite pacts. Moreover, Greece and Yugoslavia were now negotiating a border-traffic agreement: the Greek government had proceeded with these negotiations despite the adverse reactions of the Ministry of the Interior, the General Staff of National Defence and the Intelligence (KYP).[20] The Foreign Ministry pointed out that the Macedonian question focused now on the Sofia–Belgrade dispute for the Yugoslav south; Yugoslav policy on the Macedonian issue 'appears today as actively anti-Bulgarian, but has not abandoned, neither could it abandon, its fundamentally anti-Greek nature'.[21] Thus, Greek diplomacy was satisfied by the fact that Belgrade continued to avoid the embrace of the Soviets, but the Macedonian problem could always impair bilateral relations.

On the other hand, the future course of bilateral relations depended on the transformation of regional balances after the Cyprus settlement. In early March 1959, returning from a tour of Asian and African countries during which the formation of a non-aligned movement was examined, Tito met Karamanlis and Averoff in Rhodes. The relevant records suggest that the Yugoslav leader wanted to detect whether Greek policy towards Yugoslavia would change after the Cyprus settlement. Karamanlis and Averoff assured him that Greece was always interested in maintaining its Yugoslav connections, and tried to sound him out regarding possible reactivation of the 1953–54 Balkan pacts, in which Turkey was also interested. Tito rejected this latter idea, although he agreed to keep the Balkan pacts 'dormant'. The Yugoslav leader also stressed that the bilateral Greek–Yugoslav contacts 'and especially the visits and contacts of the General Staffs' should continue. Karamanlis carefully replied that these contacts had become a delicate matter after the re-establishment of Greek–Turkish relations, and Tito agreed that Greece should also notify Turkey concerning this matter.[22] Thus, Turkey wanted to reactivate the Balkan pacts, Yugoslavia disagreed, and Greece had to form a position which would preserve contacts with Belgrade without offending Ankara. In April 1959, a Greek Foreign Ministry minute described the Greek aims in the Athens–Ankara–Belgrade triangle:[23]

> Finding ourselves at the centre between the conflicting views of Turkey and Yugoslavia, we should not make an effort (which anyway will prove abortive) to press towards the one or the other direction. On the contrary, we should maintain our central position between Ankara and Belgrade, acquiring as many benefits as we can; mostly, we should continue the exchange of Greek and Yugoslav military visits, at least those which are not at the level of General Staffs. As for General Staff visits, we have a difficulty to continue them without the participation of Turkey, as the Prime Minister told Marshal Tito, and as the Minister for Foreign Affairs notified the Turkish Ambassador. The Chief of the General Staff of National Defence, Lieutenant-General Dovas, agrees that we must continue military visits.

This is exactly what Athens tried to do. During their March 1959 visit to Turkey, Karamanlis and Averoff explained Tito's position to their Turkish counterparts. The latter agreed to keep the Balkan pacts 'dormant' and accepted the continuation of Greek–Yugoslav military contacts, although they obviously did not feel very comfortable about this.[24] In July 1959, during his first meeting with the Turkish Foreign Minister, Fatin Rüştü Zorlu, who complained that the Yugoslavs were being evasive, the new Greek Ambassador to Ankara, Alexandros Matsas, cautioned him that 'Yugoslav tightrope walking is the result not of a lack of sincerity, but of an effort to balance between conflicting pressures'.[25]

On 18 June 1959, bilateral Greek–Yugoslav co-operation made a great leap forward when eleven bilateral agreements were signed in Athens by the Foreign Ministers, Averoff and Koca Popovic. These included a border-traffic agreement, a tourist agreement, compensation for the nationalization of Greek properties in Yugoslavia, economic co-operation, technical assistance and electric power.[26] This was the peak of the Greek–Yugoslav rapprochement.

However, the border-traffic agreement complicated matters. This agreement had been resisted by the Ministry of the Interior, the military and the KYP, and now attracted the fire of the leader of the Liberal Party, Sophocles Venizelos, who wrote to Karamanlis expressing his reservations and warning that the agreement could be used by Belgrade to create trouble in Greek Macedonia. Karamanlis replied that the agreement presented no such danger and that it was necessary to deepen co-operation with Yugoslavia.[27] Once more after the Cyprus upheaval (and indeed less than six months after the Cyprus settlement), the opposition began to censor the Karamanlis government for its handling of one of Greece's 'national issues'. This was becoming embarrassingly permanent, and Karamanlis evidently feared that another nationalist turmoil was in the making. Thus, the Prime Minister asked the Deputy Prime Minister, Kanellopoulos, who was paying a visit to Yugoslavia exactly at that time, to propose changes to the agreement. Kanellopoulos disagreed and pointed out to the Prime Minister that such a request could bring Greece no practical benefit, but could easily damage the climate of bilateral relations.[28] Significantly, according to the Greek Ambassador to Yugoslavia, Tsakalotos, Tito had recently described Greece as 'Yugoslavia's only friend in the Balkans'.[29] Karamanlis accepted these arguments, and the agreement remained as it stood. During the debate for its ratification by the Greek Parliament, on 17 and 18 September, the Liberal Party voted in favour of the agreement in order not to displease Yugoslavia. However, the Liberal speaker, Emmanuel Kothris, referred to documents of the General Staff which criticized the agreement, which means that during those days there were leaks of the security services to the opposition.[30]

It was on the very same days, in late summer 1959, that another extremely unfortunate incident occurred, when Greek policemen obliged Slav-speaking persons in three villages of Greek Western Macedonia to swear that they would not use the Slav-Macedonian language/dialect; arguably, this operation could not have been organized without the support of the KYP. These initiatives caused consternation in the Greek Foreign Ministry, and stopped after an extremely angry reaction by Kanellopoulos, Averoff and Tsakalotos – yet not before providing Skopje with excellent propaganda material.[31] Evidently, these incidents also alienated the Liberal Party and convinced it to stop its campaign against the border traffic agreement.

Nevertheless, the Macedonian question continued to create various difficulties in Greek–Yugoslav relations. In March 1960, Kanellopoulos rejected a Yugoslav proposal for the creation of a free trade zone between the People's Republic of Macedonia (PRM) and Greek Macedonia. The Yugoslavs then came back with a proposal for the setting up of a free trade zone on the area covered by the 1959 border-traffic agreement, which the Greek side again rejected.[32] These proposals embarrassed the Greek government. Yet, since nothing could be done about it, the Foreign Ministry stressed that this situation also presented some advantages for Greece:[33]

> But the [Yugoslav] expansionism, as manifested in the Macedonian question, is perhaps the price that Yugoslavia has to pay to de-Bulgarize Skopje; this, in turn, is the major problem between Belgrade and Sofia, and as such it is welcome to us. Furthermore, it may even be useful to maintain (within some limits) our complaints against 'Skopje', which allow us to refuse to give to Yugoslavia what we do not want to give to it.

In July 1960, Karamanlis paid his second visit to Yugoslavia. According to British sources, the Greek side did not regard the visit as necessary but the Yugoslavs insisted, because they wanted to show to the world that they had 'respectable friends'.[34] Before going to Yugoslavia, Karamanlis received a series of briefs from the Foreign Ministry which indicated that bilateral relations were excellent, although the Yugoslav tendency to raise the Macedonian issue should be closely monitored by Athens.[35] Indeed, this seems to have had much to do with Karamanlis' public reference, while in Yugoslavia, to the principle of non-interference in the internal affairs of either country. In a later note, Karamanlis indicated that, during the talks, the issue of border traffic was raised, 'which the Greek government always treated with some scepticism'.[36] Even so, the two governments continued to see eye to eye regarding the international political situation.[37]

However, the side-effects of the Macedonian question again became evident. In early October 1960, the Prime Minister of the PRM, Lazar Kolishevski (not an official of the federal government), put forward the question of a Slav-Macedonian minority in Greece; according to the Greeks, such references implied a Yugoslav tendency to view Greek Macedonia as part of a Yugoslav land. Athens immediately protested, and appeared satisfied by the Yugoslav reply that federal policy had not changed. When the Vice-President of the Yugoslav government, Alexandar Rankovic, visited Athens in May 1961, the agreement of the two governments on international issues was again manifested. Karamanlis stressed that 'Yugoslavia's neutrality and its co-operation with Greece are the key to Balkan peace'. However, he also drew Rankovic's attention to 'the need that the Yugoslav government pay more attention to the initiatives of Skopje, because it is a pity to have misunderstandings between our two countries'.[38]

In short, until 1961 the preservation of the 'special relationship' was a priority for both governments. However, the relative lessening of international tensions allowed the Yugoslavs to become more relaxed on the Macedonian affair, and some clouds appeared. This also had much to do with internal developments in Yugoslavia and the effort of the federative republics to strengthen their position towards the federal government.

The Greek–Yugoslav crisis, 1961–62

On 14 November 1961, the new Prime Minister of the PRM, Anton Grlicko, referred to 'maltreatment of the Slav-Macedonian minority of Greece'. This was a repetition of Kolishevski's statement of 1960, and the Greek government reacted in the same way: Averoff met the Yugoslav Ambassador, Petar Dapcevic, whose explanations were regarded as satisfactory by Athens. However, this time, the issue did not fade away: a strong exchange followed between the press of Thessaloniki and Skopje. In early December, when the fourth Karamanlis government was presented to Parliament, the Centre opposition expressed concern about the new PRM statement and Averoff said that the issue had been settled. Nevertheless, on 15 December, the press official of the Yugoslav

Foreign Ministry, Drago Kunc, stated that Belgrade was interested in the well-being of the Slav-speaking minority in Greece.[39]

This was the first time for many years that a federal official had publicly raised this issue, and according to Athens it signalled a major change of Yugoslav policy. Since 1957, Karamanlis had been warning the Yugoslavs that Greece would not accept a re-opening of this question. Moreover, the Kunc statement gave the opportunity for a vicious attack of the opposition against the Karamanlis government. The Centre Union had proclaimed a 'relentless struggle' for bringing Karamanlis down; accusations regarding the handling of the Macedonian question comprised a major part of this struggle in early 1962. Indeed, Sophocles Venizelos published a newspaper article denouncing government policy.[40] From the point of view of internal politics, it was Cyprus replayed.

The Kunc statement ended the golden age of Greek–Yugoslav relations and sparked a crisis which led Greece to suspend the implementation of the border-traffic agreement early in 1962.[41] Although some Western allies believed that Greece overreacted in this case, the Greek tactics were simple. In the previous two years, the Yugoslavs had circled around the Macedonian issue. Athens now tried to show to the Yugoslavs that they could either open up a Macedonian problem, or have good relations with Greece; but they could not do both, namely put forward a Macedonian problem in the 'context of good Greek–Yugoslav relations'. Karamanlis made this clear during his meeting with Ambassador Dapcevic in late February 1962:[42]

> Yugoslavia knew that Macedonia was the only issue which could endanger our relations [. . .] Everything else can be corrected. The Macedonian issue is the only one which cannot. I have been repeating this for years. This issue causes damage, and those who bring it forward must choose. They must decide whether they prefer the advantages of our co-operation, or the damage which this issue causes to our relations.

This was an unusual attempt to restrain an ally and preserve the alliance. The Karamanlis government strove to show the Yugoslavs the limits beyond which there would be a serious problem. This was why publicly the Greek government did not take a hostile position towards Yugoslavia, although this would certainly have been a popular policy, and would have countered the opposition attacks. It was mostly Averoff who faced these attacks, but kept a friendly attitude towards Belgrade. It is notable that during the NAC ministerial meeting of May 1962, Averoff insisted that despite an improvement of Soviet–Yugoslav relations, Belgrade guarded its independence; NATO should continue to regard Yugoslav independence as a useful factor.[43] The Greek government also took great care not to alarm Belgrade: when, in the summer of 1962, NATO planned large military manoeuvres in Greek Macedonia, Athens asked for special permission from the NAC to inform the Yugoslavs in advance, so as to prevent misunderstandings.[44]

The Greek government proved successful in its effort. In the autumn of 1962, the Cuban missile crisis again made Belgrade anxious to secure Athens' friendship: on 8 October, during a new Dapcevic–Karamanlis meeting, the Yugoslav Ambassador went out of his way to assure the Greeks that his country wanted to overcome the problem, and suggested that Averoff and Popovic meet in Athens.[45] An improvement of bilateral relations followed, which the British Embassy in Athens called 'unexpected': thus, in November the bilateral commercial agreement was renewed and, even more importantly, military visits were resumed.[46] Finally, Averoff and Popovic met in Athens in December and agreed that the two countries should avoid embarrassing each other on the Macedonian issue; this has perceptively been called 'an agreement of silence'.[47]

In retrospect, the Greek–Yugoslav 'special relationship' was a crucial aspect of Athens' regional policy, as it reduced geopolitical pressures on the country and increased its value as a NATO member. Common security interests pushed the two countries closer; and the Macedonian question tended to divide them. The fact is that the Greek–Yugoslav relationship depended on the international political situation. Whenever Belgrade was anxious about international affairs (and especially about Soviet intentions, as in 1956, 1958 and 1962), it tended to seek Greece's friendship. On the contrary, whenever there was relaxation of international tension, Yugoslavia tended to return to the Macedonian question.

The Turkish connection, 1959–63

The February 1959 Cyprus settlement opened the road for the revival of Greek–Turkish relations. Karamanlis expressed his views on Greek–Turkish co-operation during his visit to Ankara in May 1959: 'Greek–Turkish co-operation is a historical need. Both our governments should distribute to their citizens a map of our region. The people will then realize that we are a small island, surrounded by a Slav and communist sea.'[48] The Greek Foreign Minister, Averoff, also was an ardent supporter of Greek–Turkish friendship. Even during the difficult years of the Cyprus conflict he insisted on underlining the need for bilateral co-operation; he repeated this in an interview to the Turkish journalist Metin Toker in 1962: 'geography and history impose on us the need to co-operate'.[49]

There was more than rhetoric in these proclamations. Greece and Turkey were obvious strategic partners both in the pre-war period and in the post-war world. Despite their dispute regarding Cyprus, they were not divided by territorial claims in those years, and they both feared the Soviet Bloc. Furthermore, they were the two poorest countries of the Western alliance and often co-operated (even *during* the Cyprus crisis), trying to promote their economic interests in the alliance. After the Cyprus settlement, when Athens decided to apply for association with the EEC, it even considered a joint application with Turkey; yet the Greeks finally abandoned the idea as they were ahead of Turkey in economic development and in negotiations with the Six.[50]

Although it did not hesitate to confront Turkish policy in 1955–59, the Karamanlis government considered Turkey as an important country which could be either a valuable friend or a formidable enemy. In the late 1950s the Greek view was summed up by the Ambassador to Ankara, George Pesmazoglou, a respected political figure, whom Karamanlis had sent to the Turkish capital to work for a Cyprus settlement. In 1958, Pesmazoglou sketched the strengths and weaknesses of Turkey:[51]

> Its military forces in time of peace or war are at least equal with the forces of all the countries of the Middle East together, and its military organization improves every day. Its natural wealth is of incalculable value, and despite its present very difficult economic situation, it can and will become economically independent more quickly than is usually suggested. By constantly threatening [the West with the danger of its economic collapse] it gets more and more aid, directly or indirectly.

In the spring of 1959, shortly before Karamanlis' visit to Turkey, Pesmazoglou sent him a series of briefs on Turkish internal and external policies. Regarding internal politics, the ambassador noted that 'democracy has never functioned in Turkey until today'; he referred to the persecution of opposition leaders and to the alleged partisan role of the President of the Republic, Çelal Bayar. The ambassador noted that the only strong opposition figure was the respected statesman Ismet Inönü, who could not be persecuted, as he had been a personal associate of Kemal Atatürk. Pesmazoglou stressed that the army distrusted the government, but he did not believe that army intervention in politics was imminent. Regarding the economy, the ambassador reported that Turkey was facing a serious crisis; the government had tried to implement a large development programme, but was not successful. Still, Pesmazoglou noted, Ankara was optimistic, 'for among the Turks it is believed that, because of their strategic position, all the western countries and especially the US owe them unlimited economic assistance'. Thus, despite recent economic failures, more aid might be forthcoming: 'But the political factor of Turkey's strategic importance to the west is so important, that one could not rule out further aid to the Turkish economy, especially if one takes into account its long-term prospects'.[52]

Karamanlis' and Averoff's visit to Turkey in May 1959 confirmed the revival of the Greek–Turkish partnership. The two countries still disagreed on Middle-Eastern issues, and especially on Nasser whom Ankara strongly disliked (whereas Greece held that he could be won over for the West), but they agreed to further their common interests, mainly the preservation of balance in the Balkans. In the following years, the Turkish government allowed the Ecumenical Patriarch, Athenagoras, to travel abroad and visit the Orthodox Patriarchates in the Middle East. Furthermore, the two countries agreed to examine jointly the position of the two minorities (the Greek Orthodox in Istanbul and the Muslim in Western Thrace). This produced a document by two high-ranking diplomats, Dimitris Bitsios and Zeki Kuneralp, which became known as the Report of the Two. Athens regarded the Report as very important, but its implementation was blocked by the Turkish military coup in 1960 and then by the new crisis in Cyprus after 1963. Finally, Greece and Turkey also displayed their interest in

118 The era of functionalism, 1955–63

Cyprus developments, such as the drafting of the Cypriot constitution (both countries were represented in the constitutional committee) and the delimitation of the British bases.

Early in 1960, the Turkish Prime Minister, Adnan Menderes, faced internal problems and postponed a scheduled visit to Greece.[53] In the spring of 1960, the sudden announcement that Menderes would visit Moscow surprised and embarrassed Athens.[54] The Greek Left was also quick to note that the Turks were taking advantage of détente, while Karamanlis had failed to do so. However, as it turned out, Menderes was not destined to go on any more foreign visits. By the spring of 1960, Turkey was in serious internal turmoil. Weaknesses in the economy had forced the devaluation of the Turkish lira, with no apparent improvement in the situation (but the move hurt Greek tobacco exports). In May, there was unrest in Turkey, and Menderes sent a personal emissary, the diplomat Selim Sarper, to Athens to explain that his visit to the Greek capital should again be postponed. Karamanlis told Sarper that Athens understood Menderes' difficulties, and suggested that the only way out for the Turkish Prime Minister was to call an election immediately.[55] But Menderes was running out of time. On 27 May 1960, the army, under General Kemal Gürsel, overthrew the government and arrested Menderes, the Foreign Minister, Zorlu, and President Bayar. In 1961, Menderes and Zorlu were sentenced to death and were executed.

The Turkish coup caused great anxiety in Athens. The Greek government immediately recognized the new regime, while on 29 May the Turkish Embassy gave to Averoff a copy of the declaration of the new government which proclaimed its attachment to Greek–Turkish co-operation.[56] The Karamanlis government officially expressed its satisfaction for this, but could not conceal its concern that the new regime could prove neutralist; moreover, Athens worried about the course of events in Cyprus, since it was Menderes who had signed the 1959 agreements.[57] In a brief drafted for Karamanlis shortly before his summer 1960 visit to Yugoslavia, the Greek Foreign Ministry suggested that no one could foresee future Turkish foreign policy, the more so because there were indications that lower-rank officers were involved in the coup, as in the Nasserite model. But the brief also noted that Selim Sarper had become Foreign Minister, a development which allowed for optimism. Sarper was a staunchly pro-Western figure whom Greek diplomacy knew very well: he had proved a difficult opponent when he had led the Turkish delegation during the UN debates on Cyprus.[58] In July 1960, visiting Paris, Karamanlis told the French Prime Minister, Michel Debré, that he did not think that Turkey would drift away from the West. Although French officials thought that the coup had damaged Turkey's credibility in NATO, the Greeks downplayed the significance of developments in Ankara in the hope that Turkey's bonds to NATO would not be weakened.[59] Athens did not want to be left alone as the West's only frontline state in the region.

Greek fears were allayed during Sarper's visit to Athens on 20–22 October 1960, the first high-level bilateral meeting after the Turkish coup. The Turkish Foreign Minister again declared his country's support for Greek–Turkish co-operation. After the end of the official programme of the visit, Sarper spent some days as a personal guest of Averoff in his native Metsovo, in Epirus.[60] Thus, the Greek–Turkish relationship seemed to overcome the shock of the May coup. In March 1961, the Greek Ambassador to Ankara, Matsas, dispatched to Karamanlis a new series of memoranda on Turkish policy. These reveal the Greek relief that Turkey remained attached to the West following the 1960 coup. However, Matsas was less optimistic regarding the Turkish economy and the political scene. Although he predicted that a civilian government would soon take over, probably under Inönü, he also stressed that the Turkish military regime had failed to improve the economy or to create its own 'revolutionary' ideology. Turkey was dependent on Western aid, which would continue in the future because of Turkey's strategic importance to the West.[61] In September, from Istanbul, Matsas again expressed concern at internal political developments, when he reported the executions of Menderes and Zorlu. The ambassador made clear his dismay about the executions (which he attributed to the hard-liners, but not to the leaders of the army), and noted that Menderes and Zorlu had been immensely popular. Matsas noted that the country was bitterly divided and would continue to be so in the future:[62]

> The facets of the public deceive no one. Despite the long and tragic tradition of this city and of this country, where loss of power often entailed loss of life, millions of supporters of the executed leaders will, beginning tomorrow, plan their revenge.

Thus, the paramount consideration of Greece regarding Turkey involved Ankara's continuing attachment to the West. Significantly, when in 1962–63 Turkey decided to seek its own association with the EEC, the Karamanlis government supported this prospect, although it also indicated that it would need to monitor negotiations in order to protect the interests of Greek farmers. Karamanlis supported Turkish association during his contacts with Western European statesmen in 1963; for example, he did so during his conversation with the Dutch Prime Minister, Jan de Quay.[63] Furthermore, as the Foreign Ministry noted in a circular to the Greek Embassies, 'Greece does not believe that it has the right to block the association of any third state with the EEC'.[64]

Despite a successful visit to Ankara by Averoff in August 1962, which again confirmed the strategic partnership of the two countries,[65] Greek–Turkish relations deteriorated in 1963 because of disputes over fishing rights in the Aegean. In June 1963 the Karamanlis government fell, and in the autumn new developments brought about a new crisis in Greek–Turkish relations which, once more, radically transformed the problems of Greek security.

The Cyprus Republic: new dimensions of national security

The 1959 Cyprus settlement resulted in the establishment, for the first time in modern history, of a 'brother' state in the Eastern Mediterranean. This created one of the most delicate problems that the 1955–63 strategy of functionalism was called to face. The 1959 Zurich and London agreements provided for the setting up of an independent Cypriot state, and excluded both Enosis (union with Greece) and partition. The independence, the territorial integrity and the constitution of Cyprus were guaranteed by Britain, Greece and Turkey, while the new state formed an alliance with Athens and Ankara; the Treaties of Guarantee and of Alliance had constitutional force. Britain retained sovereign bases on the island.

The principles that guided the Karamanlis government's policy regarding Cyprus' international position deserve to be reviewed here. There were three major guiding lines. First, the Karamanlis government believed that Athens and Nicosia should avoid maximalism. Cyprus lay close to an extremely dangerous region, the Middle East, and the Greek armed forces did not have the operational capabilities to reach this area. Thus, the Karamanlis government regarded that Cyprus should avoid unnecessary entanglements in regional disputes. During the negotiations which led to the 1959 settlement, Athens resisted British participation in the Treaty of Alliance between Greece, Turkey and Cyprus. This was because Athens wanted to rule out the possibility that either itself or Cyprus would be drawn into an Anglo–Arab conflict (the Suez adventure was too recent to be ignored). Athens also ensured that Greece, Turkey and Cyprus gave a partial, not a full, guarantee of the British bases, involving only the territorial integrity of the bases but not an obligation to go to war against any power that declared war on Britain and attacked the bases.[66]

Second, the Karamanlis government fervently encouraged Archbishop Makarios to bring the new state firmly into the Western world: this was expected to strengthen Cypriot security in this troubled region. However, to integrate into the West, Cyprus needed to implement the Zurich–London agreements; this was a major precondition for a promising future. In April 1961, the Cypriot Minister of the Interior, Polykarpos Giorkatzis, spoke to Averoff about Turkish-Cypriot illegal arming, asked that Athens provide him with weapons, and threatened to denounce the Greek government if it refused to do so. Averoff literally threw him out if his office and then wrote a letter to Makarios warning that such tendencies should be checked, or else there would be a crisis in Athens–Nicosia relations.[67] The implementation of the 1959 agreements and the Western option of Cyprus were the two sides of the same coin; one could not be done without the other.

The possibility of Cypriot entry into NATO was addressed in the Zurich–London agreements. During a meeting on 29 January 1959, before the Zurich Conference, Makarios agreed with Karamanlis that Cyprus should become a NATO member. The Karamanlis–Menderes 'gentlemen's agreement', signed in Zurich, provided for Greek and Turkish support to a future Cypriot application to join NATO.[68] However, Cyprus did not enter NATO, as the US military and the British were unfavourable to such a prospect.[69] There was, however, an alternative strategy for integration into the West, namely association with the EEC, which the Karamanlis government suggested to Makarios, especially in 1962. Yet Nicosia decided to follow Britain's lead: Cyprus showed interest in association with the Community in 1961–62, when Britain had applied to accede, but when de Gaulle vetoed British entry the Cypriot interest for association also evaporated.[70]

Regional functionalism 121

The third guiding principle of the Karamanlis government involved the delicate issue of Athens–Nicosia relations. Even before 1959, the Karamanlis government did not embrace the notion that Greece was the 'national centre' which should impose its will on the Greek Cypriots. After the establishment of the Cyprus Republic the Karamanlis government projected its own view, which could be called the 'theory of the two independent states'. This held that Athens had an obligation to show concern for Cyprus, to give advice, but not to see to impose it upon the Greek Cypriots.[71] Simultaneously, the Karamanlis government carefully avoided any joint Greek–Turkish interventions in the internal Cypriot scene. During his August 1962 visit to Ankara, Averoff reminded the Turks that Greece and Turkey did not exercise any kind of imperium in Cyprus.[72]

The 'theory of the two independent states' was not a blank cheque for Makarios; it was quite the opposite. This became clear in April 1963, when Makarios suggested an extensive revision of the Cypriot constitution – an initiative with which Athens strongly disagreed, as it could spark a new crisis in the island and in Greek–Turkish relations. In a letter to Makarios, Averoff noted that if Greek–Turkish relations remained good it might even be possible to make minor revisions which would render the Cypriot regime more functional. However, if Makarios caused a crisis, the Greek government would publicly disagree and would even be prepared to hold an election on exactly this issue. Averoff then presented the heart of the 'theory of the two independent states':[73]

> I am not asking you to take any specific action. We have worked for your independence and we wish to respect it absolutely. You will do what you think right. I simply wanted you to know our views. Guided by them alone, and without allowing ourselves to de deflected by political controversy, we shall do our duty to the nation.

This point is crucial in understanding the Karamanlis government's policy towards Cyprus, as well as the magnitude of the change which occurred in 1964. The Karamanlis government regarded that Cyprus and Greece were brother, but independent, states, which meant that in case of a disagreement, Greece could threaten Nicosia with eventual abandonment. Nicosia should not be in a position to drag Athens to its own line.

Functionalism was a comprehensive and flexible response to the problems (economic, military, regional and international) of Greek national security policy of 1955–63. However, in 1963, as the Karamanlis government fell, the Centre Union won the autumn election and John F. Kennedy was assassinated in Texas, the old questions tended to emerge in new forms. Was functionalism capable of facing the problems of détente? Was Cyprus going to remain calm and, if not, how should Greece respond to a new crisis? What would be the effects of a new Cyprus crisis on the Greek public opinion? As 1963 was coming to its end, new important challenges appeared on the horizon.

Part III
The era of multiple fronts, 1963–67

11 Facing new challenges

Years of instability

In 1963–67, as the international system was moving towards détente, Greece had to adjust to a partially different world. At first sight a frontline state should have welcomed the prospect of détente, but, in practice, international developments puzzled officials in Athens. The Greek leaders – both of the Right and of the Centre – were not afraid of Bulgaria and the Soviet Bloc simply because these countries were Communist; the unfortunate legacies of southeastern Europe would not necessarily fade away in a climate of East–West détente. The new governing party in Athens, the Centre Union (CU), supported a more relaxed policy towards the East, but had never disputed the existence of a 'menace from the north', with its various historical, geographical and Cold War aspects. Furthermore, a new security problem now occurred: the new conflict in Cyprus forced Athens to face successive crises east of its borders, even the prospect of war with Turkey. Ironically, Greece's problems multiplied after 1963.

On Cyprus, things were even more complicated. In contrast to the 1950s, when it had tried to play the role of an honest broker between its allies, in the 1960s the US was directly involved in the search for a settlement. This was not surprising: the Greek–Turkish conflict of the 1950s had been waged mostly by diplomatic means; now it became a military confrontation which represented a severe threat to NATO cohesion. Thus, Washington was forced to step in: US interests and prestige came in the line of fire of the Cyprus crisis. However, the US itself was changing: without the crushing nuclear superiority of the past, entangled in Vietnam and faced with the Gaullist rebellion within NATO, Washington tended to show less tolerance for the 'special' circumstances of a local dispute in the backyard of the alliance.[1] On the part of Greece, handling this US intervention required an exceptionally high quality of leadership.

Moreover, Greece now faced an intense political crisis. During a period of four years no less than ten governments held power, including caretaker ones – which were still forced to handle explosive situations or even full-scale crises in Cyprus. The CU itself formed two governments, of which the first (November–December 1963) did not have an overall majority in Parliament. Even after its electoral triumph of February 1964, though, when it received 53 per cent of the vote and secured a large parliamentary majority, the CU continued to be a loose conglomeration of various political groups. Furthermore, the Centre soon lost its universally recognized expert on foreign affairs, Sophocles Venizelos, who died suddenly during the 1964 electoral campaign. The 1964–65 CU government faced great problems of cohesion, which culminated in the break-up of the party in July 1965. During the July–September 1965 'apostasy', important figures left the CU: the Deputy Prime Minister and Minister for Economic Co-ordination; the Speaker of Parliament; and the Ministers for Foreign Affairs, Interior, National Defence, Economy, Labour and Transport. The 1965–66 'apostates' government was in a very difficult position: it faced the onslaught of the CU, which accused the 'apostates' of treachery, depended on the vote of the Conservatives (now under the leadership of Panayiotis Kanellopoulos) and never managed to acquire popular support.[2]

These problems posed severe difficulties in foreign policy-making. Greece now faced multiple fronts on its northern border, in Cyprus and in the Aegean. Moreover, during 1952–63, under the Papagos or the Karamanlis governments, Greek policy had been centrally controlled and, despite exaggerations, phobias and mistakes, there was a single line pursued. However, in 1963–67 no person or group managed to assume full control over Greek policy. Short-lived, pressed by the internal crisis, distrustful of Makarios and Nicosia, the 1963–67 governments were forced to a piecemeal handling of individual issues and had constantly to turn their attention from one front to the other.

George Papandreou: attempting to combine rhetoric and practical needs

Few politicians of post-war Greece could boast of the indisputable pro-Western credentials of George Papandreou. After serving as a cabinet minister under Eleftherios Venizelos during the inter-war period, he became in 1943 the first leading Greek political figure to point to the danger of a Communist takeover. In a memorandum which he wrote from occupied Athens to the Greek government-in-exile and to the British authorities in Cairo, Papandreou noted that a new era of world history was beginning, as two major fronts were being formed: 'Communist Panslavism and Liberal Anglosaxonism'. He stated that Greece, together with Turkey, should be firmly on the side of the latter: 'Greece and Turkey are destined to be allies of England, as they are natural enemies of the advanced posts of Panslavism in the Balkans, and natural guardians of the exit to the Mediterranean'.[3] In 1944 he became Prime Minister of the government-in-exile. He played a major role in inflicting a political defeat on the Communist-led EAM during the May 1944 Lebanon Conference, which largely determined Greece's post-war international position. Greece was liberated during his premiership in October 1944, while in December he headed the government in the battle with EAM for the control of the capital. The political victory over EAM, liberation, the retention of Greece in the West, and the pressure on the reluctant

Bulgarian Communists to withdraw from Eastern Macedonia and Western Thrace formed Papandreou's political masterpiece, without which there could be no question of integration in the West, European options or functionalisms.

Yet, in the post-war period Papandreou did not manage to win wide popular support. His Democratic Socialist Party failed to become a major political force: the moderate reformist forces were crushed in the passions of the civil war, and then, in the early 1950s, Papagos' Rally emerged as an instrument for reform and swept away everything else. In 1952 Papandreou was elected on the Rally ticket, and in 1953 he became the co-leader of the Liberal Party. However, in the following years he was involved in a hard struggle with Sophocles Venizelos over the leadership of the Centre. The infra-Centre quarrel was relentless: it caused a split of the Liberals in 1955, reunification in 1957 and a new split in 1958, in the aftermath of the general election in which the Liberals were defeated by the EDA and came third with a mere 20 per cent of the vote. In 1959–60, disappointed by these developments, Papandreou offered to join Karamanlis' ERE, but in 1961 he became the leader of the newly-founded Centre Union. As leader of the CU he launched a fierce attack on Karamanlis, the 'relentless struggle', accusing the Right of conducting a fraudulent election in 1961, failing on social issues, being subservient to the Americans, of making grave mistakes on the Macedonian issue and betraying Cyprus. Papandreou emerged as the Centre's alternative to Karamanlis.

In 1963–64, George Papandreou once more proudly declared his major political priority, namely Greece's Western orientation. 'History and Geography have placed Greece in the Free World', he stated during the presentation of his first government to Parliament in December 1963.[4] In April 1964 he told the Secretary General of NATO, Dirk Stikker, that Greece always aimed to be a loyal NATO member,[5] and in November 1964 he told Stikker's successor, Manlio Brosio, that 'both history and geography place us in NATO, at the front of the defence of the free world'.[6] At the same time, the CU called for a new policy towards the East. The Prime Minister declared that Greece wanted to be 'an ally of the west and a friend of the east'.[7] However, these were all rather general declarations of principle, the favourite field of George Papandreou – the best orator in Greek politics in the twentieth century.

It has been noted that 'in the perception of the menace from the north, Papandreou's strategic thinking was no different from that of Karamanlis'.[8] This was an important element of continuity between these two periods. Papandreou continued to regard a localized Bulgarian attack as possible. Thus, presenting his first government in Parliament, Papandreou declared that Athens was ready to start new negotiations with Bulgaria, but also referred to the dangers for 'Peace and Freedom' arising from the possibility of general or local war.[9] He mentioned the problem of local Bulgarian attack in his conversations with the NATO Secretary General, Stikker, in April 1964, and with Stikker's successor, Brosio, in November. This was a major priority of the Prime Minister.

In late December 1963 a new crisis erupted in Cyprus, which forced Greece to face the possibility of Greek–Turkish war. Aware of the unfavourable military realities, but also focusing on the 'menace from the north', Papandreou wished to avoid this: 'It is inconceivable to think of and study the possibility of a Greek–Turkish war', he said during a meeting of the political leaders on 25 January 1964, after the first Turkish invasion scare.[10] Presenting his second government to Parliament in March 1964, Papandreou noted that Greek–Turkish friendship was necessary for both countries, but that if Ankara invaded Cyprus, a Greek–Turkish war would ensue.[11] As will be shown, this was aimed at deterring Ankara and avoiding a war.

Yet in examining Papandreou's analysis, additional factors need to be taken into consideration. First, the Prime Minister was very skilful in epigrams; it has been alleged that he liked big words that didn't necessarily have much to do with reality.[12] The US Embassy even noted that at times his rhetoric appeared to be a substitute for careful examination of issues.[13] The first view was harsh, the second unfair: Papandreou did not lack the capacity for strategic thinking but he often could not resist the temptation of a clever epigram, and this could create, for third parties, an impression that he only cared for rhetoric. Moreover, Papandreou sometimes tended to exaggerate in a manner incompatible with the pressing needs of Greek security. For example, in August 1964 he formulated the doctrine of the 'national centre' in a letter to Makarios, and referred to the eventual union of Cyprus with Greece, 'which will allow Cyprus to undertake a new historic mission: to become Hellenism's base for civilizing the East'.[14] He obviously liked this phrase and repeated it a few days later, speaking to the officers of the Third Army Corps in Thessaloniki. This was a public speech and, understandably, the Turks could hardly welcome such a suggestion,[15] which after all was insulting to third parties. Again, one should not overestimate these rhetorical excesses; they were ornaments of Papandreou's rhetoric, and did not form a practical political programme.

However, there was another level where the Prime Minister's rhetoric could prove damaging: his tendency to use foreign policy issues to gain internal political advantage. He often said that his government pursued a 'Greek foreign policy', apparently implying that the previous ones had pursued something else; this was part of the legacy of the previous years, when the Centre had attacked Karamanlis' policy as being subservient to the Americans. Throughout 1964, Papandreou kept denouncing the Karamanlis government's Cyprus policy. This was very dangerous: it unnecessarily intensified internal divisions on foreign policy issues at a time when a government dealing with a Cyprus crisis had an interest in promoting consensus. His heights of rhetoric tended to trap Papandreou in maximalist positions from which he could not easily disentangle himself. This was to become painfully evident in the case of the 1964 Acheson Plan for Cyprus.

There were other practical problems as well. The Centre had an explosive recent history of internal disputes, and Papandreou's co-ordination was not always effective, probably because the Cyprus crises distracted him; he admitted as much in a letter to the Economics Minister, Constantinos Mitsotakis, who complained about the lack of co-ordination in the government in August 1964.[16]

However, even on Cyprus, the Prime Minister's control over policy was rather loose. In spring 1964, facing repeated Turkish invasion threats, the government decided to aid the Cyprus Republic by dispatching an armed force to the island. Initially, in April, Athens sent 2,000 men, but when the third Turkish invasion scare occurred in June, the Minister of National Defence, Petros Garoufalias, took the initiative to dispatch another 6,000 men, without actually informing Papandreou – who (as Garoufalias claimed) learned the exact number of Greek troops in Cyprus in July, after Turkey protested at the UN about their presence.[17] Of course, from the operational point of view the movement of additional troops might have been considered as necessary, and Papandreou had already given orders to secure Cyprus' defence.[18] The initiative to *quadruple* the Greek troops in Cyprus without telling the Prime Minister, though, was at least unusual. Such a thing would have been totally unthinkable under Papagos or Karamanlis.

Thus a complicated picture emerges. George Papandreou's analysis was a mixture of many ingredients: rhetorical maximalism but also realism; anti-Communism and fear of the Soviet Union, but also a disposition to promote relations with the East; a priority on internal political considerations but also an ardent desire to bring about Enosis. All these could painfully prove contradictory. In an interview with this author, Constantinos Mitsotakis insisted that George Papandreou had greater abilities than people usually acknowledge.[19] However, he did not control developments, and his tendency to use foreign-policy issues (mainly Cyprus) as a stick with which to beat the Conservative opposition tended to trap him into irreversibly maximalist positions. This did not facilitate the effective handling of extremely pressing foreign policy and security problems.

Finally, George Papandreou should not be confused with his son, Andreas, who served as Minister for the Prime Minister's Office in spring 1964, and as Alternate Minister for Economic Co-ordination in the spring–autumn of 1964 and again in May–July 1965. Andreas Papandreou finally emerged in 1966 as the main leader of the Centre-left and was strongly distrusted by the Americans. In this book, the name Papandreou will refer to the Prime Minister; any reference to Andreas Papandreou will include his first name.

'Apostates'

The July–September 1965 'apostasy' resulted in three governments, under George Athanassiades-Novas, Elias Tsirimokos and Stephanos Stephanopoulos. Only the third secured an overall majority in Parliament, thanks to the support of the Conservative party, the ERE, and it remained in power until December 1966. The leaders of this government had served under George Papandreou in the CU. The Stephanopoulos government made a determined effort to reach a Cyprus settlement, which would have ended the overextension of Greece's diplomatic and military capabilities, but it was a weak administration that did not have the time or the backing fully to implement its policy. Moreover, it was burdened by one of the most painful problems of the Centre: extremely bad relations with Makarios.

130 *The era of multiple fronts, 1963–67*

The 'apostates' were a curious mix. They included major CU cabinet ministers as well as many lesser figures, whose support was necessary to build a parliamentary majority; former supporters of General Grivas's movement in 1960–61 (Stephanopoulos among them), as well as people like Athanassiades-Novas and Mitsotakis who were prominent in resisting Grivas; and, last but not least, in their ranks was found Elias Tsirimokos, a major figure of the Centre-left who had participated in the EAM resistance movement during the 1941–44 occupation. The main cabinet ministers of this government were the barons of the old Liberal Centre, of which the outward-looking, cosmopolitan and somehow aristocratic tradition they felt they represented, as inheritors of old Venizelism. Later, they put forward the view that they became involved in the apostasy in order to prevent polarization between the Centre and the Palace, which could push the latter to the imposition of a military dictatorship. However, they seriously miscalculated the effects of their move: in 1965–66 they were viciously accused by the CU and the Papandreous of treachery and of becoming puppets of the Right and the Palace. The 'apostates' failed to create a popular base, and their defection from the Centre led its masses – now radicalized through conflict with the Palace – to identify unequivocally with George Papandreou and his son, Andreas.

Stephanopoulos had Rightist roots, and had served as Papagos' Foreign Minister in 1952–55. He joined the CU in 1961, and in 1964 he became Deputy Prime Minister and Minister for Economic Co-ordination. However, as Prime Minister he remained a *primus inter pares* and a rather weak leader. The main figure of the 'apostates' government was Constantinos Mitsotakis. A Cretan with close family ties to the Venizelos family, Mitsotakis had participated in the island's resistance against the Germans in 1941–44. He had also managed to arrange a deal with the Communist resistance, and thus played a major role in the unusual Cretan achievement of avoiding civil war in the island. After the war Mitsotakis distinguished himself as a young member of the Liberals, becoming Undersecretary for the Economy in early 1951 at the age of thirty-two; a few months later he became a member of the cabinet, as Minister for Transport. Mitsotakis disagreed with Sophocles Venizelos' effort in 1960–61 to promote George Grivas as a figurehead who would unite the Centre, and thus, he played an important role in George Papandreou's prevalence over Sophocles Venizelos in the struggle for the leadership of the Centre. After the death of Sophocles Venizelos in 1964, Mitsotakis emerged as the main representative of the much-cherished Venizelist tradition of the Centre. He was Economics Minister in 1964–65, and Minister for Economic Co-ordination in 1965–66. In the apostates government he practically dominated the formulation of policy; his biographer perceptively called him 'informal prime minister' of that government. Although he mostly dealt with the home front, he also greatly influenced foreign policy: he insisted on Greece's integration in the West, on the need to revive Greek–Turkish co-operation, and on a policy of pragmatism and moderation. Furthermore, Mitsotakis tried to rationalize Greece's external trade, including commerce with the East, as a means of ensuring the country's smooth integration into the international economy. Finally, he led the effort to step up the implementation of the Association agreement with the EEC. Mitsotakis had a comprehensive view of Greece's position in the world, but his participation in the apostasy turned large parts of the public against him.[20]

A new strategy: the doctrine of the 'national centre'

In 1950–52, as agitation within Greece over Cyprus mounted, the Centre coalition governments had pursued a cautious policy: they refused to yield to Makarios' pressure to appeal to the UN, and the archbishop publicly denounced them for this.[21] However, the Centre was crushed by Papagos in the 1952 election, and in the following years its hopes for a quick return to power were dashed. After 1955, going through successive electoral defeats and internal crises, the Centre moved to much harder positions on Cyprus. Its leaders did not hold identical views: in 1957, speaking with US diplomats, Sophocles Venizelos seemed to accept the prospect of guaranteed independence for Cyprus, but George Papandreou told the British that it would be unacceptable to the Greek public.[22] In the summer of 1957, Venizelos proposed that Makarios assume the leadership of the Centre, unite the opposition and bring the Karamanlis government down, but the archbishop, who after all was not a Centrist, rejected the idea.[23] When the Cyprus settlement was reached in 1959 in Zurich, the two Centre leaders took exactly the opposing positions compared to 1957: during a Parliament debate, Venizelos (who had ousted Papandreou and now was the leader of the Liberals) noted that his party would work for the revision of the agreements when it came to power. Papandreou, who was now trying to approach Karamanlis, stressed that upsetting the agreements would be contrary to national interest, because Greece would then be 'led to the abyss': 'the struggles are being waged in the name of ideals; life materializes the possible'.[24]

Later, during the years of the 'relentless struggle', these differences were patched up and an anti-Karamanlis consensus prevailed in the Centre. In the electoral year of 1963, the attack against 'the sell out of Zurich' could greatly benefit a rising political force. Thus, now Papandreou strongly criticized the 1959 Zurich and London agreements; he even said in Parliament that the military aspect of the agreements (namely, the stationing in Cyprus of Turkish troops, along with the Greek contingent) was 'a blasphemy against the eternity of Hellenism'.[25] When Karamanlis resigned and left for Zurich in June 1963, Papandreou delivered in Parliament another of his famous aphorisms, noting that Karamanlis had 'returned to Zurich, the place of the national crime'.[26]

By 1963, many (including Makarios) took it for granted that the CU would favour an effort to overthrow the 1959 agreements.[27] Indeed, by mid-1963 Makarios' position had become bizarre: he wanted to revise the agreements. Moreover, since Karamanlis had fallen from power, the archbishop saw no reason why he alone should remain accused of having committed 'blasphemy against the eternity of Hellenism' (because he had signed the 1959 agreements). However, the CU did not want another Cyprus adventure. Venizelos, who had denounced the Cyprus settlement in 1959, now came to its defence, and Papandreou wanted to use the memories of 'Zurich' as a stick with which to beat Karamanlis, but not to plunge himself in an adventure to overthrow the Cyprus settlement.[28] In November 1963 Makarios proposed his much debated Thirteen Points for the revision of the Cypriot constitution, without notifying Athens.

Relations between the CU leaders and Makarios were strained, and the latter's unilateral initiative intensified the problem. When, in late December 1963, the inter-communal clashes erupted on the island, Papandreou stressed to the Ambassador of Cyprus, Nicos Kranidiotis, that 'every move in Cyprus must be made in concert with Athens'.[29] On 29 December 1963, in a letter to Makarios, Venizelos accused the archbishop of presenting Greece with faits accomplis. Venizelos noted that the agreements 'for independent Cyprus' could be revised only through negotiations and not through violence, and warned that both major Greek political parties would jointly oppose Makarios' policy.[30]

Makarios, though, continued his unilateral initiatives. In January 1964 he publicly appealed for Soviet support, terrifying the leaders of both the Greek Right and the Centre. From Athens' point of view, this made it important to 'control Makarios'. Thus, in February 1964, after the CU's electoral triumph, and seemingly all-powerful after the death of his old rival Venizelos, Papandreou needed to formulate a new policy. As he told the US Ambassador, Henry Labouisse, he decided to discipline the Greek Cypriots.[31] At the same time, Athens officially supported unlimited independence for Cyprus, which would include the right of self-determination. In practice, another solution was preferred, namely outright Enosis, or union with Greece. A perceptive scholar has referred to the 'fatal "unionist" euphoria' of the spring of 1964, which appeared to render Greek policy careless.[32] The Greek government told its Western allies that there was a simple dilemma: either the NATification of Cyprus through Enosis, or its transformation to another Cuba.[33]

The need to control Makarios, and the optimistic feeling that Enosis was round the corner, brought about the formulation of the doctrine of the 'national centre'. This was articulated in a letter by Papandreou to Makarios on 25 February 1964, only a few days after the CU's electoral triumph. Papandreou declared:[34]

> In the very meaning of the unity of Hellenism, and because of the increased responsibilities of Athens as the Centre of Hellenism, I wish to declare my fervent desire that full and constant contact and co-ordination exist between us. If circumstances call for it, there could even be an agreed disagreement.

Makarios had no problem with this. On 1 March he replied that he certainly wished for co-ordination with Athens: 'For I believe, as you do, that the Greek Nation is a united total, of which a part is Cyprus, looking towards Athens as the centre of united Hellenism'.[35] Nevertheless, in practice the archbishop continued to act as he pleased. In April, without prior notification to Athens, the Cyprus government forces attacked the Turkish-Cypriot enclave of St Hilarion. This precipitated a new crisis and renewed fears of a Greek–Turkish war. The NATO Secretary General, Dirk Stikker, visited Athens and told Papandreou that in the event of a Greek–Turkish conflict, the alliance would remain neutral and cease aid to both countries.[36] For Greece, which remained in a position of military inferiority vis-à-vis Bulgaria and always feared 'abandonment' by its senior NATO partners, this could have entailed a serious deterioration of its security position. From Athens' point of view, failure to 'discipline' Makarios proved extremely painful, and Greece was called to pay the price for the archbishop's unilateral initiatives. Still, in June the US prevented a Turkish invasion by the blunt letter of President Lyndon B. Johnson to the Turkish Prime Minister, Ismet Inönü.[37]

In the summer of 1964 negotiations started, aiming to reach a settlement which would provide for union of Cyprus with Greece, in exchange for the annexation or lease of the Cypriot Karpass peninsula to Turkey. This became known as the Acheson Plan. Makarios was known to reject these notions. In early August, the Greek-Cypriot National Guard launched another attack on the Turkish-Cypriot enclave in Mansura, thus embarrassing the Papandreou government, which had assured the Turks and the Americans that the island would remain calm. The Mansura attack was interpreted in Athens as an effort to torpedo the Acheson negotiations, while Makarios' simultaneous public call for Soviet assistance created alarm in Athens, which realized that it could be drawn into a war on the side of the wrong alliance. Papandreou sent an angry message to Makarios and to George Grivas, the leader of the Greek forces on the island: 'we agree on certain issues and you do otherwise'.[38] However, by the end of August Makarios forced Athens to reject the Acheson Plan and dashed Papandreou's hopes for Enosis. Once more, Athens' Cyprus policy was a shambles. Papandreou told the US Ambassador that he had been engaged in a struggle for survival with the archbishop, and asked for time to clear things with him.[39]

The Greek Prime Minister reacted with a new letter to Makarios on 29 August, which restated the national centre doctrine. Papandreou stressed that the two governments had agreed to ensure peace on the island; in case of unprovoked Turkish invasion, Enosis would be proclaimed by the Greek and the Cypriot Parliaments, and 'Greece, with all its forces, will stand by Cyprus'. Yet, there was an important question: who would be responsible for deciding the response to a Turkish initiative? Papandreou explained that this had to be clarified quickly, because if hostilities started it would be too late:[40]

> In that case, Greece will face a tragic dilemma: it will either refuse to participate [in a war] and its absence will be judged as national treason; or it will participate because it will be miserably dragged in it [...] This, Your Beatitude, cannot go on. In earlier days [...] we had agreed that the leadership of Hellenism, and the political and military initiative, should belong to Athens, which co-ordinates the struggle. But today we are not talking merely of a theoretical case. According to our decisions, which have also been made public, *an armed conflict between Turkey and Cyprus will*

immediately lead Greece into the war. And war is too big an issue for Greece to allow itself to be dragged in it, by the initiatives of others [...] I therefore ask that in the future our agreement must be respected fully and always. [This agreement] twice has already been violated. *No decision will be made in Cyprus, leading directly or indirectly to hostilities, without prior consultation and agreement with us.* If we agree, all will be good. If we disagree, Athens' view must prevail, because Athens bears the responsibility for all Hellenism. In that case, if Nicosia persists in its disagreement, this disagreement will be, honestly and in a manly way, announced to the Nation. And each will take his responsibilities and the consequences before the Nation.

Makarios delayed his reply until February 1965. In his letter the archbishop agreed that Athens should be competent to decide on any issue which could lead to war, but he also reserved his right 'to disagree with any solution leading to compromises which are unacceptable from Cyprus's point of view'.[41]

After the internal political crisis of the apostasy, which removed Papandreou from power, the Stephanopoulos government consisted of supporters of the national centre doctrine, with one important exception: the Foreign Minister, Elias Tsirimokos, who supported Makarios. However, in the spring of 1966 Tsirimokos resigned over the issue of an Athens–Nicosia disagreement regarding the Greek-Cypriot National Guard; after that, the Prime Minister, Stephanopoulos, declared that his government accepted the doctrine of the national centre.[42] The new Foreign Minister, Admiral (retd) Ioannis Toumbas, attempted to solve the Cyprus question through a bilateral Greek–Turkish negotiation.

Unlike Papandreou, who tried to get a general agreement of Makarios to the notion that Athens was the national centre of Hellenism, the 'apostates' tried to secure Makarios' assent to a specific solution, namely Enosis in exchange for ceding to Turkey one of the British bases in Cyprus. This seemed more realistic, but the Cyprus policy of the 'apostates' was burdened by their extremely bad relations with the archbishop. In 1965 Stephanopoulos had spoken of 'Luciferic' forces which had blocked the Acheson Plan, obviously meaning Makarios. In early 1965 the pro-apostates newspaper, *Eleftheria*, had suggested that 'Mr. Makarios' (which is an insulting expression in the Orthodox world) should 'simply follow orders'. Mutual trust never existed between the President of Cyprus and the Centre governments of Athens. Both Mitsotakis, the most important personality of the 'apostates' government, and Vyron Theodoropoulos, the head of the Cyprus 'desk' of the Foreign Ministry in 1965–66, point out that Makarios in effect never definitely agreed with the policy of that government, namely Enosis in exchange for giving the Turks one of the British bases. 'The time of truth had not come', Mitsotakis told this author.[43] Thus, even this more restricted version of the doctrine of the national centre failed to bring about agreement between Athens and Nicosia.

Any criticism of the national centre doctrine must take into account two important considerations. First, the doctrine was a radical break, compared to the policy of the Karamanlis governments. The latter had focused on the independent character of the Cyprus Republic, suggested that Cyprus should assume responsibility for its actions, and thus threatened to leave Makarios alone in a crisis, as Averoff did in his letter to the archbishop on 19 April 1963. However, there can be little doubt that the national centre concept was much more popular than the policy of the Karamanlis governments. Second, it should be kept in mind that the doctrine of the national centre was a refined strategy; it did not entail that Athens ruled Cyprus as a Greek province. Athens' prerogative involved two kinds of decisions: any initiative which could lead to war; and the right of Athens to negotiate with Turkey an Enosis solution. Makarios insisted that Cypriot independence should not be the subject of a Greek–Turkish negotiation. This was accepted in May 1965 by the Papandreou government, and in February 1966 by the Stephanopoulos administration.[44]

Nowadays, the doctrine of the national centre is almost universally criticized as a bad policy, certain to lead to a dead-end.[45] First, Makarios was not the kind of leader who would give Athens a free hand, and thus the national centre doctrine in fact widened an already existing gap between Athens and Nicosia. Second, the doctrine dealt a blow to Cypriot independence, since it implied that the Cyprus Republic should subject important decisions to the policy-making process of another state. For the Papandreou and the Stephanopoulos governments, which wanted to bring about Enosis (thus to abolish the Cyprus Republic), this was compatible with their policy. However, the overall picture was full of contradictions: Athens and Nicosia were going to the UN, waging Cypriot independence as their major weapon and as a rallying cry to acquire international support against the eventuality of a Turkish invasion. At the same time, Athens itself was degrading Cypriot independence and was arguing that unless Cyprus became NATO territory through Enosis, it would be transformed into a 'Mediterranean Cuba'.

More importantly, the doctrine of the national centre was a profoundly impractical concept: it never managed to keep Makarios under control. The archbishop had no problem in paying lip service to it, but in effect he did as he wished. Even in the case of an Athens–Nicosia disagreement (in which, according to George Papandreou, each would take his responsibilities towards the nation), it was Athens, not Nicosia, that would be placed in a difficult position. Athens declared that it was the 'national centre of Hellenism', and had assured Nicosia of Greek support in case of war. Athens had noted in writing that non-participation in such a conflict would amount to treason. After the outbreak of a crisis, it would be impossible under any circumstances for the 'national centre' to abandon the junior partner of this relationship. Thus, the national centre doctrine tended to limit Athens', not Makarios', options. To put it simply, if Athens wanted to be able to threaten to abandon Makarios and thus to 'control' him, it should have avoided at all costs any notion of 'national centres'.

The national centre doctrine had repercussions which were extending well beyond Cyprus, the field of its immediate implementation. Greek forces were already insufficient to cover the northern border; now they had to overextend their capabilities to cover Cyprus and the Aegean as well. After 1964, the Greek armed forces had to be present everywhere but without being sufficient anywhere. Thus, the national centre concept resulted in a defence maximalism which Greece's means – diplomatic, military or economic – simply could not support. It was Greece's most well-known *Realpolitiker*, Panayiotis Pipinelis, who stressed this during a Parliament debate on 24 April 1964. Pipinelis suggested that Greece might have to compensate Turkey for Enosis. He also noted the danger of overstretch, since the Cyprus entanglement tended to weaken Greek positions in other parts of the region: 'It is not enough to say and be content simply by saying that we are right'. In his reply, Papandreou took a different line: he said that Greece wanted peace and would defend itself if attacked. On the problem of concessions to Turkey, the Prime Minister counterattacked:[46]

> What more could we do? Should we make national sacrifices to secure Turkish acquiescence? Never [Applause]. Sacrifices have been made in the past. We do not want to remember them. But do not force us to remember them. [and, when Pipinelis said that he had not referred to such things] I will mention them since you want me to. I am talking about the concessions made by the Zurich and London treaties. [Applause].

Unlike Papandreou, who is known as the 'old man of democracy', Pipinelis has never been a likeable figure of contemporary Greek history: he was closely identified with authoritarian ideas and finally served as Foreign Minister of the military dictatorship in 1967–70. However, his remarks touched on a major problem of strategy, and in effect were never answered. Papandreou's reply was indicative of his tendency to try to solve his problems by launching attacks against Karamanlis' past policies. By the summer of 1964, when the Acheson Plan was being discussed, he realized that Greece would indeed have to compensate Turkey in order to secure Enosis. But it was already late: Makarios could be even more convincingly intransigent.

One should not be unfair towards the national centre doctrine. In 1964, the Papandreou government had to handle an already explosive Cyprus crisis. Initially, the doctrine of the national centre intended to provide the means to control the archbishop and facilitate an Enosis settlement. However, when Makarios forced Papandreou to reject the Acheson Plan, the Enosis policy practically collapsed and the national centre doctrine resulted in a permanent military entanglement of Greece in Cyprus, in conditions of crisis; crisis, that is, not only with Turkey but with Makarios as well. Thus, the national centre doctrine finally intensified the very problem that it intended to solve.

In previous decades, a debate has taken place on who was right in this dispute: Makarios or the Greek governments. In a sense, they were both right and wrong. Makarios had a point when he indicated that he could not give blank cheques or submit his country to the Athenian policy-making process, which he neither controlled nor trusted. Athens also had a point when it declared that it could not allow the regional or even local priorities of Nicosia to determine

Greek policy. And both 'centres' made grave mistakes, since they either accepted or caused the collapse of the 1959 agreements without realizing that both would then be left without a long-term policy. The intensity of the Athens–Nicosia quarrel derived from this painful lack of direction that coloured Greek policy after the collapse of 'Zurich'.

The military arm of the national centre

When writing about post-war Greek foreign and security policy, it is tempting to discuss at some length Makarios' personality. However, Makarios was the leader of another independent state; anyway, the personality of his arch-rival, General George Grivas, must also be dealt with. Grivas was the Commander-in-Chief of the Greek forces in Cyprus since the summer of 1964. He was a local commander, without wider powers in the Greek army, much less in the grand strategy of the Greek state. However, he was also a constant influence (Grivas remained on the scene even when governments fell) and his presence aggravated the Athens–Nicosia quarrel.

Grivas was born in Cyprus and had joined the Greek army at the time of the Asia Minor campaign in the early 1920s. During the occupation, he led the X, a strongly anti-Communist resistance organization. After liberation, he retired from the army with the rank of lieutenant-colonel, but his attempts to enter Greek politics in the elections of 1946 and 1950 were unsuccessful; his party got less than 1 per cent of the national vote. In 1955–59, under the name 'Digenis', he led the National Organization of Cypriot Fighters (EOKA) and its armed campaign against British rule. As the military leader of the Cyprus revolt (under Makarios' political leadership) he became a popular hero in Greece, although the Karamanlis government was clearly embarrassed by his eccentric personality. In 1956 and 1957 he called for Greece's withdrawal from NATO, an idea strongly resisted by Athens. Averoff used to describe such neutralist calls as a 'cunning' tactic on the part of the Communists, and as 'stupidity' on the part of others,[47] and it was rather clear in which category he placed Grivas. Finally, Grivas developed a paranoid belief that everyone but himself was about to betray Cyprus; in 1958 he even attacked members of AKEL, the Cypriot Communist party, ignoring the calls of Athens and Makarios not to split the internal Greek-Cypriot front. To put it simply, Grivas was a brave man, but desperately lacked political or strategic skills.

After the 1959 Cyprus settlement, the Karamanlis government made sure that Grivas left Cyprus; in Athens, the government promoted him, after retirement, to the rank of general. However, Sophocles Venizelos convinced Grivas to enter politics as a leader of the Centre. Venizelos' opinion of Grivas was extremely low: talking to British diplomats in 1959 he described the former EOKA leader as 'an arrogant fool', and went around Athens suggesting that Grivas had 'the intelligence of an infant'.[48] However, Venizelos realized that no Centre politician could oust Karamanlis, and thus tried to find a soldier-hero to play this role. Grivas duly attacked the 1959 settlement and Makarios. In 1960–61 he led the

KEA (Movement for National Rehabilitation), to which Venizelos 'lent' the twenty MPs of the Liberal Party. Grivas's attempt to pose as a Centre leader sparked serious opposition within the Centre, though, mostly from Venizelos' rival, George Papandreou. It also appears that Grivas tried to establish his own clique in the army, an attempt which the Karamanlis government neutralized by posting the pro-Grivas officers away from Athens.[49] By 1961 the KEA had failed and Venizelos was discredited, clearing the way for Papandreou to assume the leadership of the CU.

The Cyprus crisis gave new opportunities to the former EOKA leader. By December 1963, Venizelos, now Foreign Minister, toyed with the idea of helping Grivas to oust Makarios in the next Cypriot presidential election; Makarios' people were even afraid of a coup staged by the General.[50] In January 1964 Makarios publicly warned Athens that Grivas could cause civil conflict among the Greek Cypriots.[51] Despite Makarios' objections and Venizelos' death, after the February 1964 elections Papandreou decided to offer Grivas a role in the Cyprus scene, evidently hoping that the General would be able to control the Greek-Cypriot irregular bands and impose 'discipline' on the island.[52] Grivas was also useful as a lever against Makarios, while his old denunciation of the 1959 settlement made him a symbol against Karamanlis' past policies. In March 1964 the government appointed Grivas as head of the Special Joint Staff for Cyprus (EMEK), situated in Athens, but stressed that he should not move to Cyprus.[53]

Involving Grivas in the Cyprus issue proved to be a tragically mistaken decision. In May 1964, he started pressing the government to permit him to go to Cyprus 'for a limited period'. He even wrote to Papandreou, threatening publicly to denounce the government.[54] Grivas then submitted his resignation, noting that he had decided on 'separating my responsibilities, to work for the Cyprus question as my national duty imposes'.[55] On the very same day Papandreou wrote back and prevented the resignation. This was another bad start: the government of the 'national centre' had given in to blackmail by one of its military commanders.

Grivas went to Cyprus in June, but immediately afterwards the government asked him to return, fearful of international reactions if his presence on the island became known. However, when the Undersecretary for Foreign Affairs, Andreas Pappas, conveyed Papandreou's message to Grivas, the latter abruptly refused:[56]

> And I reasonably ask myself, what collusion or what else is being played around the sacred Cyprus cause? [...] I have done, now as always, my duty both to Cyprus and to Greece, and I will go on working to this direction in any way that I think best. *No force or threat is sufficient to stop me.*

Again, Grivas prevailed: the government not only allowed him to remain in Cyprus, but also appointed him Commander-in-Chief of the Greek forces there.[57] From this position, Grivas repeatedly confronted General (retd) George

Facing new challenges 139

Karayiannis, the head of the Greek Cypriot National Guard. This multiple military leadership in the island was another side-effect of Grivas's presence in Cyprus.

In early August 1964 the Mansura crisis erupted in Cyprus, when Greek-Cypriot units engaged in a local conflict with Turkish-Cypriot ones. This impaired the Greek government's policy of negotiating an Enosis settlement. Before the crisis Grivas was in Athens for consultations with the government, which urged him to avoid conflict in the island. As soon as he returned to Cyprus, though, he ignored his orders and launched the attack against the Turkish-Cypriot enclave in the Mansura area. On 8 August, George Papandreou sent to Makarios and Grivas his famous message: 'we agree on certain issues and you do otherwise'. This message has often been presented as a 'severe' attitude of the Prime Minister towards Makarios and Grivas, yet the facts paint a different picture. On 9 August Grivas submitted his resignation, and then, on the very same day, George Papandreou literally apologized and begged Grivas to remain in his place:[58]

> Please convey to General Grivas my personal appeal that in this crucial moment of Cyprus and of Mother Greece he should lay aside any personal misunderstanding and bitterness, and [...] continue his agreed leading role, according to his heroic traditions. We are in agreement with his views.

After the Mansura crisis, General Karayiannis, the head of the Greek Cypriot National Guard, who had insisted on obeying the government's orders, resigned. Arguably, this was another blow to the authority of Athens regarding the handling of the military aspects of the Cyprus question.

After August 1964, Grivas started sending reports to the Greek government, accusing Makarios of not favouring Enosis.[59] In late September, he even assured the Prime Minister that 'at any rate the army is in our hands', and concluded: 'I predict that the archbishop is currently preparing for a conflict with us. Will we allow him to choose the timing?'[60] Grivas was now seeking to precipitate an armed conflict with Makarios, which the CU government naturally refused to accept. Of course, government officials did not like Makarios either, but they did not command the Greek troops in Cyprus. In the following months, Grivas continued to report against the archbishop.[61] On his part, Makarios, not without reason, regarded Grivas as a threat and refused to place the National Guard under his orders.

Grivas also destabilized the internal political scene in Greece: he often sent his reports to the King, by-passing the Prime Minister or the Defence Minister. It is also in this context that one should place his 1965 reports about the existence of ASPIDA, the allegedly Nasserite conspiracy of young army officers, with which he finally blew up the CU government. Thus, Grivas finally struck at the very heart of the Greek political system.

Grivas continued to play an important role during the lifetime of the 'apostates' government as well. Indeed, this government tended to rely on him exactly because its relationship with Makarios was so problematic. Early in 1966 Grivas demanded that the National Guard be placed under his orders. Makarios refused, pointing out that Grivas had threatened to topple him, and expressing the fear that the General might cause civil war in the island.[62] Grivas responded with a letter to Stephanopoulos in which he called Makarios 'destroyer of the nation', and suggested that he expected the government to do its duty.[63] Grivas also insulted the Foreign Minister, Tsirimokos, who had sided with Makarios.[64] The government once more gave in to Grivas's pressures, causing Tsirimokos' resignation from the Foreign Ministry.

Grivas remained as Commander-in-Chief of the Greek forces in Cyprus even after the April 1967 Colonels' coup, and left the island only after his new attack on the Turkish-Cypriot enclave of Kophinou in November of that year, when Turkey forced Athens to withdraw its troops from the island. Grivas once again returned to Cyprus in 1971, founded the EOKA B and practically caused civil war among the Greek Cypriots. He died in January 1974, a few months before the Turkish invasion of Cyprus.

12 Multiple fronts

Problems in the army

The advent of the Centre Union brought to the forefront the issue of civilian control over the army. The CU had placed substantive reform and the strengthening of democracy high on its agenda. Since the early 1950s, the two Centre leaders, George Papandreou and Sophocles Venizelos, had openly spoken against the IDEA, the secret ultra-conservative society of officers which had appeared in the second half of the 1940s and later identified itself with Papagos. Papandreou kept denouncing the IDEA in 1964–65. However, by 1962–64 many IDEA officers, who had by now risen to the rank of general, had retired from the service. Accordingly, criticizing IDEA did not amount to much in practical political terms: army intervention in politics would not necessarily come in this form. Still, the Centre's relations with the military were strained: the CU had accused army leaders of intervening in favour of Karamanlis in the 1961 elections. The 1962–63 'relentless struggle' against Karamanlis included strong criticism of the army, and had made the military grow suspicious of the CU. In turn, the CU did not trust the army's leadership, which had been shaped by the Right since the days of Papagos.

Moreover, and despite public statements to the contrary, from the very start the CU had conceded the control of the army to the Palace. In the first CU government in November 1963, the Ministry of National Defence was assigned to General (retd) D. Papanikolopoulos, who was regarded as a 'representative' of the Crown.[1] More importantly, according to Mitsotakis, by the end of 1963 George Papandreou had managed to get the consent of King Paul for new elections, offering in return control over the army to the Palace.[2] Indeed, Andreas Papandreou also made a reference to an 'agreement of the king with the prime minister' during a discussion with the Americans in December 1963.[3] It must be noted that this agreement was not aimed against the Conservatives, but primarily against George Papandreou's major *infra-party* opponent, Sophocles Venizelos: if George Papandreou did not manage to secure an early election and an overall majority in Parliament it would be necessary to form a coalition with ERE, and the most probable head of such a 'Centre–Right' government would have been Venizelos. Although the conclusion of such an understanding between

G. Papandreou and King Paul cannot be proved by written evidence, in 1964 the Prime Minister acted as though such an agreement was in force.

Simultaneously, during the long political crisis in 1963–64, the army became increasingly autonomous from political decisions. As will be shown in the following chapter, the General Staff of National Defence took some strange initiatives on Cyprus in late 1963. Furthermore, the military slowly acquired an unprecedented freedom in the handling of the internal affairs of the army. In February 1964, the British Embassy's annual report on the Greek army noted:[4]

> The Army [...] has enormously strengthened its position in recent months. It has been able to select, post and promote officers chosen by the two senior military commanders [i.e. the chiefs of the General Staffs of National Defence and of the Army] without interference from the politicians.

After the 1964 election, the Papandreou government faced contradictory pressures. Many retired officers pressed Papandreou, Stephanopoulos and the Defence Minister, Garoufalias, with demands for their rehabilitation. A large number of these inflated expectations related to grievances dating from the 1941–52 period.[5] There were also frequent disagreements between Garoufalias and the able Undersecretary of Defence, Michalis Papaconstantinou, a young man with deep knowledge of Balkan affairs. At the same time the CU government faced a new interventionism by King Constantine, who acceded to the throne in spring 1964 following the death of his father. The government made some changes in the leadership of the army: the Chief of the General Staff of the Army, Lieutenant-General Petros Sakellariou, was replaced by Lieutenant-General Ioannis Gennimatas. Gennimatas was regarded as a political enemy of the Centre and as King Constantine's preference; indeed, his selection was the result of a negotiation between the Prime Minister and the King, which suggests that the 'army-for-elections agreement' of late 1963 remained valid. Lieutenant-General Andreas Siapkaras became Inspector General, and Lieutenant-General Ioannis Pipilis retained the post of Chief of the General Staff of National Defence. The Commander of the KYP, Lieutenant-General Natsinas, was replaced by G. Agoros.[6] This author asked Papaconstantinou why the government did not use the failures in Cyprus in order to effect more changes; Papaconstantinou replied that 'it was not in our hands'.[7]

The issue of control over the army formed part of the background of the 1965 political crisis. At the time of the CU's split in July 1965, George Papandreou was planning to make new changes in the leadership of the armed forces, while King Constantine took the view that he should have a say in this matter. The resignation of the CU government came as a result of the alleged existence of a Nasserite conspiracy of young officers in the Greek units in Cyprus, under the leadership of the Prime Minister's son, Andreas. George Papandreou decided to oust his Minister of Defence, Garoufalias, and assume the Defence Ministry himself, to which the King objected, arguing that the Andreas Papandreou affair should be cleared first; this became the breaking point between them.[8] After the

July–September 1965 crisis, the Palace appeared to consolidate its hold on the army: in October 1965 Lieutenant-General Grigorios Spantidakis was named Chief of the General Staff of the Army, while the most able pro-Centre soldier, Lieutenant-General C. Tsolakas, was practically neutralized by becoming Chief of the (relatively powerless) General Staff of National Defence. Constantinos Mitsotakis later noted that the 'apostates' government fell in December 1966, among other reasons because it planned to replace Spantidakis.[9] This implied that the King believed that he could control the army through Spantidakis and therefore wished to protect him. However, in April 1967 Spantidakis was to let the King down when he practically legitimized the Colonels' coup; the much debated Palace 'control' over the army finally proved to be a myth or a mirage. In any event, after 1963 political control over the army substantially relaxed, and this was crucial in giving the Colonels the opportunity to topple Greek democracy.[10]

The military balance, 1963–64

As shown above, in 1963 the Defence Ministry insisted that the country's military position was poor. In his memoirs, the CU Defence Minister, Garoufalias, presented similarly unfavourable figures. He noted that Greece had a land army of 116,000 men, compared to a Bulgarian army of 145,000 (not including the border army) and a Turkish army of 374,000. Greece's one armoured division possessed 409 tanks, and Bulgaria's three armoured divisions possessed 1,240 tanks. Moreover, Greece had 174 jet fighters compared to 465 Bulgarian and 307 Turkish. The Greek navy had twelve destroyers and five patrol boats, while the numbers for Turkey were eighteen and twenty respectively. Garoufalias also quoted military documents which suggested that in late 1963 the Greek army did not have ammunition and spare parts for more than 7–10 days of war.[11] This seems to have been an exaggeration, although shortages in such material had not been uncommon in the Greek forces since 1952.

On the other hand, the evaluation of comparative strength cannot be based on numbers alone. For example, the Turkish armed forces had to cover many fronts and thus were compelled to disperse over a larger area than those of Greece and Bulgaria. However, the military balance between Greece and Turkey was decisively influenced by an additional factor: the distance between Greece and Cyprus, which made it impossible for the Greek air force to operate there. Thus, in August 1964, during the Mansura crisis, the Turkish air force bombed inhabited areas on the island. During an important conference in Athens, the Chief of the Air Staff, Lieutenant-General George Antonakos, indicated to the Greek government and to the Cypriot Foreign Minister, Spyros Kyprianou, that the Turkish air force, which was stronger than the Greek, could reach Cyprus in a matter of minutes, while 'our great weakness lies in the factor of distance'. Antonakos said that the Greek jets could not stay over Cyprus for more than seven minutes; if they engaged the Turkish jets or if they spent more than ten minutes in search for a land target, they would not have enough fuel to return to their bases. Thus, the Greek air force could not be used in support of land operations in Cyprus.[12] Throughout the Cyprus crises, this was an ongoing problem for the Greek air force. Indeed, in January–June 1964 American officials assumed that in a war over Cyprus the Turks would prevail exactly because of their air superiority.[13]

The military balance with Bulgaria was also unfavourable. Sofia had more and better tanks and artillery, and in 1964 Greek capabilities against Bulgaria deteriorated further, as some Greek units were moved to Cyprus.[14] On 23 April 1964, in a report to Papandreou, Stephanopoulos and Garoufalias, the General Staff of National Defence sketched a gloomy picture:[15]

> A. The land and air forces of the Balkan Satellites enjoy a crushing superiority over Greek forces in numbers, mobilization capability, modern equipment, firepower and mechanized means. B. The Bulgarian forces enjoy a three to one superiority in tanks and aircraft.

More importantly, the Greek military were convinced that the readiness of the Bulgarian forces was far higher than that of the Greek army. The Greeks estimated that in the first crucial days of a war they could engage only three divisions out of a total of twelve infantry divisions and an armoured one, while half of the Bulgarian army could enter the conflict immediately.[16] In December 1965 the Greeks presented a paper to the NAC, setting out their estimations of Bulgarian military capabilities. The Greek paper took it for granted that, in case of war, Albania would fight on the side of the Warsaw-Pact forces. It also noted that eleven Bulgarian divisions could participate in a future surprise attack against Greece; as these units already were at a high combat readiness (75–80 per cent of their full strength) and also had adequate mobility and a high strike capability, they could attack 'without any preparatory measures'.[17] Even allowing for some alarmism, this meant that the capabilities of the Bulgarian army could prove crushing and decisive.

Post-1963 threat perception

Throughout these years Greece continued to regard the menace from the north, and especially the danger of localized war, as present and pressing. As shown in previous chapters, the perception of the menace from the north combined historical, geographical and strategic factors, to which the CU leadership and George Papandreou personally were very sensitive. Furthermore, the CU leaders resented the fact that Greece did not have the capability to implement the forward defence strategy which NATO supported. On the other hand, it should be taken into account that, although the Americans themselves regarded a local war as improbable, the NATO military authorities or other countries did not rule out such a possibility.[18] Greece was not alone in its fears; in a sense, it took the worst scenario into account.

The CU ministers kept stressing the problem of localized war. During the extraordinary NAC ministerial meeting of November 1963, the Minister of Economic Co-ordination, George Mavros, said that détente did not provide for security for Greece.[19] In December 1963, George Papandreou asked for an American assurance that the US would repel any violation of Greek territory.[20] As had happened with similar previous requests by Karamanlis, the Americans were not forthcoming. During the December 1963 NATO ministerial meeting, the Foreign Minister, Sophocles Venizelos, noted that the Soviet Bloc could easily create faits accomplis in NATO's southeastern flank, and asked for the strengthening of alliance forces there. Significantly, the Turkish Foreign Minister, Feridun Kemal Erkin, supported Venizelos' arguments; it was only a few days before the start of the inter-communal clashes in Cyprus.[21] Thus, the CU started its period in office trying to strengthen Greek security in the north.

A few days later, however, inter-communal clashes erupted in Cyprus; the new crisis opened new fronts and overstretched Greek defence. At a meeting of political and military leaders on 25 January 1964, the Chief of the General Staff of the Army, Lieutenant-General Sakellariou, pointed out that, in case of a Greek–Turkish conflict, the Greek forces would not be in a position to cover the Bulgarian border. The meeting concluded that a Greek threat to go to war might deter a war; however, the meeting also noted that a Greek–Turkish conflict could give the Soviet Bloc an excellent pretext to launch a local attack.[22] Thus, according to the Greek political and military leadership, the Cyprus crisis not only created new threats but could also further intensify old ones. The national centre doctrine was intended to limit these dangers, by preventing Nicosia from triggering a wider conflict.

During their meeting in Athens in late April, the NATO Secretary General, Dirk Stikker, indicated to George Papandreou that the alliance would not interfere in a Greek–Turkish war, and that it might consider terminating military aid to both countries. The Greek Prime Minister complained bitterly about this, noting that the alliance could not remain indifferent in the case of a conflict between two of its members. He also referred to the danger of a Bulgarian local attack. In that case, he noted, security could be achieved either by a provision for an automatic intervention by the alliance or by the strengthening of the Greek army. Papandreou asked for NATO aid to increase Greece's defence capability:[23]

> We do not have the economic capability to secure our full defence against a local attack solely by our own means. Perhaps we could do this, if we devoted to defence the largest part of our budget; but our distinguished guest knows well, and we know it too – after three internal revolutions within a decade – that the threat of communism appears in both fronts, external and internal. If we devoted a larger part of our budget to military expenditure in order to prevent an external invasion, we would then drive our people to misery and thus we would be certain to succumb to the internal front of communism.

In May 1964, the NAC entrusted Stikker with a 'Watching Brief' – namely a mandate to monitor Cyprus and Greek–Turkish relations and prevent the deterioration of the situation. However, the Watching Brief was merely a monitoring mission, and did not commit the alliance to stopping a Greek–Turkish war.[24]

The Greek leaders were shocked to hear that the alliance would not interfere in a Greek–Turkish war. It is true that, in June, President Johnson averted a Turkish invasion of Cyprus by his letter to the Turkish Prime Minister, Inönü. The Greeks knew, though, that similar US interventions depended on circumstances and on the political will of the US administration. On the contrary, Stikker's April message referred to a general principle laid down by the alliance, and could not be ignored. Thus, both during his 10 June meeting with the US Undersecretary of State, George Ball, and two weeks later, during his visit to Washington, Papandreou protested about NATO's line of neutrality in case of a Greek–Turkish war.[25] Successive crises erupted in Cyprus in summer 1964, threatening to lead to war, and in early July the US State Department estimated the possibility of a Greek–Turkish war at 50 per cent.[26] During the Mansura crisis in August 1964, the Turkish air force bombed inhabited areas in Cyprus, while Greece and Turkey placed their air forces under national command, as a prelude to their possible use against one another. The crisis was finally overcome, but when the new NATO Secretary General, Manlio Brosio, praised Athens for its restraint, he used wording that the Greek leaders found less than satisfactory: he noted that NATO intended to prevent *to the extent that this was possible*, any military act which could endanger peace.[27] Last but not least, the rejection of the Acheson Plan in August 1964 meant that Athens would now have to face a long-term military entanglement in Cyprus, and therefore a permanent dispersion of its armed forces, which were never strong enough alone to deal with the Bulgarians.

In November 1964, Brosio visited Athens. Papandreou repeated his protests regarding the projected NATO neutrality in case of a Greek–Turkish war, and also raised the problem of Bulgarian local attack. The Greek Prime Minister repeated that credible defence could be secured either by a provision for immediate intervention of NATO forces, or by the strengthening of the Greek army to the point that it could, alone, repel the Bulgarians.[28] It appears that Papandreou raised the issue of immediate NATO intervention, trying to argue, indirectly, that since Article 5 of the NATO Treaty did not provide for automatic intervention, the Greek army should be strengthened by the alliance. This, of course, meant that the maximalist Enosis rhetoric, which the Greek government was simultaneously employing, was simply out of touch with reality. The 'national centre' was simply too exposed and too overstretched in too many ways.

The July–September 1965 political crisis brought the CU government down, but did not dramatically change Athens' threat perception. Presenting his government during a turbulent Parliament session, Stephanopoulos indicated that Greece would remain loyal to its alliances, but did not mention the menace from the north; this was the first time in post-war Greek history that the menace from the north was not mentioned in such a Parliamentary statement.[29] However, its existence was taken for granted. The Foreign Minister, Ioannis Toumbas, expressly mentioned this to Makarios in successive meetings. Thus, on 2 September 1966, Toumbas rejected Makarios' idea to compensate Turkey with Greek land in case of Enosis; Toumbas said that this would create a precedent of changing borders in the Balkans, and might give ideas to Greece's northern neighbours.[30] Athens also had to take into account the military balance with Turkey, and Toumbas, as a former military officer, paid much attention to this. On 9 November, in a new meeting with Makarios, the Greek Foreign Minister raised this point:[31]

> [Toumbas] discussed the military situation, pointing to the factor 'time' and its likely effect on a future agreement. In particular, he examined the present balance of power between Greece and Turkey in all sectors – military, population, economy etc. – and the projected balance after a decade. He concluded, and this was accepted by everybody, that this balance will steadily become unfavourable for Greece.

Similar remarks were made to Makarios during the Council of the Crown (a meeting of Makarios, Greek political leaders and the King) on 6 February 1967.[32] Even if the Greek leaders were trying to scare Makarios by such remarks, these considerations reflect the magnitude of the pressures on Greek security policy during this period of multiple fronts.

NATO and the northern front, 1964–66

The CU government tried to strengthen Greek security vis-à-vis Bulgaria mainly through closer co-operation with NATO. Athens pointed out to the alliance that the Greek forces could not implement a forward defence doctrine. However, whereas the US itself implemented a flexible response, NATO was rather slow in adopting it, and often Greek requests exceeded alliance capabilities or fell on deaf ears. On the other hand, the Cyprus crisis forced the Greek government to move troops not only to Cyprus but also to Western Thrace, to deal with a possible Turkish strike.[33] This meant that Greece practically had to implement a kind of forward strategy *against Turkey*, at a moment that it was in no position to do it in the Bulgarian border. This was another contradiction of Greek defence policy in the era of multiple fronts. All these underlined the need for reform of the country's security policy.

In 1964 the Greek army was supplied with new M-48 tanks for the XX Armoured Division, whereas the older M-47s were moved to the infantry formations. The army also acquired new armoured vehicles, M-59s and M-113s. However, the navy was not strengthened: Greece received only an old US submarine. Moreover, the CU government's efforts to buy small craft such as patrol or torpedo boats (which would be useful in a war in the Aegean) led nowhere; evidently, the British and the Americans did not want to strengthen Greek and Turkish naval capabilities which could be employed against one another. The air

148 *The era of multiple fronts, 1963–67*

force also received new types of aircraft: F-104s, which arrived in 1964 and F-5As in 1965,[34] but these still were not enough. In 1963–65, Greece failed to report to NATO its force plans for the immediately following years. The Greek military authorities accepted in principle the minimum requirements of NATO force goals, but always noted that their implementation would depend on the receipt of external aid.[35]

Initially, the Greeks thought that NATO could provide for a solution to these problems. Following the December 1963 decision of the NAC to give priority to the study of the problems on the southeastern flank, NATO's Defence Planning Committee (DPC) set up a working group on the defence of the region. It is interesting that, during the DPC sessions which dealt with this issue, the Greek and the Turkish representatives were usually in agreement, despite the ongoing crises in Cyprus.[36] The DPC also initiated a general study for the future organization of NATO forces until 1970. Greece, like other countries, responded to the DPC questionnaires stating its preferred force goals, but was evasive on the issue of funding them; the Greeks were once more counting on foreign aid to strengthen their army.[37]

The working group on the defence of the southeastern region commenced its study in the spring of 1964, and established two working parties for Greece and Turkey respectively. The working party for Greece accepted Athens' argument that Western Thrace had to be defended 'as far to the North and East as possible'. The working party noted the problems in the Greek army, which lacked adequate mobility and armour. The vessels of the Greek navy were old, while there was a shortage of strike aircraft in the Greek air force, which also was vulnerable to a surprise attack. The working party stressed that 'a lack of armour and mobility reduces the capability of the Greek forces to employ mobile defence tactics', while the terrain in Northern Greece was highly compartmented and precluded the quick shift of the defending forces. The study concluded that 'there is only a marginal capability for current forces to control Hellenic Thrace and prevent a gap between Greek and Turkish forces in that area'. On the other hand, Greece's long-term plans for its army were partially incompatible with NATO requirements. By late 1964, SHAPE had formulated two alternative scenarios for the NATO forces until 1970: the 'Alpha' and the 'Bravo' postures. The former involved retention of much larger conventional forces than the latter, but the 'Bravo' posture also required a sharp rise of defence expenditure by the member states in order to meet the high qualitative standards which the alliance considered necessary. For Greece, the 'Alpha' posture involved the creation of a new mechanized division and a new armoured brigade, modernization of the units and an increase of air force jets under NATO command from 168 to 198. The 'Bravo' posture called for a modernization of the land army, which would remain at its present numerical strength, but provided for a reduction in the air force to 127 jets assigned to NATO by 1970.[38]

However, the reply of the Greek government to the DPC questionnaire indicated that Athens was thinking along different lines: Greece wanted to have larger forces than those required even by the 'Alpha posture' (an additional armoured brigade), but these forces would be of significantly lower quality even compared to the 'Bravo' goals. The Greeks wanted to create, by 1970, a new mechanized division, two new armoured brigades and an air force of 220 aircraft, while they also suggested that they needed new vessels for their navy. The NATO working party noted that the greatest problem involved resources: the Greeks took it for granted that they would continue to receive military aid in the future, but this was an insecure prediction; even the free delivery of military hardware might be terminated. At any rate, the cost of the Greek programme was estimated at $1,220 million for the following six years, while the 'Bravo' posture (which was the cheaper of the two NATO scenarios) would require $1,400. Additionally, Greece would also need $80 million of financial aid annually; it should be remembered that in the past, US defence support (which had already been terminated) was $20–25 million. As could be expected, the working party saw no way of dealing with this problem. There was little point in strengthening the already existing but insufficient forces; the assignment of allied forces in the region was unlikely, and even those which had been earmarked to reinforce Greece might not 'in certain circumstances' be available; finally, the fortification of the border, which the Greeks also raised, was considered as an outdated concept. The working group suggested that in any scenario Greece would have to increase its defence expenditure; it might also need to give priority to certain aspects, for example armour, while another idea involved a reduction of the internal security forces to allow for an increase in the land army. The DPC suggested a further study of the resources that Greece and Turkey could devote to their defence. This would be carried out in the spring of 1965.[39]

The studies of the working group and the deliberations in the DPC showed that the Greeks were anxious to increase the firepower of their army, which could prove crucial in a short, sudden local war. However, this was considered inadequate by the NATO military authorities, who were also thinking in terms of a general conflict. At any rate, it was improbable that Greece would secure the amount of military aid necessary to achieve these goals. There seemed to be two solutions to this problem: a heavier reliance on nuclear weapons, or the coverage of the southeastern region by NATO's mobile forces.

After this rebuff from the alliance, the Greek government approached the Americans, asking both for more military aid and for a more practical NATO guarantee. Thus the Foreign Minister, Stavros Costopoulos, and the Defence Minister, Petros Garoufalias, met the US Secretary of Defence, Robert Macnamara, on 11 December 1964, prior to the NATO ministerial meeting. Garoufalias asked for US assistance to strengthen the capabilities of the Greek army; if this could not be done, Athens would be content with a NATO plan for alliance intervention in case of a war with Bulgaria. Macnamara replied that a local Bulgarian attack was improbable, but if it occurred, the US would intervene on the side of Greece, committing the aircraft of the Sixth Fleet. When Garoufalias remarked that the old bonds seemed to have become loose, Macnamara said that the Sixth Fleet was in the Mediterranean to help US allies. Yet Macnamara refused to make an official statement along these lines. The Greek Defence Minister suggested that a simple provision for NATO intervention in a crisis was not enough, exactly because NATO could not act automatically, according to Article 5 of the NATO Treaty: 'the Bulgarians will have occupied our country before the NATO Council makes a decision'.[40]

A few days later, during the NAC session, the Greek ministers insisted on the danger of local war and tried to impress upon their NATO colleagues that Bulgarian military capabilities allowed Sofia to attack Greece and create a fait accompli. Garoufalias repeated that either the Greek army should be strengthened, or NATO should be able to strengthen Greek forward defence. He also asked for NATO assistance to modernize Greek equipment, so that Athens could transform two of its infantry divisions into an armoured and a mechanized one. Finally, Garoufalias suggested calling a NATO Defence Ministers' conference to deal with the problems of the southeastern flank.[41]

To be sure, Athens would have preferred to receive NATO or US aid in order to strengthen its own army; however, since this seemed improbable, the only other option was to rely on an alliance mobile force, which would be able to intervene quickly in case of local war. As the British Embassy in Athens noted in early 1965, the Greeks were still afraid that such assistance might not arrive 'on time or in sufficient numbers'. According to the British Embassy, 'Greece, like Turkey, has spent the past year rattling a sabre in one hand [on the Cyprus conflict] and a begging bowl in the other'.[42] Last but not least, the alliance considered a rapid mobile force to be a much more practical option than a 'Maginot line mentality'.[43] In other words, if Greece were to adjust to the needs of forward defence, this would be in the form of a NATO mobile force.

In February and March 1965, NATO military experts visited Athens to study the problem of resources. The Greek government appeared anxious about alliance intentions, since the 'Bravo' posture called for a reduction in the air force. In May, the Greek government presented a memorandum to the working party on the defence problems of the southeastern region. Athens argued that it was impossible to increase substantially its defence spending in the following years, as this would result in serious cuts in public investment. The Greek government also noted that the country had not received the already approved NATO defence support aid.[44] However, these were contradictory arguments: Greece could not increase its defence budget, but wanted to set up additional mechanized and armoured units at a time when military aid was not forthcoming.

In May 1965, during a NAC session of Defence Ministers which discussed the future force goals of the alliance, Garoufalias again raised the issue of the southeastern flank. The alliance agreed to draw contingency plans for Greek Western Thrace, which would also be covered by the NATO mobile forces; this was regarded as the most effective way of setting up forward defence for this region.[45] This NAC meeting was a significant step forward. It was the first time that the alliance had committed itself to strengthening the Greek front in the early stages of a war. Following this, NATO's DPC decided to lay emphasis on the flanks, including their coverage by mobile forces.[46]

However, the CU fell from power in July, and the implementation of this decision was left to the 'apostates' government. The contingency planning for the defence of Greek Western Thrace started in summer 1965; another study involved Northern Norway.[47] The 1965 NATO annual review noted that Greece had made some progress compared to previous years, mostly in the air force, as the new types of jet aircraft were now becoming operational and combat readiness improved; two infantry divisions had been modernized, while one squadron of Hawk missiles and two parachute battalions had been formed. Still, the NATO military also noted the shortages in self-propelled artillery, heavy guns and communications equipment, as well as in regulars. The 1965 annual review considered that the country had a 'limited operational capability' to perform the tasks assigned by NATO.[48]

The Greeks continued unsuccessfully to ask for NATO aid in order to strengthen the capabilities of their army, especially to create a second armoured division.[49] By late 1965 the DPC suggested to the NAC the adoption of the 'Bravo' posture for NATO forces; new studies would be undertaken and the final decision would be reached later, but, as the relevant DPC memorandum noted, Greece and Turkey were omitted from the study 'since their national resources do not permit them to sustain their defence programmes without external aid'.[50]

Thus the mobile force concept again appeared as the only way out, and in this respect significant progress was made. Two exercises of the NATO mobile forces, Summer Express and Marmara Express, were planned for late summer 1966, involving operations of the NATO mobile force in Greek and Turkish Thrace respectively. By mid-1966 a mobile force deployment was established in Micra in Northern Greece, and Summer Express took place in September.[51] According to a July 1966 public statement by the Defence Minister, Costopoulos, Athens regarded the mobile force as adequate to cover the needs of Greek security.[52] It is indicative that Summer Express was financed on an ad hoc basis, to which Athens agreed. The Greeks wanted the exercise to take place anyway, as it might boost morale in the country; indeed, Greek newsreels strongly publicized the exercise.[53] By late 1966 Greece had also become part of the agreement to install the NADGE, the air defence system in Western Europe.[54]

The NATO mobile force concept was discussed and agreed during the lifetime of the CU government and materialized in the days of the 'apostates'; there was notable continuity in the policies of these two administrations, which are usually regarded as mortal political enemies. The mobile force arguably was the only way for Greece to implement forward defence and to achieve additional security regarding the Soviet Bloc. It certainly did not fully cover Greek worries, if only because the intervention of a NATO mobile force depended on the availability of forces at a given moment. However, taking into account the obligations of the Greek army on the Bulgarian border, Thrace, the Aegean and Cyprus, the mobile force was the only solution to the country's problem. It is also true that it entailed an additional dependence on the alliance, but this was the result of the overstretch of the Greek armed forces in those years.

Military expenditure and NATO aid

Before its electoral victory in 1963, the CU had repeatedly referred to the need to reduce defence spending. After his ascent to the premiership, George Papandreou indicated that his government would try to secure NATO defence support aid for Greece. During the December 1963 NATO ministerial meeting, Sophocles Venizelos managed to get a promise that NATO would again provide $23.5 million defence support aid for 1964.[55] However, this promise proved illusory: by the summer of 1964 no alliance member had contributed any money, and the Ministry for the Economy estimated that, at best, Greece would finally receive not more than $15 million for that year, which meant that a large deficit would appear in the budget.[56] Furthermore, the West Germans contributed some funds on a bilateral basis, aiming to balance anti-NATO feeling in Greece because of the Cyprus question. The Americans expressed their appreciation for the Greek defence effort, but offered no money.[57]

The government tried to reduce defence spending. On 4 June 1964, the Economics Minister, Constantinos Mitsotakis, tabled the 1964 budget and referred to the need to reform the organization of the armed forces. The effort to modernize the country, Mitsotakis noted, was not compatible with high defence expenditure, for which Athens expected some assistance from the other NATO members.[58] Immediately afterwards, though, the third Turkish invasion scare occurred in Cyprus and thus the government decided to send additional troops there. This brought about an expansion of the Greek defence effort and prevented cuts in the defence budget. In early August Mitsotakis wrote to Papandreou, suggesting cuts in defence expenditure,[59] but again the Mansura crisis, the rejection of the Acheson Plan and the continuation of the military entanglement in Cyprus rendered this next to impossible.

In December 1964, tabling the 1965 budget in Parliament, Mitsotakis repeated that Greece could only maintain an armed force proportional to its economic capabilities.[60] A few days earlier, the NATO ministerial meeting again had promised to offer Greece $23.5 million as defence support aid for the following year. The 1965 budget counted very much on that provision, but throughout that year Greece did not receive a single dollar; by May 1965 the CU government was very upset at this and protested to the Americans, while Garoufalias strongly raised the issue during the NATO Defence Ministers' conference.[61] Greece and Turkey also asked the NATO Secretary General, Brosio, to remind the allies of the December 1964 decision to give defence support aid to the two countries; Brosio duly made a plea to the NATO members to provide aid, and the May 1965 Defence Ministers' conference recommended that aid be given, but this too led nowhere.[62]

After the advent of the Stephanopoulos government to power, the problem became even more difficult. By late 1965 the country faced a severe currency crisis, as a result of the expansionist economic policy of the previous two years.[63] The December 1965 crisis was overcome thanks to tough government measures, while an announcement that the US would provide economic aid also helped to improve the psychological climate.[64] However, the crisis also called for prudence regarding defence spending. Once more, the government submitted to the NAC a request for defence support aid.[65] It is also notable that, prior to and during the NAC meeting (which also discussed the 'Bravo' posture of NATO forces), Greece and Turkey declared that they would not be able to meet the alliance's force goals unless they received 'adequate and timely external aid'.[66] The Greek government notified NATO that it could not resort again to the practice of covering defence costs by extra payments through the budget (to compensate for the non-receipt of NATO defence aid), 'since this practice very seriously hinders the implementation of the nation's economic and social development programme'.[67] For his part, Brosio made a new plea to the NATO members to provide aid.[68] The NAC again decided that Greece and Turkey should receive defence support aid, but this time Athens, in the midst of the currency crisis, placed little trust in such promises. The pro-government daily, *Eleftheria*, published a bitter editorial asking for 'Justice in Sacrifices' between NATO members. Mitsotakis, presenting the government's economic measures in Parliament, noted that Greek economic estimates for 1966 would take it for granted that no NATO defence aid would be given. Mitsotakis also indicated that defence expenditure would remain at the levels of the previous years. Yet the Conservatives (who supported the government in Parliament) stressed that they would not tolerate a reduction of the army.[69]

In 1966, the Stephanopoulos government continued its efforts to secure aid. In early 1966 the Ambassador to Washington, Alexandros Matsas, asked US officials to convince the NATO allies to contribute to NATO defence support aid for Greece. Matsas also said that if the US gave some money the others would follow; the Americans offered to advise the allies to give money, but refused to do so themselves.[70] In May 1966 the Alternate Minister of Economic Co-ordination, Ioannis Tsouderos, gave the Americans a memorandum outlining the Greek economic effort and arguing that the country needed defence support aid in order to continue its economic development.[71] The US Embassy in Athens considered that the memorandum was an accurate description of the Greek economic problem, but again Washington was not forthcoming.[72] At the same time, the Greeks tried to reactivate the old idea of the OECD consortium which would provide loans to Greece, but the allies only promised to offer small amounts of money.[73] In Washington Matsas requested US loans, but the Americans replied that they could not give favourable loans to a country with such impressive development rates.[74]

By late 1966, Athens made a final effort to convince the NATO allies that it desperately needed financial assistance. In a new memorandum, the government noted that Greece was not in a position to support its social and economic development and its military effort without some help. The memorandum also noted that Northern Greece bordered on Communist countries, and this impeded its economic development; the twelve prefectures of the Greek North amounted to the 25 per cent of the country's territory and 17 per cent of its population, but the Greek defence effort had created in the north of the country a 'poverty

154   *The era of multiple fronts, 1963–67*

belt'.[75] Then, in December 1966, the Ministers of Co-ordination (Mitsotakis), Foreign Affairs (Toumbas), Defence (Costopoulos) and Economics (George Melas) tried once more to convince their NATO counterparts to offer economic assistance.[76] However, the overthrow of Greek democracy in April 1967 created a completely different scene.

Still, since 1964 it had become clear that these requests for aid involved great effort and produced little result; sometimes, the Greek leaders felt insulted by the whole affair. During his December 1964 meeting with Macnamara, Garoufalias said that 'it is inconceivable that Greece should beg in order to strengthen its defence'.[77] In his memoirs, Christos Xanthopoulos-Palamas, who had served as Director General of the Foreign Ministry, permanent representative to NATO and Foreign Minister in caretaker governments of the mid-1960s, noted his discomfort regarding 'this constant bargaining for US and then for NATO aid'.[78] It is also important to note the difference of tone in successive speeches by Mitsotakis to the Greek School of National Defence in 1964–66: in the first one, as Minister for the Economy in the CU government, he stressed that defence spending 'should be in some balance' with the country's capabilities, but Athens hoped to get NATO defence support. In March 1965, again as a member of the CU government, he noted that the Cyprus crisis had burdened the economy, but NATO had promised some defence support aid. In March 1966, he mentioned nothing about NATO defence support; his disappointment was obvious.[79] Of course, this involved a special type of aid, defence support; throughout this period the US provided military hardware to Greece.

Between de Gaulle and NATO, 1963–67

European policy was a crucial aspect of any Greek government's perception of the post-war world. In 1963–67 this was even more important, as Greece was also an associate member of the EEC. Despite its warm rhetorical support for Greece's orientation towards European integration, the CU government did not manage to pursue a practical and systematic policy towards the EEC, perhaps because the successive Cyprus crises turned George Papandreou's attention to another pressing front. Indeed, in 1964 the implementation of the Association Agreement almost stagnated, especially regarding the Community's funding of Greek projects, the harmonization of agricultural policy and the possible participation of Greece in the projected Common Agricultural Policy (CAP). In 1965 the CU government tried to make a fresh start in its relations with the EEC, but many issues remained pending. The 'apostates' government made a determined effort to step up the implementation of the Association Agreement and much progress was made in 1966, including EEC funding of Greek projects, but the Association with the EEC was 'frozen' after the April 1967 military coup.[80]

The CU government was much more Atlanticist than European-oriented. Moreover, it often expressed discomfort about the policies of the French President, General de Gaulle, who caused problems in NATO. Thus, the CU Defence Minister, Garoufalias, indicated his disagreement with de Gaulle's policies during his meeting with Macnamara in December 1964, and Papandreou made similar remarks to the US Ambassador, Henry Labouisse, in January 1965.[81] This was a significant difference compared to the policy of the Karamanlis governments, which had appeared anxious to minimize the importance of the disagreements between the French President and the Americans; according to Karamanlis' functionalism, Greece should not take positions in a quarrel between the great powers of the alliance.

There were various sets of considerations which account for the attitude of the CU government towards Gaullist France. The years 1964–65 were an era of internal difficulties in the Community, and this evidently made it less appealing to many CU leaders, who in any event placed their emphasis on the US. Furthermore, the Greek leaders felt that de Gaulle blocked the defence planning of the alliance in which Greece was interested; criticizing de Gaulle might also have been a way for the Greeks to show that they were in favour of alliance cohesion, even if the Cyprus issue caused problems in NATO. The Greeks were disappointed by de Gaulle, who during Papandreou's June 1964 visit to Paris failed to fully support the Greek position on Cyprus. Last but not least, the CU leaders evidently (though erroneously) believed that the Americans had brought Karamanlis down because of his rapprochement with France, and thus they were trying to show that they would not follow his path.

The 'apostates' government took much more careful positions on the problems posed by French policy. In November 1965, in an interview with Marc Marceau of *Le Monde*, the Prime Minister, Stephanopoulos, stressed that Greece regarded the EEC and NATO as complementary and not antagonistic organizations; he avoided any criticism of de Gaulle and suggested that 'the expansion of the European economic space will advance the economic and political interests of the EEC members'.[82] The 'apostates' administration also dealt with the crisis of the French withdrawal from the military structure of the alliance in the spring of 1966. Immediately after receiving the news, the Foreign Minister, Tsirimokos, told the US Ambassador, Phillips Talbot, that Greece would not side with de Gaulle, but hoped that the 'unity' of France with the alliance would be maintained.[83] In the following months, the new Foreign Minister, Toumbas, continued to express the hope that France could be persuaded to keep in line with the alliance, especially on the West German front; he took this line during his meetings with the British Foreign Secretary, Michael Stewart, in June, with the British Minister for Foreign Affairs, George Thomson, in September, and with the West German Foreign Minister, Gerhard Schröder, in October.[84]

At the same time, however, the Stephanopoulos government regarded European integration as a priority, and did not hesitate to differ with de Gaulle on issues regarding the organization of Western Europe. Thus this government strongly supported Britain's accession to the Community: as Toumbas told the British Minister for Foreign Affairs, George Thomson, Greece regarded that tensions with de Gaulle should be avoided, but Britain should join the EEC because 'the existence of two separate economic groups [i.e. EEC and EFTA] in Europe must be ended'.[85] This government therefore tried to return to a kind of functional perception regarding Europe, stepped up the contacts with the major Western European countries (including Britain) and focused on the smooth implementation of the Association Agreement with the EEC, as a tool for the long-term integration of Greece in the West. However, this strategy was blocked by the military coup in April 1967.

The revival of anti-Americanism: the political climate as part of the security problem

In 1964, the Cyprus crisis created a new wave of anti-Americanism in Greece. In the spring, large demonstrations in Athens were dominated by anti-American slogans, which irritated President Johnson personally; a visit of the Sixth Fleet to Greece was cancelled, and American officials were speaking of a 'new atmosphere' prevailing in Athens.[86] In August 1964, at a moment when the Soviets issued a public warning against a Turkish invasion of Cyprus, an opinion poll showed that a majority of Greeks considered the Soviet Union as 'Greece's best friend'. This view changed in the following months, mainly because of the autumn 1964 pro-Turkish turn of Soviet policy in Cyprus, but this was a difficult period in Greek–US relations.[87] As had happened in the 1950s, fears were expressed that the public's excitement could lead to a disengagement of Greece from the West.

Apart from the general public, important personalities with strong pro-Western credentials now expressed disappointment with the West. Thus, in May 1964, Lieutenant-General Andreas Siapkaras, the Inspector General of the army and certainly no left-winger, suggested that the Greek officers should be withdrawn from the NATO Headquarters at Izmir, because this would act as a brake 'on Turkey and the great imperialist power hiding behind it'.[88] In March 1965, the Ambassador to Washington, Alexandros Matsas, told the US Undersecretary of State, George Ball, that NATO had become a paradox for Greece: it offered 'defence from a non-threatening opponent and danger from a threatening ally [i.e. Turkey]'.[89] It should be remembered that in the 1950s Matsas had shown a profoundly combatant Cold War mentality and had played a role in the rejection, if not the torpedoing, of proposals for normalization of relations with Bulgaria.

There also were leading politicians who showed impatience with NATO. Andreas Papandreou was Minister for the Prime Minister's Office in the spring of 1964 when he had a row with the head of the USIS in Greece because of the unfavourable coverage of events in Cyprus by the 'Voice of America' radio.[90] Andreas Papandreou was one of the CU's experts on Greek–US relations: he had spent many years in the US and had been a Professor of Economics at Berkeley. In the CU government, and regardless of post, he always had a say in relations with the US, and for that reason, as Alternate Minister for Economic Co-ordination, he accompanied his father to Washington in June 1964. Still, in 1964–66 Andreas Papandreou publicly called for the disengagement of Greece from dependence on the US, which made him extremely popular with the public and quite unpopular with the US Embassy.

Nor was Andreas Papandreou alone in expressing dissatisfaction with NATO. The Cypriot-born Undersecretary for Education, Loukis Akritas, was a major figure of Greek letters and a close associate of George Papandreou; during the 1944 Liberation, as George Papandreou's personal envoy to Athens, he had played a major role in the struggle to keep Greece in the West. Yet, on 3 April 1964, speaking in Parliament, he accused NATO of adopting a pro-Turkish attitude and praised Tito and Nasser, implying that they could become a model for Greece.[91] Petros Garoufalias, a businessman with strong anti-Communist credentials, told Macnamara in December 1964 that NATO was 'unfavourable' to Greece on Cyprus.[92] In August 1964, during the Mansura crisis in Cyprus, the Foreign Minister, Stavros Costopoulos, complained to Brosio that the alliance and its members discriminated in favour of Turkey.[93] It should be remembered that Garoufalias and Costopoulos were among the leading 'apostates' in 1965, and they were denounced by the CU as puppets of the Palace, the US, NATO, etc. Finally, George Papandreou himself, one of the country's most ardently pro-Western politicians, appeared disappointed during the meeting of the government Political Committee on 6 May 1965: 'NATO is not friendly [...] NATO is pro-Turkish'.[94]

To be sure, leading Greek personalities had expressed some disappointment with NATO in 1955–58. However, such views were now being expressed by persons who had been prominent supporters of the West even during the first Cyprus dispute of the 1950s. As a result, the strain on Greek–NATO relations was probably more dangerous than before. In 1955–58, under the strong leadership of the Karamanlis government, any explicit reference to withdrawal from NATO had caused an immediate reaction by those who supported the alliance. In 1964–67, although the danger of drifting away from the West seemed less immediate, the problem went deeper. Indeed, following the summer of 1964, Greek–US relations seemed to move from one problem to the next: Greek disappointment in the US over Cyprus was matched by US disappointment in Greece over the rejection of the Acheson Plan. Andreas Papandreou's claims in the autumn of 1964 that he was forced to resign from the government because of US pressure (which was inaccurate) caused US resentment; indeed, the US Embassy protested to the government regarding Andreas's allegations.[95] In the spring of 1965, during the crisis over the Cypriot SAMs (see Chapter 13), American officials adopted an extremely harsh attitude towards the Greeks. Ironically, at the very same time Greece was increasingly turning towards NATO to cover its defence needs. This made Greek policy appear schizophrenic, but it was another consequence of the existence of multiple fronts.

The July–September 1965 apostasy complicated things even further, if only because it effected a radicalization of Centrist public opinion. The US Embassy was accused of having 'planned' this crisis, causing the downfall of the CU, because the latter had supposedly 'defied' American pressure on Cyprus. This was inaccurate: in the summer of 1965 the US Embassy was afraid that if King Constantine toppled George Papandreou, a kind of Popular Front would emerge. It was only after his resignation, when they considered that a Popular Front was in the making, that the Americans accepted the idea of a temporary solution which would pave the way for new elections. Even then, the State Department instructed the Embassy to avoid anything which could be interpreted as intervention in the Greek crisis; the expression of opinion by US diplomats should also be avoided. Still, after the summer 1965 crisis the US Embassy appeared to fear George and Andreas Papandreou and their possible alliance with the Left.[96]

At the same time, the Conservative opposition was also facing its own dead-ends. The Conservatives had lost their leader, Karamanlis (who now lived in Paris), and had then suffered a disaster at the February 1964 elections when they received a mere 35 per cent of the vote. Their new leader, Kanellopoulos, a distinguished intellectual, could not unite all factions of the party. Thus, in 1964–66 the Conservative leaders found it difficult to defeat CU policies, and appeared fearful of a possible resurgence of a left-wing vote and, worse, of Communist infiltration of state agencies. Finally, during 1952–63 the Conservatives, under Papagos and Karamanlis, had kept the army outside the control of the Palace, whereas in 1964–65 they conveniently came to view such control as a bulwark against the CU. In the years that followed, the Conservatives' unspoken assumptions would also prove painfully mistaken.[97]

Finally, the Palace proved much more interventionist, but also less effective, than before. King Paul was politically much more experienced than King Constantine. For example Paul had managed to cause Karamanlis' fall in June 1963 behind the scenes, with minimal damage to his own position. By contrast, in the summer of 1965 King Constantine would literally massacre the CU's majority for two long months, before the eyes of an exasperated public, and this would finally prove fatal for the monarchy. As a result of all these developments, in the mid-1960s the political system suddenly collapsed, giving the Colonels the opportunity to seize power.

American attitudes towards developments in Greece in 1964–67 were also seriously defective. Entangled in Vietnam, concerned about and irritated over the eruption of a dangerous crisis in Cyprus, the Johnson administration did not resist the temptation to deal roughly with a CU government which could not deliver in Cyprus. Personal attitudes, or misunderstandings about personal intentions, also played a role. President Johnson's abrupt behaviour during George Papandreou's June 1964 visit to Washington was interpreted by many Greeks as an anti-Greek attitude, not as a sign of the President's known discomfort and clumsiness when meeting foreign leaders. Finally, as the available bibliography correctly indicates, throughout this period the US laboured under an erroneous assumption. American officials tended to view Greece and Turkey merely as parts of a strategic equation, and to play down or disregard important historical and regional issues which for Athens and Ankara represented matters of prime importance.[98]

As anti-Americanism in Greece reached a new peak after mid-1965, the Americans decided to maintain a close relationship with the power centre which they regarded as more permanent, namely the Palace. Although this issue should be researched further, the available evidence suggests that neither Washington nor the US Embassy were involved; neither wanted or expected the Colonels' coup of April 1967. The Americans expected a coup by the Palace, although when King Constantine approached it in the spring of 1967 the Embassy would not give him a green light to proceed.[99] More significantly, on 20 April, literally a few hours before the coup, the State Department instructed the Embassy to try to play the role of an honest broker between King Constantine and George Papandreou.[100] This was the first time in years that Washington had instructed the Embassy to interfere in Greek politics. It also suggests that American officials believed that a coup could only come from the Throne, and that they wanted to prevent it. However, by then it was already too late. Recent Greek bibliography tends to stress the importance of national, rather than foreign, factors in the road to the dictatorship.[101] Still, after the Colonels' coup the Americans decided to safeguard their own strategic interests and tolerate, if not embrace, the dictatorship. This fuelled Greek anti-Americanism even more; the circle had become vicious.

13 Maximalism and dead-end
The Cyprus entanglement

Losing control, 1963–64

In late 1963, Athens completely lost control over developments in Cyprus. This was a period of internal crisis in Greece: the inconclusive November 1963 election brought the CU to power without an overall majority in Parliament, then, in late December, a new election was proclaimed and a caretaker government was appointed. In the meantime, in late November, Makarios proposed his Thirteen Points for revising the Cypriot constitution.[1] The proposal was rejected by Turkey before the Turkish Cypriots had the chance to comment on it. Intercommunal clashes broke out in late December. By that time, both sides in Cyprus were armed to the teeth and had plans for action against each other. In September, Turkish-Cypriot armed groups had prepared for confrontation. Immediately after the eruption of the clashes, such armed groups created enclaves which did not recognize the authority of the government, and the Turkish-Cypriot leadership also encouraged its people to withdraw into these enclaves.[2] The Greek Cypriots also had plans for armed action – for example, the infamous 'Akritas Plan', drafted by the Minister of the Interior (and, from spring 1964, also of Defence) Polykarpos Giorkatzis. The Akritas Plan is indicative of the confusion and wishful thinking of the Greek-Cypriot side at that crucial moment. The plan suggested that the Greek Cypriots should aim at a quick victory: 'if we prevail within one or two days, no outside intervention will be possible, probable or justified'.[3]

The situation had been complicated further by the fact that, according to the available evidence, armed Greek-Cypriot groups had received some support from military circles in Athens. Until June 1963, the Karamanlis government was certain to react decisively to any idea of armed conflict in Cyprus; however, immediately following Karamanlis' downfall, from July 1963, it appears that the Greek General Staff of National Defence supplied arms to Greek Cypriots. Since Cyprus was another independent state, it fell under the jurisdiction of this Staff. According to a June 1964 paper of the General Staff of National Defence:[4]

> The General Staff of National Defence correctly assessed the situation before December 1963 and proceeded in most cases on its own initiative to

the organization and utilization of the Greek Cypriot element; this enabled us to deal effectively with enemy action.

In early December 1963, the General Staff of National Defence suggested a limited engagement in Cyprus, based on wildly mistaken assumptions. For example, it was argued that Turkey was in no position 'strategically and militarily' to intervene in Cyprus; Greece was seen as capable of meeting any dangers in such a crisis; the threats against Greece from the Soviet Bloc were seen as diminishing and the Communist countries were viewed as benevolent to a Greek bid for Enosis, while Britain was regarded as almost certain to acquiesce to such a policy.[5] Within a few weeks, all these assumptions proved wrong: Turkey was capable of threatening an invasion, and in the following months the General Staff of the Army (which was the competent staff) noted that Greece did not have the capability to undertake action in Cyprus, or to cover effectively the northern border as well as the Aegean and Cyprus; the Communist countries certainly did not support Enosis, which would turn Cyprus into NATO territory; and Britain did not support the Thirteen Points. The Papandreou government rejected these plans, but the damage had already been done since some military had appeared to encourage Greek-Cypriot hopes. As George Papandreou stressed in the dramatic meeting of party leaders of 25 January 1964, 'irresponsible officers are gravely mistaken when encouraging the [Greek] Cypriots that we can aid them effectively'.[6] It is indeed difficult to grasp how this very same Staff which in 1963 and 1964 sounded alarmist regarding Greek–Bulgarian balances now suggested that Athens could undertake operations in Cyprus. Greek army documents (at least on such a high level) were notable for high-quality analysis, and the December 1963 texts are a painful exception. In the following months, the General Staff of the Army (the operational head of the land army) proved extremely suspicious of any idea coming from the General Staff of National Defence.

It is not easy to explain the initiatives of the General Staff of National Defence in the second half of 1963. The most plausible explanation is that the fall of Karamanlis led to a relaxation of the political control over the army during the long political crisis that followed. In this context, some high-placed officers led themselves to believe that they could engineer a limited, 'surgical' action in Cyprus, ignoring international balances or even the possibility of Turkish reaction. Repeatedly in 1964 the British and the US Embassies noted that there were 'senior Army officers' who might want to force the government to follow such a course.[7]

The inter-communal clashes in Cyprus displayed the dangers of this adventurism. The Greek-Cypriot groups managed tactically to defeat the Turkish Cypriots, but the latter (and the Turkish army detachment in Cyprus, which managed to occupy a strategic position north of Nicosia) retained the control of areas which did not recognize the government's authority; the British interfered from their bases and separated the combatants.[8] The Greek-Cypriot 'victory' was not strategic but only Pyrrhic, and led to an early form of partition.

Moreover, the Greek Cypriots suffered a disaster in international public opinion, which denounced their actions. The broadcasts of the 'Voice of America', which caused Andreas Papandreou's wrath, were not an isolated phenomenon. Last but not least, Greece was moving towards a general election and proved unprepared to handle the crisis. In January, the confusion was at its peak: Greece was in the middle of an electoral campaign, the caretaker government under Ioannis Paraskevopoulos participated in the London Five-Party Conference on Cyprus, and when the Turks threatened with an invasion of Cyprus, Athens replied that this would mean war. The SACEUR, General Lyman Lemnitzer, travelled to Ankara to prevent a Turkish invasion.[9]

On 25 January and 1 February, dramatic meetings were held in Athens in which the leaders of the two major parties, Papandreou and Kanellopoulos, participated. It was ironic that these people had to campaign for the election in the morning and then sit together at night to handle this desperate situation. In these meetings, authorities in Athens initially decided to accept the dispatch of a NATO force in Cyprus, but Makarios rejected it and the Greeks finally followed his line. During the meeting of 25 January the Chief of the General Staff of the Army, Lieutenant-General Sakellariou, briefed the political leaders about the military situation. Papandreou then summarized:[10]

> I heard that we clearly are not in a position to fight the Turks in Cyprus [...] If we are at a disadvantage, it is clear that we have to avoid a clash and to seek a political solution. Regarding dynamic solutions, we have to make a distinction between preventive and decisive methods. I think that preventively, it is necessary to give the impression that we are determined to fight, so as to deter a war. This is a strong deterrence. But we must be very careful in the ways that we implement this preventive strategy, because we need to avoid a war.

Thus, by early February Makarios had dragged Athens in the direction he wanted. He blocked the NATO force idea, and also appealed for Soviet diplomatic support and got it in the form of a letter by Nikita Khrushchev to the UN Secretary General, U Thant. In early March, Makarios managed to secure a favourable decision of the UN Security Council.[11] However, from Athens' point of view, it was not possible for a small state to play such dangerous games in the Eastern Mediterranean. Mostly, Makarios' appeal to Moscow terrified Athens.[12] Thus, by late February the newly elected CU government was determined to 'discipline' the archbishop.

The failure to regain control

The national centre doctrine which Papandreou introduced in his February 1964 letter to Makarios was an effort to respond to this dangerous situation. At the same time, the CU government decided to help Cyprus to organize an autonomous defence (the National Guard). The idea was that by increasing

Greek-Cypriot deterrence, it would be easier both to prevent a Turkish invasion and to avoid a Greek–Turkish war.[13]

However, Athens needed to be very careful: at that moment the National Guard was not yet ready, and thus Turkey had the chance to invade. Indeed, Ankara threatened to do so in early March 1964. This second invasion scare was also overcome thanks to US intervention, as the US funded the transportation of the first UN forces (UNFICYP) to the island.[14] Still, Makarios did not stop his unilateral initiatives. In early April he declared that the 1960 Treaty of Alliance between Greece, Turkey and Cyprus was null and void.[15] On 25 April, without consultation with Athens, the Greek Cypriots launched an attack against the Turkish-Cypriot enclave at St Hilarion, which failed and displayed the inadequacy of the Greek-Cypriot forces. It was then that Athens decided to bring Grivas on the scene as head of the Special Joint Staff for Cyprus (EMEK). At the same time, Athens decided that since the Greek-Cypriot armed groups were inadequate, it had to send a Greek army detachment to the island; initially, 2,000 men were sent.

In later years, the dispatch of this force to Cyprus was severely criticized as a grave mistake: the detachment had no air cover; its presence in fact increased Makarios' chances to drag the Greek government in the direction he preferred (because Athens found it difficult publicly to confront Makarios with a withdrawal of these troops, whatever the archbishop did); the presence of the Greek detachment intensified Ankara's suspicions that Athens was trying strategically to encircle Turkey; and the presence of the Greek troops intensified the illusions that Enosis was round the corner.[16] Initially, though, this force aimed to buy time for the completion of the organization of the National Guard, thus deterring a Greek–Turkish conflict.

Yet the planning for Cyprus' autonomous defence collapsed because of the third Turkish invasion scare in early June. Although the Turkish Prime Minister, Inönü, appeared to wish to avoid such an international adventure, he also was under pressure from public opinion and from the military to react strongly to the Cyprus crises; thus in early June the Turks prepared to invade the island.[17] The invasion was averted thanks to the intervention of President Johnson, while General Lemnitzer also made his usual trip to Ankara. However, the crisis showed that the National Guard had not been given time to organize itself; in case of a Turkish attack, Greece would not have the time to send reinforcements to the island.[18] This meant that Greece had to send its troops to Cyprus before the beginning of a Turkish invasion. Thus Garoufalias sent another 6,000 men. It is interesting that Garoufalias failed to notify both Papandreou and the Greek Cypriots about this: 'I am sorry for not informing you about the arrival of the troops. We should have', he wrote to the Greek Cypriot Defence Minister, Giorkatzis, in late June.[19] At the same time, the Turks appeared to have sent an additional 1,000 troops to the island.[20] In other words, the June 1964 Turkish invasion scare caused a dramatic expansion of the Greek military involvement in Cyprus.

The dispatch of Greek troops to Cyprus was not enough to alter the unfavourable overall balance between Greece and Turkey. Western Thrace and

Cyprus could be shielded, but the Aegean could not. The eastern Aegean islands were partially demilitarized, and Turkey could always select a target, concentrate the necessary forces and strike there. However, this meant that Greece did not have the power to impose Enosis. This had not been fully appreciated in Athens in the spring of 1964, at the time of the 'fatal Enosis euphoria'. It was only after the third Turkish invasion scare and following George Papandreou's visit to Washington that Athens realized that it could not impose Enosis, and that the Americans would not do this on Greece's behalf. By that time, late July and August 1964, the Greek government accepted the idea that Turkey would have to be compensated for agreeing to Enosis, probably with a large base in Cyprus.

Thus when, in mid-1964, deliberations with the Americans on a Cyprus settlement started, Athens and Ankara seemed to have reached a strategic stalemate: Athens had to take into account that the Turkish threat to Cyprus and the Aegean was always clear and present. For its part, Turkey had suffered a serious political setback as a result of the Johnson letter. The Americans tried to use this deadlock in order to find a solution. On 10 June, meeting George Papandreou in Athens, the US Undersecretary of State, George Ball, indicated that Turkey did not bluff and that therefore a solution could not fully satisfy either country. Ball toyed with the idea of a meeting of the Greek and the Turkish Prime Ministers, but Papandreou rejected this, noting that such a meeting should be prepared in advance; otherwise it would fail and make things worse.[21]

By the end of June, George Papandreou, the Foreign Minister, Costopoulos, and Andreas Papandreou visited Washington to confer with President Johnson, who had also just met the Turkish Prime Minister, Inönü. Johnson suggested to Papandreou a meeting between representatives of the Greek and the Turkish governments under the chairmanship of Dean Acheson, the former US Secretary of State. Subsequently, many on the Greek side (including George Papandreou in his 3 July statement in Parliament and Andreas Papandreou in his *Democracy at Gunpoint*) accused Johnson of trying to 'impose' a meeting of the Prime Ministers of Greece and Turkey (this implied that the US was trying to bring about another 'sell out' such as the 1959 Zurich agreements, which had been concluded at Prime Ministers' level). However, both the Greek and the US records of the talks have now been published, and show that Johnson did not press for a Prime Ministers' meeting but for a negotiation through representatives (which is what finally took place).[22] Johnson, Ball, Acheson and other US officials stressed to Papandreou that they had averted a Turkish invasion for the third time, but that they might not be able to do so again in the future. George Papandreou finally accepted the idea of parallel talks through Dean Acheson, who would formally assist the UN mediator on Cyprus.[23] During the talks, George Papandreou strongly protested that the US was blackmailing Greece with the threat of a Turkish invasion. It is not clear whether he really believed that the US was obliged to stop future Turkish invasions; he was probably merely trying to raise his price and to extract greater concessions. After the Washington talks Johnson wrote to George Papandreou, again underlining the danger of a Greek–Turkish war and urging for a quick settlement on Cyprus.[24]

Johnson was far from being an example of diplomatic leader, but he really believed that he would not be able to prevent a war in the future, and his letter was not an 'ultimatum', as the pro-government press in Athens claimed.[25] For his part, Papandreou responded in two ways: on the internal front he played the card of his defiant 'resistance' to American pressures, but as an experienced politician he understood that Johnson was making a point which could not be ignored. Papandreou wanted a serious negotiation through Acheson.

However, the Greek Prime Minister had already trapped himself: in the previous months he had accused the Conservatives of having made painful sacrifices in the 1959 agreements. Even on 3 July, after triumphantly returning to Athens, he pointed out that he had defied US pressure, while he added that no compensation could be given to Turkey for Enosis and that his government pursued a 'Greek foreign policy'. In other words, Papandreou had painted a heroic picture of national intransigence which was not compatible with compensations or realistic solutions, and now he would find out that he could not impose a less than ideal solution on a reluctant Makarios. Furthermore, the public campaign to present the Prime Minister as having said the 'big no' to the Americans also backfired internally: in an atmosphere of revival of anti-Americanism, the municipal elections of 5 July resulted in an impressive strengthening of the EDA vote – something which had not happened since 1958.[26] Evidently, this also increased the internal pressures on Papandreou.

Meanwhile, in Cyprus, Grivas's arrival and his appointment as Commander-in-Chief of the Greek forces had created further problems. These became apparent in early August during the Mansura crisis, when Grivas launched his attack, contrary to the orders of the Greek government. The Mansura crisis was a disaster for Greece. During the crisis, the Turkish air force used napalm bombs against inhabited areas in Cyprus, the Greek air force was unable to respond, and Greek-Cypriot morale collapsed. In its agony to stop the Turkish bombings, Athens declared that their continuation would be a *casus belli*.[27] The bombings stopped, but not before their impact had been felt. The fact that the Greek government had found it necessary to threaten war had shown that it could easily be dragged into a conflict. During the Mansura crisis, Athens suspected Makarios and Grivas of trying to lure the Greek forces in Cyprus into the battle.[28] Moreover, Makarios again appealed for Soviet support, and Moscow readily stated that it would intervene against an invasion. This also created waves of horror in the Greek government, which realized that, in the case of Soviet intervention, Greece would indeed be dragged into a conflict, on the side of Moscow and against the Turks and the Americans. Last but not least, the Greek government protested to NATO's Secretary General, Brosio, that during the NAC meetings, when the crisis was discussed, the alliance had taken a pro-Turkish attitude.[29] However, this put the Greeks in an extremely embarrassing position, since at the very same time they were trying to convince NATO to provide more aid for the strengthening of the Greek armed forces. The Mansura crisis resulted in the cancellation of two important NATO exercises – Eastern Express in Turkey and Deep Furrow in Greece – which were important for the improvement of these countries' defence against the Soviet Bloc.[30] The whole affair threatened to blow up Greece's foreign and security policies.

In short, Athens had completely failed to control Nicosia's initiatives. In a meeting with the Cypriot Foreign Minister, Spyros Kyprianou, on 11 August, the Greek Prime Minister was furious. He brushed aside Kyprianou's argument that prior to the Mansura attack Nicosia had spoken 'with an officer at the General Staff':[31]

> I do not know if there was a conversation or what it was. There was no consultation with us, the responsible leadership of the country. And we were faced with dilemmas. I was presented to the international public opinion as an impostor, because I had assured everybody that peace would prevail on the island. From that moment onwards, the prestige of the Greek government suffered, not of the Cypriot one. At the same time, we were horrified at the danger of a holocaust of [Greek] Cypriot civilians and at the danger that communism would appear as the only patriotic force and Moscow as the sole protector.

The Greek government tried to keep the Acheson negotiation alive. Acheson duly proposed Enosis, while Turkey would be compensated with sovereignty over the Karpass Peninsula; in a second version of his plan, he suggested that the Karpass be leased to Turkey for fifty years. Initially the Greek Cabinet welcomed the plan, while George Papandreou is reported as saying that 'we are being offered an apartment building and subletting only one penthouse to our neighbors, the Turks'.[32] However, Makarios – and, according to other sources, Andreas Papandreou as well – reacted against the plan and the Greek government felt unable to accept it. Then a naive idea about 'imposing' Enosis was put forward (probably by Garoufalias), which Makarios rejected, fearing that it would lead to the implementation of the Acheson Plan through the back door. This was a moment of ultimate confusion, and it was then that Papandreou's second letter to Makarios was sent, elaborating the national centre doctrine.

With the rejection of the Acheson Plan, and at a moment when the Turkish air force had exposed the vulnerability of Cyprus, Athens' military entanglement became permanent. Until August, the Greek strategy aimed at deterring a Turkish invasion and at bringing Enosis closer. The August failures changed all this. The Greek forces remained in the island, in constant crisis with Turkey and as a guarantee against unilateral moves of Makarios. The strategic overstretch of the Greek armed forces was complete.

Deadlocks, 1964–65

After the summer of 1964, new factors emerged on the scene. In June 1964 the Turkish government started expelling Greek citizens, members of the Greek Orthodox minority of Istanbul. In September 1964 Athens even appealed to the UN Security Council on this, but did not respond with similar measures against the Muslim minority in Greek Thrace.[33] In the following years, Ankara stepped up the pressures on the minority each time it wanted to press Athens on Cyprus; the members of the Greek Orthodox minority began an exodus from Turkey. In September 1964, Papandreou again appealed to NATO, asking the alliance to deal with the danger of a Greek–Turkish war. This also backfired: Brosio offered his 'good offices' in accordance with NATO's 1956 Resolution for the peaceful settlement of disputes; Turkey accepted the proposal but Greece rejected it, as this procedure was unacceptable to Makarios and might result in having Cyprus discussed in NATO rather than the United Nations.[34]

Militarily, the Greek forces had a clear superiority against the Turks in Cyprus itself. However, this meant that Cyprus' defence would not be autonomous; it would be based on the so-called Greek 'division'. (The Greek forces in Cyprus were not equivalent to a division, but often Greek analysts referred to them using this term.) And yet, this local superiority was not enough. The Turkish air strikes of August 1964 and the pictures of civilians burned by the Turkish napalm bombs showed that the Turkish military had found alternative ways to intervene in the island. The Greek side faced an important operational problem: the range of the Greek jets did not permit them to remain over Cyprus for more than a few minutes, and this could prove fatal in case of a Turkish military operation. Athens and Nicosia discussed this problem at length. The Greek Cypriots made the naive suggestion that the Greek jets could use Syrian airfields. This embarrassed Athens, as Syria was a pro-Soviet country, but (as could be predicted) the Egyptians and the Syrians rejected the Greek-Cypriot request, because they were not prepared to get into trouble with Turkey for the sake of non-aligned Cyprus.[35] The problem of air cover was never solved.

Additionally, Athens needed to take into account the overall balance of power with Turkey. On that level, the problem manifested itself mostly in the partially demilitarized islands of the eastern Aegean, which could fall easy prey to a Turkish attack. In the autumn of 1964, the government assigned a regiment to the wider area of the Aegean and created a strategic reserve whose task would be to counterattack in the event of a Turkish invasion there.[36] Yet in the spring of 1965 the Greek military authorities were warning that the Greek army was present everywhere, but nowhere in sufficient force.[37] The problem of security in the Aegean also remained unsolved. Vyron Theodoropoulos, the head of Turkish and Cypriot affairs in the Foreign Ministry in 1965–66, noted in an interview with this author that Thrace and Cyprus were theoretically secure, but the Aegean remained a huge problem.[38]

As if these burdens were not enough, Makarios seemed to fail to understand the problem of the overall Greek–Turkish balance. The archbishop appeared satisfied with his local superiority in Cyprus, and regarded that it was only a matter of time for the Turkish Cypriots to concede their defeat. This too was wishful thinking: 'By offering the Turkish-Cypriots nothing better than terms of surrender, Makarios unwittingly drove them closer to Ankara'.[39] The archbishop overestimated his own personal abilities and underestimated the problems that a small state could face in one of the most turbulent parts of the globe. Athens, on the other hand, could not lose sight of the overall balances; this was another major difference between Athens and Nicosia during that period.

In the autumn of 1964, the issue of Nicosia's relations with Moscow became much more pressing. Makarios' decision to seek verbal Soviet support has been criticized on the grounds that it provided little practical benefit to Cyprus, but turned the US against Nicosia.[40] It also made Athens even more anxious. The Papandreou government repeatedly indicated to Makarios that appealing to Moscow was a very dangerous policy. When the Greek Cypriots considered sending Kyprianou to Moscow to purchase Soviet arms, the Greek government suggested that this should be done through quiet diplomacy, not by a much-publicized visit of the Foreign Minister. In early September 1964 in Nicosia, speaking on Papandreou's instructions, Garoufalias told Makarios that 'Russia may be wielded as a threat, but it is not in our interest to force it to define its position'.[41] Still, Kyprianou went to Moscow. Immediately afterwards, Athens discovered that the Greek Cypriots had ordered Soviet surface-to-air missiles. Fearful of Greek-Cypriot use of these weapons, Athens demanded that they be manned by Greek personnel.[42] In order fully to appreciate the pressures that Makarios' Soviet opening created for Athens, one has to take into account that the purchase of Soviet SAMs finally sparked a crisis in *Greek–US relations*. Athens had focused its attention on the political importance of Kyprianou's visit, and did not realize the strength of US objections regarding the missiles. On their part, the Americans would not tolerate the purchase of Soviet missiles by Cyprus, but they did not realize that Cyprus had ordered such weapons.[43] This double misunderstanding was in the basis of the Greek–US crisis of the spring of 1965.

Meanwhile, the Greek Cypriots faced an important setback. In late 1964, after Khrushchev's fall, the Soviet Union changed its policy on Cyprus and accepted the Turkish view for a federation of the two Cypriot communities within an independent Republic.[44] When Papandreou and Costopoulos protested to the Soviet Ambassador, N. Koriukin, about the change of Soviet policy, they received a simple answer: Moscow did not want Cyprus to become NATO territory.[45] By early 1965, Athens' disappointment about Nicosia's policy could not be concealed. In a meeting between Papandreou, Costopoulos and Garoufalias, there were expressions of bitterness:[46]

> The Greek Government will neither allow nor tolerate any initiative on the part of the archbishop which could lead directly or indirectly to war. A similar initiative by the archbishop will be immediately followed by a public separation of responsibilities and a break of relations. Regarding other political initiatives, our views will be made clear and our responsibilities will be separated. This remark was caused by the realization of the failure and damaging consequences of the archbishop's policy towards Moscow. As is known, the archbishop had followed this policy despite the repeated disagreements of the Greek Government.

Then, in March 1965, the Americans found out that Cyprus had purchased Soviet T-34 tanks, which raised no serious objections in Washington, as well as surface-to-air missiles, which were, for the moment, transported to Egypt. Until then, the Americans had not realized that Cyprus had bought these weapons, and the Greeks had not realized the strength of US feelings on this issue. Moreover, the US was evidently afraid that when the missiles arrived in Cyprus, the Turkish response would be violent and uncontrollable. During successive meetings with the Greek Ambassador, Matsas, the US Undersecretary of State, George Ball, expressed worries about information that Greek officers had been trained in the use of Soviet weapons. Ball said that Greek officers who in the past had been trained in US Nike missiles, could by their very knowledge reveal secrets of Nike technology to their Soviet trainers. Ball demanded to know whether there were any secret agreements between Greece, Egypt or the Soviet Union.[47] This started a Greek–US crisis, at a moment when the Greeks were asking the Americans and NATO to help in the defence of the Greek North (see Chapter 12).

On 13 March, George Papandreou used his favourite 'right/wrong' rhetoric to reply to the US demarche: he disclaimed that Greece had made any secret agreements and indicated that these were defensive weapons, which Cyprus had every right to possess in the exercise of its solemn right of self-defence; the missiles would be 'a guarantee of peace' in Cyprus. He reminded the Americans that the Turks had used US-built jets to bomb inhabited areas in Cyprus, and finally noted that former, not active, Greek officers had been trained in the Soviet missiles.[48] However, Papandreou had disappointed the Americans in the case of the Acheson Plan, and Washington would not be drawn into a discussion about high principles, when it believed that the confidentiality of US military technology was at stake. Evidently, after the Papandreou message, the US position hardened. On 15 March, Ball told Matsas that this affair could even lead to the termination of Greek–US co-operation.[49] On 16 March, the US Secretary of Defence, Robert Macnamara, sent a message to Garoufalias, referring to the 'shock' that this affair had caused in Washington; Macnamara also refused to meet his Greek counterpart until the issue was cleared up.[50] On 17 March, Macnamara told Matsas that the missile affair could lead to the 'destruction of Greece',[51] a threat that the US had never made before. Matsas reported to Athens that the Americans felt that they had been deceived. Talking to the Americans, Matsas took the line that if the Greek government had not stepped in to acquire control of the SAMs, these would have fallen into the hands of Greek-Cypriot extremists or even of Soviet officers.[52] This seemed to calm Ball. Then Garoufalias wrote to Macnamara, noting that no Greek officers with previous Nike experience had been trained in Soviet weapons; simply, some officers who had taken part in manoeuvres with Nikes had been sent to Egypt. Garoufalias reminded his American counterpart that the Greek Cypriots had tasted Turkish napalms and could not be expected to be left unprotected from the Turkish air force. Following this, Garoufalias went to Cyprus and made sure that the missiles would not arrive in Cyprus for six months (in fact, the missiles never reached Cyprus).[53] This was how the crisis was overcome. However, the whole affair had revealed that the efforts of the Athens government to control Nicosia had again failed. Indeed, this time they backfired.

Faced with such difficulties, in the spring of 1965 Athens decided to negotiate a Cyprus settlement directly with Turkey, and consulted Makarios on this. During the first meeting, on 6 May, the differences between the two governments became clear. Makarios appeared content with the present balance of forces within Cyprus, and suggested that the Greek Cypriots could wait until the Turkish Cypriots decided to make concessions. However, George Papandreou replied that this was an incomplete analysis:

> The internal balance has been decided, but you cannot ignore the existence of a Turkish State which will not remain idle. You are not alone. If this were simply an internal problem, it would already have been solved. Just as we tell the Turks that they cannot ignore Cyprus, which is a UN member, in the very same way we cannot say that this is simply an internal issue and ignore the Turkish State which is vigilant and threatens to intervene whenever the Turkish minority is pressed. And how is it possible that the suppression of the Turkish minority will not have repercussions at the United Nations, where good government is a precondition for self-determination? Therefore, there is the threat of the Turkish State, and there are the United Nations, and both will play a role in the final outcome. This is why the internal aspect is one, but not the only aspect. [...] We must bring Enosis about, but also we have to avoid war, which will bring about the death of Enosis and slaughter in Cyprus, Thrace and Istanbul. A war could lead to Enosis only if it resulted in a crushing victory of Greece against Turkey. But today this is out of the question.

Makarios said that 'we have come to the edge of the cliff but did not fall', to which Papandreou replied: 'playing with fire all the time is dangerous'. Papandreou's analysis also had some defects, though: during this meeting the Prime Minister launched another verbal attack against the 1959 agreements and suggested that the Turks wanted to revert to them; Makarios corrected him, pointing out that Turkey would not accept a return to a Cypriot unitary state, but wanted the creation of a federal system.[54]

On the next day, a new meeting was held at the Palace, with the participation of King Constantine and of former Prime Ministers Pipinelis and Kanellopoulos. Makarios once more said that he regarded Athens as the centre of Hellenism, but made it clear that he preferred the status quo rather than a compromise according to which Turkey would be compensated with territory in Cyprus. Kanellopoulos, the Conservative leader, supported Papandreou's views by stressing that the Aegean islands were exposed to Turkish attack, and 'we cannot defend ourselves effectively everywhere'. King Constantine said that the Greek Orthodox minority of Istanbul would be destroyed without a Cyprus settlement. The Cypriot Foreign Minister, Kyprianou, suggested compensating Turkey with Greek, not Cypriot, territory, for example an island, but Papandreou and Kanellopoulos ruled this out. Faced by a common stance of both major Greek parties, Makarios agreed that Athens could negotiate with Ankara an Enosis solution, but he ruled out a Greek–Turkish agreement on the constitutional status of an independent Cyprus.[55]

Thus, the Greek and Turkish Foreign Ministers, Stavros Costopoulos and Hasan Işik, met and agreed to initiate negotiations; these took place in Ankara between the Greek Ambassador, Alexandros Sgourdaios and Işik, but led nowhere. The Turks asked for a large compensation, even in Greek territory. The Greeks aired the idea that Turkey should receive the British base of Dhekelia in Cyprus; at some point, Sgourdaios and Costopoulos examined the possibility of giving to Turkey a small area (about 100 square kilometres) of Greek territory in Thrace. However, the internal Greek crisis of summer 1965 put an end to this process.[56]

Trying to break the deadlock, 1966

After September 1965, the Stephanopoulos government tried to terminate the strategic overstretch of the Greek army and to close the eastern front through a Greek–Turkish agreement on Cyprus which would provide for Enosis with some compensation for Turkey. This government strongly believed in the necessity of Greek–Turkish co-operation: Stephanopoulos himself, in an interview to the Turkish journalist, Abdi Ipeçki, noted that history and geography called for Greek–Turkish co-operation.[57] Moreover, Mitsotakis, the strong man of this government, was a known supporter of Greek–Turkish friendship and played a role in the start of the 1966 negotiation. Last but not least, in the autumn of 1965, during NAC sessions, many NATO countries encouraged Athens and Ankara to resume talks, and the December 1965 Watching Brief of the Secretary General also contained a similar appeal.[58] A negotiated settlement in Cyprus could thus play a role in furthering Greek and Turkish relations with the alliance.

Still, the Stephanopoulos government considered that a negotiation with Ankara called for the parallel strengthening of Greek defence capabilities. This was possible, as the December 1965 currency crisis was overcome, and the country could afford the cost; 'we could stand it', Mitsotakis told this author.[59] Thus, in 1966 the Stephanopoulos government bought fast patrol boats, torpedo boats and aircraft, all suitable for a war in the Aegean. The CU government had tried to order such hardware in 1964, but the British and the Americans had refused to sell any to Greece. The 'apostates' bought fast patrol boats from other sources (Norway, a NATO ally), and thus the British and the Americans decided not to be left behind.[60]

Once more, the major problem concerned the Athens–Nicosia dimension: the apostates' relations with Makarios were even worse than the archbishop's relations with Papandreou. The Stephanopoulos government started deliberations with Nicosia in October 1965, when Mitsotakis went to Cyprus, on his way to a private trip to the Middle East.[61] In November, Tsirimokos visited Cyprus and stated that Nicosia should have the lead in its 'struggle for liberation' (a view – and wording – which rather embarrassed his colleagues in the government). Then, on 18 December 1965, the UN General Assembly passed a Resolution favourable to Cyprus. This was a victory for Makarios, but also revealed the limits of his policy: the Resolution had been supported only by the non-aligned; the Americans voted against the Greek-Cypriot item, while the Soviets abstained. Thus, the December 1965 UN Resolution did not solve anything, although it could become a useful lever for the Greek side in a future negotiation with Ankara.

The Greek government tried to secure Makarios' consent for a new Greek–Turkish negotiation. In early February 1966, in Athens, Makarios accepted the idea, again making clear that these negotiations should deal with eventual Enosis, not with the constitutional problems of independent Cyprus. It was also agreed to define the status of the Greek officers serving in the Greek-Cypriot National Guard.[62] However, this latter issue proved extremely thorny. Grivas demanded that the National Guard be placed under his command even in peacetime; Stephanopoulos gave in to this demand, Makarios protested and Tsirimokos resigned. The suspicions between Athens and Nicosia did not go away; they deepened.

The Stephanopoulos government went on with its effort to settle Cyprus. The initiative was carefully prepared, with Mitsotakis holding the first exploratory meetings, in December 1965, with the Turkish Tourism Minister, Nihat Kursat, and in March 1966 with the Foreign Minister, the able Ihsan Sabri Çaglayangil. During his meeting with the latter, Mitsotakis stressed that the negotiations should aim at Enosis, and that the deportation of Greeks from Istanbul should cease. When the Turkish Foreign Minister raised the issue of the Greek forces in Cyprus, Mitsotakis noted that these troops had provided a check on Makarios and indirectly prevented the deterioration of the position of the Turkish Cypriots.[63] It is of course doubtful whether this last argument could have convinced Ankara, although a prominent Turkish writer has argued that Ismet Inönü also shared a similar view.[64]

A Toumbas–Çaglayangil meeting took place in June, and representatives of the two governments were appointed to continue the talks. During the ensuing negotiation, the Greeks did not rule out a federal union of Cyprus with Greece, which would provide for a local Cypriot Parliament with Turkish-Cypriot representation; Athens proposed that Turkey be compensated with the British base at Dhekelia (this base could be under Turkish sovereignty). Finally, the Greeks ruled out the full demilitarization of Cyprus; Athens indicated that it could not accept the withdrawal of Greek troops from an island on which the Turks would have a large base.[65]

To be sure, the idea of giving Turkey a British base meant that the whole affair was dependent on a British decision which could not be taken for granted. However, once more, another major problem came up between Athens and Nicosia. During Makarios' meeting with the Greek ministers in early September, the climate was not good. Athens raised the issue of 'communist infiltration' of the National Guard; this, together with Athens' support of Grivas, made Makarios suspicious that the Stephanopoulos government was conspiring against him. The archbishop rejected the idea of Turkey receiving a sovereign base, but accepted the installation of a NATO base manned by Turkish troops.[66] A new meeting took place in November, when Makarios again stressed his disagreement on a Turkish sovereign base. This central problem was not solved.[67]

Toumbas and Çaglayangil were to meet in December, during the NATO ministerial meeting. However, a few days earlier a new Athens–Nicosia crisis erupted, when the Cypriot government purchased firearms from Czechoslovakia. Athens regarded this as an attempt to torpedo the negotiations, and feared that these weapons could be used to create a paramilitary force loyal to the archbishop. The Chief of the General Staff of National Defence, Lieutenant-General Tsolakas, immediately flew to Cyprus and got Makarios' agreement that the arms would remain under lock and key and would not be distributed.[68] Immediately afterwards, though, Makarios backtracked from his agreement with Tsolakas; Grivas submitted his usual resignation to the Greek government, for not taking measures against the archbishop; and Toumbas sent two severe messages to Makarios, threatening with a withdrawal of the Greek Ambassador from Nicosia. Makarios again promised to abide by his agreement with Tsolakas, but evidently he had already distributed many of the Czech weapons to his supporters.[69]

Thus, Toumbas and his Turkish counterpart met again on 17 December. The Turkish side aired ideas about Greek–Turkish condominium, suggested that it wanted a base in any event (not only in an Enosis solution), and asked for the demilitarization of Cyprus, which Toumbas rejected. Yet, it was agreed to make further contacts with the British, in order to determine whether London would indeed be prepared to cede the Dhekelia base to Turkey in the case of an Athens–Ankara agreement.[70] However, the Stephanopoulos government fell on 20 December, following a George Papandreou–Kanellopoulos agreement to lead the country to elections. The negotiations would be continued by the caretaker government under Ioannis Paraskevopoulos.

However, during a meeting of the Council of the Crown on 6 February 1967 Makarios again said that he would accept the installation of a NATO, not a Turkish, base in Cyprus.[71] Thus, he rejected the minimum demand of Ankara. Moreover, Toumbas, Markezinis and Stephanopoulos, independently of each other, told the US Ambassador, Talbot, that during the Council meeting Makarios had claimed that the Americans had promised him they would stop a Turkish invasion, which Talbot of course disclaimed.[72] This was indicative of the illusions that constantly appeared on the Greek side (Greeks and Greek Cypriots) regarding the US attitude. Anyway, in April 1967 the Colonels' coup put an end to the Greek–Turkish talks.

Arguably, the 1966 negotiation was the last chance for an Enosis settlement with some compensation for Turkey. Of course, Turkey had not definitely agreed to this idea and the British attitude had not been quite clear about ceding Dhekelia to Ankara. Still, there had been prospects, which in the following years would disappear. The failure of this negotiation signalled the definite collapse of Athens' Cyprus policy. By 1967, Athens had achieved none of its aims in Cyprus. On the contrary, there was constant friction with Nicosia, the Greek strategic overstretch continued, Greek–Turkish relations remained bad, and the Greek Orthodox minority of Istanbul was driven out of Turkey. More Cyprus crises lay in the years ahead.

14 The effort to adjust Greece's Eastern policy

The Eastern policy of the CU, 1964–65

The CU appeared to be much better placed than the Karamanlis government to pursue a comprehensive new Eastern policy. In 1963–64, George Papandreou often declared that Greece wanted to be an ally of the West and a friend of the East. However, Papandreou himself was always suspicious of the Soviet Bloc. Among the Centre leaders it was Sophocles Venizelos who had argued for an opening to the East, but he died early during the 1964 electoral campaign. Moreover, the Cyprus crises in 1964 further complicated Greece's Eastern policy.

After the February 1964 election, the CU government scored an important success: the full normalization of Greek–Bulgarian relations. In 1962, Averoff had proposed a 'package deal' to Sofia. The Bulgarians accepted the idea in the summer of 1963, and a new round of negotiations started in April 1964. The Bulgarians now offered a small amount of money as reparation and, as the Cyprus crises were mounting in those months, their bargaining position was rather strong. The CU government showed resolve and decided to go ahead. On 28 June 1964, twelve Greek–Bulgarian agreements were signed, settling all pending issues: reparations (the Bulgarians agreed to pay $7 million); commercial exchanges; the use of the port of Thessaloniki by the Bulgarians; the re-establishment of railway and air traffic communications as well as of mail, telegraph and telephone communications; and the common exploitation of the water of the rivers running through the territory of both countries. Even after the settlement, Athens still tried to keep the Bulgarians at arms' length as far as political relations were concerned: in September 1964, George Papandreou rejected overtures by Sofia to form a common attitude in case of a Greek–Turkish war. In the same month, though, during the visit to Sofia of the Foreign Minister, Costopoulos, the Greeks scored an important success: in the communiqué, the Bulgarians officially stated that they claimed no Greek territory. This was a declaration that the Greeks had been trying to get since 1919. Thus, Greek policy towards Bulgaria resulted in a major success for the CU.[1]

The Greek–Soviet relationship was a more complicated affair. The Papandreou government distrusted Moscow, was embarrassed by Makarios' bids for Soviet support and strongly resented the change of Soviet policy on Cyprus in the autumn of 1964. Greek–Soviet interests diverged on Cyprus, an issue of prime importance to Athens. Thus, in 1964 the Greeks preferred to focus on commercial relations: in October a new five-year trade agreement was concluded, providing for an increase of 33 per cent in trade by 1969.[2] In December a delegation of the Supreme Soviet visited Athens and, according to press reports, invited Papandreou to Moscow.[3] This transferred the focus of attention from the economic to the political level.

The official invitation was conveyed by Ambassador Koriukin in early March; Papandreou accepted it in principle, although the dates were to be set later.[4] A visit of the Greek Prime Minister to Moscow would have been the most impressive development in Greek–Soviet relations since 1945. Top diplomats were in favour of the visit, and indeed Christos Xanthopoulos-Palamas, the former Director General of the Foreign Ministry and now permanent representative to NATO, told the Prime Minister that Greece should not confine itself to the 'ghetto' of the West, which was the legacy of the civil war.[5] However, the visit to Moscow provoked various external as well as internal pressures on the Greek government.

First, the new Soviet line on Cyprus had embittered Athens and added to its suspicions. Second, the Soviets themselves again intensified Greek reserve: in mid-March a Moscow Radio broadcast and an article in *Pravda* suggested that the Greek government should suppress the legislation of previous conservative administrations, legalize the Communist Party and withdraw from NATO.[6] This was self-defeating: throughout the post-civil war period, George Papandreou himself had been prominent in resisting the legalization of the KKE and had strongly supported Greece's Western orientation. Moreover, the Soviet remarks gave to the conservative opposition grounds strongly to oppose the Papandreou visit. By now the ERE was mounting a major political counteroffensive against the CU. The Conservative leader, Kanellopoulos, stated that although a visit by a Greek Prime Minister to Moscow might be beneficial, a visit by Papandreou was out of the question, especially after the recent Soviet comments on Greek internal affairs. The respected Conservative daily *Kathimerini* even wrote that if Papandreou went to Moscow, he would not return to Greece as Prime Minister. The opposition attacks were widely held to be the main reason why the visit never took place.[7] Certainly, the Conservative attack formed an important obstacle to the visit, and was a telling example of the tendency of Greek opposition parties to create internal trouble on issues of foreign policy; it was also indicative of the mounting internal tension of those months, which would culminate in the break-up of the CU in summer.

However, the attitude of the opposition was not the only reason that the Moscow visit did not take place. There were additional problems. In fact, Papandreou himself was not sure whether he should proceed with the visit. Immediately after receiving the formal Soviet invitation, the Foreign Minister, Costopoulos, told the British Ambassador, Sir Ralph Murray, that the government was highly sceptical about the visit. According to Costopoulos, Athens feared that this was simply a Soviet effort to play Greece against Turkey and blackmail Ankara in order to force it to make more concessions to Moscow. Murray alleged that the invitation made the Conservative wing of the CU anxious that the Soviets were trying to build bridges with members of the party who might then accept a future governmental alliance with the Left.[8] In a loose conglomeration such as the CU, this was a major problem.

Thus the government publicly appeared in favour of the visit, but in practice it proved reluctant to fix its dates. To make matters worse, Papandreou told the US Ambassador, Henry Labouisse, that he doubted whether he would go to Moscow. This was leaked to the press, offended the Soviets and provoked a representation by the Soviet Ambassador, Koriukin, to Costopoulos. The British Embassy, a careful observer of Greek affairs, reported that the Prime Minister had not made up his mind about going to the Soviet capital, but he would consider 'as always' whether he could turn the visit to 'local political advantage' and whether 'he could really diminish the Turkish success, such as it is, with the Russians [on Cyprus], or would be merely used by the latter to keep up pressure on the Turks'.[9] Last but not least, on the very same days in mid-March 1965, the crisis in Greek–US relations erupted when Washington discovered that Cyprus had purchased surface-to-air missiles from the Soviet Union. This was hardly a time when Athens would want to further provoke the US with visits to Moscow. The CU government fell in July, and the visit never took place.

To be sure, the CU government, like its Conservative predecessors, did not attempt to play the East against the West over Cyprus. Apart from Bulgaria and the Soviet Union, the CU government concluded commercial or economic agreements with East Germany, Czechoslovakia, Poland and Hungary.[10] However, this administration was under the constant pressure of successive crises in Cyprus or (in 1965) internally, and did not have the opportunity fully to implement a comprehensive policy towards the Communist East.

However, beyond Moscow and Sofia there were other important Greek interests in Eastern Europe. Tito's Yugoslavia was now a leading member of the non-aligned and was going through important internal changes, including the relative strengthening of the federative republics, such as the now Socialist Republic of Macedonia (SRM), vis-à-vis the federal government in Belgrade. Moreover, as was usually the case in Greek–Yugoslav relations, during a period of relative relaxation of East–West tensions the Yugoslavs tended to place less emphasis on the strategic value of their Greek connections and to put forward issues relating to the Macedonian problem, which embarrassed Athens. Impressive rhetoric, such as George Papandreou's reference to Tito as 'the Apostle of Peace', involved appearances rather than substance.

In the autumn of 1964, Greece and Yugoslavia agreed to reactivate the 1959 bilateral border agreement but also to proceed to an exchange of land estates, so as to reduce the need for border traffic.[11] Greece reduced tariffs for Yugoslav products transported through Thessaloniki, whereas Belgrade doubled the number of passes to Greek lorries driving through Yugoslavia.[12] Then, in February 1965, George Papandreou visited Belgrade. According to Costopoulos and Greek diplomats who spoke with the British after the visit, the Yugoslavs were against NATification of Cyprus through Enosis, and intended to come out in favour of the federalization of Cyprus – that is, to follow the Soviets in supporting the Turkish position. The Greeks managed to avert this. Regarding bilateral relations, the Greeks rejected Yugoslav suggestions for the creation of a free trade zone in the common border (this was also incompatible with Greece's association with the EEC), for the expansion of the Yugoslav free zone in the port of Thessaloniki, and for the settlement of additional Yugoslav monks in the Helandari Monastery at Mount Athos. The Greeks suggested the expansion of bilateral co-operation on tourism, cultural exchanges and industry, which Belgrade accepted. Thus, it could be argued that Papandreou succeeded in furthering Greek–Yugoslav relations in the pace and the sectors that Athens preferred, while he also averted a switch of Yugoslav diplomacy on Cyprus. However, the visit became a very embarrassing affair for the Greek government when the Yugoslav Deputy Minister for Foreign Affairs stated that a problem existed regarding the treatment of the Slav-Macedonian minority in Greece.[13] This was the first time that a Yugoslav federal official had made a similar statement with the Greek leaders present in Belgrade. During the 1962–63 'relentless struggle' the CU had strongly attacked Karamanlis on this issue, and now it was the Conservatives' turn to make some very bitter observations about Papandreou's policy.[14] Thus the Papandreou visit ended in creating another internal problem for the Greek Prime Minister.

Finally, relations with Tirana remained non-existent. In 1964–65, the CU government maintained that Greece would have to secure some fundamental human rights for the Greeks of Northern Epirus before abandoning the claim over this territory. In July 1964, Papandreou also stated that the issue of Northern Epirus was still pending in the four-power CFM since 1946.[15] This reference to the CFM was reminiscent of the Pipinelis line on Northern Epirus, and could easily be misunderstood. However, the lack of progress in Greek–Albanian relations was primarily the result of Tirana's extreme isolationism.

The 'apostates' and the attempt to shape a new Eastern policy, 1966

The Stephanopoulos government tried to shape a more comprehensive policy towards Moscow and its allies, while it also attempted, for the first time since the civil war, to expand this opening to the political level. By 1966, the international climate was more favourable for an opening to the East. Concerning strategy, the 'apostates' government regarded that, although there was no prospect for a 'desatellization' of the Soviet allies in Eastern Europe, these countries would have a greater degree of economic independence in the future; this created opportunities for the West.[16] However, a more relaxed policy towards the East should be based on the strengthening of Western unity: as Toumbas told the British Foreign Secretary, Michael Stewart, in June 1966, Athens welcomed moves to lessen East–West tension, 'provided that it was made by the NATO Governments in concert'.[17]

Although Elias Tsirimokos, a major figure of the Centre-left, was Foreign Minister of this government, he was not the driving force behind its Eastern opening; indeed, the major successes of this policy came after his resignation from the Foreign Ministry. The main influence in Eastern policy was that of the Minister of Economic Co-ordination, Constantinos Mitsotakis, who personally handled some crucial issues. The guiding line of his policy could be found in the priority to rationalize the country's external economic relations, as a means to ensure Greece's integration in the international economy. Indeed, in order to pursue a new policy Greece would have to complement the old logic of military confrontation with a new one, which would recognize the common interest of East and West in the development of economic co-operation. Thus, in 1966 Greece concluded economic or commercial agreements with the Soviet Union, Hungary, Romania, Yugoslavia, Bulgaria and Czechoslovakia; Greece also initiated exports of wheat to the Soviet Bloc, which were paid in currency, not through clearing agreements. Last but not least, Athens tried to facilitate deals of Greek businessmen in the Soviet-Bloc countries, such as the building of Greek commercial ships in Soviet docks. The latter effort brought no significant results, but was indicative of the search for new forms of co-operation. A major study on Greece's Eastern policy noted that 1966 was the 'apogee' of the country's Eastern trade.[18]

The Soviet Union itself was very important in this new policy. In March 1966, Tsirimokos stated that the government wished to improve relations with Moscow and its allies. He also played down the importance of the Soviet position on Cyprus, arguing that at any rate Moscow was opposed to a Turkish invasion of the island.[19] This was probably the most positive statement on the Soviet Union by a Greek Foreign Minister since the second half of the 1940s. However, Tsirimokos resigned one month later, after disagreeing with the government's Cyprus policy. Evidently his replacement by a Centre-right politician and former naval officer, Toumbas, disappointed Moscow: in April, *Pravda* published an article criticizing the internal policy of the Greek government as well as its policy on Cyprus.[20] In the autumn of 1966 Mitsotakis stepped in and negotiated a new agreement: the Soviets would build a large electricity power station in the wider Athens area (Keratsini), which would be paid for by Greek tobacco.[21] This was the first Western purchase of a Soviet power generator; never before had Athens concluded an agreement of this magnitude with the Soviet Union. Thus, no political initiative was undertaken towards Moscow, but bilateral economic and technical co-operation made a great leap forward.

The Balkans was another major field of diplomatic activity. Although some tension appeared in Greek–Bulgarian relations in 1965, when the magazine of the Bulgarian army criticized the Greek government and Greek intelligence arrested the Bulgarian military attaché for espionage, these incidents did not lead to a crisis in bilateral relations. In 1966 a Greek parliamentary delegation visited Sofia for the first time since 1945, and cultural exchanges were initiated.[22] The 'apostates' government also tried to revive Greek–Yugoslav co-operation. In October 1966, the President of the Executive Council of Yugoslavia, Petar

Stambolic, and the Economics Minister, Kiro Gligorov, visited Athens. Before this visit, a leading member of the Communist Party of the SRM again put forward the existence of a Macedonian issue. This time the statement was not made by a federal official, but the CU still took the opportunity to denounce government policy. The Greek government now changed its line and raised this issue during the Stambolic visit, trying to make it clear that similar initiatives could adversely affect bilateral relations. Things became even more difficult when, during the visit, the Yugoslavs proposed the abolition of visas for travel between the two countries; the Greeks feared that this would allow many former Communist guerrillas (who now had Yugoslav citizenship) to enter the country. Still, despite these problems, Athens continued to aim at the improvement of bilateral relations. As the British Embassy in Athens put it, this was one of the major aims of all Greek governments.[23] Notably, the Stephanopoulos government was successful on another level: in 1966 the military co-operation of the two countries revived, when the military visits were resumed.[24] This suggests that for the 'apostates' government, the movement towards détente had to be combined with a strengthening of the country's regional position.

As always, Albania was the most difficult case in Greece's Eastern policy. According to Greek diplomats, the Stephanopoulos government wanted to normalize relations with Tirana, and considered that the state of war between the two countries was 'ridiculous'.[25] In early 1966, Athens asked the French government to act as an intermediary with Tirana. In March, the Greek and the Albanian Chambers of Commerce signed a commercial agreement. This was the first Greek–Albanian agreement in the post-war period, but was never implemented because Tirana finally refused to sign the necessary payments agreement. Still, Greek ministers stated that this was the first step towards the restoration of relations, and referred to the possibility of abolishing the state of war. However, this was immediately resisted by Pipinelis, who kept supporting the claim on Northern Epirus.[26] The 'apostates' government had a majority of one in Parliament, and this meant that Pipinelis alone could bring it down. Thus the effort could not continue, although one should keep in mind that throughout this process the Albanians themselves did not show much willingness to proceed to the normalization of relations.

Athens' most impressive initiative concerned Romania. Bucharest had by now claimed relative independence from Moscow in foreign affairs, and a political opening to Eastern Europe could usefully begin from there. Greek–Romanian relations had been normalized in 1956, when agreement had also been reached on compensation for Greek properties destroyed during the Second World War. The 1956 agreement did not cover compensation for the post-war nationalization of Greek properties, but Bucharest had agreed in principle that this should be settled as well. In the summer of 1966, new negotiations started. It was also announced that after the conclusion of a settlement, the Romanian Prime Minister, Gheorghe Maurer, would visit Greece. This was going to be the first visit of a Communist Prime Minister to Athens, and Greek Foreign Ministry officials cautiously stressed to Western diplomats that it was similar to other such exchanges between the Soviet Bloc and the Western countries; Greece was merely taking the opportunity to improve relations with the East.[27]

Indeed, nine bilateral agreements were signed during Maurer's visit to Athens in early September 1966, including: compensation; a long-term commercial agreement; a payments agreement; an agreement on industrial, economic and technical co-operation; a programme for cultural and scientific exchanges; and a maritime agreement. During the visit the Romanians, evidently trying not to embarrass Athens, did not press their favourite proposal for a Balkan nuclear-free zone. Stephanopoulos accepted Maurer's invitation to visit Bucharest. According to the British Embassy, the visit was in line with Greek policy to improve relations with the country's northern neighbours; it was natural for Greece to try to make use of its own advantage, as a Balkan country, in the improved East–West climate.[28]

Following the Maurer visit, the Greek government accelerated political (not merely economic) contacts with the Soviet-Bloc countries. In October, the Minister of Commerce, Emmanuel Kothris, visited Hungary.[29] In November, Kothris and Mitsotakis visited Czechoslovakia – a country with which, according to the Greek government, commercial relations could substantially develop further.[30] At the same time, autumn 1966, the Greek government invited the Bulgarian President, Todor Zhivkov, to visit Greece.[31] This would be the first Greek–Bulgarian state visit ever, but it did not take place; the Greek government fell in late December, and in April 1967 the country's democratic regime was toppled by the Colonels. Thus, the adjustment of Greece's Eastern policy was not completed before the dictatorship; this was left for the post-1974 governments.

15 The mid-1960s
A re-evaluation

The years 1963–67 were an era of contradictions and upheaval. Short-lived or caretaker governments were called upon to handle tense and dangerous problems, which were being anxiously followed by an excited and bitterly divided public opinion. Not unexpectedly, these governments were not very successful. They had little control over events, faced multiple fronts and were plagued by internal crises which in turn tended to maximize the difficulties in formulating a comprehensive response to problems.

It is perhaps surprising that limited control was a characteristic of the CU government, the most popular Greek administration of the early post-war period. It has been noted that this administration had an 'unclear perception about Greece's strategic priorities'.[1] Its aims were largely contradictory: the desire to reduce defence expenditure was incompatible with the multiple fronts in the north, in the Aegean and in Cyprus; the inability to control Makarios could always spark crises even with the US; and the misunderstandings with the Americans, together with the revival of anti-Americanism, were contradictory with the effort to persuade Washington to provide additional guarantees for Greek security, which were indispensable in these years of strategic overstretch and multiple fronts. However, in an overall re-evaluation it can be argued that, at the end of the day, there was a specific crucial turning point – literally a 'fatal moment' – for the CU government: the rejection of the Acheson Plan in August 1964.

Sections of older Greek bibliography regarded the Acheson Plan as a partitionist scheme which the Americans tried to 'impose' on a proud and defiant CU government. According to this thesis, when this government, protecting the national interest, resisted American pressure, the US brought it down through the 'apostasy' (thus, the 'apostasy' was also regarded as part of this American conspiracy). Then, the Americans imposed, facilitated or welcomed the imposition of the military dictatorship. Largely, this 'revisionist' thesis was based on Andreas Papandreou's writings, mainly his *Democracy at Gunpoint*.[2] The Greek post-revisionist bibliography questioned the validity of this interpretation. The problem of the conspiracy theory lies in the fact that the CU government itself wanted, but felt unable to accept, the Acheson Plan. The Centre had already aroused Greek public sentiment against 'the sell out of Zurich'; the Centre leaders had declared that they would work for the undoing of the 1959 settlement, and had contributed to the maximalism of Greek public opinion. In August 1964, the CU government finally discovered that its options were severely limited precisely because of the maximalism which it had encouraged. In a sense, the CU was trapped by, and fell victim to, its own propaganda of the previous years.

The rejection of the Acheson Plan mortgaged the CU government's policy as a whole. Indeed, until the summer of 1964 the Papandreou administration centred all its efforts on the Cyprus question, hoping to achieve absolute political dominance in the country, if it could get Enosis and score an impressive national victory. This strategy collapsed in August 1964. Until then, the US and Britain had considered that Athens created faits accomplis, but would finally manage to get Enosis. The CU government's inability to accept the Acheson Plan, at the very moment when Enosis appeared to be very close, created the impression (to West as well as East) that Athens was either extremely weak or highly ambivalent. Indeed, US and British attitudes towards the Papandreou government started changing exactly from that moment. Soviet policy also changed, and tried to block NATification of the island through Enosis. Until August 1964 the CU government's initiatives proved successful; this was the case, for example, in the Greek–Bulgarian settlement, despite the fact that the sum of Bulgarian reparations was rather low. However, after August 1964 no comparable success was scored; the government lacked the air of a winner and was regarded by all as a vulnerable player. Witness, for example, the abrupt US behaviour during the March 1965 crisis over the Soviet SAMs.

The rejection of the Acheson Plan dealt a severe blow to the CU on the internal front as well: the public was confused and anti-Americanism was strengthened, greatly embarrassing the Papandreou government; the Conservatives organized their counterattack; the internal quarrels in the CU became more tense, especially over the role of Andreas Papandreou, who was reputed to have resisted acceptance of the Acheson Plan; Grivas followed his own line in Cyprus and made relations with Makarios even more difficult; finally, Grivas destroyed the Papandreou government with the ASPIDA affair. Thus, the rejection of the Acheson Plan was indeed a turning point in the history of the CU government. However, this was not because the Americans became 'angry', conspired against it and toppled it, as a number of analysts assert; it was the CU government itself that lost its major political investment, and presented to friend and foe, both internal and external, a picture of weakness which finally caused it to disintegrate.

Of course, by the spring of 1965 George Papandreou had realized the need to pursue a more realistic policy, including direct Greek–Turkish negotiation on Cyprus, which he so proudly claimed to have rejected less than a year before, pursuing his 'Greek foreign policy'. For various reasons, though, internal as well as external, spring 1965 was too late. If nothing else, Athens now was forced to accept a bilateral negotiation, without having the Americans on its side pressing for an immediate Enosis solution.

To put it simply, in 1964 Athens and Nicosia had to make a compromise: neither the international political situation nor the regional balance of power allowed any hope for a crushing diplomatic victory. Athens should have known that the Cyprus crisis could only end with a compromise. In August 1964 it might have been a favourable compromise, but it would still require a difficult decision. Thus, the long debate in the Greek bibliography as to whether the Acheson Plan was 'good' is, at the end of the day, misleading: this Plan (or, more generally, the idea of compensating Turkey to get Enosis) was the maximum that the Greek side could achieve in the mid-1960s. This is why this government was criticized for lack of realism.[3] Other critics have taken an even stronger line: they held that in 1964 George Papandreou pursued an 'inconsiderate policy' and an 'Enosist demagoguery', 'feeding from fatal illusions and giving life to equally tragic hallucinations'.[4] This book has supported a different view: in 1964 Papandreou was trapped by his own maximalist propaganda. In that climate it was very difficult to make a decision for a favourable, and yet still painful, compromise. Given the forces that the CU's rhetoric had unleashed in the country, this proved fatal for the overall course of the CU government.

Evaluating the other relatively 'long-lived' government of this period, the 'apostates', is an equally interesting challenge. This administration was always on the verge: it constantly faced the onslaught of the CU, it failed to create its own popular base, and was forced to rely on the Conservatives (the old enemies) in Parliament. It inherited the multiple fronts and the Cyprus entanglement. Still, there was a notable continuity in the CU and the 'apostates' policy in many respects, such as the deliberations with NATO on the organization of Greek defence and on military aid. Moreover, on other issues the 'apostates' pursued a more refined and comprehensive policy than that of the CU: they tried to close fronts, to rationalize Greek security policy, to reactivate Greece in Europe and effectively to reform the country's Eastern policy. None of these aims was fully achieved; the 'apostates' fell before having the time to complete their policy. In the 1965–67 climate, their prospects for success had never been great.

Thus, Greek policy in 1963–67 was a mixture of realism and wishful thinking, maximalism and sentimentalism (on Cyprus), fear of the political cost, and limited control of events by short-lived or weak governments. Furthermore, there was a lack of accurate assessment of the balance of power, interests and objectives of actors such as the US, Britain, Turkey and the Soviet Union. Naturally, this was an explosive mixture. By 1966–67, détente seemed to prevail internationally. However, the problem of the multiple fronts was not solved. Needless to say, in terms of grand strategy, the existence of multiple fronts is a serious mistake and a source of weakness, especially for a small and geographically exposed country.

Conclusions

The formulation of foreign and security policy is a very complicated affair, touching upon the functions of a modern state: a complex administrative or military system, a relatively developed economy and a refined policy-making process. It also involves various sets of considerations: geographical, historical, diplomatic, economic, psychological, the availability of means and the stability of the state's political system. On a purely military level, it involves the capability of the state and its society to withstand the enormous burdens of modern war: economic potential, strategic planning, communications, education, technology and morale. For a small state trying to find its way in the Cold War, these were mounting challenges. Still, this book has argued that, in the mid-twentieth century, a small state in the front line of the Western world still had considerable space for manoeuvre on the international scene.

This chapter will discuss some wider issues regarding Greek policy in 1952–67. First, how real was the 'menace from the north'? In later years, especially after the experience of the 1967–74 dictatorship, many Greeks tended to believe that it was exaggerated or, as the Soviet Foreign Minister, Shepilov, told Karamanlis in summer 1956, that it was 'imaginary'.

The thesis of this book is that the 'menace from the north' perception was not the result of a fanatical, one-sided, simplistic anti-Communism (although internally it certainly was useful for, and was used by, the extreme Greek anti-Communists). In fact, the 'menace from the north' was a pre-war concept of Greek national security policy which was transformed and acquired greater intensity in the post-war period. As a threat perception, the post-war 'menace from the north' was a refined concept based on three sets of considerations, history, geography and the Cold War, with ideology being a part, though an important one, of the third set. The 'menace from the north' also combined two important historical experiences: the burdened Balkan legacy of the first half of the twentieth century, and the experience of the Cold War, in which Greece had been the first battleground. This book has claimed that regional legacies, the intensity of the Cold War, Bulgaria's emergence as the main Soviet ally in the region, the constant military inferiority of Greece, its geographical exposure and its inability to defend long and strategically thin borders made it impossible for Greek policy-makers to assume that the country was not facing a clear and present danger. Moreover, since Greece aimed at integration with the West, it was only natural that it attracted the hostility of the West's enemies. It was not possible to become part of the West without sharing its dangers; anything else would run counter to the logic of the constantly tense, ideologically polarized post-war world. At the end of the day, the 'menace from the north', even with its exaggerations or its contradictions, was based on a realistic reading of international affairs. Needless to say, a neutralist Greece would have faced even greater threats, if only because it would not have been covered by NATO and would have possessed a negligible military or political deterrent capability.

It has also been argued in this book that, despite the intensity or even the exaggerations of internal Greek power struggles, Greece's search for security in the Cold War was part of a rational policy-making process. In the post-war era, Athens could achieve security in two ways. The first involved participation in a traditional balance-of-power system: NATO membership; the relationship with the US; contacts with Western European power centres; constant monitoring of regional developments; and the effort to reduce the number of potential adversaries through friendship with Yugoslavia. This meant that Athens placed its emphasis on political and diplomatic, rather than military, deterrence: at no time during 1952–67 were the Greek armed forces strong enough to repel an attack in the exposed northern frontier. However, there also was a second option: integration into the West. The effort to achieve economic development and to integrate into the Western European system was based on the view that Europe was Greece's 'natural space', a view shared both by the Right and the Centre. The Karamanlis governments, in particular, saw European integration, among others, as a way to overcome the seemingly insoluble problem of geographical detachment from the West. This is another reason why the 1961 Association Agreement with the EEC was a major achievement, designed to determine the course of the country for many years to come. Karamanlis' functionalism provided Greece with imaginative concepts and practical results regarding its integration in Europe and in the West. This was the only conceivable means to stop being a frontline state – the ultimate Greek strategy in the post-war world.

This book has also argued that for Greek policy, NATO played a dual role, military and political. Militarily, it offered participation in the strategic planning of the alliance, military aid, while it also turned the Greek army into a trip-wire mechanism, which was the best deterrent Greece could hope to get. One would have to think twice before striking against a NATO army. More importantly, it was mostly in terms of grand strategy that NATO was indispensable for Greek policy: it offered participation in an alliance together with the great powers of the West, something which Greece did not enjoy even during the two world wars. Indeed, whenever the Greeks doubted Western solidarity (1953, 1959–60, 1964–65), Athens' fear was of an existential nature. This is why this book claims that mistakes in the Cyprus question (in 1954–55 and in 1963–64) led to deep crises in the country's overall security and foreign policies: these mistakes endangered Greece's very relationship with the West.

Even so, Greece was a relatively minor partner of the Western alliance, and

186 Conclusions

NATO membership was often held responsible for the country's dependence on the US. Such views seemed to be strengthened after 1967, when a large part of Greek public opinion considered that the US and NATO were responsible for the imposition of the humiliating military dictatorship. For the historian, it is very difficult accurately to evaluate dependence, if only because dependence existed; it existed in the case of major Western European powers, and it could not but exist in the case of Greece. However, it is one thing to proceed with a critical and detached study of this phenomenon, and quite another to deify (or demonize) it.

It is true that Greek defence was part of NATO planning, which was decided through Paris or (regionally) Naples. This meant that, from an operational point of view, Greek defence interests could be disregarded in the name of the wider defence priorities of the West. It is also clear that all the military hardware of the country came from NATO (and, something which is often ignored, it came for free). However, these observations do not necessarily mean that the Greek–NATO or Greek–US relationship was as one-sided as sometimes suggested. Often, Greek policy found itself in a dilemma, in a conflict between national and alliance priorities. In 1955–59 because of Cyprus, in 1959–63 because of the fear of local aggression, and in 1964–67 because of both, Greece felt that it needed extra guarantees. Thus, despite operational dependence, in the formulation of Greek policy the national priority usually prevailed over the alliance priority.

It is also true that in the Greek–US relationship some blackmail was present, although research shows that since 1951 it had often been the minor partner, Greece, that proved more eager to resort to such means. It was only in the mid-1960s that the US assumed a more aggressive tone – for example, Ball and Macnamara during the March 1965 Cyprus missile crisis. This suggests that, in Greek–US relations, Washington showed some restraint in the 1950s and early 1960s, but the style of its policy changed in the years of Vietnam. On the other hand, it is also true that even during the 1950s the Greek policy-makers normally kept in the back of their minds this dependence on the US. Thus, it may be argued that the US restraint of 1952–63 might have been a more efficient tool for the projection of US interests in Greece than the more aggressive tone of the mid-1960s.

Finally, one should keep in mind that the Greek–US relationship did not remain unchanged throughout 1952–67: in times of stability, the country tended to assert its relative independence. On the contrary, in periods of instability or serious strategic mistakes, it was only natural that this minor partner tended to become more vulnerable to outside pressures. All these display how important it is for a small country to pursue a comprehensive, prudent and realistic policy. This is perhaps the most important conclusion of this book.

Notes

Introduction

1 C.A. Karamanlis, *O Eleftherios Venizelos kai oi Exoterikes mas Scheseis, 1928–1932* [Eleftherios Venizelos and our External Relations], Athens: Helleniki Evroekdotiki, 1986, pp. 73–97; E. Hatzivassiliou, *O Eleftherios Venizelos, he Hellenotourkiki Prosegisi kai to Provlima tis Asfaleias sta Valkania, 1928–1931* [Eleftherios Venizelos, the Greek–Turkish Rapprochement and the Problem of Security in the Balkans], Thessaloniki: Institute for Balkan Studies, 1999.
2 E. Dimitrakopoulos, *Ta Chersaia Synora tis Helladas* [Greece's Land Borders], Thessaloniki: Institute for Balkan Studies, 1991, p. 60; see also the analysis in J. Koliopoulos and Th. Veremis, *Greece: the modern sequel. From 1831 to the present*, London: Hurst, 2002, pp. 327–47.
3 C. Svolopoulos, *He Helleniki Exoteriki Politiki meta tin Synthikin tis Lozanis: he krisimos kampi, Ioulios–Dekemvrios 1928* [Greek Foreign Policy after the Treaty of Lausanne: the turning point, July–December 1928], Thessaloniki: Institute of Public International Law and International Relations, 1977.
4 E. Kofos, *Nationalism and Communism in Macedonia*, Thessaloniki: Institute for Balkan Studies, 1964, pp. 66–89.
5 C. Svolopoulos, 'Le problème de la sécurité dans le sud-est européen de l'entre-deux-guerres: à la recherche des origines du Pacte Balkanique de 1934', *Balkan Studies*, 14, 1973, 247–92.
6 J. Koliopoulos, *Greece and the British Connection, 1935–1941*, Oxford: Clarendon Press, 1977.
7 There is a huge bibliography on the 1940s. See, among others, H. Fleischer, *Stemma kai Swastica: he Hellada tis katochis kai tis antistasis, 1941–1944* [The Crown and the Swastika: Greece of occupation and resistance], two vols, Athens: Papazisis, 1995; M. Mazower, *Inside Hitler's Greece: the experience of occupation, 1941–44*, New Haven: Yale University Press, 1993; J.O. Iatrides, *Revolt in Athens: the Greek Communist 'second round'*, Princeton: Princeton University Press, 1972; S. Kalyvas, 'Red terror: leftist violence during the occupation', in M. Mazower (ed.), *After the War was Over: reconstructing the family, nation, and state in Greece, 1943–1960*, Princeton: Princeton University Press, 2000, pp. 142–83; A. Lykogiannis, *Britain and the Greek Economic Crisis, 1944–1947: from liberation to the Truman Doctrine*, Columbia and London: The University of Missouri Press, 2002; D.H Close, *The Origins of the Greek Civil War*, London and New York: Longmann, 1995; Koliopoulos and Veremis, *Greece: the modern sequel*, pp. 68–98; J.O. Iatrides, 'Revolution or self-defense? Communist goals, strategy and tactics in the Greek civil war', *Journal of Cold War Studies*, 7, 2005, 3–33.
8 B. Kondis, *He Angloamerikaniki Politiki kai to Helleniko Provlima, 1944–1949* [Anglo–American Policy and the Greek Problem], Thessaloniki: Paratiritis, 1984, pp. 33–9; G.A. Kazamias, 'To diethnes diplomatiko paraskinio kai he apochorisi ton

Voulgaron apo tin Anatoliki Makedonia kai ti Thraki' [The international context and the Bulgarian evacuation of Eastern Macedonia and Thrace], in X. Kotzageorgi-Zymari, *He Voulgariki Katochi stin Anatoliki Makedonia kai ti Thraki, 1941–1944* [The Bulgarian Occupation in Eastern Macedonia and Thrace], Thessaloniki: Institute for Balkan Studies and Paratiritis, 2002, pp. 235–72.
9 B. Kondis, 'The "Macedonian question" as a Balkan problem in 1940s', *Balkan Studies*, 28, 1987, 151–60; I.D. Michailides, *Ta Prosopa tou Ianou: he helleno–yugoslavikes scheseis tis paramones tou hellenikou emfyliou polemou (1944–1946)* [The Faces of Janus: Greek–Yugoslav Relations before the Greek Civil War], Athens: Patakis, 2004, p. 224.
10 B. Kondis and S. Sfetas (eds), *Emphylios Polemos: eggrafa apo ta yougoslavika kai voulgarika archeia* [The Civil War: documents from the Yugoslav and Bulgarian archives], Thessaloniki: Paratiritis, 1999.
11 Kondis, *He Angloamerikaniki Politiki*; A. Nachmani, *International Intervention in the Greek Civil War: the United Nations Special Committee on the Balkans, 1947–1952*, New York: Praeger, 1990.
12 E. Kofos, *The Impact of the Macedonian Question on Civil Conflict in Greece (1943–1949)*, Athens: ELIAMEP, 1989.
13 GES, *Historia tis Organoseos tou Hellenikou Stratou, 1821–1954* [A History of the Organization of the Greek Army], Athens: Army History Directory, 1957, pp. 153–92; D.H. Close and Th. Veremis, 'The Military Struggle, 1945–9', in D.H. Close (ed.), *The Greek Civil War, 1943–1950: studies of polarization*, London: Routledge, 1993, pp. 97–155; A. Nachmani, 'Civil war and foreign intervention in Greece, 1946–49', *Journal of Contemporary History*, 25, 1990, 489–522.
14 V.G. Afinian, B. Kondis, C. Papoulides, N.D. Smirnova and N. Tomilina (eds), *Oi Scheseis KKE kai KK Sovietikis Enosis sto Diastima 1953–1977: symfona me ta eggrafa tou Archeiou tis KE tou KKSE* [Relations between the KKE and the CPSU in the Years 1953–1977: according to documents of the Archive of the Central Committee of the CPSU], Thessaloniki: Institute for Balkan Studies, 1999. There have been attempts to study the rise of anticommunism in Greece. The best, focusing on the civil war years, is Basil K. Gounaris, *Egnosmenon Koinonikon Fronimaton: koinonikes kai alles opseis tou anticommounismou stin Makedonia tou emfyliou polemou* [Of known Social Beliefs: social and other aspects of anticommunism in (Greek) Macedonia during the civil war], Thessaloniki: Paratiritis, 2002.
15 P. Kazakos, *Anamesa se Kratos kai Agora: oikonomia kai oikonomiki politiki sti metapolemiki Hellada, 1944–2000* [Between the State and the Market: economy and economic policy in post-war Greece], Athens: Patakis, 2001, pp. 70–123; S. Zachariou, 'Struggle for survival: American aid and Greek reconstruction', in M. Schain (ed.), *The Marshall Plan: fifty years after*, New York and Basingstoke: Palgrave, 2001, pp. 153–63; C. Svolopoulos, *He Helleniki Exoteriki Politiki* [Greek Foreign Policy], Vol. 2 (1945–1981), Athens: Hestia, 2001, pp. 25–9.
16 See, among others, Th.A. Couloumbis, J. Petropoulos and H. Psomiades (eds), *Foreign Interference in Greek Politics*, New York: Pella, 1976; J.O. Iatrides, 'American attitudes toward the political system of postwar Greece', in Th.A. Couloumbis and J.O. Iatrides (eds), *Greek–American Relations: a critical review*, New York: Pella, 1980, pp. 49–73; J.O. Iatrides, 'Britain, the United States and Greece, 1945–9', in D.H. Close (ed.), *The Greek Civil War*; A.A. Fatouros, 'Building formal structures of penetration', in J.O. Iatrides (ed.), *Greece in the 1940s: a nation in crisis*, Hanover, NH and London: University Press of New England, 1978, pp. 239–58.
17 P. Pipinelis, *Historia tis Exoterikis Politikis tis Hellados, 1923–1941* [A History of Greek Foreign Policy], Athens: Saliveros, 1948, p. 372.
18 I.D. Stefanidis, *Apo ton Emfylio ston Psychro Polemo: he Hellada kai o symmachikos paragontas (1949–52)* [From Civil War to Cold War: Greece and the allied factor], Athens: Proskinio, 1999, pp. 29–30, 39.

19 J.O. Iatrides, 'The United States, Greece and the Balkans', in V. Coufoudakis, H.J. Psomiades and A. Gerolymatos (eds), *Greece and the New Balkans*, New York: Pella, 1999, p. 274.
20 On NATO accession, see Th.A. Couloumbis, *Greek Political Reaction to American and NATO Influences*, New Haven and London: Yale University Press, 1966, pp. 34–50; Stefanidis, *Apo ton Emfylio ston Psychro Polemo*, pp. 67–91; Y.G. Valinakis, *Eisagogi stin Helleniki Exoteriki Politiki, 1949–1988* [An Introduction to Greek Foreign Policy], Thessaloniki: Paratiritis, 1989, pp. 47–51; Svolopoulos, *He Helleniki Exoteriki Politiki*, pp. 30–5.
21 Stefanidis, *Apo ton Emfylio ston Psychro Polemo*, p. 85.
22 I.D. Stefanidis, 'United States, Great Britain and the Greek–Yugoslav rapprochement', *Balkan Studies*, 27, 1986, 315–43.
23 Venizelos to Peurifoy, 29 September 1950, in F. Tomai-Constantopoulou (ed.), *He Hellada sto Metaichmio enos Neou Kosmou: Psychros Polemos, Dogma Truman, sxedio Marshall, 1943–1951* [Greece in the Threshold of a New World: the Cold War, the Truman Doctrine, the Marshall Plan], Vol. III, Athens: Foreign Ministry and Castaniotis Publications, 2002, pp. 235–6.
24 Stefanidis, *Apo ton Emfylio ston Psychro Polemo*, pp. 209–12.
25 Y. Roubatis, *Doureios Hippos: he amerikaniki dieisdysi stin Hellada, 1947–1967* [The Trojan Horse: US penetration in Greece], Athens: Odysseas, 1987, pp. 92–8; Stefanidis, *Apo ton Emfylio ston Psychro Polemo*, pp. 71–2.
26 Kallergis to Berry, 11 September 1951, Politis to Washington Embassy, 8 September 1951, Note (Venizelos), 6 November 1951, in Constantopoulou (ed.), *He Hellada sto Metaichmio*, Vol. III, pp. 255–60.
27 Stefanidis, *Apo ton Emfylio ston Psychro Polemo*, pp. 73, 76.
28 See Record (Averoff–Birgi), Athens, 24 April 1952, in Athens, Constantinos G. Karamanlis Foundation, Evangelos Averoff-Tossizza Political Archive file 111 (hereafter Averoff Archive).

1 Attempting to adjust to the post-war world

1 Special Report Prepared by the Psychological Strategy Board, 11 September 1953, *FRUS* 1952–54, I, pp. 1515–17.
2 S. Markezinis, *Sygchroni Politiki Historia tis Hellados, 1936–1975* [Contemporary History of Greece], Vol. C, Athens: Papyros, 1994, pp. 50–3.
3 Quoted in Th.A. Couloumbis, *The Greek Junta Phenomenon: a professor's notes*, New York: Pella, 2004, p. 93.
4 *Greek Parliamentary Records* (GPR), period C, synod A, pp. 10–12.
5 *Kathimerini*, 17 November 1953.
6 *Kathimerini*, 18 November 1951.
7 Ibid.
8 *Kathimerini*, 13 February 1955.
9 *Kathimerini*, 5 January 1954.
10 P. Kanellopoulos, *Historika Dokimia* [Historical Essays], Athens: Hestia, 1975.
11 Kanellopoulos, speech at the Press Club in Washington DC, 8 March 1954, in Athens, Constantinos G. Karamanlis Foundation, Anastasios Kanellopoulos Collection, file 24 (hereafter Kanellopoulos Collection).
12 *GPR, Special Committee of Article 35,* period C, synod A, pp. 1353–4; Kanellopoulos, speech at the Press Club, 8 March 1954, Kanellopoulos Collection, file 24.
13 Kanellopoulos, *Historika Dokimia*, pp. 165–6.
14 C. Xanthopoulos-Palamas, *Diplomatiko Triptycho* [Diplomatic Triptych], Athens: Ekdoseis ton Filon, 1979, pp. 134, 169.
15 A. Kyrou, *Oneira kai Pragmatikotis: chronia diplomatikis zois (1923–1953)* [Dreams and Reality: years of diplomatic life], Athens: n.p., 1972, pp. 369–70.

190 Notes

16 E. Hatzivassiliou, *Britain and the International Status of Cyprus, 1955–59*, Minneapolis: Minnesota Mediterranean and East European Monographs, 1997, p. 11; I.D. Stefanidis, *Isle of Discord: nationalism, imperialism and the making of the Cyprus problem*, London: Hurst, 1999, pp. 262–3.
17 Anonymous [A. Kyrou], *Exoteriki Politiki kai Ethnikai Diekdikiseis: fantasia kai pragmatikotis* [Foreign Policy and National Claims: fantasies and reality], Athens: Greek Blood Publications, April 1944, p. 5.
18 A. Kyrou, *Helleniki Exoteriki Politiki* [Greek Foreign Policy], Athens: Hestia, 1955, pp. 126, 128.
19 Ibid, p. 217.
20 Ibid, pp. 194–6.
21 A. Kyrou, *Oi Valkanikoi mas Geitones* [Our Balkan Neighbours], Athens: n.p., 1962, pp. 202–20.
22 A. Kyrou, *Helleniki Exoteriki Politiki*, pp. 162–3.

2 A new NATO member, 1952–55

1 Th. Veremis, *The Military in Greek Politics: from independence to democracy*, London: Hurst, 1997, pp. 70–133.
2 N. Alivizatos, *Oi Politikoi Thesmoi se Krisi, 1922–1974: opseis tis hellenikis empeirias* [The Political Institutions in Crisis, 1922–1974: aspects of the Greek experience], Athens: Themelio, 1983, pp. 191–202, 260–1.
3 Veremis, *The Military in Greek Politics*, p. 152. On IDEA, see also Nicholas A. Stavrou, *Symmachiki Politiki kai Stratiotikes Epemvaseis: o politicos rolos ton Hellenon stratiotikon* [Allied Politics and Military Interventions: the political role of the Greek military], Athens: Papazisis, 1976.
4 Yost to State Department, 19 November 1952, *FRUS*, 1952–54, VIII, pp. 810–11.
5 P. Kanellopoulos, *Historika Dokimia* [Historical Essays], Athens: Hestia, 1975, pp. 28–9, 165–6.
6 Alivizatos, *Politikoi Thesmoi*, pp. 262–5.
7 C. Sazanides, *Xenoi, Vaseis kai Pyrinika stin Hellada* [Foreign Powers, Bases and Nuclear Weapons in Greece], Thessaloniki: Altintzis, 1985, p. 342.
8 Papagos, speech in Parliament, 19 March 1953, *Greek Parliamentary Records* (GPR), period C, synod A, pp. 593–4.
9 I.D. Stefanidis, *Asymmetroi Etairoi: oi Enomenes Politeies kai he Ellada ston psychro polemo, 1953–1961* [Unequal Partners: The US and Greece in the Cold War], Athens: Patakis, 2002, p. 278.
10 See NAC memoranda, 'Second Report on the Annual Review Part I', NATO Archives, CM (53) 35, 15 April 1954; Annual Review 1953: Country Chapter on Greece, CM (53) 150, Part III, 24 November 1953.
11 *Kathimerini*, 18 November 1951.
12 *GPR*, period C, synod A, pp. 593–4.
13 See J.O. Iatrides, 'Failed Rampart: NATO's Balkan Front', paper presented at a conference on NATO and the Warsaw Pact: Intra-Bloc Conflicts, Lemnitzer Center for NATO and European Union Studies, Kent State University, 23–24 April 2004.
14 See A. Papagos, *O Polemos tis Hellados, 1940–1941* [The War of Greece], Athens: Filoi tou Vivliou, 1945, pp. 26–42; A. Papagos, *O Hellenikos Stratos kai he pros Polemos Proparaskevi tou: apo Avgoustou 1923 mechri Octovriou 1940* [The Greek Army and its Preparation for War: from August 1923 to October 1940], Athens: Pyrsos, 1945, pp. 305–25.
15 *Kathimerini*, 18 November 1951.
16 Peurifoy to State Department, 6 May 1952, and McGhee to State Department, 6 February 1953, *FRUS*, 1952–54, VIII, pp. 592–3, 616–19.
17 Peurifoy to State Department, 14 February 1953, *FRUS*, 1952–54, VIII, pp. 621–3.

18 Peurifoy to State Department, 28 May 1953, *FRUS*, 1952–54, VIII, pp. 834–7.
19 Stefanidis, *Asymmetroi Etairoi*, p. 89.
20 GES, *Historia tis Organoseos tou Hellenikou Stratou, 1821–1954* [A History of the Organization of the Greek Army], Athens: Army History Directory, 1957, p. 207; GES, *Historia tou Hellenikou Stratou, 1821–1997* [A History of the Greek Army], Athens: Army History Directory, 1998, p. 283.
21 *GPR*, period C, synod B, pp. 32–46; Kanellopoulos Collection, file 19 (November 1953); See also NAC memorandum, 'Infrastructure payments to Greece', NATO Archives, CM (53) 94, 23 July 1953.
22 *GPR*, period C, synod A, p. 408.
23 Records Markezinis–Jenergan and Markezinis–Eisenhower, 7 May 1953, *FRUS*, 1952–54, VIII, pp. 822–5; Baxter to Peurifoy, 12 May 1953, *FRUS*, 1952–54, VIII, pp. 826–30; Stefanidis, *Asymmetroi Etairoi*, pp. 254–5.
24 NAC ministerial meeting records, NATO Archives CVR (53) 20 and 21, 23 April 1953; CVR (53) 23, 24 April 1953.
25 Peurifoy to State Department, 28 May 1953, *FRUS*, 1952–54, VIII, pp. 834–7.
26 See NAC, Permanent representatives session, NATO Archives, CR (53) 32, 30 June 1953.
27 Kanellopoulos Collection, file 16 (May 1953); Hoyer-Millar (NATO) to FO, 27 May 1953, FO 371/107909/1.
28 Kanellopoulos Collection, file 16 (summer 1953); Stefanidis, *Asymmetroi Etairoi*, p. 257.
29 See Peake to Hood, 22 and 24 September 1953, and the records of Montgomery's talks with Papagos, Kanellopoulos and Kitrilakis, 21 September 1953, FO 371/108018/2.
30 NAC ministerial meeting records, NATO Archives, CVR (53) 55 and 56, 15 December 1953.
31 *Kathimerini*, 23 January–4 February 1954. See also NAC memorandum, 'Report on the 1954 Annual Review: Country Report on Greece', NATO Archives, CM (54) 100, Part III, 20 November 1954.
32 See NAC memorandum, 'Report on the 1954 Annual Review', NATO Archives, CM (54) 100, Part I, 20 November 1954.
33 Editorial, 'The cost of defence', *Kathimerini*, 13 February 1954.
34 See the US Embassy's comments on the Greek memorandum, in Cannon to State Department, 27 February 1954, *FRUS*, 1952–54, VIII, pp. 857–8; a summary of the Greek memorandum can be found in Athens to FO, 10 March 1954, FO 371/112896/1. The memorandum gave exaggerated figures for Greek defence expenditure.
35 Editorial, 'New look ...', *Kathimerini*, 21 March 1954.
36 Records (Kanellopoulos–Stassen and Eisenhower), 18 March 1954, *FRUS*, 1952–54, VIII, pp. 859–62; Kanellopoulos Collection, file 23 (March–April 1954).
37 *Kathimerini*, 4, 5 and 6 May 1954; GES, *Historia tou Hellenikou Stratou*, p. 279.
38 Cannon to State Department, 8 May 1954, *FRUS*, 1952–54, VIII, pp. 862–4.
39 Editorial, 'The army', *Kathimerini*, 13 June 1954. See also the newspaper's comments and reports on 4, 18 and 27 July.
40 Olson (USIS) to Kanellopoulos, 27 July 1954, in Athens, Association of Friends of Panayiotis Kanellopoulos, Panayiotis Kanellopoulos Archive, file 'Archive of letters of the Defence Minister' (hereafter Kanellopoulos Archive).
41 Gruenther to the military representative of Greece, 26 August 1954, Kanellopoulos Archive, file 'Correspondence and other diplomatic documents'.
42 NAC memorandum, 'Report on the 1954 Annual Review: Country Report on Greece', NATO Archives, CM (54) 100, Part III, 20 November 1954.
43 Draft memorandum (Allen), 14 February 1955, *FRUS*, 1955–57, XXIV, pp. 530–1; Kanellopoulos Collection, file 26 (September 1954).

44 Record (Stephanopoulos–Dulles), 10 May 1955, and Cannon to State Department, 20 May 1955, *FRUS*, 1955–57, XXIV, pp. 535–8.
45 See articles by Lieutenant-Admiral (retd) Metzeviris and Admiral (retd) Alexandris, in Kanellopoulos Collection, file 26A.
46 Kanellopoulos to Mountbatten, 26 March 1953, Kanellopoulos Archive, file 'Archive of letters of the Defence Minister'.
47 Stefanidis, *Asymmetroi Etairoi*, pp. 231–3.
48 NAC memorandum, 'Report on the 1954 Annual Review, Country Report on Greece', NATO Archives, CM (54) 100, Part III, 20 November 1954.
49 See NAC ministerial meeting records, NATO Archives CVR (52) 37 and 38 (Revised), 16 December 1952; CVR (53) 53, 14 December 1953; CVR (54) 17, 23 April 1954; CVR (54) 39, 22 October 1954.
50 Stefanidis, *Asymmetroi Etairoi*, pp. 201–6.
51 See the text of the agreement in *GPR, Special Committee of Article 35*, period C, synod B, pp. 1374–7.
52 Th.A. Couloumbis, *Greek Political Reaction to American and NATO Influences*, New Haven and London: Yale University Press, 1966, pp. 77–89; *GPR, Special Committee of Article 35*, period C, synod A, pp. 1353–77.
53 Record (Stephanopoulos–Dulles), 30 October 1953, *FRUS*, 1952–54, VIII, pp. 852–7.
54 See the press reports in Kanellopoulos Collection, file 20 (October 1953).
55 H. Fleischer, 'Post-war relations between Greece and the two German states: a re-evaluation in the light of German unification', *The Southeast European Yearbook*, 2, 1991, 163–78.
56 Raphail (Paris) to Foreign Ministry, 30 January 1951 and Politis (Athens) to London Embassy, 4 February 1951, in F. Tomai-Constantopoulou (ed.), *He Symmetochi tis Helladas stin Poreia pros tin Evropaiki Oloklirosi* [Greece's participation in the course towards European integration], Vol. I: 1948–1968, Athens: Foreign Ministry and Castaniotis Publications, 2003, pp. 167–9.
57 Averoff to Paris Embassy, 8 March 1952, in Constantopoulou (ed.), *He Symmetochi tis Helladas*, pp. 187–9.
58 See, for example, Stephanopoulos' position during the April 1954 NATO ministerial meeting: NATO Archives CVR (54) 17, 23 April 1954.
59 Peake to Eden, 27 March 1954, FO 371/112834/1.
60 NAC ministerial meeting records, NATO Archives CVR (54) 39, 22 October 1954.
61 *GPR*, period C, synod A, pp. 32–46, 84–5.

3 The regional balance: the tripartite Balkan pacts

1 G. Dafnis, *Sophocles E. Venizelos, 1894–1964*, Athens: Ikaros, 1970, pp. 497–8; Record (Averoff–Birgi), Athens, 24 April 1952, Averoff Archive, file 111.
2 Minute (Averoff), June 1952, Averoff Archive, file 98.
3 Pipinelis to Foreign Ministry, 24 July 1952, Averoff Archive, file 111.
4 J.O. Iatrides, *Balkan Triangle: birth and decline of an alliance across ideological boundaries*, The Hague: Mouton, 1968, pp. 70–3, 83, 91, 95–9; Anschuetz to State Department, 22 January 1953, 665.81/1-2253.
5 This was mentioned in Record (Averoff–Birgi), 24 April 1952, Averoff Archive, file 111.
6 Dundas (British Consulate, Thessaloniki) to Galsworthy (British Embassy, Athens), 29 June 1953, FO 371/107522/3. It is notable, however, that the Greeks did not allow the Yugoslavs to own the buildings of the free zone. This suggests that Athens had not forgotten the Yugoslav policy of the 1920s, when Belgrade had claimed sovereignty, not merely ownership, over the free zone.
7 Acheson to US Embassy, Athens, 2 December 1952 and 7 January 1953, *FRUS*, 1952–54, VIII, pp. 598–600 and 605–7.

8 Peake to Eden, 15 January, Mallet (Rome) to Eden, 26 January and Young to Cheetham, 2 February 1953, FO 371/107492/2 and 5; Anschuetz to State Department, 22 January 1953, 665.81/1-2253; Iatrides, *Balkan Triangle*, p. 93.
9 Peurifoy to State Department, 31 December 1952, 28 January 1953 and 26 February 1953; McGhee to State Department, 6 January 1953; Dulles to US Embassy, Athens, 21 February 1953, *FRUS*, 1952–54, VIII, pp. 600–4, 613–14, 623–6.
10 See the comments in Iatrides, *Balkan Triangle*, pp. 104–7. See also Minute (Foreign Ministry), no date (possibly 1955), in Athens, Constantinos G. Karamanlis Foundation, Constantinos Karamanlis Archive, file 1A (hereafter Karamanlis Archive).
11 *Greek Parliamentary Records* (GPR), period C, synod A, pp. 405–9, 683–9.
12 Record (Papagos–Menderes), 18 June 1953, Averoff Archive, file 111.
13 Iatrides, *Balkan Triangle*, pp. 119–20.
14 Ibid, pp. 121–3, 126.
15 Galsworthy to May, 3 September 1953, and Moss (Belgrade) to May, 18 September 1953, FO 371/107489/1 and 2; Yost to State Department, 2 September 1953, 668.81/9-253; Anschuetz to State Department, 2 September 1953, 668.81/9-253. On the failure of the resettlement programme, see Ireland (Thessaloniki) to State Department, 7 November 1956, 781.022/11-756.
16 Mallet (Rome) to Salisbury, 30 September 1953, and Peake to FO, 8 October 1953, FO 371/107492/6 and 7.
17 Cannon to State Department, 1 December 1953, *FRUS*, 1952–54, VIII, pp. 634–6; Iatrides, *Balkan Triangle*, pp. 125–7.
18 Record (Stephanopoulos–Dulles), 30 October 1953, *FRUS*, 1952–54, VIII, pp. 852–7.
19 *GPR*, period C, synod B, p. 43.
20 Rumbold (Paris) to Cheetham, 28 January 1954, FO 371/112834/4.
21 Cannon to State Department, 20 April 1954, *FRUS*, 1952–54, VIII, pp. 642–3, and the comment 'The Objections', *Kathimerini*, 23 May 1954.
22 Dulles to US Embassies Athens and Belgrade, 17 May 1954, *FRUS*, 1952–54, VIII, pp. 643–6.
23 On Tito's visit see Peake to FO, 4 June 1954, FO 371/112826/12; Royce (Athens) to Eden, 11 June 1954, and Peake to Harrison, 11 June 1954, FO 112838/3 and 4. See also Kanellopoulos Collection, file 22 (June 1954); *Kathimerini*, 6 June 1955.
24 On the Menderes visit, see Kanellopoulos Collection, file 22 (June 1954). In these days, the British, the French and the Americans also held talks in London monitoring the tripartite discussions: see *FRUS*, 1952–54, VIII, pp. 651–6 and the British FO 371/113222 and 113223.
25 Aldrich to State Department, 17 June 1954, *FRUS*, 1952–54, VIII, pp. 654–6; Lambert (Athens) to FO, 17 July 1954, FO 371/112826/15; Lambert to FO, 26 June and 6 July, Lambert to Eden, 7 July, and FO to Ankara Embassy, 12 July 1954, FO 371/113222/9, 17, 23 and 26.
26 Dulles to US Embassy, Athens, 2 July and Dulles to US Embassy, London, 8 July 1954, *FRUS*, 1952–54, VIII, pp. 659–62, 665.
27 See Lambert to FO, 15 and 16 July, Bowker (Ankara) to FO, 17 July, and Minute (Harrison, FO), 17 July 1954, FO 371/113222/28; Scott Fox (Ankara) to Young, 16 July 1954, FO 371/113223/55.
28 Iatrides, *Balkan Triangle*, p. 136; Editorial, 'Why not bilateral?', *Kathimerini*, 17 July 1954.
29 Warren (Ankara) to State Department, 16 July 1954, *FRUS*, 1952–54, VIII, pp. 666–7.
30 Minute (Foreign Ministry), no date (possibly 1955), Karamanlis Archive, file 1A.
31 Minute (Matsas, Foreign Ministry), 27 February 1959, Karamanlis Archive, file 8A.
32 *GPR*, period C, synod C, pp. 479–88.
33 Minute (General Staff of National Defence, Siapkaras), 19 February 1959, Karamanlis Archive, file 8A.

194 *Notes*

34 See Minute on the Cultural and Economic Committee of the Permanent Secretariat of the Ankara Pact (Foreign Ministry, 1959) Karamanlis Archive, file 2A.
35 Th.A. Couloumbis, *Greek Political Reaction to American and NATO Influences*, New Haven and London: Yale University Press, 1966, p. 93.

4 Greece and peaceful co-existence

1 Holt to State Department, 16 October 1953, 669.81/10-1653.
2 Greek memorandum to the US government, 23 December 1955, 667.8124/12-2355.
3 See, among others Athens to FO, 14 January, 4 and 12 February 1954, FO 371/112916/1, 2 and 3. See also I. Lagani, *To 'Paidomazoma' kai oi Helleno–yugoslavikes scheseis, 1949–1953* [The Abduction of children and Greek–Yugoslav Relations], Athens: Sakkoulas, 1996; M. Ristovic, *A Long Journey Home: Greek refugee children in Yugoslavia, 1948–1960*, Thessaloniki: Institute for Balkan Studies, 2000.
4 S. Wallden, *Hellada kai Anatolikes Chores, 1950–1967: oikonomikes scheseis kai politiki* [Greece and the Eastern countries: economic relations and politics] Vol. A, Athens: Odysseas and Foundation for Mediterranean Studies, 1991, pp. 79–86.
5 Peurifoy to State Department, 5 May 1953, 661.81/5-553.
6 Anschuetz to State Department, 2 November 1953, 661.81/11-253.
7 Galsworthy to May, 21 October 1953, FO 371/107497/2; Peake to FO, 10 November 1953, FO 371/107493/1.
8 Cannon to State Department, 29 October 1953, 661.81/10-2953; Anschuetz to State Department, 5 November 1953, 661.81/11-553; Schnee to State Department, 1 March 1954, 661.81/3-154.
9 Peake to Eden, 20 January 1954, FO 371/112891/2.
10 Wallden, *Hellada kai Anatolikes Chores*, Vol. A, pp. 86–9.
11 E. Hatzivassiliou, 'Greek–Bulgarian and Greek–Soviet relations, 1953–1959: a view from the British archives', *Modern Greek Studies Yearbook*, 8, 1992, 119–37 (128).
12 Anschuetz to State Department, 10 September 1953, 669.81/9-1053.
13 Anschuetz to State Department, 28 July 1953, 669.81/7-2853 and 26 August 1953, 669.81/8-2653.
14 Anschuetz to State Department, 12 September 1953, 669.81/9-1253; Cannon to State Department, 17 September 1953, 669.81/9-1753; Lourie (Washington DC) to US Embassy, Athens, 10 September 1953, 669.81/9-1053; Cannon to State Department, 8 October 1953, 669.81/9-1053; Dulles to US Embassy, Athens, 10 and 15 October 1953, 669.81/10-1053 and 10-1553.
15 E. Dimitrakopoulos, *Ta Chersaia Synora tis Helladas* [Greece's Land Borders], Thessaloniki: Institute for Balkan Studies, 1991, pp. 100–2.
16 Hatzivassiliou, 'Greek–Bulgarian and Greek–Soviet Relations', p. 124.
17 Athens to FO, 12 June 1954, FO 371/112842/6.
18 Schnee to State Department, 20 November 1954, 666.81/11-2054; Marcy (The Hague) to State Department, 18 July 1955, 666.81/7-1855.
19 Record (Averoff–Birgi), 24 April 1952, Averoff Archive, file 111.
20 Dunn (Paris) to State Department, 5 July 1952, *FRUS*, 1952–54, VIII, pp. 797–9.
21 Makins to FO, 12 January 1953, FO 371/107291/1; Anschuetz to State Department, 7 March 1953, 667.811/3-753.
22 *Greek Parliamentary Records* (GPR), period C, synod A, pp. 10–12.
23 Greek memorandum to the US government, 25 May 1953, 667.81/5-2553.
24 Lambert to Cheetham, 28 May and Greek memorandum to the British government, 12 June 1953, FO 371/107289/13 and 14.
25 Record (Hasan Dosti, Free Albania Committee–Recknagel), 3 June 1953, 667.81/6-353; Record (Dosti–Peters), 18 September 1953, 667.81/9-1853.
26 Mallet (Rome) to Salisbury, 30 September 1953, FO 371/107492/6; J.O. Iatrides,

Balkan Triangle: birth and decline of an alliance across ideological boundaries, The Hague: Mouton, 1968, p. 122.
27 Makins to FO, 17 March 1953, FO 371/107289/4.
28 Minute (Galsworthy, Foreign Office), 7 July 1953, FO 371/107289/17.
29 A. Kyrou, *Helleniki Exoteriki Politiki* [Greek Foreign Policy], Athens: Hestia, 1955, p. 200.
30 Record (Cavalieratos–Wood), 12 July, Record (Cavalieratos–Balfour), 14 July, 667.81/7-1255 and 667.81/7-1455; Metcalf to State Department, 18 July 1955, 667.81/7-1855.
31 Lambert to Macmillan, 24 August 1955, and Peake to Ward, 30 September 1955, FO 371/117603/5 and 6.

5 Disaster in 1955

1 S.G. Xydis, *Cyprus: Conflict and Conciliation, 1954–1958*, Columbus, Ohio: The Ohio State University Press, 1967, pp. 9–11; I.D. Stefanidis, *Isle of Discord: nationalism, imperialism and the making of the Cyprus problem*, London: Hurst, 1999, pp. 262–76.
2 Mallet (Belgrade) to FO, 10 September 1954, FO 371/112860/502.
3 Xydis, *Cyprus*, pp. 11–23; R. Holland, *Britain and the Revolt in Cyprus, 1954–1959*, Oxford: Clarendon Press, 1998, pp. 41–4.
4 Stefanidis, *Isle of Discord*, pp. 282–3.
5 J.O. Iatrides, *Balkan Triangle: birth and decline of an alliance across ideological boundaries*, The Hague: Mouton, 1968, pp. 158–64.
6 See a reference to Greek anxieties in Metcalf (Athens) to State Department, 2 August 1955, 668.81/8-255.
7 Minute (Ward, Foreign Office), 6 June and Steel to Ward, 22 June 1955, FO 371/118653/1 and 2.
8 Peake to Selwyn Lloyd, 23 March 1956, Annual Review for Greece, 1955, FO 371/123844/1.
9 E. Hatzivassiliou, *He Anodos tou Constantinou Karamanli stin Exousia, 1954–1956* [The Advent of Constantinos Karamanlis to Power], Athens: Patakis, 2001, pp. 149–52.
10 There is a large bibliography on the Istanbul riots. See mostly A. Alexandris, *The Greek Minority of Istanbul and Greek–Turkish Relations, 1918–1974*, Athens: Centre for Asia Minor Studies, 1983, pp. 256–66.
11 Thurston to Baxter, 12 September 1955, *FRUS*, 1955–57, XXIV, p. 543.
12 See the text of Dulles's message in *Kathimerini*, 20 September 1955.
13 Th.A. Couloumbis, *Greek Political Reaction to American and NATO Influences*, New Haven and London: Yale University Press, 1966, pp. 95–6; Hatzivassiliou, *He Anodos tou Karamanli*, pp. 200–2.
14 Hatzivassiliou, *He Anodos tou Karamanli*, p. 204.
15 Editorial, 'Elections', *Eleftheria*, 23 September 1955; Editorial, 'A government of Quislings?' *Hestia*, 26 September 1955.
16 Editorials, 'Shame', *Kathimerini*, 22 September and 'Realists', 25 September 1955. See also Couloumbis, *Greek Political Reaction*, pp. 96–7; Y.G. Valinakis, *Eisagogi stin Helleniki Exoteriki Politiki, 1949–1988* [An Introduction to Greek Foreign Policy], Thessaloniki: Paratiritis, 1989, p. 73.
17 *Kathimerini*, 4 October 1955.
18 Hatzivassiliou, *He Anodos tou Karamanli*, pp. 227–9.

6 The search for a long-term strategy

1. See A.I. Svolos, *Gia ti Makedonia kai ti Thraki* [For Macedonia and Thrace], Athens, n.p., 1945.
2. Karamanlis, Speech, 16 October 1950, in C. Svolopoulos (ed.), *Constantinos Karamanlis: archeio, gegonota kai keimena* [Constantinos Karamanlis: archive, events and texts], Vol. 1, Athens: C.G. Karamanlis Foundation and Ekdotike Athenon, 1992, pp. 133–4 (hereafter referred to as *Karamanlis*).
3. Karamanlis, interview with Mario Modiano, 30 September 1950, *Karamanlis*, Vol. 1, p. 131.
4. E. Hatzivassiliou, *He Anodos tou Constantinou Karamanli stin Exousia, 1954–1956* [The Advent of Constantinos Karamanlis to Power], Athens: Patakis, 2001, pp. 45–54.
5. E. Hatzivassiliou, 'Greek–Bulgarian and Greek–Soviet relations, 1953–1959: a view from the British archives', *Modern Greek Studies Yearbook*, 8, 1992, 119–37 (129).
6. Karamanlis to Stoica, 23 September 1957, *Karamanlis*, Vol. 2, p. 421.
7. Record (Karamanlis–Makarios), 19 September 1958, *Karamanlis*, Vol. 3, pp. 227–9.
8. Record (Karamanlis–Erhard), 11 November 1958, *Karamanlis*, Vol. 3, p. 278.
9. Record (Karamanlis–Eisenhower), 15 December 1959, *Karamanlis*, Vol. 4, pp. 222–6.
10. Record (Karamanlis–J.F. Kennedy), 19 April 1961, *Karamanlis*, Vol. 5, p. 43.
11. E. Averoff, *Union douanière Balkanique*, Paris: Sirey, 1933.
12. E. Averoff, *Symvoli eis tin Erevnan tou Plithysmiakou Provlimatos tis Hellados* [A Contribution to the Research on the Demographic Problem of Greece], Athens: Christou, 1939.
13. E. Hatzivassiliou, *Evangelos Averoff-Tossizza, 1908–1990: politiki viographia* [A Political Biography], Athens: C. Karamanlis Institute and Sideris Publications, 2004, pp. 13–44, 95–100.
14. E. Averoff-Tossizza, *By Fire and Axe: the Communist Party and the civil war in Greece, 1944–1949* (trans. Sarah Arnold Rigos), New Rochelle, NY: Caratzas, 1978, p. 1. The book was first published in French: *Le feu et la hâche: Grèce, 1946–1949*, Paris: éditions Breteuil, 1973.
15. E. Averoff-Tossizza, '*He nea morfi tou ethnous*' [The new form of the nation], *Kathimerini*, 30 April 1961.
16. E. Hatzivassiliou, 'Security and the European option: Greek foreign policy, 1952–1962', *Journal of Contemporary History*, 30, 1995, 187–202.
17. Averoff to Karamanlis, (summer 1956), *Karamanlis*, Vol. 2, p. 114.
18. Records of the talks of the Greek government with Richards, 30 April–2 May 1957, *Karamanlis*, Vol. 2, p. 331.
19. Note by the Greek Delegation, NATO Archives, AC/052(SP)D1, 14 May 1958; records of the Committee on Information and Cultural Relations, AC/52-R(58)9, 12 May 1958.
20. See, for example, NAC ministerial meeting records, NATO Archives, CVR (61) 17, 8 May 1961.
21. NAC ministerial meeting records, NATO Archives, CVR (59) 45 and 49, 15 and 16 December 1959.
22. C. Svolopoulos, *He Helleniki Exoteriki Politiki* [Greek Foreign Policy], Vol. 2 (1945–1981), Athens: Hestia, 2001, pp. 89–132; Hatzivassiliou, *Averoff*, pp. 45–95.
23. On Greece's Association with the EEC, see K. Botsiou, *Griechenlands Weg nach Europa: von der Truman-Doctrin bis zur Assoziierung mit der EWG, 1947–1961*, Frankfurt-am-Main: Peter Lang, 1998; Svolopoulos, *He Helleniki Exoteriki Politiki*, pp. 114–32; P. Kazakos, *Anamesa se Kratos kai Agora: oikonomia kai oikonomiki politiki sti metapolemiki Hellada, 1944–2000* [Between the State and the Market: economy and economic policy in post-war Greece], Athens: Patakis, 2001,

pp. 231–45; M. Vaïsse, 'La France et l'Association de la Grèce au Marché Commun', in C. Svolopoulos and C. Morelle (eds), *De Gaulle et Karamanlis: La nation, l'état, l'Europe*, Athens: C.G. Karamanlis Foundation and Patakis Publications, 2002, pp. 155–66.
24 Karamanlis, speech after the signature of the Association Agreement, 9 July 1961, *Karamanlis*, Vol. 5, pp. 110–12.
25 Xanthopoulos-Palamas (Foreign Ministry) circular telegram to the Greek Embassies, 11 July 1961, Philon (Paris) to Foreign Ministry, 2 February 1962 and Minute (Foreign Ministry, Second Political Directory), 12 February 1962, in F. Tomai-Constantopoulou (ed.), *He Symmetochi tis Helladas stin Poreia pros tin Evropaiki Oloklirosi* [Greece's Participation in the Course towards European Integration], Vol. I: 1948–1968, Athens: Foreign Ministry and Castaniotis Publications, 2003, pp. 386–9, 404–7, 407–10; quotation from p. 405.
26 A. Papahelas, *O Viasmos tis Hellenikis Dimokratias: o amerikanikos paragon, 1947–1967* [The Rape of Greek Democracy: the American factor], Athens: Hestia, 1997, p. 175.
27 See Memorandum of retd officers to Defence Ministry, 31 March 1964, in Athens, Michalis Papaconstantinou Archive, at the hands of the owner, file 'Undersecretariat of Defence (a)' (hereafter Papaconstantinou Archive).

7 New security problems

1 S.G. Xydis, *Cyprus: conflict and conciliation, 1954–1958*, Columbus, Ohio: Ohio State University Press, 1967, pp. 84–96; J.O. Iatrides, *Balkan Triangle: birth and decline of an alliance across ideological boundaries*, The Hague: Mouton, 1968, p. 172.
2 I.D. Stefanidis, *Asymmetroi Etairoi: oi Enomenes Politeies kai he Ellada ston psychro polemo, 1953–1961* [Unequal Partners: the US and Greece in the Cold War], Athens: Patakis, 2002, pp. 184, 267.
3 Record (Karamanlis–Collins), 13 October 1955, in C. Svolopoulos (ed.), *Constantinos Karamanlis: archeio, gegonota kai keimena* [Constantinos Karamanlis: archive, events and texts], Vol. 1, Athens: C.G. Karamanlis Foundation and Ekdotike Athenon, 1992, pp. 278–80 (hereafter referred to as *Karamanlis*).
4 Strange (Athens) to State Department, 13 October 1955, *FRUS*, 1955–57, XXIV, pp. 547–9.
5 Cannon to State Department, 16 March 1956, 781.00(W)/3-1656.
6 *Karamanlis*, Vol. 2, p. 24.
7 Minute (Averoff), 24 August 1956, Averoff Archive, file 106.
8 Minute (Thomson, Foreign Office), 19 September 1956, FO 371/124812/2.
9 Th.A. Couloumbis, *Greek Political Reaction to American and NATO Influences*, New Haven and London: Yale University Press, 1966, pp. 93–109.
10 Penfield to State Department, 4 November 1957, 611.81/11-457.
11 National Intelligence Estimates, 18 January 1955 and 26 June 1956, *FRUS*, 1955–57, XXIV, pp. 527–9 and 566–7; NSC 5718/1, 5 August 1957, 'US Policy toward Greece'.
12 Penfield to State Department, 25 April 1958, 681.00/4-2558.
13 E. Nicolakopoulos, *He Kachektiki Dimokratia: kommata kai ekloges, 1946–1967* [The Sickly Democracy: parties and elections], Athens: Patakis, 2001, pp. 236–46; Couloumbis, *Greek Political Reaction*, pp. 119–32.
14 I.D. Stefanidis, '"Telling America's story": US propaganda operations and Greek public reactions', *Journal of the Hellenic Diaspora*, 30, 2004, 39–95.
15 NAC memorandum, 'Report on the 1955 Annual Review', NATO Archives, CM (55) 101 Part I, 10 November 1955.
16 Note, no date, evidently autumn 1955, Karamanlis Archive, file 1A.

198 *Notes*

17 See Notes (General Staff of National Defence) to Karamanlis, 12 October and 7 November 1955, Karamanlis Archive, file 1A; Table, (autumn 1955) Karamanlis Archive, file 1A.
18 NAC memoranda, 'Annual Review 1955, Country Chapter: Greece', NATO Archives, CM (55) 101, Part II, 10 November 1955; 'Report on the 1956 Annual Review, Country Chapter on Greece', CM (56) 132, Part II, 1 December 1956.
19 OCB Report, Operations Plan for Greece, 21 May 1958, *FRUS*, 1958–60, X, part 2, pp. 620–31.
20 J.O. Iatrides, 'Failed Rampart: NATO's Balkan Front', paper presented at a conference on NATO and the Warsaw Pact: Intra-Bloc Conflicts, Lemnitzer Center for NATO and European Union Studies, Kent State University, 23–24 April 2004.
21 Record (Karamanlis–Collins), 13 October 1955, *Karamanlis*, Vol. 1, pp. 278–80.
22 Karamanlis to Cannon, 14 October 1955, and Greek aide memoire to the US government (autumn 1955), Karamanlis Archive, file 1A.
23 Record (Karamanlis–Hoover), 15 November 1956, *Karamanlis*, Vol. 2, p. 198.
24 See the Greek memorandum, January 1957, *Karamanlis*, Vol. 2, pp. 256–8.
25 Penfield to State Department, 31 January 1957, 781.5/1-3157.
26 Armour Report (extract), March 1957, *Karamanlis*, Vol. 2, p. 290.
27 Note (General Staff of National Defence), 27 November 1957, Karamanlis Archive, file 4A; Note (no date, probably 1959), Karamanlis Archive, file 8A; *Kathimerini*, 17 February 1957; 344; GES, *Historia tou Hellenikou Stratou, 1821–1997* [A History of the Greek Army], Athens: General Staff of the Army, Army History Directory, 1998, p. 302.
28 Briefing Note, late 1959, Karamanlis Archive, file 10A.
29 P. Nicolopoulos, 'Ypourgos Ethnikis Amynis' [Minister of National Defence], in *Aristeidis Protopapadakis, 1903–1966*, Athens: n.p., 1967, pp. 70–72.
30 C. Sazanides, *Xenoi, Vaseis kai Pyrinika stin Hellada* [Foreign Powers, Bases and Nuclear Weapons in Greece], Thessaloniki: Altintzis, 1985, pp. 312–13, 344.
31 Dovas to Karamanlis, 14 July 1958, *Karamanlis*, Vol. 3, pp. 167–9.
32 NAC memorandum, 'Report on the 1957 Annual Review, Country Chapter on Greece', NATO Archives, CM (57) 143, Part II, 9 December 1957.
33 NSC 5718/1, 5 August 1957, 'US Policy toward Greece'.
34 Operations Plan for Greece, *FRUS*, 1955–57, XXIV, p. 605.
35 *Karamanlis*, Vol. 4, pp. 84–90.
36 *Karamanlis*, Vol. 4, pp. 212–13.
37 'Preparation of the Summit Meeting: Text of reply by Greece', NATO Archives, PO/60/166, 10 February 1960.
38 *Karamanlis*, Vol. 5, pp. 153–4.
39 Briggs to State Department, 13 September 1961, John F. Kennedy Library, National Security Files (NSF), Country File: Greece, General, Box 100.
40 NAC ministerial meeting records, NATO Archives CVR (59) 45, 15 December 1959.
41 See the attitude of the Undersecretary of National Defence, Georgios Themelis, in NAC ministerial meeting records, NATO Archives CVR (60) 13, 31 March 1960.
42 NSC-6101, 4 January 1961, 'US Policy toward Greece'.
43 S. Rizas, *He Hellada, oi Enomenes Politeies kai he Evropi, 1961–1964: politikes kai oikonomikes opseis tou provlimatos asfaleias sto metaichmio psychrou polemou kai yfesis* [Greece, the US and Europe, 1961–1964: political and economic aspects of the security problem in the passing from Cold War to détente], Athens: Patakis, 2001, p. 81.
44 Bennett (Athens) to State Department, 1 July 1961, Kennedy Library, NSF Country File: Greece, General, Box 100.
45 E. Averoff-Tossizza, *Lost Opportunities: the Cyprus question, 1950–1963* (trans. Timothy Cullen and Susan Kyriakidis), New Rochelle: A. Karatzas, 1986, p. 407; Record (Averoff–Koriukin), 26 October 1962, Averoff Archive, file 9.

46 *Karamanlis*, Vol. 4, pp. 298–300.
47 Minute (Xanthopoulos-Palamas), summer 1960, Karamanlis Archive, file 12A.
48 Economou-Gouras (New York) to Averoff, 24 March 1961, Averoff Archive, file 8.
49 Note by Averoff, 'Thoughts, potentially useful for the Washington talks', spring 1961, Averoff Archive, file 8.
50 See the rationale behind MC 70, as explained by the SACEUR, General Lauris Norstad, during the Defence Ministers' meeting of April 1958: NAC ministerial meeting, NATO Archives, CVR (58) 21, 15 April 1958.
51 NAC memoranda, 'Report on the 1958 Annual Review, General Chapter', NATO Archives, CM (58) 141, 5 December 1958; 'Annual Political Appraisal: Report by the Secretary General', CM (59) 27, 17 March 1959; 'Report on the 1959 Annual Review, General Chapter', CM (59) 94, Part I, 3 December 1959.
52 NAC memoranda, 'Report on the 1958 Annual Review, Country Chapter on Greece', NATO Archives, CM (58) 141 Part II, 5 December 1958 and 'Report on the Annual Review, Country Chapter on Greece', CM (59) 94 Part II, 3 December 1959.
53 NAC ministerial meetings, NATO Archives, CVR (58) 63 and 64, 17 December 1958; CVR (59) 47, 16 December 1959; CVR (60) 21 and 51, 3 May and 17 December 1960.
54 Memorandum (Frontistis) to Karamanlis, April 1960, Karamanlis Archive, file 12A.
55 B. Kardamakis, 'To epi tis ypourgeias tou epitelesthen ergon' [The work of his ministry], in *Aristeidis Protopapadakis, 1903–1966*, Athens: n.p., 1967. Kardamakis was the chief of the GES in 1959–62.
56 NAC memorandum, '1961 Interim Review: Chapter on Greece', NATO Archives, CM (61) 115, 4 December 1961.
57 Memorandum (General Staff of National Defence), 27 April 1959, Karamanlis Archive, file 8A; Note to Karamanlis, September 1961, Karamanlis Archive, file 16A.
58 Rizas, *He Hellada, oi Enomenes Politeies kai he Evropi*, pp. 45–6; see also Athens to FO, 31 July 1961, FO 371/160424/1.
59 Panas to Karamanlis, 4 September 1962, Karamanlis Archive, file 18A; Labouisse to State Department, 6 March 1962, Kennedy Library, NSF, Country File: Greece, General, Box 100.
60 NAC memorandum, 'Triennial review 1962: international staff appreciation of NATO military authorities' Initial Country Force Programmes 1963–1964, Greece', NATO Archives, CM (62) 24, 12 March 1962.
61 NAC memoranda, 'Implementation of the resolution on the defence problems of Greece', NATO Archives, CM (62) 87, 24 August 1962; Triennial Review 1962: Chapter on Greece, CM (62) 121, 11 December 1962.
62 Briggs to State Department, 30 January 1962, Kennedy Library, NSF, Country File: Greece, General, Box 100.
63 Stefanidis, *Asymmetroi Etairoi*, p. 282.
64 Johnson to Karamanlis, 22 October 1962, Karamanlis Archive, file 18A.
65 Memorandum (General Staff of National Defence), January 1963, Karamanlis Archive, file 20A.
66 Protopapadakis to Karamanlis, 24 and 29 April 1963, Karamanlis Archive, file 20A.
67 NAC ministerial meeting records, NATO Archives, CVR (58) 61, 16 December 1958.
68 Karandreas (Berlin) to Foreign Ministry, 19 July 1961, Averoff Archive, file 8.
69 Melas (NATO) to Foreign Ministry, 1 September 1961, Averoff Archive, file 8.
70 Karandreas (Bonn) to Ministry for the Prime Minister's Office, 6 April 1962, Averoff Archive, file 9.
71 H. Fleischer, 'Post-war relations between Greece and the two German states: a re-evaluation in the light of German unification', *The Southeast European Yearbook*, 2, 1991, 163–78.

8 Functionalism in action

1 Karamanlis, speech in Parliament, 10 October 1955, in C. Svolopoulos (ed.), *Constantinos Karamanlis: archeio, gegonota kai keimena* [Constantinos Karamanlis: archive, events and texts], Vol. 1, Athens: C.G. Karamanlis Foundation and Ekdotike Athenon, 1992, pp. 272–3 (hereafter referred to as *Karamanlis*).
2 See E. Hatzivassiliou, *Britain and the International Status of Cyprus, 1955–59*, Minneapolis: Minnesota Mediterranean and East European Monographs, 1997, pp. 115–16, 142–51; R. Holland, 'NATO and the struggle for Cyprus', *Journal of Modern Greek Studies*, 13, 1995, 33–61; R. Holland, *Britain and the Revolt in Cyprus, 1954–1959*, Oxford: Clarendon Press, 1998, p. 283.
3 Karamanlis, intervention in Cabinet, 13 September 1955, *Karamanlis*, Vol. 1, p. 257.
4 Karamanis, speech in Thessaloniki, 22 January 1956, *Karamanlis*, Vol. 1, p. 353.
5 Karamanlis, speech in Parliament, 25 April 1956, *Karamanlis*, Vol. 2, p. 73.
6 Averoff to Vlachos (Nicosia), 2 October 1956, Averoff Archive, file 102.
7 M. Melas to Foreign Ministry, 1 November 1957, Karamanlis Archive, file 4A.
8 Hatzivassiliou, *Britain and the International Status of Cyprus*, p. 118.
9 Karamanlis to Spaak, 9 September 1958, *Karamanlis*, Vol. 3, pp. 223–4.
10 Hatzivassiliou, *Britain and the International Status of Cyprus*, pp. 140–1.
11 M. Melas, *Anamniseis enos Presveos* [The Memoirs of an Ambassador], Athens: Rodis, 1966, p. 203.
12 NAC ministerial meeting records, NATO Archives, CVR (55) 59 and 60, 15 and 16 December 1955; CVR (56) 21 final and 23 final, 4 and 5 May 1956.
13 Record (Karamanlis–Hoover), 15 November 1956, *Karamanlis*, Vol. 2, p. 196.
14 Karamanlis, speech in NATO summit, 16 December 1957, *Karamanlis*, Vol. 2, pp. 477–80.
15 See the common Greek–Turkish memorandum (autumn 1958), Karamanlis Archive, file 7A.
16 Record (Karamanlis–Eisenhower), 15 December 1959, *Karamanlis*, Vol. 4, pp. 222–6.
17 Karamanlis to Spaak, 5 December 1960, *Karamanlis*, Vol. 4, p. 464.
18 Record (Karamanlis–Rusk), 18 April 1961, *Karamanlis*, Vol. 5, p. 35.
19 Record (Averoff–Allen), 3 November 1956, Averoff Archive, file 102.
20 Record (Karamanlis–J.F. Kennedy), 19 April 1961, and Note (Karamanlis), *Karamanlis*, Vol. 5, p. 44.
21 S. Rizas, *He Hellada, oi Enomenes Politeies kai he Evropi, 1961–1964: politikes kai oikonomikes opseis tou provlimatos asfaleias sto metaichmio psychrou polemou kai yfesis* [Greece, the US and Europe, 1961–1964: political and economic aspects of the security problem in the passing from Cold War to détente], Athens: Patakis, 2001, pp. 46–7.
22 See Foreign Ministry Brief, 'Note on the position of West Germany in NATO', autumn 1958, Karamanlis Archive, file 7A.
23 H. Fleischer, 'Post-war relations between Greece and the two German states: a re-evaluation in the light of German unification', *The Southeast European Yearbook*, 2, 1991, 163–78.
24 Philon to Foreign Ministry, 5 March 1959, *Karamanlis*, Vol. 4, pp. 20–3; on Greece's French opening see mostly, C. Svolopoulos, 'La perspective européene de la politique extérieure grecque et le général de Gaulle (1959–1963)', in *De Gaulle en son siècle: 5. L'Europe*, Paris: Plon, 1992, pp. 247–55.
25 Minute (Foreign Ministry, Second Political Directory), 16 June 1960, Karamanlis Archive, file 12A.
26 Speeches by Karamanlis and de Gaulle and communiqué, 19 May 1963, *Karamanlis*, Vol. 5, pp. 637–40.

27 Record (Karamanlis–J.F. Kennedy), 19 April 1961, and Note (Karamanlis, late 1960s), *Karamanlis*, Vol. 5, pp. 44, 60.
28 Philon to Foreign Ministry, 20 February 1961, *Karamanlis*, Vol. 4, pp. 521–2.
29 Record (Karamanlis–Spaak), 3 April 1962, *Karamanlis*, Vol. 5, p. 340.
30 Record (Karamanlis–Merchant), 22 April 1963, *Karamanlis*, Vol. 5, p. 614.
31 Note (Karamanlis, late 1960s), and Record (Karamanlis–de Gaulle), 19 May 1963, *Karamanlis*, Vol. 5, pp. 580, 637. See also E. Hatzivassiliou, 'Security and the European option: Greek foreign policy, 1952–1962', *Journal of Contemporary History*, 30, 1995, 187–202.
32 *Karamanlis*, Vol. 5, p. 644.
33 Rizas, *He Hellada, oi Enomenes Politeies kai he Evropi*, pp. 142–51. See also Labouisse to State Department, 12 March and 20 May 1963, Kennedy Library, NSF Country File: Greece, General, Box 100.
34 P. Kazakos, *Anamesa se Kratos kai Agora: oikonomia kai oikonomiki politiki sti metapolemiki Hellada, 1944–2000* [Between the State and the Market: economy and economic policy in post-war Greece], Athens: Patakis, 2001, pp. 163–250; G. Alogoskoufis, 'The two faces of Janus: institutions, policy regimes and macroeconomic performance in Greece', *Economic Policy*, 20, 1995, 149–92.
35 C. Svolopoulos, *He Helleniki Exoteriki Politiki* [Greek foreign policy], Vol. 2 (1945–1981), Athens: Hestia, 2001, p. 101.
36 Memorandum (Allen) 2 July 1956 and Allen to State Department, 3 October 1956, *FRUS*, 1955–57, XXIV, pp. 568–9, 572–3.
37 Greek memorandum, January 1957, *Karamanlis*, Vol. 2, pp. 256–8.
38 NSC 5718/1, 5 August 1957; S. Zachariou, 'The road to the garrison state: an overview of Greek–American relations during the Eisenhower and Kennedy administrations (1952–1963)', *Modern Greek Studies Yearbook*, 14/15, 1998/1999, 241–60.
39 Greek memorandum, 26 May 1958, *Karamanlis*, Vol. 3, pp. 133–5.
40 Greek aide-memoire to the US government, 781.5MSP/9-158.
41 *Karamanlis*, Vol. 3, pp. 220, 268, 378–9. See also Riddleberger to State Department, 4 November 1958, 781.00(W)/11-458; Record (Karamanlis–McGhee), 29 January 1959, Karamanlis Archive, file 8A.
42 See the figures in Th.A. Couloumbis, *The United States, Greece and Turkey: the troubled triangle*, New York: Praeger, 1983, p. 178.
43 Minute, 'Caramanlis visit: United States Military Aid', spring 1961, Kennedy Library, NSF Country File: Greece, Caramanlis Briefing Book, 17–20 April 1961, Box 101.
44 Zachariou, 'The road to the garrison state', pp. 241–60.
45 Allen Dulles to John Foster Dulles, 26 May 1956, *FRUS*, 1955–57, XXIV, pp. 562–3; Record (Karamanlis–Dulles), 19 December 1957, *Karamanlis*, Vol. 2, p. 502.
46 Liatis to Karamanlis, 16 September 1959, *Karamanlis*, Vol. 4, pp. 163–6.
47 Th. Grigoropoulos, *Apo tin Koryfi tou Lofou: anamniseis kai stochasmoi, 1914–1952 kai 1959–1962* [From the top of the hill: memories and thoughts], Athens: n.p., 1966, pp. 548–56.
48 Note, 15 December 1959, *Karamanlis*, Vol. 4, p. 214.
49 Briggs to State Department, 7 January 1960, *FRUS*, 1958–60, X, part 2, p. 696.
50 Record (Karamanlis–Herter), 4 May 1960, *FRUS*, 1958–60, X, part 2, pp. 718–19.
51 Minute (Goustis), 8 March 1961, *Karamanlis*, Vol. 5, pp. 27–30.
52 Record (Karamanlis–Johnson), 22 May 1961, *Karamanlis*, Vol. 5, p. 88.
53 Karamanlis to Rusk, 22 July 1961 and Greek memoranda, *Karamanlis*, Vol. 5, pp. 121–5.
54 Greek aide-memoire to the US government, 12 January 1962, Karamanlis Archive, file 17A.
55 Labouisse to State Department, 6 March 1962, Kennedy Library, NSF, Country File: Greece, General, Box 100. Also published in *FRUS*, 1961–63, XVI, pp. 630–1.

202 Notes

56 NAC memorandum, 'Report of the Committee of Economic Advisers', NATO Archives, CM (59) 90, 21 October 1959.
57 See Note, NATO Archives, AC/200 (Revised), 5 April 1961.
58 NAC ministerial meeting records, NATO Archives, CVR (61) 19, 9 May 1961; CVR (61) 67, 14 December 1961.
59 See NATO Archives, PO (61) 693, 28 August 1961.
60 NAC memorandum, 'Report on Greece of the Mission Appointed in Accordance with the Resolution of the NATO Council on 9th May, 1961', NATO Archives, CM (62) 32, 18 April 1962.
61 Record (Karamanlis–Labouisse), 11 April 1962, *Karamanlis*, Vol. 5, pp. 353–6.
62 Rizas, *He Hellada, oi Enomenes Politeies kai he Evropi*, pp. 50–1, 75–81.
63 'Note by the Secretary General to the Council on the Report of the NATO Mission (Greece)', NATO Archives, PO/62/265, 17 April 1962.
64 Record (Karamanlis–Rusk), 3 May 1962, *Karamanlis*, Vol. 5, p. 371.
65 NAC ministerial meeting records, NATO Archives, CVR (62) 24, 5 May 1962.
66 Stikker to permanent representatives, 'Implementation of the Resolution on the Defence Problems of Greece', NATO Archives, PO/62/298, 18 May 1962.
67 See Note, NATO Archives, AC/213-D1, 5 June 1962; AC/213-D2 (Revised), 20 June 1962 and AC/213-D3 (Revised) 16 July 1962; AC/213-D5, 31 July 1962; NAC memorandum, 'Implementation of the Resolution on the Defence Problems of Greece', NATO Archives, CM (62) 87, 24 August 1962.
68 NAC ministerial meeting records, NATO Archives, CVR (62) 63, 14 December 1962; NAC memorandum CM (62) 154 final, 18 December 1962.
69 See Xanthopoulos-Palamas to Stikker, NATO Archives, PO (63) 073, 29 January 1963.
70 Greek Note, 4 June 1959, *Karamanlis*, Vol. 4, p. 88.
71 I.D. Stefanidis, *Asymmetroi Etairoi: oi Enomenes Politeies kai he Ellada ston psychro polemo, 1953–1961* [Unequal Partners: The US and Greece in the Cold War], Athens: Patakis, 2002, pp. 183–8.
72 S.G. Xydis, *Cyprus: conflict and conciliation, 1954–1958*, Columbus, Ohio: The Ohio State University Press, 1967, pp. 96–8.
73 Stoica to Karamanlis, 10 September and Karamanlis to Stoica 23 September 1957, *Karamanlis*, Vol. 2, pp. 417–21.
74 Memorandum of the Romanian Foreign Ministry to the Central Committee of the CPSU (not later than 8 August 1957), in B. Kondis, Y. Mourelos, C. Papoulides, M.G. Prozoumentsikov, N.D. Smirnova and N. Tomilina (eds), *Sovietiki Enosi kai Valkania stis Dekaeties 1950 kai 1960: syllogi eggrafon* [The Soviet Union and the Balkans in the 1950s and the 1960s: a collection of documents], Thessaloniki: Institute for Balkan Studies, 2003, pp. 138–43.
75 NAC ministerial meeting records, NATO Archives CVR (59) 45, 15 December 1959.
76 Michael Melas to Karamanlis, 25 November 1957, Karamanlis Archive, file 4A; Melas, *Anamniseis*, pp. 209–10.
77 Minute (General Staff of National Defence), 30 November 1957, Karamanlis Archive, file 4A.
78 Minute (Foreign Ministry), 16 January 1958, Karamanlis Archive, file 5A.
79 Th.A. Couloumbis, *Greek Political Reaction to American and NATO Influences*, New Haven and London: Yale University Press, 1966, p. 111.
80 Stefanidis, *Asymmetroi Etairoi*, p. 166.
81 Karamanlis, speech in NATO summit, 16 December 1957, and Note (Karamanlis, late 1960s), *Karamanlis*, Vol. 2, pp. 477–80, 497–8. For a criticism of this position, see Melas, *Anamniseis*, p. 210.
82 Record (Karamanlis–Eisenhower), 18 December 1957, *Karamanlis*, Vol. 2, pp. 500–2.

Notes 203

83 Bulganin to Karamanlis, 12 December 1957 and 14 January 1958, Karamanlis to Bulganin, 5 February 1958, *Karamanlis*, Vol. 2, pp. 486–98.
84 Averoff to Greek Embassy, Budapest, 12 January 1958, Averoff Archive, file 5.
85 *Karamanlis*, Vol. 3, pp. 120–1.
86 Stefanidis, *Assymetroi Etairoi*, pp. 170–83.
87 See Markezinis's articles in *Hestia*, 25–27 May 1959.
88 J. Melissen, *The Struggle for Nuclear Partnership: Britain, the United States and the making of an ambiguous alliance, 1952–1959*, Groningen: Styx, 1993, p. 105; Ph. Nash, *The Other Missiles of October: Eisenhower, Kennedy, and the Jupiters, 1957–1963*, Chapel Hill and London: The University of North Carolina Press, 1997, pp. 60–5.
89 Stefanidis, *Asymmetroi Etairoi*, pp. 170–82.
90 See, among others, the Parliamentary debates in November 1959 and April 1960 in *Greek Parliamentary Records* (GPR), period E, synod B, pp. 54–228, 524–693.
91 Record (Karamanlis–Rusk), 18 April 1961, *Karamanlis*, Vol. 5, p. 35.
92 Averoff, circular telegram to the Greek Embassies, 19 January 1963, Karamanlis Archive, file 20A. See also Averoff's speech in NAC ministerial meeting records, NATO Archives, CVR (63) 28, 22 May 1963.

9 The limits of functionalism: security and détente

1 E. Hatzivassiliou, 'Greek–Bulgarian and Greek–Soviet relations, 1953–1959: a view from the British archives', *Modern Greek Studies Yearbook*, 8, 1992, 129.
2 S. Wallden, *Hellada kai Anatolikes Chores, 1950–1967: oikonomikes scheseis kai politiki* [Greece and the Eastern Countries: economic relations and politics], Vol. A, Athens: Odysseas and Foundation for Mediterranean Studies, 1991, pp. 121–2.
3 S.G. Xydis, *Cyprus: Conflict and Conciliation, 1954–1958*, Columbus, Ohio: The Ohio State University Press, 1967, pp. 61–3.
4 Hatzivassiliou, 'Greek–Bulgarian and Greek–Soviet relations', pp. 125–7.
5 Record of the meeting, 17 October 1958, Averoff Archive, file 5.
6 Mackenzie (Athens) to Galsworthy, 17 May 1957 and FO minute (Goodall) 21 May 1957, FO 371/129997/2.
7 Herter to US Embassy, Athens, 24 May 1958, 667.81/5-2458.
8 Allen to State Department, 6 March 1957, 781.00/3-657; Athens to FO, 8 January 1960, FO 371/152818/1.
9 Hatzivassiliou, 'Greek–Bulgarian and Greek–Soviet relations', p. 133.
10 Record (Averoff–Koriukin), 26 October 1962, Averoff Archive, file 9.
11 S. Venizelos, 'Entyposeis kai porismata apo ena taxidi' [Impressions and conclusions from a journey], *To Vima*, 26–30 June 1960; S. Venizelos, 'Diati prepei na anagnoristhei to KKE' [Why the KKE should be legalized], *To Vima*, 3 July 1960.
12 Tables of exports (December 1958), in C. Svolopoulos (ed.), *Constantinos Karamanlis: archeio, gegonota kai keimena* [Constantinos Karamanlis: archive, events and texts], Vol. 4, Athens: C.G. Karamanlis Foundation and Ekdotike Athenon, 1994, pp. 210–12 (hereafter referred to as *Karamanlis*); Roberts (Thessaloniki) to State Department, 1 November 1959, 781.00/11-159 and 7 December 1959, 781.00/12-759; S. Rizas, *He Hellada, oi Enomenes Politeies kai he Evropi, 1961–1964: politikes kai oikonomikes opseis tou provlimatos asfaleias sto metaichmio psychrou polemou kai yfesis* [Greece, the US and Europe, 1961–1964: political and economic aspects of the security problem in the passing from Cold War to détente], Athens: Patakis, 2001, p. 40.
13 *Greek Parliamentary Records* (GPR), period E, synod B, pp. 54–228.
14 GPR, period E, synod B, pp. 524–693.
15 Karamanlis to the heads of governments of the Six, 26 November 1960, *Karamanlis*, Vol. 4, pp. 451–2.

16 Record (Xanthopoulos-Palamas–Briggs), 9 December 1960, *Karamanlis*, Vol. 4, pp. 465–6.
17 *Karamanlis*, Vol. 4, pp. 466–7.
18 Minute (Foreign Ministry), 21 January 1961, Karamanlis Archive, file 14A.
19 M. Melas (NATO) to Foreign Ministry, 1 September 1961, Averoff Archive, file 8.
20 NAC memorandum, Report by the Working Group on Economic Countermeasures', NATO Archives, CM (61) 114, 20 November 1961.
21 Averoff to Rusk, 22 December 1962, Averoff Archive, file 9 (original text in English, emphasis in the original).
22 E. Hatzivassiliou, 'Negotiating with the enemy: the normalization of Greek–Bulgarian relations, 1960–1964', *Southeast European and Black Sea Studies*, 4, 2004, 138–59.
23 Allen to Tomkins, 6 May 1961, FO 371/160409/2.
24 Briggs to State Department, 18 November 1961, Kennedy Library, NSF Country File: Greece, General, Box 100; Athens to FO, 29 November and 5 December 1961, FO 371/160409/3 and 4.
25 Athens to FO, 3 January 1962, FO 371/163481/1.
26 Curle (Athens) to Tomkins, 3 January 1962, FO 371/165803/1.
27 Bespalov (Tirana) to Soviet Foreign Ministry, 31 June 1961, in B. Kondis, Y. Mourelos, C. Papoulides, M.G. Prozoumentsikov, N.D. Smirnova and N. Tomilina (eds), *Sovietiki Enosi kai Valkania stis Dekaeties 1950 kai 1960: syllogi eggrafon* [The Soviet Union and the Balkans in the 1950s and the 1960s: a collection of documents], Thessaloniki: Institute for Balkan Studies, 2003, pp. 325–41.
28 Carr (Brussels) to Symon, 27 April 1962 and Murray to Tomkins, 4 June 1962, FO 371/165803/3 and 6.
29 P. Pipinelis, *Europe and the Albanian Question*, Chicago: Argonaut, 1963.
30 Athens to FO, 13 September, Greek memorandum 23 August and Minute (Viney, FORD), 30 August 1963, FO 371/169072/1 and 2.

10 The regional aspect of functionalism: Yugoslavia, Turkey, Cyprus

1 Record (Karamanlis–Averoff–Menderes–Zorlu), 8 May 1959, in C. Svolopoulos (ed.), *Constantinos Karamanlis: archeio, gegonota kai keimena* [Constantinos Karamanlis: archive, events and texts], Vol. 4, Athens: C. G. Karamanlis Foundation and Ekdotike Athenon, 1994, p. 66 (hereafter referred to as *Karamanlis*).
2 E. Hatzivassiliou, 'Security and the European option: Greek foreign policy, 1952–1962', *Journal of Contemporary History*, 30, 1995, 193.
3 Record (Karamanlis–J.F. Kennedy), 19 April 1961, *Karamanlis*, Vol. 5, p. 43.
4 E. Hatzivassiliou, *Britain and the International Status of Cyprus, 1955–59*, Minneapolis: Minnesota Mediterranean and East European Monographs, 1997, pp. 73–4, 79–80.
5 Lambert to Young, 5 April 1956, FO 371/123858/20; Lambert to Young, 20 June 1956, FO 371/123858/24; Ireland (Thessaloniki) to State Department, 26 September 1956, 781.00/9-2656.
6 See Lambert to FO, 31 July 1956, FO 371/123860/4; Roberts (Belgrade) to FO, 9 August 1956, FO 371/123860/7; Cannon to State Department, 3 August 1956, 781.00(W)/8-356.
7 Records (Karamanlis–Tito), 5–6 December 1956, *Karamanlis*, Vol. 2, pp. 224–33.
8 Elting to State Department, 13 December 1956, 681.00/12-1356.
9 See Minute (Matsas, Foreign Ministry), 14 February 1959, Karamanlis Archive, file 8A.
10 Records (Karamanlis–Kardelj), 22–23 October 1957, *Karamanlis*, Vol. 2, pp. 439–49.
11 Belgrade to FO, 20 June 1958, FO 371/136232/3.
12 Athens to FO, 2 July 1958, FO 371/136232/4.

13 Lambert to Selwyn Lloyd, 12 April and Minute (Goodall, Foreign Office), 16 April 1957, FO 371/130026/2.
14 NSC-5718/1, 5 August 1957; NSC-6101, 4 January 1961.
15 Ankara to FO, 30 July 1958, FO 371/136232/8.
16 Hatzivassiliou, *Britain and the International Status of Cyprus*, p. 149.
17 Minute (Foreign Ministry, NATO Directory), February 1959, Karamanlis Archive, file 8A.
18 Hayman to Addis, 2 November 1957, FO 371/130027/7.
19 Penfield to State Department, 25 April 1958, 681.00/4-2558.
20 Minute, 14 February 1959, Karamanlis Archive, file 8A.
21 See extracts of the Foreign Ministry minutes by Ambassador Matsas, in *Karamanlis*, Vol. 4, p. 110.
22 Record (Karamanlis–Tito), 3 March 1959, *Karamanlis*, Vol. 4, p. 18.
23 Minute (Matsas, Foreign Ministry), 23 April 1959, *Karamanlis*, Vol. 4, p. 19.
24 Record (Karamanlis–Averoff–Menderes–Zorlu), 8 May 1959, *Karamanlis*, Vol. 4, pp. 64–7.
25 Matsas to Foreign Ministry, 24 July 1959, Averoff Archive, file 6.
26 *Karamanlis*, Vol. 4, pp. 108–11.
27 Venizelos to Karamanlis, 4 August and Karamanlis to Venizelos, 20 August 1959, *Karamanlis*, Vol. 4, pp. 137–9.
28 Kanellopoulos to Karamanlis and Kanellopoulos to Averoff, 9 September 1959, *Karamanlis*, Vol. 4, pp. 160–1. On Kanellopoulos' visit to Yugoslavia, see also Kanellopoulos Archive, file 'ERE government (1959). Diplomatic documents on Yugoslavia'.
29 Garvey (Belgrade) to Selwyn Lloyd, 16 September 1959, FO 371/144550/3.
30 *Greek Parliamentary Records* (GPR) *Special Committee of Article 35*, period E, synod A, pp. 471–97; S. Wallden, *Hellada kai Yugoslavia: gennisi kai exelixi mias krisis* [Greece and Yugoslavia: birth and evolution of a crisis], Athens: Themelio, 1991, p. 15.
31 On the reaction of Greeks leaders and officials regarding these, see Markantonakis to Belgrade Embassy, 21 August and 2 September 1959, Kanellopoulos Archive, file 'ERE government (1959). Diplomatic documents on Yugoslavia', where Kanellopoulos minuted in his own handwriting his angry reaction. See also, in the same file, the appeals of Ambassador Tsakalotos from Belgrade to stop these police initiatives.
32 *Karamanlis*, Vol. 4, p. 266.
33 Minute (Cambiotis, Foreign Ministry), 21 June 1960, Karamanlis Archive, file 12A.
34 Garvey to Barnes, 8 June 1960, FO 371/152976/4.
35 See the minutes in Karamanlis Archive, file 12A.
36 *Karamanlis*, Vol. 4, pp. 330–3.
37 Crosswell (Belgrade) to Selwyn Lloyd, 13 July 1960, FO 371/152976/9; Curle to Sarell 6 July 1960 and Crosswell to Selwyn Lloyd, 13 July 1960 FO 371/152976/7 and 9.
38 Record (Karamanlis–Rancovic), 4 May 1961, *Karamanlis*, Vol. 5, pp. 72–5.
39 *Karamanlis*, Vol. 5, pp. 264–5.
40 S. Venizelos, 'Astochiai eis ton cheirismon ton ethnikon mas thematon' [Mistakes in the handling of our national issues], *To Vima*, 7 January 1962.
41 Wallden, *Hellada kai Yugoslavia*, pp. 75–6.
42 Record (Karamanlis–Dapcevic), 28 February 1962, *Karamanlis*, Vol. 5, p. 307.
43 NAC ministerial meeting records, NATO Archives, CVR (62) 22, 3 May 1962.
44 NAC, Permanent representatives session, NATO Archives, CR (62) 41, 17 August 1962.
45 Record (Karamanlis–Dapcevic), 8 October 1962, *Karamanlis*, Vol. 5, pp. 475–7.
46 Barnes to Jamieson, 17 October 1962, FO 371/163453/5; Brigadier Snowball to Murray, 31 January 1963, Annual report on the Greek Army, FO 371/169091/1.

47 Wallden, *Hellada kai Yugoslavia*, pp. 98–101.
48 *Karamanlis*, Vol. 4, pp. 62, 64.
49 Averoff, hand-written notes for the conversation with Toker, and text of the interview, March 1962, Averoff Archive, file 9.
50 See Minute (Foreign Ministry, Economic Affairs Directorate), 18 April 1959, and Minute (Ioannis Pesmazoglou) to Karamanlis, 27 April 1959, Karamanlis Archive, file 8A.
51 Minute (George Pasmazoglou), early 1958, Karamanlis Archive, file 9A.
52 Minutes (George Pesmazoglou), April 1959, and G. Pesmazoglou to Karamanlis, 21 April 1959, Karamanlis Archive, file 9A.
53 *Karamanlis*, Vol. 4, pp. 233–4.
54 See the records of Averoff's two conversations with the US Ambassador, Ellis Briggs, on 14 and 19 April 1960, in *Karamanlis*, Vol. 4, pp. 283–5.
55 Menderes to Karamanlis, 24 May 1960, and Note (Karamanlis, late 1960s), *Karamanlis*, Vol. 4, pp. 307–9.
56 *Karamanlis*, Vol. 4, pp. 308–9.
57 Minute (Cambiotis, Foreign Ministry), 16 June 1960, Karamanlis Archive, file 12A.
58 Brief 'The change of regime in Turkey', 16 June 1960, Karamanlis Archive, file 12A.
59 Record (Karamanlis–Debré), 11 July 1960, *Karamanlis*, Vol. 4, p. 352.
60 *Karamanlis*, Vol. 4, pp. 423–7.
61 Minutes (Matsas), 27 March 1961, Averoff Archive, file 8.
62 Matsas to Foreign Ministry, 15 September 1961, Averoff Archive, file 8.
63 Verykios to Foreign Ministry, 5 March 1963, *Karamanlis*, Vol. 5, p. 566.
64 Sgourdaios, circular telegram to the Greek Embassies in the EEC member states, 12 March 1963, Karamanlis Archive, file 97A.
65 Note (Averoff), 10 August 1962, Averoff Archive, file 110.
66 E. Hatzivassiliou, *The Cyprus Question, 1878–1960: the constitutional aspect*, Minneapolis: Minnesota Mediterranean and East European Monographs, 2002, pp. 73–81.
67 A. Heraclides, *Kypriako: sygrousi kai epilysi* [The Cyprus question: conflict and resolution], Athens: Sideris, 2002, p. 82.
68 Hatzivassiliou, *The Cyprus Question: the constitutional aspect*, pp. 78–9.
69 C. Nicolet, *United States Policy towards Cyprus, 1954–1974: removing the Greek–Turkish bone of contention*, Manheim und Möhnesee: Bibliopolis, 2001, pp. 160–3.
70 J. Joseph, *Cyprus: ethnic conflict and international politics. From independence to the threshold of the European Union*, London: Macmillan, 1997, pp. 116–17.
71 Regarding the debate about whether Athens 'imposed' the 1959 agreements on Makarios, see Hatzivassiliou, *The Cyprus Question: the constitutional aspect*, pp. 82–3.
72 Note (Averoff), 10 August 1962, Averoff Archive, file 110.
73 Averoff to Makarios, 19 April 1963, in E. Averoff-Tossizza, *Lost Opportunities: the Cyprus question, 1950–1963* (trans. Timothy Cullen and Susan Kyriakidis), New Rochelle: A. Karatzas, 1986, p. 430.

11 Facing new challenges

1 Th.A. Couloumbis, *The United States, Greece and Turkey: the troubled triangle*, New York: Praeger, 1983, p. 45.
2 On the internal crisis, see mostly Th. Diamantopoulos, *He Helleniki Politiki Zoi: eikostos aionas* [The Greek Political Life: the twentieth century], Athens: Papazisis, 1997, pp. 188–92, 367–479; E. Nicolakopoulos, *He Kachektiki Dimokratia: kommata kai ekloges, 1946–1967* [The Sickly Democracy: parties and elections], Athens: Patakis, 2001, pp. 303–71.
3 George Papandreou, memorandum to the Greek and the British governments (1943),

in P. Petrides and G. Anastasiades (eds), *Georgios Papandreou: o politikos logos* [G. Papandreou: political discourse], Thessaloniki: University Studio Press, 1995, pp. 247–8.
4 George Papandreou, speech in Parliament, 20 December 1963, *Greek Parliamentary Records* (GPR), period Z, synod A, pp. 11–22; also published in Petrides and Anastasiades (eds), *Papandreou: politikos logos*, pp. 470–506.
5 Record (Papandreou–Stikker), 30 April 1964, in S. Papageorgiou (ed.), *Ta Krisima Documenta tou Kypriakou (1959–1967)* [The crucial documents of the Cyprus question], Vol. A, Athens: Ladias, 1983, pp. 312–19 (hereafter referred to as *Cyprus Documents*).
6 Record (Papandreou–Brosio), 4 November 1964, *Cyprus Documents*, Vol. C, pp. 40–4.
7 Papandreou, speech in Parliament, 20 December 1963, *GPR*, period Z, synod A, pp. 11–22; Papandreou, speech in Parliament, 30 March 1964, *GPR*, period H, synod A, pp. 16–23.
8 S. Rizas, *He Hellada, oi Enomenes Politeies kai he Evropi, 1961–1964: politikes kai oikonomikes opseis tou provlimatos asfaleias sto metaichmio psychrou polemou kai yfesis* [Greece, the US and Europe, 1961–1964: political and economic aspects of the security problem in the passing from Cold War to détente], Athens: Patakis, 2001, p. 182.
9 Papandreou, speech in Parliament, 20 December 1963, *GPR*, period Z, synod A, pp. 11–22.
10 Record of the meeting of 25 January 1964, in P. Petrides (ed.), *O Georgios Papandreou kai to Kypriako Zitima (1954–1965): documenta* [George Papandreou and the Cyprus question, 1954–1965: documents], Thessaloniki: University Studio Press, 1998, pp. 274–81 (hereafter referred to as *Papandreou–Cyprus*).
11 Papandreou, speech in Parliament, 30 March 1964, *GPR*, period H, synod A, pp. 16–23.
12 S. Linardatos, *Apo ton Emfylio sti Junta* [From the Civil War to the Junta], Vol. E, 1964–1967, Athens: Papazisis, n.d., p. 221.
13 A. Papahelas, *O Viasmos tis Hellenikis Dimokratias: o amerikanikos paragon, 1947–1967* [The Rape of Greek Democracy: the American factor], Athens: Hestia, 1997, p. 141.
14 Papandreou to Makarios, 29 August 1964, *Cyprus Documents*, Vol. B, pp. 323–5. Emphasis in the original.
15 See, for example, the comment in T. Bahcheli, *Greek–Turkish Relations since 1955*, Boulder: Westview Press, 1990, p. 65.
16 Mitsotakis to Papandreou, 4 August and Papandreou to Mitsotakis, 5 August 1964, in Th. Diamantopoulos, *Costas Mitsotakis, Politiki Viographia: apo ton anendoto sti dictatoria* [Costas Mitsotakis, Political Biography: from the relentless struggle to the dictatorship], Athens: Papazisis, 1990, appendix.
17 P. Garoufalias, *Hellas kai Kypros: tragika sfalmata, efkairies pou chathikan* [Greece and Cyprus: tragic mistakes, lost opportunites], Athens: Bergadis, 1982, pp. 99–101, 125–6.
18 Constantinos Mitsotakis, interview with the author, 2 October 2002; Michalis Papaconstantinou, interview with the author, 30 April 2002.
19 Constantinos Mitsotakis, interview with the author, 2 October 2002.
20 On Mitsotakis's views, see Diamantopoulos, *Mitsotakis*; E. Hatzivassiliou, *Helleniki Evropaiki Politiki, 1965–1966: epanadrastiriopoiisi sto Koinotiko plaisio* [Greece's European Policy, 1965–1966: re-activation in the community context], Athens: C. Mitsotakis Foundation, 2003, pp. 33–42.
21 I.D. Stefanidis, *Isle of Discord: nationalism, imperialism and the making of the Cyprus problem*, London: Hurst, 1999, pp. 30–1.
22 E. Hatzivassiliou, *Britain and the International Status of Cyprus, 1955–59,*

Minneapolis: Minnesota Mediterranean and East European Monographs, 1997, p. 99; Minute (Sir Roger Allen), 3 July 1957, FO 286/1416.
23 N. Kranidiotis, *Diskola Chronia: Kypros, 1950–1960* [Difficult Years: Cyprus, 1950–1960], Athens: Hestia, 1981, pp. 278–80.
24 *GPR*, period E, synod A, pp. 286–341.
25 *Papandreou–Cyprus*, pp. 191–2.
26 S. Linardatos, *Apo ton Emfylio sti Junta* [From the Civil War to the Junta], Vol. D, 1961–1964, Athens: Papazisis, 1986, p. 300.
27 D. Markides, *Cyprus, 1957–1963: from colonial conflict to constitutional crisis. The key role of the municipal issue*, Minneapolis: Minnesota Mediterranean and East European Monographs, 2001, p. 138.
28 S. Rizas, *Enosi, Dichotomisi, Anexartisia: oi Enomenes Politeies kai he Vretania stin anazitisi lysis gia to Kypriako, 1963–1967* [Enosis, Partition, Independence: the US and Britain in search of a solution for the Cyprus question], Athens: Vivliorama, 2000, pp. 36–7.
29 N. Kranidiotis, *Anochyroti Politeia: Kypros, 1960–1974* [Unfortified State: Cyprus, 1960–1974], Vol. A, Athens: Hestia, 1985, pp. 94, 98.
30 Venizelos to Makarios, 29 December 1963, *Cyprus Documents*, Vol. A, pp. 285–6.
31 Labouisse to State Department, 21 February 1964, *FRUS*, 1964–68, XVI, pp. 34–7.
32 P. Tzermias, *Historia tis Kypriakis Dimokratias* [A History of the Cyprus Republic], Vol. A, 2nd edn, Athens: Libro, 2001, p. 562.
33 Rizas, *Enosi, Dichotomisi, Anexartisia*, pp. 89–90; C. Nicolet, *United States Policy towards Cyprus, 1954–1974: removing the Greek–Turkish bone of contention*, Manheim und Möhnesee: Bibliopolis, 2001, pp. 233–4.
34 Papandreou to Makarios 25 February 1964, *Cyprus Documents*, Vol. A, pp. 300–1.
35 Makarios to Papandreou, 1 March 1964, *Cyprus Documents*, Vol. A, pp. 301–6; also published in *Apanta Archiepiskopou Makariou III* [Collected texts of archbishop Makarios III], Vol. 6, Nicosia: Foundation of Archbishop Makarios III, 1996, pp. 194–200 (hereafter referred to as *Makarios*).
36 Record (Papandreou–Stikker), 30 April 1964, *Cyprus Documents*, Vol. A, pp. 312–19.
37 See the analysis and the discussion about the impact of the Johnson letter to Turkey in S. Bolukbasi, *The Superpowers and the Third World: Turkish–American relations and Cyprus*, New York and London: University Press of America, 1988, pp. 1, 72–9, 115–16; Bahcheli, *Greek–Turkish Relations*, pp. 62–3.
38 See the message in Costopoulos to Greek Embassy, Nicosia, 8 August 1964, *Cyprus Documents*, Vol. B, pp. 112–13.
39 Labouisse to State Department, 25 August 1964, *FRUS*, 1964–68, XVI, pp. 289–92.
40 Papandreou to Makarios, 29 August 1964, *Cyprus Documents*, Vol. B, pp. 323–5. Emphasis in the original.
41 Makarios to Papandreou, 21 February 1965, *Cyprus Documents*, Vol. B, pp. 327–33.
42 *GPR*, period H, synod C, pp. 1659–60.
43 Constantinos Mitsotakis, interview with the author, 2 October 2002; Vyron Theodoropoulos, interview with the author, 8 October 2004.
44 Records of the Government Political Committee, 6 May 1965, *Cyprus Documents*, Vol. C, pp. 170–81, and Records of the meeting in the Palace, 7 May 1965, *Papandreou–Cyprus*, pp. 351–76; Record (Stephanopoulos–Makarios–Tsirimokos–Kyprianou), 2 February 1966, *Makarios*, Vol. 9, pp. 70–2.
45 See, among others, Tzermias *Historia tis Kypriakis Dimokratias*; C. Svolopoulos, *He Helleniki Exoteriki Politiki* [Greek Foreign Policy], Vol. 2 (1945–1981), Athens: Hestia, 2001, p. 164; Th.A. Couloumbis, 'Cyprus Policy Errors', *Epetirida Kentrou Epistimonikon Erevnon* (Bulletin of the Cyprus Research Centre), 20, 1993/1994, 643–8. Greek analysts also cannot forget that an extremist version of the concept of 'national centre' finally became the basis for the Greek junta's coup against Makarios

in 1974 which gave the pretext for the Turkish invasion of Cyprus. Still, they correctly stress that a differentiation must be made between the moderate national centre doctrine as put forward by the governments of Greek democracy and the extremist views of the dictators; there is no indication that a democratic Greek government ever planned to use armed force against Makarios.
46 *GPR*, period H, synod A, pp. 530–2.
47 See, for example, the article which Averoff published under the name 'Diplomat' in *Kathimerini* on 6 and 9 July 1958, reprinted in C. Svolopoulos (ed.), *Constantinos Karamanlis: archeio, gegonota kai keimena* [Constantinos Karamanlis: archive, events and texts], Vol. 3, Athens: C.G. Karamanlis Foundation and Ekdotike Athenon, 1994, pp. 157–62.
48 Brigadier Hobbs (British Embassy, Athens) to Addis, 12 October 1959, FO 371/144519/29.
49 Linardatos, *Apo ton Emfylio sti Junta*, Vol. D, pp. 48–9.
50 Rizas, *Enosi, Dichotomisi, Anexartisia*, pp. 52–3; Kranidiotis, *Anochyroti Politeia*, Vol. A, pp. 125–7.
51 Makarios, public statement, 21 January 1964, *Makarios*, Vol. 6, pp. 361–4.
52 Labouisse to State Department, 21 February 1964, *FRUS*, 1964–68, XVI, pp. 34–7.
53 Grivas, report to the Greek government, 29 March 1966, *Cyprus Documents*, Vol. C, pp. 226–54.
54 Grivas to Papandreou, 23 May 1964, *Cyprus Documents*, Vol. A, pp. 331–5.
55 Garoufalias to Grivas and Grivas to Papandreou, 28 May 1964, *Cyprus Documents*, Vol. A, pp. 339–43.
56 Grivas to Papandreou, 20 June 1964, *Cyprus Documents*, Vol. B, pp. 15–18. Emphasis in the original.
57 Garoufalias to Grivas, 3 July 1964, *Cyprus Documents*, Vol. B, pp. 76–7.
58 Signal ELDYK to General Staff of National Defence, 9 August 1964, 10.30 a.m., and Papandreou to Greek Embassy, Nicosia, message to Grivas, 9 August 1964, *Cyprus Documents*, Vol. B, pp. 115–16.
59 Grivas to Papandreou, 9 September 1964, *Cyprus Documents*, Vol. B, pp. 336–8.
60 Grivas to Papandreou, 28 September 1964, *Cyprus Documents*, Vol. B, pp. 345–6.
61 Grivas to Papandreou, 2 October 1964; Grivas to Garoufalias, 4 October 1964; Grivas to Papandreou, 19 October 19, and 21 October 1964; Grivas to King Constantine, 11 December 1964, *Cyprus Documents*, Vol. B, pp. 356–62 and Vol. C, pp. 24–33, 50–2. See also Vol. C, pp. 58–62, 125–44, 166–9, 180–1.
62 Makarios to Stephanopoulos, 16 March 1966, *Cyprus Documents*, Vol. C, pp. 209–11.
63 Grivas to Stephanopoulos, 19 March 1966, *Cyprus Documents*, Vol. C, pp. 216–17.
64 See Tsirimokos to Alexandrakis (Nicosia), 21 March and Grivas to Tsirimokos, late March 1966, *Cyprus Documents*, Vol. C, pp. 221–4.

12 Multiple fronts

1 S. Linardatos, *Apo ton Emfylio sti Junta* [From the Civil War to the Junta], Vol. D, 1961–1964, Athens: Papazisis, 1986, pp. 328–9.
2 Th. Diamantopoulos, *Costas Mitsotakis, Politiki Viographia: apo ton anendoto sti dictatoria* [Costas Mitsotakis, Political Biography: from the relentless struggle to the dictatorship], Athens: Papazisis, 1990, pp. 79–80.
3 A. Papahelas, *O Viasmos tis Hellenikis Dimokratias: o amerikanikos paragon, 1947–1967* [The Rape of Greek Democracy: the American factor], Athens: Hestia, 1997, pp. 98–9.
4 The report attached to Murray to Butler, 24 February 1964, FO 371/174829/1.
5 See the memoranda of the former officers, immediately after the February election, in Papaconstantinou Archive, file 'Undersecretariat of Defence (a)'.

6 On the issue of changes in the military leadership, see M. Papaconstantinou, *He Taragmeni Exaetia (1961–1967)* [The Turbulent Six Years], Vol. A, Athens: Proskinio, 1997, Chapter 5; P. Garoufalias, *Hellas kai Kypros: tragika sfalmata, efkairies pou chathikan* [Greece and Cyprus: tragic mistakes, lost opportunities], Athens: Bergadis, 1982, pp. 30–1, 106–7; Papaconstantinou to George Papandreou and Garoufalias, 31 March 1964, Papaconstantinou Archive, file 'Undersecretariat of Defence (c)'.

7 Michalis Papaconstantinou, interview with the author, 30 April 2002.

8 See the Papandreou–Constantine correspondence in S. Linardatos, *Apo ton Emfylio sti Junta* [From the Civil War to the Junta], Vol. E, 1964–1967, Athens: Papazisis, n.d., pp. 210–18.

9 Diamantopoulos, *Mitsotakis*, pp. 258–62.

10 Th. Veremis, *The Military in Greek Politics: from independence to democracy*, London: Hurst, 1997, pp. 153–8. On developments in the army, see also E. Hatzivassiliou, 'The dark side of the force: losing control over the army, 1963–1964', *Modern Greek Studies Yearbook*, 18/19, 2002/2003, 225–38.

11 Garoufalias, *Hellas kai Kypros*, pp. 36–42.

12 Record of the meeting of 11 August 1964, in S. Papageorgiou (ed.), *Ta Krisima Documenta tou Kypriakou (1959–1967)* [The Crucial Documents of the Cyprus Question], Vol. B, Athens: Ladias, 1983, pp. 206–16 (hereafter referred to as *Cyprus Documents*).

13 S. Rizas, *Enosi, Dichotomisi, Anexartisia: oi Enomenes Politeies kai he Vretania stin anazitisi lysis gia to Kypriako, 1963–1967* [Enosis, Partition, Independence: the US and Britain in search of a solution for the Cyprus question], Athens: Vivliorama, 2000, pp. 132–4.

14 British Embassy, annual report for the Greek army (1964), in Sykes to Stewart, 4 February 1965, FO 371/180024/1.

15 Quoted in Garoufalias, *Hellas kai Kypros*, pp. 47–8.

16 Tables, 1964, Papaconstantinou Archive, file 'Undersecretariat of Defence (a)'.

17 See the Greek memorandum in NATO Archives, PO (65) 636, 14 December 1965.

18 See, for example, NATO Archives, Draft Report to Ministers by the DPC, DPC-D (65) 4, 30 April 1965. See also the views of high-ranking NATO military in NAC ministerial meeting records, CVR (63) 75, 17 December 1963.

19 NAC ministerial meeting records, NATO Archives, CVR (63) 66, 18 November 1963.

20 Papahelas, *Viasmos tis Hellenikis Dimokratias*, p. 96.

21 NAC ministerial meeting records, NATO Archives, CVR (63) 74, 16 December 1963; G. Dafnis, *Sophocles E. Venizelos, 1894–1964*, Athens: Ikaros, 1970, pp. 580–1.

22 Record of the meeting of 25 January 1964, in P. Petrides (ed.), *O Georgios Papandreou kai to Kypriako Zitima (1954–1965): documenta* [George Papandreou and the Cyprus Question, 1954–1965: documents], Thessaloniki: University Studio Press, 1998, pp. 274–81 (hereafter referred to as *Papandreou–Cyprus*).

23 Record (Papandreou–Stikker), 30 April 1964, *Cyprus Documents*, Vol. A, pp. 312–19.

24 See the analysis of the mandate in Manlio Brosio's first Watching Brief, NATO Archives, PO/64/688, December 1964.

25 Record (Papandreou–Ball), 10 June 1964, *Cyprus Documents*, Vol. A, pp. 361–8; Records (Papandreou–Johnson), 24 June, (Papandreou–Ball), 24 June, (Papandreou–Stevenson), 28 June 1964, in *Papandreou–Cyprus*, pp. 233–50, 265–70.

26 Rizas, *Enosi, Dichotomisi, Anexartisia*, p. 132.

27 Brosio to Papandreou, 24 August 1964, *Papandreou–Cyprus*, pp. 299–300.

28 Record (Papandreou–Brosio), 4 November 1964, *Cyprus Documents*, Vol. C, pp. 40–4.

Notes 211

29 Stephanopoulos, speech in Parliament, 22 September 1965, *Greek Parliamentary Records* (GPR), period H, synod B, pp. 243–5.
30 Record (Stephanopoulos–Toumbas–Makarios–Kyprianou), 5 September 1966, in I. Toumbas, *Apo to Imerologion enos Ypourgou* [From a Minister's Diary], Athens: Ekdoseis ton Filon, 1986, pp. 65–71.
31 Record (Stephanopoulos–Toumbas–Makarios–Kyprianou), 9 November 1966, in Toumbas, *Apo to Imerologio*, pp. 101–3. Vyron Theodoropoulos, who in 1965–66 was head of the Turkish and Cypriot affairs in the Foreign Ministry, told the author on 8 October 2004 that the services had not made an extensive study on future Greek and Turkish military capabilities; he attributed this presentation to Toumbas's experience as a naval officer.
32 Council of the Crown records (extract), 6 February 1967, in *Apanta Archiepiskopou Makariou III* [Collected texts of Archbishop Makarios III], Vol. 10, Nicosia: Foundation of Archbishop Makarios III, 2000, pp. 71–108 (hereafter referred to as *Makarios*).
33 Garoufalias, *Hellas kai Kypros*, pp. 89–90.
34 C. Sazanides, *Xenoi, Vaseis kai Pyrinika stin Hellada* [Foreign Powers, Bases and Nuclear Weapons in Greece], Thessaloniki: Altintzis, 1985, pp. 279–80, 313–14, 344–7.
35 NAC memoranda, 'Intermediate Review 1963: Chapter on Greece', NATO Archives, CM (63) 93, 25 November 1963; '1964 Annual Review: Chapter on Greece', CM (64) 119, 30 November 1964.
36 See NATO Archives, DPC-D (64) 3, 31 January 1964; DPC-R (64) 4 and 5, 12 and 25 March 1964.
37 NATO Archives, DPC-D (64) 6, 23 July 1964.
38 Note of the Working Party on the Defence Problems of the South-eastern region, NATO Archives, AC/248-D (64) 2, 24 November 1964; DPC memorandum, 'Progress Report by the Defence Planning Committee on the Defence Problems of the South-eastern region', CM (64) 121, 4 December 1964.
39 Ibid.
40 Record (Garoufalias–Costopoulos–Macnamara–Vance) 11 December 1964, in Garoufalias, *Hellas kai Kypros*, pp. 75–83.
41 NAC ministerial meeting records, NATO Archives CVR (64) 55 and 56, 15 December 1964.
42 British Embassy, annual report on the Greek army (1964), in Sykes to Stewart, 4 February 1965, FO 371/180024/1.
43 Minute (Makins, Foreign Office), 12 February 1965, FO 371/180024/1.
44 Greek memorandum, NATO Archives, AC 248-D (65) 1, 13 May 1965.
45 NAC ministerial meeting records, NATO Archives CVR (65) 26, 31 May 1965; Garoufalias, *Hellas kai Kypros*, pp. 84–6.
46 'Defence Planning Exercise: Follow up of Defence Ministers' Meeting', NATO Archives, DPC-D (65) 5, 22 June 1965.
47 See NATO Archives, DPC-R (65) 5, 9 July 1965; 'Progress Report on Contingency Studies by the Defence Planning Working Group', DPC-D (65) 6, 23 July 1965.
48 NAC memorandum, '1965 Annual Review: Chapter on Greece', NATO Archives, CM (65) 121, 26 November 1965.
49 *Eleftheria*, 15 December 1965; Petersen to Dodson, 10 March 1966, FO 371/185672/10; NAC ministerial meeting records, NATO Archives CVR (65) 52, 14 December 1965.
50 'Non-military Implications of the Major NATO Commanders' Force Goal Proposals', NATO Archives, DPC-D (65) 8, 7 December 1965; DPC-R (65) 11, 9 December 1965.
51 See Records of the Working Group on Allied Command Europe Mobile Forces, NATO Archives, AC/212-R/9, 21 October 1965 and AC/212-R/10, 26 October

1965. See also memorandum, 'Financing of the ACE Mobile Force Exercises, in Particular Exercises Summer Express and Marmara Express', AC/212-D/20, 2 June 1966.
52 *Eleftheria*, 29 July 1966.
53 Murray to Brown, 1 March 1967: annual report for Greece for 1966, FCO 9/202/5; D. Pantavos, 'He "diafotisi" tou koinou: kinimatographika epikaira schetika me tis scheseis tis Helladas me to NATO, 1961–1968' [The 'enlightenment' of the public: newsreels on Greece's relations with NATO], *Helleniki Epitheorisi Politikis Epistimis* [Greek Review of Political Science], 21, 2003, 70–91.
54 Sazanides, *Xenoi, Vaseis kai Pyrinika*, pp. 383–4.
55 NAC ministerial meeting records, NATO Archives, CVR (63) 76, 17 December 1963; Greek memorandum, in CM (63) 132, 14 December 1963. See also Dafnis, *Venizelos*, pp. 580–1.
56 See the anxieties of Greek officials in Minute (General Accountancy of the State) to Mitsotakis, 21 July 1964, in Athens, Constantinos Mitsotakis Foundation, Constantinos Mitsotakis Archive, Pol. 63-67, file 23 (hereafter Mitsotakis Archive).
57 See among others, Papaconstantinou to Papandreou and Garoufalias, 21 March 1964, Papaconstantinou Archive, file 'Undersecretariat of Defence (c)'; Minute (Hood, Foreign Office), 4 May 1964, FO 371/174828/8.
58 Mitsotakis, speech in Parliament, 4 June 1964, *GPR*, period H, synod A, pp. 102–26.
59 Mitsotakis to Papandreou, 4 August 1964, in Diamantopoulos, *Mitsotakis*, appendix.
60 Mitsotakis, speech in Parliament, 22 December 1964, *GPR*, period H, synod B, pp. 710–46.
61 On Greece's efforts to secure NATO defence support aid, see Xanthopoulos-Palamas (NATO) to Foreign Ministry, 31 May 1965, *Cyprus Documents*, Vol. C, pp. 191–2; NAC ministerial meeting records, NATO Archives, CVR (65) 26, 31 May 1965.
62 See the Greek memorandum to Brosio in NATO Archives, PO (65) 227, 16 April 1965.
63 On the December 1965 currency crisis, see Tsouderos to Raymond Hare, 4 May 1966, Tsouderos to Rostow, 10 May 1966, Johnson Library, NSF Country File: Greece, Box 126, Memoranda and Misc.
64 Butler to Talbot 11 May 1966, Note (Saunders), 22 June 1966, Johnson Library, NSF Country File: Greece, Box 126, Memoranda and Misc.
65 NAC ministerial meeting records, NATO Archives, CVR (65) 53, 15 December 1965; see also *Eleftheria*, 27 November and 16 December 1965.
66 NAC memorandum, 'Resolution on 1965 Annual Review', NATO Archives, CM (65) 134, 1 December 1965.
67 NAC memorandum, '1965 Annual Review: Chapter on Greece', NATO Archives, CM (65) 121, 26 November 1965.
68 NAC memorandum, 'Defence Aid to Greece and Turkey for 1965', NATO Archives, CM (65) 140, 10 December 1965.
69 Editorial, 'Justice in Sacrifices', *Elefhteria*, 19 December 1965; Mitsotakis, speech in Parliament, 20 December 1965, *GPR*, period H, synod C, pp. 397–410. See also Minutes 'Implementation of the State Budget' and 'Prospects of the State Budget 1966', 18 December 1965, Mitsotakis Archive, Pol. 63-67, file 18.
70 Record (Matsas–Mann), 11 January 1966, Johnson Library, NSF Country File: Greece, Box 126.
71 Tsouderos to Hare, 4 May 1966, Tsouderos to Rostow, 10 May 1966, Butler to Talbot 11 May 1966, Johnson Library, NSF Country File: Greece, Box 126.
72 Butler to Talbot 11 May 1966, Johnson Library, NSF Country File: Greece, Box 126.
73 Nicolareizis (London) to Foreign Ministry, 9 May; Christides (OECD) to Foreign

Ministry, 10 May 1966; Minute on French aid through the Consortium, no date (1966), Mitsotakis Archive, Pol. 63-67, file 23.
74 Record (Matsas–Rostow), 22 June 1966, Johnson Library, NSF Country File: Greece, Box 126.
75 Draft memorandum to NATO (1966), Mitsotakis Archive, Pol. 63-67, file 23.
76 *Eleftheria*, 18 December 1966.
77 Record (Garoufalias–Costopoulos–Macnamara–Vance), 11 December 1964 in Garoufalias, *Hellas kai Kypros*, pp. 75–83.
78 C. Xanthopoulos-Palamas, *Diplomatiko Triptycho* [Diplomatic triptych], Athens: Ekdoseis ton Filon, 1979, p. 213.
79 Mitsotakis, speeches to the School of National Defence, 1964, March 1965, March 1966, Mitsotakis Archive, Pol. 63-67, file 12.
80 E. Hatzivassiliou, *Helleniki Evropaiki Politiki, 1965–1966: epanadrastiriopoiisi sto Koinotiko plaisio* [Greece's European policy, 1965–1966: re-activation in the Community context], Athens: C. Mitsotakis Foundation, 2003, pp. 11–80.
81 Garoufalias, *Hellas kai Kypros*, pp. 75–83; Papahelas, *Viasmos tis Hellenikis Dimokratias*, p. 155.
82 Stephanopoulos, interview to Marc Marceau, *Eleftheria*, 13 November 1965.
83 Talbot to State Department, 9 March 1966, Lyndon B. Johnson Library, National Security Files (NSF)/Country File: Greece, Box 126, Cables and Memoranda.
84 See the records of Toumbas's conversations with Stewart, 3 June 1966, FO 371/185667/21; Thomson, 12 September 1966, FO 371/185666/12; on his talks with Schröder, see Sykes to Brown, 24 October 1966, FO 371/185658/1.
85 Record (Toumbas–Thomson), 12 September 1966, FO 371/185666/12.
86 C. Nicolet, *United States Policy towards Cyprus, 1954–1974: removing the Greek–Turkish bone of contention*, Manheim und Möhnesee: Bibliopolis, 2001, pp. 218–19; Papahelas, *Viasmos tis Hellenikis Dimokratias*, pp. 112–13, 139–40.
87 I.D. Stefanidis, '"Telling America's story": US propaganda operations and Greek public reactions', *Journal of the Hellenic Diaspora*, 30, 2004, 39–95.
88 Siapkaras to Garoufalias, 14 May 1964, *Cyprus Documents*, Vol. A, pp. 327–8.
89 Matsas to Papandreou and Costopoulos, 12 March 1965, *Cyprus Documents*, Vol. C, pp. 62–4.
90 Linardatos, *Apo ton Emfylio sti Junta*, Vol. D, pp. 432–3.
91 Th.A. Couloumbis, *Greek Political Reaction to American and NATO Influences*, New Haven and London: Yale University Press, 1966, pp. 181–2.
92 Record (Garoufalias–Costopoulos–Macnamara–Vance) 11 December 1964, in Garoufalias, *Hellas kai Kypros*, pp. 75–83.
93 See Brosio's reply to Costopoulos, on 17 August 1964, NATO Archives, PO/64/454.
94 Records of the government Political Committee, 6 May 1965, *Cyprus Documents*, Vol. C, pp. 170–81.
95 See A. Papandreou, *He Dimokratia sto Apospasma* [Democracy at Gunpoint], Athens: Karanassis, 1974, pp. 203–5; Labouisse to State Department, 19 November 1964, *FRUS*, 1964–68, XVI, pp. 330–2.
96 Anschuetz to State Department, 30 June, 9 July, 23 July, 10 August, 20 August 1965, *FRUS*, 1964–68, XVI, pp. 416–30; Papahelas, *Viasmos tis Hellenikis Dimokratias*, pp. 181–226. Still, Papahelas considers that the US diplomat had moved in crucial moments in favour of the apostates.
97 S. Rizas, 'Koinovouleftismos i "ektropi"? He Ethniki Rizospastiki Enosis kai he politiki krisi, 1964–1967' [Parliamentarianism or 'deviation'? The National Radical Union and the political crisis], *Bulletin of the Centre for the Study of Modern Hellenism* (Academy of Athens), 3, 2003, 355–78.
98 M. Stearns, *Entangled Allies: US policy toward Greece, Turkey and Cyprus*, New York: Council of Foreign Relations Press, 1992, p. 16.

214 *Notes*

99 Papahelas, *Viasmos tis Hellenikis Dimokratias*, pp. 295–303.
100 State Department to US Embassy, Athens, 20 April 1967, *FRUS*, 1964–68, XVI, pp. 577–9.
101 S. Rizas, 'He krisi tou koinovouleftismou kai to stratiotiko praxikopima, 1965–67' [The crisis of Parliamentarianism and the military coup], *Cleio*, 1, 2004, 89–121.

13 Maximalism and dead-end: the Cyprus entanglement

1 On Makarios' proposal, see mostly D. Markides, *Cyprus, 1957–1963: from colonial conflict to constitutional crisis. The key role of the municipal issue*, Minneapolis: Minnesota Mediterranean and East European Monographs, 2001.
2 P. Tzermias, *Historia tis Kypriakis Dimokratias* [A History of the Cyprus Republic], Vol. A, 2nd edn, Athens: Libro, 2001, pp. 526–40. See the Turkish Cypriot documents in *Apanta Archiepiskopou Makariou III* [Collected Texts of Archbishop Makarios III], Vol. 6, Nicosia: Foundation of Archbishop Makarios III, 1996, pp. 446–9, 484–92 (hereafter referred to as *Makarios*).
3 Akritas Plan late 1963, in S. Papageorgiou (ed.), *Ta Krisima Documenta tou Kypriakou (1959–1967)* [The Crucial Documents of the Cyprus Question], Vol. A, Athens: Ladias, 1983, pp. 250–57 (hereafter referred to as *Cyprus Documents*). See also the analysis in S. Bolukbasi, *The Superpowers and the Third World: Turkish–American relations and Cyprus*, New York and London: University Press of America, 1988, p. 57; T. Bahcheli, *Greek–Turkish Relations since 1955*, Boulder: Westview Press, 1990, p. 56.
4 Note, (Pipilis) to Garoufalias, 6 July 1964, *Cyprus Documents*, Vol. B, pp. 83–7.
5 Note (Pipilis) to the Minister of National Defence, and Note (General Staff of National Defence) 'Evolution of the Situation in Cyprus', 6 December 1963, *Cyprus Documents*, Vol. A, pp. 259–72.
6 Record of the meeting, 25 January 1964, in P. Petrides (ed.), *O Georgios Papandreou kai to Kypriako Zitima (1954–1965): documenta* [George Papandreou and the Cyprus question, 1954–1965: documents], Thessaloniki: University Studio Press, 1998, pp. 274–81 (hereafter referred to as *Papandreou–Cyprus*).
7 British Embassy, annual report on the Greek army (1963), in Murray to Butler, 24 February 1964, FO 371/174829/1; Moberly (Athens) to Brown, 6 July 1964, FO 371/174829/4; British Embassy, annual report on the Greek army (1964), in Sykes to Stewart, 4 February 1965, FO 371/180024/1; Memorandum of Conference with President Johnson, 25 January 1964, *FRUS*, 1964–68, XVI, pp. 4–7.
8 J. Ker-Lindsay, *Britain and the Cyprus Crisis, 1963–1964*, Manheim und Möhnesee: Bibliopolis, 2004, pp. 34–41.
9 C. Nicolet, *United States Policy towards Cyprus, 1954–1974: removing the Greek–Turkish bone of contention*, Manheim und Möhnesee: Bibliopolis, 2001, pp. 198–9.
10 Record of the meeting, 25 January 1964, *Papandreou–Cyprus*, pp. 274–81.
11 Nicolet, *United States Policy towards Cyprus*, pp. 199–221; Ker-Lindsay, *Britain and Cyprus*, pp. 79–99.
12 Record of the meeting, 1 February 1964, *Papandreou–Cyprus*, pp. 282–6.
13 Garoufalias to Grivas, 28 May 1964, *Cyprus Documents*, Vol. A, pp. 339–42.
14 Nicolet, *United States Policy towards Cyprus*, pp. 222–4.
15 Makarios to Inönü, 4 April 1964, *Makarios*, Vol. 6, pp. 259–66.
16 See, among others, the views of three high-ranking diplomats in M. Alexandrakis, V. Theodoropoulos and E. Lagakos, *To Kypriako, 1950–1974: mia endoskopisi* [The Cyprus Question, 1950–1974: an introspection], Athens: Helleniki Evroekdotiki, 1987, pp. 102–4.
17 Bolukbasi, *The Superpowers and the Third World*, pp. 72–9 and 115–16.
18 Michalis Papaconstantinou, interview with the author, 30 April 2002.

19 Garoufalias to Giorkatzis, 30 June 1964, *Cyprus Documents*, Vol. B, pp. 69–71.
20 Brosio, Watching Brief, NATO Archives, PO/64/688, December 1964.
21 Record (Papandreou–Ball), 10 June 1964, and Papandreou to Johnson (extract), 15 June 1964, *Cyprus Documents*, Vol. A, pp. 361–9.
22 See the US record in *FRUS*, 1964–68, XVI, pp. 151–5. The Greek in *Papandreou–Cyprus*, pp. 233–9. See also A. Papandreou, *He Dimokratia sto Apospasma* [Democracy at Gunpoint], Athens: Karanassis, 1974, pp. 198–9; Nicolet, *United States Policy towards Cyprus*, pp. 254–5.
23 See the records of the Greek–US talks, 24–28 June 1964, *Papandreou–Cyprus*, pp. 233–70.
24 Johnson to Papandreou, 2 July 1964, *Papandreou–Cyprus*, pp. 294–6.
25 *Vima*, 4 July 1964.
26 S. Linardatos, *Apo ton Emfylio sti Junta* [From the Civil War to the Junta], Vol. E, 1964–1967, Athens: Papazisis, n.d., pp. 25–8.
27 D. Bitsios, *The Vulnerable Republic*, Thessaloniki: Institute for Balkan Studies, 1975, pp. 170–6; Bolukbasi, *The Superpowers and the Third World*, pp. 81–5.
28 Minute (Garoufalias) on the events of 9 August 1964, *Cyprus Documents*, Vol. B, pp. 114–15. See also M. Papaconstantinou, *He Taragmeni Exaetia (1961–1967)* [The Turbulent Six Years], Vol. A, Athens: Proskinio, 1997, p. 206.
29 Brosio to Costopoulos, NATO Archives, PO/64/454, 17 August 1964. Turkey also complained about the alliance's attitude on the Cyprus issue.
30 Brosio, Watching Brief, NATO Archives, PO/64/688, December 1964.
31 Record of the meeting of 11 August 1964, *Cyprus Documents*, Vol. B, pp. 206–16.
32 Quoted in Th.A. Couloumbis, *The United States, Greece and Turkey: the troubled triangle*, New York: Praeger, 1983, p. 47. See also Papaconstantinou, *Taragmeni Exaetia*, Vol. A, p. 207.
33 Bitsios, *Vulnerable Republic*, pp. 177–90.
34 Brosio, Watching Brief, NATO Archives, PO/64/688, December 1964.
35 Labouisse to State Department, 2 September 1964, *FRUS*, 1964–68, XVI, pp. 298–9.
36 P. Garoufalias, *Hellas kai Kypros: tragika sfalmata, efkairies pou chathikan* [Greece and Cyprus: tragic mistakes, lost opportunities], Athens: Bergadis, 1982, pp. 34–5, 89–94.
37 'Memorandum on the present state of the army' spring 1965, Papaconstantinou Archive, file 'Undersecretariat of Defence (c)'.
38 V. Theodoropoulos, interview with the author, 8 October 2004.
39 Bahcheli, *Greek–Turkish Relations*, p. 71.
40 C. Svolopoulos, *He Helleniki Exoteriki Politiki* [Greek Foreign Policy], Vol. 2 (1945–1981), Athens: Hestia, 2001, p. 159.
41 Garoufalias, *Hellas kai Kypros*, pp. 215–18.
42 Garoufalias to Grivas, 3 October 1964, *Cyprus Documents*, Vol. B, p. 359.
43 Nicolet, *United States Policy towards Cyprus*, pp. 274, 309.
44 Bolukbasi, *The Superpowers and the Third World*, pp. 116–18.
45 Record (Papandreou–Koriukin), 25 January 1965, *Papandreou–Cyprus*, pp. 313–16.
46 Record of the meeting of 18 January 1965, *Papandreou–Cyprus*, pp. 310–12.
47 Matsas (Washington) to Papandreou and Costopoulos, 12 March 1965, *Cyprus Documents*, Vol. C, pp. 62–4.
48 Papandreou, message to the US government, 13 March 1965, *Cyprus Documents*, Vol. C, pp. 65–6.
49 Matsas to Papandreou and Garoufalias, 15 March 1965, *Cyprus Documents*, Vol. C, pp. 67–70. See also Labouisse to State Department, 16 March 1965, *FRUS*, 1964–68, XVI, pp. 372–6.
50 The message was quoted in Costopoulos to Greek Embassy Washington, 16 March 1965, *Cyprus Documents*, Vol. C, pp. 70–1.
51 Matsas to Papandreou, Costopoulos and Garoufalias, 17 March 1965, *Cyprus Documents*, Vol. C, pp. 72–4.

216 *Notes*

52 Matsas to Papandreou and Costopoulos, 15 March 1965, *Cyprus Documents*, Vol. C, pp. 67–70.
53 Record (Makarios–Garoufalias), 22 March 1965, *Cyprus Documents*, Vol. C, pp. 83–4.
54 Records of the government Political Committee, 6 May 1965, *Cyprus Documents*, Vol. C, pp. 170–81.
55 Records of the meeting in the Palace, 7 May 1965, *Papandreou–Cyprus*, pp. 351–76.
56 S. Rizas, *Enosi, Dichotomisi, Anexartisia: oi Enomenes Politeies kai he Vretania stin anazitisi lysis gia to Kypriako, 1963–1967* [Enosis, Partition, Independence: the US and Britain in search of a solution for the Cyprus question], Athens: Vivliorama, 2000, pp. 184–8; Nicolet, *United States Policy towards Cyprus*, pp. 318–21.
57 Parsons to Edes, 28 June and 5 July 1966, FO 371/185662/3.
58 Brosio, Watching Brief, NATO Archives, PO/65/593, December 1965.
59 Constantinos Mitsotakis, interview with the author, 2 October 2002.
60 See the relevant British FO documents in FO 371/174830 (1964), 180025 (1965), 185675, 185676 (1966).
61 Constantinos Mitsotakis, interview with the author, 2 October 2002.
62 Record (Stephanopoulos–Makarios–Tsirimokos–Kyprianou), 2 February 1966, *Cyprus Documents*, Vol. C, pp. 206–8.
63 Record (Mitsotakis–Çaglayangil), 19 March 1966, in G. Clerides, *He Katathesi moy* [My Deposition], Vol. 2, Nicosia: Alitheia, 1989, pp. 190–4.
64 Bolukbasi, *The Superpowers and the Third World*, p. 128.
65 Rizas, *Enosi, Dichotomisi, Anexartisia*, pp. 199–211.
66 Record (Stephanopoulos–Makarios–Toumbas–Kyprianou), 5 September 1966, in I. Toumbas, *Apo to Imerologion enos Ypourgou* [From a Minister's Diary], Athens: Ekdoseis ton Filon, 1986, pp. 65–71.
67 Record (Stephanopoulos–Makarios–Toumbas–Kyprianou), 9 November 1966, in Toumbas, *Apo to Imerologio*, pp. 101–3.
68 Record, 7 December 1966, in Toumbas, *Apo to Imerologio*, pp. 116–19.
69 Alexandrakis, Theodoropoulos and Lagakos, *Cyprus*, pp. 49–51; Clerides, *Katathesi*, Vol. 2, pp. 188–9; Toumbas, *Apo to Imerologio*, pp. 122–4.
70 Record (Toumbas–Çaglayangil), 17 December 1966, and Minute (Foreign Ministry), 20 December 1966, *Cyprus Documents*, Vol. C, pp. 297–306.
71 Record, Crown Council (extract), 6 February 1967, *Makarios*, Vol. 10, pp. 71–108.
72 Talbot to State Department, 10 February 1967, *FRUS, 1964–68*, XVI, pp. 536–40.

14 The effort to adjust Greece's Eastern policy

1 E. Hatzivassiliou, 'Negotiating with the enemy: the normalization of Greek–Bulgarian relations, 1960–1964', *Southeast European and Black Sea Studies*, 4, 2004, 151–6; S. Perrakis, 'He valkaniki politiki tou Georgiou Papandreou (1963–1965)' [George Papandreou's Balkan Policy], in P. Petrides and G. Anastasiades (eds), *Georgios Papandreou: 60 chronia parousias kai drasis stin politiki zoi* [George Papandreou: 60 years of presence and action in political life], Thessaloniki: University Studio Press, 1994, pp. 541–50.
2 Murray to Gordon-Walker, 6 November 1964, FO 371/174825/1.
3 Moberly (Athens) to Wood, 9 July, and Moberly to Parsons, 23 December 1964, FO 371/174812/2.
4 Murray to FO, 6 March 1965, FO 371/180012/1.
5 C. Xanthopoulos-Palamas, *Diplomatiko Triptycho* [Diplomatic Triptych], Athens: Ekdoseis ton Filon, 1979, pp. 166–7, 210–12.
6 Alexander (Moscow) to Parsons, 18 March 1965, FO 371/180012/2.
7 S. Wallden, *Hellada kai Anatolikes Chores, 1950–1967: oikonomikes scheseis kai*

politiki [Greece and the Eastern Countries: economic relations and politics], Vol. A, Athens: Odysseas and Foundation for Mediterranean Studies, 1991, pp. 270–1.
8 Murray to FO, 6 March 1965, FO 371/180012/1.
9 Sykes to Dodson, 16 March 1965, FO 371/180012/1.
10 Wallden, *Hellada kai Anatolikes Chores*, Vol. A, pp. 286–95.
11 It should be remembered that the Centre had strongly denounced the border traffic agreement at the time of its conclusion.
12 S. Wallden, *Hellada kai Yugoslavia: gennisi kai exelixi mias krisis* [Greece and Yugoslavia: birth and evolution of a crisis], Athens: Themelio, 1991, p. 119; Sykes to Brown, 6 November 1964, FO 371/174815/3.
13 Sykes to Davidson, 9 February 1965, and Wilson (Belgrade) to Stewart, 10 February 1965, FO 371/180015/2 and 3.
14 Wallden, *Hellada kai Yugoslavia*, pp. 123–7.
15 Perrakis, 'He valkaniki politiki', pp. 545–6; Sykes to Brown, 6 November 1964, FO 371/174815/3.
16 See the views of Greek ministers as expressed in NAC, in NATO Archives, CVR (65) 51, 14 December 1965.
17 Record (Toumbas–Stewart), 3 June 1966, FO 371/185667/21.
18 Wallden, *Hellada kai Anatolikes Chores*, Vol. A, pp. 250–3, 297–302.
19 Moberly to Edes, 22 March 1966, FO 371/185661/1.
20 Wood (Moscow) to FO, 21 April 1966, FO 371/185661/2.
21 Wallden, *Hellada kai Anatolikes Chores*, Vol. A, pp. 297–8.
22 Thomas (Sofia) to Rhodes, 29 December 1965, FO 371/182589/2; Thomas to Rhodes, 12 July 1966 and Thomas to Harvey, 13 December 1966, FO 371/188624/1 and 4.
23 Sykes to Brown, 3 November 1966, FO 371/185663/1.
24 British Embassy, annual report on the Greek army (1966), in Murray to Brown, 1 March 1967, FCO 9/202/5.
25 Murray to FO, 1 March 1966, FO 371/188529/1.
26 See Moberly to Edes, 13 April 1966, FO 371/188536/2; Wallden, *Hellada kai Anatolikes Chores*, Vol. A, pp. 275–6.
27 Sykes to Rhodes, 3 August 1966, FO 371/185660/2.
28 Murray to Brown, 10 September 1966, FO 371/188820/3; I. Toumbas, *Apo to Imerologion enos Ypourgou* [From a Minister's Diary], Athens: Ekdoseis ton Filon, 1986, pp. 78–81.
29 Greek Embassy, Budapest, to Foreign Ministry, 19 October 1966, Mitsotakis Archive, Pol. 63-67, file 23.
30 Note (Ministry of Commerce), 'Commercial exchanges with Czechoslovakia', 24 October 1966, Mitsotakis Archive, Pol. 63-67, file 27.
31 Wallden, *Hellada kai Anatolikes Chores*, Vol. A, p. 274.

15 The mid-1960s: a re-evaluation

1 S. Rizas, *He Hellada, oi Enomenes Politeies kai he Evropi, 1961–1964: politikes kai oikonomikes opseis tou provlimatos asfaleias sto metaichmio psychrou polemou kai yfesis* [Greece, the US and Europe, 1961–1964: political and economic aspects of the security problem in the passing from Cold War to détente], Athens: Patakis, 2001, p. 161.
2 A. Papandreou, *He Dimokratia sto Apospasma* [Democracy at Gunpoint], Athens: Karanassis, 1974, mostly pp. 209, 258–9.
3 Rizas, *He Hellada, oi Enomenes Politeies kai he Evropi*, p. 173; A. Heraclides, *Kypriako: sygrousi kai epilysi* [The Cyprus Question: conflict and resolution], Athens: Sideris, 2002, pp. 115–16.
4 P. Tzermias, *Historia tis Kypriakis Dimokratias* [A History of the Cyprus Republic], Vol. A, 2nd edn, Athens: Libro, 2001, pp. 584, 587–93.

List of sources

Unpublished

A Greek

Panayiotis Kanellopoulos Archive, Association of Friends of Panayiotis Kanellopoulos, Athens
Constantinos Karamanlis Archive, Constantinos G. Karamanlis Foundation, Athens
Constantinos Mitsotakis Archive, Constantinos Mitsotakis Foundation, Athens
Michalis Papaconstantinou Archive, at the hands of the owner, Athens
Evangelos Averoff-Tossizza Political Archive, Constantinos G. Karamanlis Foundation, Athens
Anastasios Kanellopoulos Collection, Constantinos G. Karamanlis Foundation, Athens

B British

FO 371: Foreign Office, general political correspondence, 1952–67, National Archives, London.

C US

State Department Papers, RG 59, Greece, general political correspondence, 1952–59, National Archives, Washington DC.
John F. Kennedy Library, National Security Files/Country File: Greece (1961–63)
Lyndon B. Johnson Library, National Security Files/Country File: Greece (1966)

D NATO

NATO Archives, International Staff, 1952–65, Brussels.
    NAC   (North Atlantic Council)
                      CVR: verbatim records of the ministerial meetings
                      CR: records of the meetings of the permanent representatives
                      CM: memoranda to the North Atlantic Council
    DPC   (Defence Planning Committee, 1963–65)
                      DPC-R: Records
                      DPC-D: memoranda
    PO   Private Office of the General Secretary

AC/52	Joint Working Group on Information Policy and Cultural Co-operation
AC/52 (SP)	Joint Working Group on Information Policy and Cultural Co-operation. Working Group on the Proposal by the Greek Delegation
AC/200	Ad Hoc Study Group on the Economic Problems of Greece and Turkey (1961)
AC/212	Working Group on Allied Command Europe Mobile Forces (1962–65)
AC/213	Working Group on the Defence Problems of Greece (1962)
AC/248	Working Party on the Defence Problems of the South-eastern Region (1964–65)

Published

A Greek

Apanta Archiepiskopou Makariou III [Collected Texts of archbishop Makarios III], Vols 6–10, Nicosia: Foundation of Archbishop Makarios III, 1996–2000. Referred to as *Makarios*.

Greek Parliamentary Records (GPR): *Episima Praktika ton Synedriaseon tis Voulis* [Official Records of Parliament Sessions], Athens: Greek Parliament, 1952–67.

Papageorgiou, S. (ed.), *Ta Krisima Documenta tou Kypriakou (1959–1967)* [The Crucial Documents of the Cyprus Question], 3 vols, Athens: Ladias, 1983. Referred to as *Cyprus Documents*.

Petrides, P. (ed.), *O Georgios Papandreou kai to Kypriako Zitima (1954–1965): documenta* [George Papandreou and the Cyprus Question, 1954–1965: documents], Thessaloniki: University Studio Press, 1998. Referred to as *Papandreou–Cyprus*.

Petrides, P. and Anastasiades, G. (eds), *Georgios Papandreou: o politikos logos* [G. Papandreou: political discourse], Thessaloniki: University Studio Press, 1995.

Svolopoulos, C. (ed.), *Constantinos Karamanlis: archeio, gegonota kai keimena* [Constantinos Karamanlis: archive, events and texts], 12 vols, Athens: C.G. Karamanlis Foundation and Ekdotike Athenon, 1992–97. Referred to as *Karamanlis*.

Tomai-Constantopoulou, F. (ed.), *He Hellada sto Metaichmio enos Neou Kosmou: Psychros Polemos, Dogma Truman, sxedio Marshall, 1943–1951* [Greece in the Threshold of a New World: the Cold War, the Truman Doctrine, the Marshall Plan], 3 vols, Athens: Foreign Ministry and Castaniotis Publications, 2002.

Tomai-Constantopoulou, F. (ed.), *He Symmetochi tis Helladas stin Poreia pros tin Evropaiki Oloklirosi* [Greece's Participation in the Course towards European Integration], Vol. I: 1948–1968, Athens: Foreign Ministry and Castaniotis Publications, 2003.

Athens Press (selection of articles and editorials)
Eleftheria
Hestia
Kathimerini
Vima

B US

Department of State, *Foreign Relations of the United States (FRUS)*, Washington DC:
1952–54, Volume VIII (1988)
1952–54, Volume I (1983)
1955–57, Volume XXIV (1989)
1958–60, Volume X, part 2 (1993)

1961–63, Volume XVI (1994)
1964–1968, Volume XVI (2002)

C Soviet/Soviet Bloc

Afinian, V.G., Kondis, B., Papoulides, C., Smirnova, N.D. and Tomilina, N. (eds), *Oi Scheseis KKE kai KK Sovietikis Enosis sto Diastima 1953–1977: symfona me ta eggrafa tou Archeiou tis KE tou KKSE* [Relations between the KKE and the CPSU in the Years 1953–1977: according to documents of the Archive of the Central Committee of the CPSU], Thessaloniki: Institute for Balkan Studies, 1999.

Kondis, B. and Sfetas, S. (eds), *Emphylios Polemos: eggrafa apo ta yougoslavika kai voulgarika archeia* [The Civil War: documents from the Yugoslav and Bulgarian archives], Thessaloniki: Paratiritis, 1999.

Kondis, B., Mourelos, Y., Papoulides, C., Prozoumentsikov, M.G., Smirnova, N.D. and Tomilina, N. (eds), *Sovietiki Enosi kai Valkania stis Dekaeties 1950 kai 1960: syllogi eggrafon* [The Soviet Union and the Balkans in the 1950s and the 1960s: a collection of documents], Thessaloniki: Institute for Balkan Studies, 2003.

Bibliography

Alexandris, A., *The Greek Minority of Istanbul and Greek–Turkish Relations, 1918–1974*, Athens: Centre for Asia Minor Studies, 1983.

Alivizatos, N., *Oi Politikoi Thesmoi se Krisi, 1922–1974: opseis tis hellenikis empeirias* [The political Institutions in Crisis, 1922–1974: aspects of the Greek experience], Athens: Themelio, 1983.

Alogoskoufis, G., 'The two faces of Janus: institutions, policy regimes and macroeconomic performance in Greece', *Economic Policy*, 20, 1995, 149–92.

Averoff-Tossizza, E., *Lost Opportunities: the Cyprus question, 1950–1963* (trans. Timothy Cullen and Susan Kyriakidis), New Rochelle: A. Karatzas, 1986.

Bahcheli, T., *Greek–Turkish Relations since 1955*, Boulder: Westview Press, 1990.

Botsiou, K., *Griechenlands Weg nach Europa: von der Truman-Doctrin bis zur Assoziierung mit der EWG, 1947–1961*, Frankfurt-am-Main: Peter Lang, 1998.

Couloumbis, Th.A., *Greek Political Reaction to American and NATO Influences*, New Haven and London: Yale University Press, 1966.

Couloumbis, Th.A., *The United States, Greece and Turkey: the troubled triangle*, New York: Praeger, 1983.

Couloumbis, Th.A and Iatrides, J.O. (eds), *Greek–American Relations: a critical review*, New York: Pella, 1980.

Couloumbis, Th.A., Petropoulos, J. and Psomiades, H., *Foreign Interference in Greek Politics*, New York: Pella, 1976.

Diamantopoulos, Th., *He Helleniki Politiki Zoi: eikostos aionas* [The Greek Political Life: the twentieth century], Athens: Papazisis, 1997.

General Staff of the Army (GES), *Historia tis Organoseos tou Hellenikou Stratou, 1821–1954* [A History of the Organization of the Greek Army], Athens: Army History Directory, 1957.

General Staff of the Army (GES), *Historia tou Hellenikou Stratou, 1821–1997* [A History of the Greek Army], Athens: Army History Directory, 1998.

Hatzivassiliou, E., 'Security and the European option: Greek foreign policy, 1952–1962', *Journal of Contemporary History*, 30, 1995, 187–202.

Hatzivassiliou, E., *Britain and the International Status of Cyprus, 1955–59*, Minneapolis: Minnesota Mediterranean and East European Monographs, 1997.

Holland, R., *Britain and the Revolt in Cyprus, 1954–1959*, Oxford: Clarendon Press, 1998.

Iatrides, J.O., *Balkan Triangle: birth and decline of an alliance across ideological boundaries*, The Hague: Mouton, 1968.

Joseph, J., *Cyprus: ethnic conflict and international politics. From independence to the threshold of the European Union*, London: Macmillan, 1997.

222 Bibliography

Kanellopoulos, P., *Historika Dokimia* [Historical Essays], Athens: Hestia, 1975.

Kazakos, P., *Anamesa se Kratos kai Agora: oikonomia kai oikonomiki politiki sti metapolemiki Hellada, 1944–2000* [Between the State and the Market: economy and economic policy in post-war Greece], Athens: Patakis, 2001.

Kofos, E., *Nationalism and Communism in Macedonia*, Thessaloniki: Institute for Balkan Studies, 1964.

Koliopoulos, J. and Veremis, Th., *Greece: the modern sequel. From 1831 to the present*, London: Hurst, 2002.

Mazower, M. (ed.), *After the War was Over: reconstructing the family, nation, and state in Greece, 1943–1960*, Princeton: Princeton University Press, 2000.

Nicolakopoulos, E., *He Kachektiki Dimokratia: kommata kai ekloges, 1946–1967* [The Sickly Democracy: parties and elections], Athens: Patakis, 2001.

Nicolet, C., *United States Policy towards Cyprus, 1954–1974: removing the Greek–Turkish bone of contention*, Manheim und Möhnesee: Bibliopolis, 2001.

Rizas, S., *Enosi, Dichotomisi, Anexartisia: oi Enomenes Politeies kai he Vretania stin anazitisi lysis gia to Kypriako, 1963–1967* [Enosis, Partition, Independence: the US and Britain in search of a solution for the Cyprus question], Athens: Vivliorama, 2000.

Rizas, S., *He Hellada, oi Enomenes Politeies kai he Evropi, 1961–1964: politikes kai oikonomikes opseis tou provlimatos asfaleias sto metaichmio psychrou polemou kai yfesis* [Greece, the US and Europe, 1961–1964: political and economic aspects of the security problem in the passing from Cold War to détente], Athens: Patakis, 2001.

Stefanidis, I.D., *Apo ton Emfylio ston Psychro Polemo: he Hellada kai o symmachikos paragontas (1949–52)* [From Civil War to Cold War: Greece and the allied factor], Athens: Proskinio, 1999.

Stefanidis, I.D., *Isle of Discord: nationalism, imperialism and the making of the Cyprus problem*, London: Hurst, 1999.

Stefanidis, I.D., *Asymmetroi Etairoi: oi Enomenes Politeies kai he Ellada ston psychro polemo, 1953–1961* [Unequal Partners: The US and Greece in the Cold War], Athens: Patakis, 2002.

Svolopoulos, C., 'La perspective européene de la politique extérieure grecque et le général de Gaulle (1959–1963)', in *De Gaulle en son siècle: 5. L' Europe*, Paris: Plon, 1992.

Svolopoulos, C., *He Helleniki Exoteriki Politiki* [Greek Foreign Policy], Vol. 2 (1945–1981), Athens: Hestia, 2001.

Svolopoulos, C. and Morelle, C. (eds), *De Gaulle et Karamanlis: La nation, l'état, l'Europe*, Athens: C.G. Karamanlis Foundation and Patakis Publications, 2002.

Tzermias, P., *Historia tis Kypriakis Dimokratias* [A History of the Cyprus Republic], 2 vols, 2nd edn, Athens: Libro, 2001.

Valinakis, Y.G., *Eisagogi stin Helleniki Exoteriki Politiki, 1949–1988* [An Introduction to Greek Foreign Policy], Thessaloniki: Paratiritis, 1989.

Veremis, Th., *The Military in Greek Politics: from independence to democracy*, London: Hurst, 1997.

Wallden, S., *Hellada kai Anatolikes Chores, 1950–1967: oikonomikes scheseis kai politiki* [Greece and the Eastern Countries: economic relations and politics], Vol. A, Athens: Odysseas and Foundation for Mediterranean Studies, 1991.

Xydis, S.G., *Cyprus: conflict and conciliation, 1954–1958*, Columbus, Ohio: The Ohio State University Press, 1967.

Index

Acheson, Dean 37, 164, 165, 166
Acheson Plan 128, 133, 134, 146, 164–6, 181–3
Acropolis 41
Adenauer, Konrad 33, 34
Aegean islands 164, 167
Agoros, G. 142
AKEL (Cypriot Communist Party) 137
Akritas, Loukis 157
Albania 12, 73; armed forces 25, 70, 144; and Italy 48; and Kosovo 111; and UN 49; *see also* Greek–Albanian relations
Allen, George 69
Anglo-Greek relations 34–5, 58, 63, 126
anti-Americanism 62, 67, 156–9, 165; *see also* neutralism
anti-Communism 5, 8, 24
anti-Western sentiment 83
Antonakos, George 143–4
'apostates' 126, 129–31, 139–40, 143, 154, 157, 177–80, 183; *see also* Stephanopoulos, Stephanos
Arab relations 61, 63, 71
archival sources 2–3
Armour Report 71, 89
ASEA (Supreme Council of National Defence) 25
ASPIDA (Nasserite group of officers) 139, 142, 182
Atatürk, Kemal 117
Athanassiades-Novas, George 129, 130
'Athena' project 78, 93
Athenogoras, Patriarch 117
Averoff-Tossizza, Evangelos: Foreign Minister 56–64, 66, 68, 74, 76, 79, 82–3, 86–8, 90–5, 98–102, 104–5, 107–21, 137; Under-Secretary for Foreign Affairs 34, 36, 47

Balkan Pacts: (1934) 7, 27, 39; (1953) 13, 27, 36–8, 40, 46, 51, 110; (1954) 39–42, 51, 66, 73, 108, 111–12
Balkan Wars (1912–13) 6
Ball, George 146, 156, 164, 169
Bank of Greece 5
Bayar, Çelal 36, 117, 118
Bebler, Alexander 39, 41
Berlin Wall 74, 79, 104
Birgi, Nuri 41
Bitsios, Dimitris 117
Bled Treaty *see* Balkan Pacts: (1954)
Briggs, Ellis O. 86, 102
Britain: and Cyprus 50, 51, 67, 68, 82, 120, 161; EEC 155; Macmillan Plan 58, 67, 80, 83, 96; policy 3, 4; *see also* Anglo-Greek relations
Brosio, Manlio 127, 146, 152, 157, 165, 167
Bulganin, Nikolai 51, 96
Bulgaria 12; armed forces 25, 69–70, 71, 77, 78, 143, 144; Communist regime 7–8, 22; invasions of Greece 7; nationalism 21; re-armament 10–11; *see also* Greek–Bulgarian border; Greek–Bulgarian relations
Bulgarian Peace Treaty (1947) 10, 45

Çaglayangil, Ihsan Sabri 172–3
Cannon, Cavendish 30, 32, 67, 70
Centre coalition governments 11, 17, 25, 28, 30, 33–4, 47, 131
Centre Union (CU): (1961–63) 74, 91, 93, 101, 115; (1963–67) 125–6, 128, 130, 131, 141, 144–5, 154, 181–3; Eastern policy (1964–65) 174–7
Choidas, Constantinos 65
civil war (1946–49) 7, 8–9, 10, 11, 12, 43, 73, 145

224 *Index*

Collins, J. Lawton 67, 70
Colonels' coup (1967) 143, 158, 159
Comintern 7
Communism 61, 62, 74; *see also* anti-Communism; Greek Communist Party (KKE)
Communist Democratic Army of Greece (DSE) 8, 43
Communist Party of the Soviet Union (CPSU) 9
Constantine, King 142–3, 147, 157, 158–9, 170
Costopoulos, Stavros: Defence Minister 151, 154; Foreign Minister 149, 157, 164, 168, 171, 174–6
CU *see* Centre Union
Cuban missile crisis 74, 101, 104, 116
Cyprus: (1931) Greek-Cypriot revolt 21; (1954) appeal to UN 21, 23, 34, 45, 50, 52, 80, 99; (1955–59) 'in the framework of the country's alliances' 50–1, 73, 80, 108, 185; (1959) independence 119–21; (1963–64) losing control 127–8, 129, 131–3, 144, 145–6, 160–6, 185; (1964–65) deadlocks 166–71; (1966) negotiation 171–3; Acheson Plan 128, 133, 134, 146, 164–6, 181–3; AKEL 137; Akritas Plan 160; British role 50, 51, 67, 68, 82, 120, 161; constitution 118; EEC interest 120; EMEK 138, 163; Enosis 50, 120, 129, 132, 135, 146, 161, 163, 164, 166, 170–1, 172; EOKA 51, 67, 82, 137, 140; Karpass Peninsula 166; London Five-Party Conference 162; London Tripartite Conference 51–3, 67; Macmillan Plan 58, 67, 80, 83, 96; Mansura crisis 133, 139, 143, 146, 165; 'national centre' doctrine 131–40, 162, 166; National Guard 162–3, 172; NATO policy 45, 68, 80, 120, 167, 171; St Hilarion 132–3, 163; theory of the two independent states 121; Thirteen Points 160, 161; Treaty of Alliance (1960) 120, 163; UNFICYP 163; US role 50, 125, 164–5, 168–9; weapons 168–9, 173; Zurich–London agreements 120
Czechoslovakia 173; *see also* Greek–Czechoslovakian relations

Daily Mail 13
Dapcevic, Petar 114, 115, 116
de Gasperi, Alcide 33, 38
de Gaulle, Charles 86–7, 88, 97, 120, 154–6
de Quay, Jan 119
Debré, Michel 87, 118
defence expenditure 27*t*, 28, 30, 71, 77, 88, 89*t*, 94, 151, 152–4
defence policy 63, 64; 1957 reform 71–2, 89
defence support aid 77, 78, 88, 90–4, 145, 152–4
Democratic Party 32, 52
Democratic Socialist Party 127
Democratic Union 81
Development Loan Fund (DLF) 90
Dillon, Douglas 103
Diomidis, Alexandros 11
Dovas, Constantinos 24, 42, 72, 84, 112
DSE *see* Communist Democratic Army of Greece
Dulles, John Foster 27, 29, 33, 40, 52, 90

EAM *see* National Liberation Front
East Germany 43, 176
Eastern Macedonia (Greek) 8, 13, 26, 36, 43, 45, 71, 127
Eastern Thrace (Turkish) 27, 36
economic aid 8, 9, 17, 28, 90, 152–3
Economou-Gouras, Pavlos 75–6, 99
economy 7, 9, 88, 92–3
EDA *see* United Democratic Left
EDC (European Defence Community) 33, 34
Eden, Anthony 12
EEC *see* European Economic Community
EENA (Union of Young Greek Officers) 64–5
Egypt 34, 67, 85–6, 110
Eisenhower, Dwight D. 17, 29, 30, 32, 59, 85, 90, 96
Eleftheria 52, 134, 153
Eliou, Elias 102
EMEK (Special Joint Staff for Cyprus) 138, 163
Engin, Octay 108
EOKA (National Organization of Cypriot Fighters) 51, 67, 82, 137, 140
EPEK *see* National Progressive Centre Union
Epirus 5, 60; *see also* Northern Epirus
ERE *see* National Radical Union
Erhard, Ludwig 59
Erkin, Feridun Kemal 145
European Defence Community (EDC) 33, 34

European Economic Community (EEC): Britain 155; Cyprus 120; and de Gaulle 155; Greek Association 64, 84, 86, 88, 102–3, 154, 156, 185
European integration 64
European Political Cooperation 64
European Recovery Pogramme (ERP) 9

famine (1941–42) 7
Faure, Edgar 92
Ferguson, John H. 92
Finletter, Thomas 93
First World War 43
Foreign Ministry 4, 21, 75
foreign policy 1, 2, 4, 6, 21, 59, 60–1, 63, 184
Fouchet Plan 64
France *see* Greek–French relations
Frederica, Queen 33, 36, 63, 109
French National Assembly 34
Frontistis, Athanassios 77
functionalism: defence policy 64; national security 62–5; NATO 64, 83–5; regional aspect 107–21

Garoufalias, Petros 129, 142–4, 149–50, 152, 154–5, 157, 163, 168–9
General Staff of National Defence 25, 46, 78, 84, 111, 142–4, 160–1
General Staff of the Army 25, 143, 161
Gennimatas, Ioannis 142
geography 57, 58, 59, 60, 62, 64, 116
Germany 7, 10, 34, 74, 104; *see also* East Germany; West Germany
Ghikas, Solon 18, 24
Giorkatzis, Polykarpos 120, 160, 163
Glezos, Manolis 101
Gligorov, Kiro 179
government: (1952–63) 4–5; (1963–67) 125–6, 181; *see also* 'apostates'; Centre coalition governments
Greek Central Intelligence Service (KYP) 2, 24–5, 99–100, 111, 113, 142
Greek Communist Party (KKE) 2, 7, 8–9, 32, 58, 101, 175
Greek Macedonia 5–8, 12, 37, 41, 48, 58, 72, 107, 109, 113–15
'the Greek problem' 8
Greek Rally 13, 17, 28, 52, 127
Greek–Albanian border 26, 48–9
Greek–Albanian relations 32, 43, 47–9, 76, 99, 100, 105–6, 177, 179
Greek–Bulgarian border 5, 6, 26, 45–6, 70
Greek–Bulgarian relations 13, 21–2, 32,

Index 225

43, 45–7, 61, 73–4, 86, 96, 99–100, 104–5, 145–6, 174, 178–9
Greek–Czechoslovakian relations 63, 176, 178, 179
Greek–Eastern European relations 101
Greek–French relations 40–1, 86–8
Greek–Hungarian relations 63, 96, 176, 178, 179
Greek–NATO relations 52–3, 156–7
Greek–Romanian relations 7, 47, 63, 73, 94–6, 98, 109, 178–9
Greek–Soviet relations: (1946–49) 10; (1953–55) 43–5; (1955–59) 61–2, 68, 69, 73, 98–100; (1959–63) 75–6, 96, 100–6; (1964–66) 156, 174–6, 178; commercial relations 43, 63, 98, 101–2, 103, 178
Greek–Turkish relations: (1922–30) 6; (1933) 7, 26–7; (1952) 36, 47; (1955–59) 22–3, 51–3, 66–7, 81–2, 100, 107–8; (1959–63) 77, 84–5, 92, 111–12, 116–19; (1964–66) 128, 145–8, 166–73
Greek–Turkish–Yugoslav Pact of Friendship and Collaboration (1953) 13, 27, 36–8, 40, 46, 51, 110; Council of Foreign Ministers 38, 39, 42, 48
Greek–US relations 6; (1950–55) 11, 20, 31–3, 35, 52; (1955–63) 68–9, 168; conspiracy theory 181–2; defence support aid 77, 78, 88, 92, 145, 153; dependence of Greece 9, 186; economic aid 17, 28, 90, 152–3; extraterritoriality 32, 51, 81; guarantee of Greek territorial integrity 85–6; installation of US bases 31–3; military aid 12, 13, 28, 31, 70–1, 77, 85, 88–90, 149; and tripartite alliance 40–1; USIS opinion polls 68–9, 82, 95; *see also* anti-Americanism
Greek–Yugoslav relations: (1950–53) 11–12, 36, 37, 39–40; (1956–58) bilateral partnership 61, 63, 72, 107, 108–11; (1959–61) rapprochement 111–14; (1961–62) crisis 22, 114–16; (1963–67) 176–7, 178–9; *see also* Balkan pacts
Greek–Yugoslav–Egyptian talks 67, 110
Grigoropoulos, Theodoros 24, 65, 90
Grivas, George 82, 101, 130, 133, 137–40, 163, 165, 172–3, 182
Grlicko, Anton 114
Gruenther, Alfred 28, 29, 30–1
Gürsel, Kemal 118

Hadjivassiliou, Nicolaos 62

Harding, Sir John 82
Hellenikon Aima 21
Herter, Christian 75, 90
Hestia 21, 50, 52
Heuss, Theodor 64
Hoxha, Enver 48, 105
Hungary: Soviet invasion 108; *see also* Greek–Hungarian relations

Iceland 45, 50
IDEA (Sacred Bond of Greek Officers) 20, 24, 25, 64, 141
Inönü, Ismet 6, 117, 119, 133, 146, 163–4, 172
institutions 4–5
Ipeçki, Abdi 171
Işik, Hasan 171
Ismay, Lord 29
Italy: (1940s) 7, 10; and Albania 48; nuclear weapons 110; Trieste dispute 12, 33, 37–8, 40, 48; and tripartite Balkan pacts 41; and Yugoslavia 40

Johnson, Lyndon B.: Vice-President 78, 91; President 133, 146, 156, 158, 163, 164–5

Kafantaris–Moloff agreement (1927) 46
Kanellopoulos, Panayiotis 19–20, 23; Conservative leader 126, 158, 162, 170, 175; Defence Minister 24–5, 27–32, 34, 40, 51; Deputy Prime Minister 57, 113
Karamanlis, Constantinos: Defence Minister 72; government 49, 53, 57–9, 61–5, 67–72, 74–6, 78, 80–97, 98–106, 107–21, 131, 141, 155, 160; Minister of Public Works 80–1; retirement 158
Karayiannis, Georgios 139
Kardelj, Edvard 108, 109
Kathimerini 25, 30, 41, 52, 175
Kavala 7, 79
KEA (Movement for National Rehabilitation) 138
Kennedy, John F. 59, 74, 85–7, 90–1, 97, 107, 121
Khrushchev, Nikita 51, 73–5, 96–7, 101, 103, 105, 162
Kitrilakis, Stelios 24, 29
KKE *see* Greek Communist Party
Kolishevski, Lazar 114
Komitsas, Ioannis 99
Köprülü, Fuat 36, 38, 39, 41
Korean War 11, 12, 13, 75, 81
Koriukin, N. 101, 168, 175, 176

Kothris, Emmanuel 113, 180
Kountoumas, Alexandros 44
Kranidiotis, Nicos 132
Kunc, Drago 115
Kuneralp, Zeki 117
Kursat, Nihat 172
Kuznetsov, Vassili 98–9
KYP *see* Greek Central Intelligence Service
Kyprianou, Spyros 143, 166, 168, 170
Kyrou, Alexis 21–3, 40, 41, 43–4, 46, 48, 50

Labouisse, Henry 91, 92, 93, 132, 155, 176
Le Monde 88
League of Nations 7
Lebanon Conference 126
Lemnitzer, Lyman 162, 163
Liatis, Alexis 90
Liberal Anglosaxonism 126
Liberal Democratic Union 11, 32, 52, 60, 69, 113, 127
Lloyd, Selwyn 63
London Five-Party Conference 162
London Tripartite Conference 51–3, 67

Macedonia 6, 8, 12, 39, 57, 111, 113–16; *see also* Eastern Macedonia; Greek Macedonia
Macedonian Struggle (1904–08) 6, 57
McElroy, Neil 89
McGhee, George 89
Macnamara, Robert 149–50, 154, 155, 157, 169
Makarios, Archbishop: appeal to Moscow 162, 165, 168; exile 63, 66, 67, 82; and Karamanlis government 58–9, 83, 110, 120, 121, 131; and NATO 162; and Papandreou government 128–9, 131–40, 147, 162, 167–8, 170; and Stephanopoulos government 171–3; Thirteen Points 160; and Treaty of Alliance 163
Mangoldt-Reiboldt, Hans Karl von 92
Marceau, Marc 155
Markezinis, Spyros: Minister of Economic Co-ordination 17–18, 28, 30, 32–3; in opposition 96, 101–2, 173
Marshall Plan 9, 13, 33
Matsas, Alexandros 100, 112, 119, 153, 156, 169
Maurer, Gheorghe 179–80
Mavros, George 47, 145

MDAP (Mutual Defence Assistance
  Program) 13
Megali Idea 6
Melas, George 154
Melas, Michael 79, 82, 83–4, 95
Menderes, Adnan 36, 41, 50, 52, 118, 119, 120
Menderes, Ethem 41
Merchant, L. 87
Metaxas Line 5
Middle Eastern defence organization 34
military 4–5, 24–31; air force 25, 27, 31, 70–2, 77–8, 143, 147–8, 151, 171; civilian control 4–5, 141–3, 158; EENA 64–5; foreign aid 72, 77; influence 4–5, 24; institutional role 25; land army 25, 27, 29–31, 70–2, 77–8, 142–3, 147–8, 151; mobilization 26, 31, 73; Naples Headquarters 25; National Guard Defence (TEA) 70; NATO and the northern front (1964–66) 147–51, 185; navy 31, 70, 72, 143, 147, 148, 171; officers 24–5, 64–5, 142; political role 24–5; project 'Athena' 78, 93; reduction of forces 76; regional balance (1963–64) 143–4; US aid 12, 13, 28, 31, 70–1, 77, 85, 88–90, 149; war strategy 25–6; *see also* ASPIDA; defence expenditure; defence policy; defence support aid; IDEA
military dictatorship (1967–74) 5, 184
Minchev, N. 105
Ministry of National Defence 141, 143
Ministry of the Land Forces (1940s) 20
Mitsotakis, Constantinos 134, 141, 143; Economics Minister and Minister of Economic Co-ordination 128–31, 152–4, 178, 180; in opposition 32
Montgomery, Sir Bernard 29
Moscow Radio 73, 94, 175
Mostras, Vassilios 50
Mountbatten, Admiral Lord 25
multilateralism 62
Murray, Sir Ralph 175–6
Mutual Defence Assistance Program (MDAP) 13

NAC *see* North Atlantic Council
Nagy, Imre 101
Nasser, Gamal Abdel 109, 110, 117, 157
'national centre' doctrine 131–7
National Guard Defence (TEA) 70
National Liberation Front (EAM) 7, 24, 126

National Progressive Centre Union (EPEK) 11, 32, 52
National Radical Union (ERE) 57, 60, 69, 127, 129, 130, 175
National Schism 24
national security 1, 3–4, 184; 1950–54 11–13, 23; 1955–59 66–73; post-1963: threat perception 144–7; balance of power 185; external security 2; functionalism 62–5; internal security 2, 11; 'menace from the north' 1, 2, 5–11, 125, 144, 146, 184–5; Western integration 185
NATO (North Atlantic Treaty Organization): aid and military expenditure 145, 151, 152–4; armed forces 25, 70, 72, 76, 77, 92, 149–51; Cyprus policy 45, 68, 80, 120, 167, 171; and de Gaulle 154–6; Deep Furrow 165–6; defence effort 28–9; Defence Planning Committee (DPC) 148–9, 150, 151; Eastern Express 165–6; flexible response strategy 74, 97; functionalism 64, 83–5; Greek accession 2, 11–13, 18, 20, 25; Greek membership 59, 67–8, 72, 77–8, 80, 83, 92, 111; manoeuvres 115; Multilateral Force 97; neutrality 146; and the northern front (1964–66) 147–51, 185; proposed study of Soviet propaganda 63; role in Greek policy 185–6; SACEUR 28, 74, 78, 89, 93, 162; SHAPE 148; Soviet protests 74; standard of living 28; and tripartite Balkan pacts 37, 41; Turkish membership 11–12, 20, 92, 118; and Yugoslavia 39, 42; *see also* Greek–NATO relations; North Atlantic Council
Natsinas, A. 24, 142
neutralism 80–3, 89, 90
New Look strategy 29, 30
Nicolopoulos, Petros 71–2
Norstad, Lauris 78, 89, 93
North Atlantic Council (NAC) 11, 72, 76, 78–9, 84, 92–3, 115, 144–6, 150, 153
Northern Epirus 8, 47, 48, 49, 100, 105–6
Northern Greece xvii, 153–4; *see also* Greek Macedonia; Thrace
Norway 151, 171
nuclear weapons 66, 73, 87–8, 94–7, 104, 110

occupation (1941–44) 7, 59–60

228 Index

OECD (Organization for Economic Co-operation and Development) 93, 153

Panslavism 21, 126
Papaconstantinou, Michalis 142
Papagos, Alexandros 17–19; government 4, 23–35, 36–7, 40–1, 44–5, 47, 49, 50, 52, 65, 81; Greek Rally 13; in military 4, 8, 12, 24
Papaligouras, Panayis 57, 69, 92, 102
Papandreou, Andreas 129, 130, 141–2, 156–8, 164, 181–2
Papandreou, George 126; Centre Union 74, 101–3; government 126–9, 132–6, 138–9, 141–2, 145–6, 152, 154–5, 157–9, 161–70, 174–7, 182–3; Liberal Party 32, 52; in opposition 130–2, 141, 162
Papanikolopoulos, D. 141
Pappas, Andreas 138
Paraskevopoulos, Ioannis 162, 173
Paris Peace Conference (1946) 8
Passalides, Ioannis 45, 52, 102
Paul, King: and the army 24, 141–2; overseas visits 33, 36, 51, 63, 109; politics 47, 50, 53, 58, 65, 100, 158; death 142
Penfield, James 68, 69, 98
Pentzopoulos, Th. 24
People's Republic of Macedonia (PRM) 8, 113, 114
Pesmazoglou, George 117
Philon, Philon 86
Pipilis, Ioannis 142
Pipinelis, Panayiotis 10, 36–7, 97, 105, 136, 170, 179
Plastiras, Nicolaos 12, 17
Poland 43, 45, 176
policy research 2–3
Popovic, Koca 112, 116
Pravda 175, 178
PRM *see* People's Republic of Macedonia
pro-Soviet leagues 68
Protopapadakis, Aristeides 78–9, 102, 103

Rallis, George 69
Rankovic, Alexandar 114
Report of the Three 92
Report of the Two 117
Richards, James 62
Rodopoulos, Constantinos 109
Romania 7, 12, 47; *see also* Greek–Romanian relations
Rusk, Dean 85, 86, 91, 93, 104

Sakellariou, Petros 142, 145, 162
Sarper, Selim 92, 118–19
Sceferis, Pericles 96
Schröder, Gerhard 155
Sergueev, Mikhail 44–5, 74, 94, 98
Sgourdaios, Alexandros 171
Shepilov, Dmitri 58, 61, 98, 184
Siapkaras, Andreas 142, 156
Slav-Macedonian groups 12
'Socialist Union' 57
Southern Albania *see* Northern Epirus
Soviet Union 10, 22, 28, 32, 39, 43, 168; *see also* Greek–Soviet relations
Soviet–Egyptian relations 85–6
Soviet–Yugoslav relations 51, 115
Spaak, Paul-Henri 80, 83, 85, 87
Spantidakis, Grigorios 143
Sputnik 94, 95
Stalin, Joseph 8, 28, 39
Stambolic, Petar 178–9
Stephanopoulos, Stephanos 53, 130, 142; Foreign Minister 21, 28, 31–4, 38–40, 50–1; government 129–30, 134–5, 146, 152–3, 155, 171–3, 177–80
Stewart, Michael 155, 177
Stikker, Dirk 93, 127, 133, 145, 146
Stoica, Chivu 58, 94–5
Strymon/Struma River 26, 72
Suez crisis 108, 120
Supreme Council of National Defence (ASEA) 25
Supreme Military Council 20
Svolos, Alexandros 57
Symeon, former King of Bulgaria 99
Syria 167

Talbot, Phillips 155, 173
Taray, Kemal 41
TEA *see* National Guard Defence
Test Ban Treaty (1963) 97
Thant, U 162
Theodoropoulos, Vyron 134, 167
Theotokis, Spyros 82, 84
Thessaloniki 6, 7, 37, 44, 45, 79, 81, 108, 114, 174
Thomson, George 155
Thrace 7, 27, 36, 39, 45; *see also* Eastern Thrace; Western Thrace
Thurston, Ray 52, 68
Tito, Josip Broz 8, 37, 40, 41, 51, 104, 108–13, 157
Toker, Metin 116
Toumbas, Ioannis 134, 147, 154–5, 172–3, 177–8

Index 229

Tranos, Constantinos 99
Treaty of Alliance, Political Co-operation and Mutual Assistance (Bled 1954) 39–42, 51, 66, 73, 108, 111–12
Treaty of Alliance between Greece, Turkey and Cyprus (1960) 120, 163
Treaty of Lausanne (1923) 6, 7
Treaty of Washington 2
Trieste dispute 12, 37–8, 40, 48
Truman Doctrine 8, 9, 35
Tsakalotos, Thrassyvoulos 24, 65, 110, 113
Tsaldaris, Constantinos 52
Tsatsos, Constantinos 57
Tsigounis, Alexandros 24
Tsirimokos, Elias: Democratic Union 102; Foreign Minister 134, 140, 155, 171, 172, 178; government 129, 130
Tsolakas, C. 143, 173
Tsouderos, Ioannis 153
Turkey: armed forces 25, 70, 78, 143; and Cyprus 50, 120, 163–4; and the Dodecanese 31; Eastern Thrace 27, 36; expulsion of Greek citizens 166; in Korean War 12; military coup (1960) 73, 118; in NATO 11–12, 20, 92, 118; riots (1955) 67, 108; *see also* Balkan Pacts; Greek–Turkish relations
Turko–Soviet border 39

unemployment 89
United Democratic Left (EDA) 8, 32, 45, 52, 63, 69, 73, 81–3, 89, 95–7, 101, 127
United Nations: Albanian accession (1955) 49; Cyprus debate (1954–55) 21, 23, 34, 45, 50, 52, 80, 99; Security Council 162; UNFICYP 163
United Nations Relief and Rehabilitation Administration (UNRRA) 7
United States: Armour Report 71, 89; and Cyprus 50, 125, 164–5, 168–9; and Greek–Soviet relations 44; and Greek–Yugoslav rapprochement 109, 110; missiles 73, 82; National Security Council (NSC) 13, 69, 72–4, 110; policy 3, 4; Sixth Fleet 70, 149, 156; *see also* Greek–US relations
United States Information Service (USIS) 30

Vasilas, E. 24
Venizelos, Eleftherios 4, 6, 7
Venizelos, Sophocles 28, 141; Foreign Minister 11–13, 17, 36, 126, 138, 145, 152; leader of opposition parties 52–3, 60, 101–3, 112, 115, 130–2, 137; Prime Minister 11, 58; death 126
Vlachos, Angelos 82
Voice of America 32, 156, 162
Vovolinis, Constantinos 32
Vukmanovic-Tempo, Svetozar 109

West Germany 33, 41, 77, 79, 86, 152
Western Europe 33–5, 63
Western Thrace 5, 6, 8, 13, 22, 26, 36, 45, 69, 71–2, 77, 127, 147–8, 150–1, 163–4

Xanthopoulos-Palamas, Christos 75, 102–3, 154, 175

Yost, Charles 24
Yugopress Agency 39
Yugoslav–Albanian relations 47, 105
Yugoslavia: armed forces 25, 70, 78; Balkan Pact (1934) 7; and Cyprus 50; Greek–Yugoslav–Egyptian talks 67, 110; and Italy 40; and NATO 39, 42; and Soviet Bloc 51, 115; Thessaloniki 7; *see also* Greek–Turkish–Yugoslav Pact of Friendship and Collaboration (1953); Greek–Yugoslav relations; People's Republic of Macedonia (PRM)
Yugov, Anton 104

Zhivkov, Todor 104, 180
Zorlu, Fatin Rüştü 112, 118, 119

eBooks – at www.eBookstore.tandf.co.uk

A library at your fingertips!

eBooks are electronic versions of printed books. You can store them on your PC/laptop or browse them online.

They have advantages for anyone needing rapid access to a wide variety of published, copyright information.

eBooks can help your research by enabling you to bookmark chapters, annotate text and use instant searches to find specific words or phrases. Several eBook files would fit on even a small laptop or PDA.

NEW: Save money by eSubscribing: cheap, online access to any eBook for as long as you need it.

Annual subscription packages

We now offer special low-cost bulk subscriptions to packages of eBooks in certain subject areas. These are available to libraries or to individuals.

For more information please contact webmaster.ebooks@tandf.co.uk

We're continually developing the eBook concept, so keep up to date by visiting the website.

www.eBookstore.tandf.co.uk